The World is a Stage

My Life in the Performing Arts:

Theater, Advertising, and Other Strange Callings.

By Jerry Inglehart

Cambria Free Press
88005 Overseas Highway
Suite 9
Islamorada, FL 33036
U.S.A.

Library of Congress Cataloging-in-Publication Data
available upon request.

ISBN: 0-9749099-1-2

Jacket design by Lain & Associates
Cover photo by PictureQuest

Copyright © MMIII, MMIV by Jerry Inglehart
ALL RIGHTS RESERVED

No part of this book may be used, reproduced, stored in a retrieval system, or transmitted in any form or by any means, electronic, mechanical, photocopying, recording, or otherwise, without prior written permission of Jerry Inglehart.

For Christie

Contents

Opening Night	In Milwaukee	3
Atwater Beach	In Over My Head	14
Dr. Rahn's Role	In Glencoe, IL	27
In Search of Sharon Bates	As a Freshman	40
Discovering Show Biz	As a Wise Fool	53
Trying to Undo Gloria	As a Junior	65
The Nashville Jail	Big Man on Campus	83
Marlon and Me	In College	100
Missed Cues	In Pittsburgh	131
Wrong Show	In the Drug Biz	144
Miscast	At Sears	153
Awakening from the New Trier Dream	In Wilmette, IL	165
Will it Play in Rockford?	Small Town Blues	180
Setting it to Music	Lilienfeld & Co.	192
Playing in the Majors	Young & Rubicam	200
The Writing on the Wall	Nader-Lief	217
Bringing Home the Bacon	On My Own	225
Rebirth	By My Bootstraps	250
"Seeking the Bubble, Reputation"	The Awards Circuit	271
Survival	Over My Head Again	296
Scene Change	Bankruptcy	318
The Phoenix	Starting Over	331
"They Have Their Exits and Their Entrances"	Goodbye and Hello	346
A Different Drummer	Competition	350
Rewriting the Scripts	Publishing	354
Madeline and Other Challenges	Ups and Downs	378
The Big Apple	Success	405
Right on the Money	Sale and Sail	429
"Last Scene of All that Ends this Strange, Eventful History"	Final Curtain	448
Index		**455**

Jacques: All the world's a stage,
And all the men and women merely players.
They have their exits and their entrances;
And one man in his time plays many parts,
His acts being seven ages. At first the infant,
Mewling and puking in the nurse's arms.
Then the whining school-boy, with his satchel
And shining morning face, creeping like snail
Unwillingly to school. And then the lover,
Sighing like furnace, with a woeful ballad
Made to his mistress' eyebrow. Then a soldier,
Full of strange oaths, and bearded like the pard,
Jealous in honour, sudden and quick in quarrel,
Seeking the bubble reputation
Even in the cannon's mouth. And then the justice,
In fair round belly with good capon lin'd,
With eyes severe and beard of formal cut,
Full of wise saws and modern instances;
And so he plays his part. The sixth age shifts
Into the lean and slipper'd pantaloon,
With spectacles on nose and pouch on side,
His youthful hose, well sav'd, a world too wide
For his shrunk shank; and his big manly voice,
Turning again toward childish treble, pipes
And whistles in his sound. Last scene of all,
That ends this strange eventful history,
Is second childishness and mere oblivion;
Sans teeth, sans eyes, sans taste, sans everything.

William Shakespeare
As You Like It
Act II, Scene VII

ACT I

SCENE 1

PLACE: Upscale suburbs north of Milwaukee and Chicago

TIME: Autumn 1937 to spring 1957

Chapter 1

Opening Night

Wednesday October 13, 1937 Storm clouds had been developing over southeastern Wisconsin since about noon, adding a threatening dimension to the intensity of labor pains my mother had been feeling since before dawn. She didn't share with my father her suspicion that I might be about to emerge into the world sometime that evening or early next morning because she had always felt a degree of guilt about her pregnancies, all of which were unplanned. Three generations before, Inglehart babies were considered an asset to the family because they increased the productivity of the family farm. But now we'd become an urban family dependent for our daily bread on the profits of a drugstore, and the Great Depression had been testing the mettle of the metropolitan middle class for nearly a decade. Children were now regarded as liabilities rather than assets. My eldest brother had been born in 1931, just ten months after my parents had taken a morning off from work at the drugstore for a Justice of the Peace wedding. Three years later came Brother Ron, insisting on his right to life as the ravaged economy hit rock bottom.

My 29-year-old father, following his well-established routine, arose at 6 A.M., bathed, dressed, and headed out to start his sporty little 1937 Ford V8, a luxury he'd allowed himself in the early spring, because even though the economic woes were showing no response to Franklin D. Roosevelt's programs, the Walgreens store he managed at 3rd and North Avenues in Milwaukee was generating record sales and profits. He'd be due for a promotion and a raise soon and the snappy new Ford V8 seemed justified. But he would never have bought it had he known that his wife was six weeks late at the time, a detail she declined to tell him because this latest pregnancy was the result of an adventurous cloud of seed winning a competition with a poorly seated diaphragm.

At 4 P.M. the Dow closed at 138, losing two points in an ominous tailspin that had plummeted the market 10% downward in two weeks.

By 6 P.M. the skies were black and the labor pains were five minutes apart. Mom called Dad at work to let him know (also informing the rest of the neighborhood that was listening in on the party line). Dad's workday was only three-quarters finished—he customarily put in a 16-hour day filling prescriptions, managing the store, maintaining morale for workers who were glad simply to be among the employed, and checking for shoplifting and shrinkage. Sometimes he'd stay even later to supervise the flood of soda fountain business from the after-movie crowd at about 10 P.M., but the driving rain kept the moviegoers at home this night. So at ten P.M. he stepped through the puddles between the stockroom door and the Ford V8 parked in the alley and headed home to drive his wife, now in almost constant pain, to the nearby Catholic hospital.

Religion did not influence my parents' choice of hospitals. Dad always shopped to find the physician with the lowest fee. The discipline of obstetrics was far too new and costly, and Daddy would never consider hiring a pricey specialist for anything as routine as childbirth. Besides, in the 1930s, general practice doctors delivered most babies, and if you remembered to give the doctor a cigar, he'd perform the circumcision for

Opening Night

free. Dr. Heinrich Pfeifer, the general practice doctor who came in with the lowest bid, happened to deliver babies at St. Joseph Catholic Hospital.

Dr. Pfeifer arrived to make a preliminary check on my progress into the world—he was an obese fellow with Mephistophelean eyebrows and a permanent scowl intensified by the realization that my earthly debut would disturb his night's sleep. I was struggling down a birth canal designed for a seven-pound baby at best, but I would weigh in at 10 pounds and probably should have been taken by caesarian hours earlier.

At 2 A.M., with the thunder, lightning, and rain at its greatest, Dr. Pfeifer continued to withhold anesthesia despite my mother's intense screams which, together with the loud storm outside, were disturbing not only the sleep of other patients in the hospital but also that of the German immigrant families living in bungalows just across the street. This Catholic doctor believed that a mother's birth agony was her payment for original sin, and she deserved it.

A minute or so later the doctor determined that I would crown shortly and signaled the nurse to apply the anesthesia mask, thus eliminating one violent sound from this tempestuous night. As my mother and I drifted into welcome sleep, the doctor reached for his shiny, evil-looking stainless steel forceps. Moments later I was extracted like a molar.

Now came the part that Dr. Pfeifer probably enjoyed most. Holding me up by the ankles he slapped me smartly on my bottom, the first of many spankings I would grow accustomed to. Waking from a pleasant sleep to the sharp smarting on my lean buttocks, I filled my lungs with my first gasp of air and let out a mighty scream. My outburst went unheard, because one moment earlier the tempest outdoors climaxed into a multi-million-volt sizzle in a pattern looking like varicose veins across the autumn sky, followed in a fraction of a second by an angry, resentful, deafening thunderclap that drowned out my scream, as it shook the windows of Milwaukee, waking the Germans all over town, many of whom were applauding the political thunderclouds simultaneously rolling across the European continent.

In this Wagnerian manner I gained my first extra-uterine perceptions: the doctor and his diabolical, Frankensteinesque delivery room with its glaring lights, green-tiled walls, and stainless steel stirrups (you can see excellent re-creations of these mid-1930s torture chambers in many outstanding period films nowadays), followed a few days later by views of pre-war Milwaukee as the clouds of both winter and war boiled over the Northern Hemisphere.

In the course of time I would also discover exciting Chicago, the pastoral Midwest, the diversified eastern U.S., and ultimately the world, each new discovery more challenging, broadening, and exciting than the last. But one step at a time—I have a book full of empty pages to fill. Back to the delivery room. . . .

I was born a mid-October Libra, supposedly a person as well balanced as the Libra scales. Years later, when astrology became chic, I inquired how this birth sign determined my personality (I had clearly grown up very un-balanced and of minimal stability) and was told by a gullible but cute female Scorpio that the gravitational effect of the constellation of my birth sign predetermined my personality. With a pocket calculator I determined that the gravitational effect of Dr. Heinrich Pfeifer was several million times greater than the gentle pull of the benign stars in that distant constellation.

*

My earliest recollection focuses on a chocolate Easter bunny.

It was in the spring of 1941. I was three years old. My family was living in the downstairs level of a humble Milwaukee two-flat on North Frederick Avenue. Both of my brothers and I received Easter baskets in which stood large, solid chocolate Easter bunnies. By weight each bunny probably contained as much chocolate as a dozen Hershey bars. I was awestruck. So much chocolate in a world still recovering from the Great Depression.

My Easter bunny enriched the next few days of my life with a delightful chocolaty hubbub of sweet taste in my mouth. By Wednesday after Easter my chocolate bunny was nothing but a memory. And Brother Bill had long since ingested his also.

But Brother Ron had taken a far more conservative, Depression-era attitude toward his candy bunny. He kept it wrapped in wax paper in his underwear drawer in the bedroom we brothers shared. Perhaps six times a day he'd unwrap it, admire it, sniff it, then nibble a tiny bite of chocolate ear, mix it in his mouth with copious quantities of saliva, then squish the solution back and forth to savor the taste before finally, reluctantly swallowing. In this parsimonious manner he'd managed to consume no more than the ears and part of the head by Wednesday.

I watched him. I suffered. This was somehow *wrong!* Chocolate was something to be *scarfed down*, not saved.

Thursday morning before school Ron went through his chocolate communion ritual once again, then wrapped the remainder in the wax paper, securing each corner carefully before returning the thing to his underwear drawer and heading off to his first grade classes.

I was too young for school, but not too young to scheme. There was no lock on that underwear drawer, and it was low enough for me to reach. Besides, these were the liberal Roosevelt years of class struggle between the haves and the have-nots. I was definitely a have-not, and was determined to do something about it.

In the afternoon my mother went down to the basement to do laundry. This would afford me the privacy I needed. She'd spend the rest of the afternoon either in the basement or the backyard where she hung the wet laundry on clothes lines. I removed the bunny from the drawer and retired to the living room where I could hide behind the sofa. For most of the early afternoon I was in undisturbed privacy, joyously devouring Ron's bunny as quickly as I could.

Then I heard footsteps on the front porch. Ron, home from school! I munched faster and faster—both of the bunny's fat haunches and his thick chocolate tail still remained. I heard Ron walk into our bedroom. I began swallowing whole bites of chocolate haunch. I heard the drawer being opened. And I heard the scream— "***MOM!***"

She bounded up the stairs, witnessed Ron's tearful discovery, and yanked me out from behind the sofa. My mouth was full and there were streams of chocolaty spit drooling down my cheeks and onto my bib overalls.

After that incident Ron learned to eat candy quickly and immediately, before I got to it. Today Ron is 69 and he can devour an entire plate of chocolate brownies in a matter of minutes.

During the summer that followed I learned to expand my horizons. First I ventured upstairs to the Nicholsons' flat where a lovely blonde Swedish woman named Erika lived with her husband and two daughters. Mrs. Nicholson occasionally fixed me a sandwich of peanut butter that she spread on white bread. White bread! I'd had no idea bread came this way since my mother purchased nothing but whole wheat, which I assumed had been invented by the same people who came up with spinach, liver, and other awful-tasting foods. By contrast, Mrs. Nicholson's white bread was wonderfully soft, and tasted *good!*

She also had a bathroom with a high tank toilet that flushed with a pull of a long chain, making such a loud rushing sound, it terrified me. And she had an icebox with a huge block of ice in it. During the hot, sweaty days of July I'd go up to Mrs. Nicholson's flat and she'd take an ice pick and knock off a wedge of ice for me to rub on my cheeks for coolness. It was very comforting. Decades later when I was a stressed-out advertising man in Chicago, I'd go after work for a highball in the Drake Hotel bar. Occasionally I'd take an ice cube out of my drink and rub it on my forehead because it reminded me of pretty Mrs. Nicholson's kindness and comfort. And her white bread.

My next horizon was venturing down the sidewalk to the corner. I was not allowed to cross the street, but I could turn the corner. It was a little frightening because around the corner I could not see our porch. And there was a strange girl living in an apartment building. She was a year or two older. She was mean. When she saw me she'd walk up to me and push me so that I'd fall on my fanny. This caused me to burst into tears and run home to the comfort of my mother. Wandering too far from home could be dangerous. But eventually I grew up and discovered hitchhiking. Then automobiles. Then airplanes. Then all seven continents, including Antarctica.

In 1941 our family moved to the Milwaukee suburb of Shorewood, where my father had built a pleasant little red brick colonial house. On December 7 of that year my brothers and I were running from house to house informing our friends of what we had just heard on the radio: the Japanese surprise attack on Pearl Harbor. I'd just turned four and had no awareness of world events—*who* the Japanese were, or *why* they would attack an old lady. We had a phlegmatic aunt named Pearl Hanson, and I assumed that Pearl Harbor was someone else's cranky old aunt.

*

By then I was beginning to feel an affinity for the performing arts. Prior to attending kindergarten I'd learned to sing two songs that I was often asked to perform for neighbors and dinner guests. The first was "Casey Would Waltz With the Strawberry Blond and the Band Play Don." I wondered about that song title. I knew songs were often written about people like *Clementine, Nola,* and *Patricia.* Presumably the band was playing a song celebrating someone named Don. I had an uncle named Don who was a bombardier in the air force, flying missions out of Southeast England. I asked Brother Ron about it. He was already a scholar at age eight and I figured he'd have the answer.

Ron considered a moment, then explained, "Band instruments are non-verbal. If I was singing 'God Bless America,' it would go *God bless America, land that I love*...but," he continued, "a band would play it as...(and he sang as if he were a trumpet) *Don don don don da-don*...see?"

"The band was playing 'God Bless America?' " I asked.

"No, in fact they were probably playing a waltz. But it sounded like that."

The other song I knew was "The Old Gray Mare," which I performed on request as an encore to "Casey Would Waltz," but the lyrics I knew were not about a tired old horse—they were about an old lady who "*went to the county fair, sat on a 'lectric chair, burnt off her underwear.*" It invariably elicited a titter. And my performances caused me to feel like a big shot in the neighborhood.

Until I entered school.

Whereas our early 1940s dinner guests, houseguests, relatives, and neighbors thought I was the cutest thing since the teddy bear, I was shocked to discover that my kindergarten teachers, Miss Jensen and Miss Tank, didn't think I was cute at all. What had gone wrong? I couldn't very well sing "Casey Would Waltz" all the time, but I did know how to make funny comments that disrupted the class and made the other kids laugh. Why weren't the teachers laughing too?

Actually, Tank and Jensen were minor league compared to Gladys Horn, my first grade teacher, who detested me with a passion that I found intimidating. Three weeks after the start of class, she began answering my questions with a scowl and a snarl, or dragging me off by my arm to stand me in the corner. Somehow I really got under that woman's skin.

Opening Night

Miss Horn was a published author of a children's book called *Bounce* about a kitten of that name owned by a sweet little girl. The book was illustrated with darling drawings of Bounce playing innocently (with a ball of yarn, of course). I didn't like the book at all. It wasn't funny. The little girl never made clever comments. She was just a cute kid with her cute cat. Boring!

There were at least twelve students who prepared book reports on *Bounce* that year. Perhaps they got elected to Congress when they grew up. I was more interested in comedy than politics.

After a day of browbeating and intimidation by Miss Horn, I would often wander down to the other end of the hall after school (it was on the way home anyway) and into the classroom of Miss Tuhill, the music teacher. I don't know exactly when my friendship with Miss Tuhill began, but it lasted most of the year. I'd simply hang around her empty classroom and watch her. She was young and pretty. And she seemed to think I was as cute as Bambi. Mind you, I was making no effort whatsoever to *try* to be cute. (I never once performed "Casey Would Waltz" for her.) I was simply sitting there watching her at her desk correcting papers, watering her plants, erasing the blackboard, and generally wrapping up her day, as I enjoyed a pleasant respite from evil Miss Horn. Miss Tuhill would give me candy and find things to entertain me while she worked. She never once sent me on my way; she was clearly enjoying my company as much as I was enjoying hers. Once she even took a snapshot of me.

Occasionally she would give me gifts. Actually, they weren't gifts—just things to keep a little boy occupied—things she took out of the second desk by the window. They were little toys and gadgets, like a cast-iron military tank, a metal racing car, or a comic book. When I took these things home with me, my sixth grade brother Bill would claim the items. He was in Miss Tuhill's homeroom and she was taking the things from his desk.

Perhaps I should dedicate this book to little brothers everywhere, those younger siblings who recognize the challenges of being the youngest, when all you want to do is what your older brothers can do, and you're not yet old enough to do.

In my case this meant wanting to swim at age six like my brothers, but I couldn't. When I finally did learn to swim, all I wanted in life was a bicycle, like my brothers had.

At age nine when I got my first bike, I decided life wouldn't be complete until I had a paper route and could earn money. But I had to be twelve to have a paper route.

On reaching age 12 and finally getting a paper route, the most important thing in life was having a driver's license—and for that I had to be 16.

On becoming a licensed driver, my goal was to own my own car—one with a beer tap in it, like the car owned by Brother Bill's friend Bill Worthington. The car itself would impress teenage girls, but the beer tap would turn them to putty. I'd figured out how to buy beer when I was only fifteen, and I was certain I could work out the logistics of installing the beer tap in the car. But car ownership required an initial capital outlay and working capital—something I never seemed to have.

Brother Bill subsequently set another nearly unattainable goal—he was traveling around the country. The summer of his junior year in high school he and a friend traveled by Greyhound bus to Louisville, Kentucky, over spring break. Louisville! That was in the South, practically the Confederacy! They served mint juleps down there!

Then during Bill's third year in college, over spring break he traveled by Greyhound bus to Ft. Lauderdale, Florida. That was on the Atlantic! Salt water, with crabs and sharks and tides!

A year later, Bill landed the impossible dream—a summer job as a dishwasher on the *El Capitan,* the crack Santa Fe express train out of Chicago. Every week he traveled to Los Angeles and back—a city on the West Coast, the Pacific Ocean, across a continent and a mountain range! I'd never even *seen* an ocean. I'd never been outside of five Midwestern states! Bill's amazing travel accomplishments presented moving targets that overwhelmed and defeated me. The Santa Fe wasn't hiring sixteen-year-old boys. Would my Little Brother complex never end?

But I've jumped ahead again. This is supposed to be a chronology. Where was I?

Oh yes—1944....

Chapter 2

Atwater Beach

Shorewood is on Lake Michigan. Our family did not visit the beach very often, partly because it involved a trek of at least 14 blocks from our house on Ardmore Avenue (we were a one-car family), but mostly because Lake Michigan, being a glacial lake, never warmed up much since the Ice Age. Most summer days the water temperatures hover at a sobering chill that keeps beer cold, but makes it difficult for teenage beach bums to impress the girls because the frigid waters shrink their manliness to embarrassing insignificance.

One summer day in 1944 remains lodged in my memory like a scorpion sting. My mother and brothers and I had hiked down to Atwater Beach. Mother put out a towel and lay on her belly in the sun to read a book while we three boys ran down to the water.

We discovered that the lake water was an almost acceptable 69 degrees. I'd taken swimming lessons at the Shorewood High School pool, but hadn't yet gotten the hang of swimming. My brothers, splashing and playing ever deeper into the surf, soon disappeared from my view. I courageously tried following them, but soon found myself in water up to my neck, although my toe could still touch that reassuring sandy bottom.

across a continent and a mountain range! I'd never even *seen* an ocean. I'd never been outside of five Midwestern states! Bill's amazing travel accomplishments presented moving targets that overwhelmed and defeated me. The Santa Fe wasn't hiring sixteen-year-old boys. Would my Little Brother complex never end?

But I've jumped ahead again. This is supposed to be a chronology. Where was I?

Oh yes—1944....

Chapter 2

Atwater Beach

Shorewood is on Lake Michigan. Our family did not visit the beach very often, partly because it involved a trek of at least 14 blocks from our house on Ardmore Avenue (we were a one-car family), but mostly because Lake Michigan, being a glacial lake, never warmed up much since the Ice Age. Most summer days the water temperatures hover at a sobering chill that keeps beer cold, but makes it difficult for teenage beach bums to impress the girls because the frigid waters shrink their manliness to embarrassing insignificance.

One summer day in 1944 remains lodged in my memory like a scorpion sting. My mother and brothers and I had hiked down to Atwater Beach. Mother put out a towel and lay on her belly in the sun to read a book while we three boys ran down to the water.

We discovered that the lake water was an almost acceptable 69 degrees. I'd taken swimming lessons at the Shorewood High School pool, but hadn't yet gotten the hang of swimming. My brothers, splashing and playing ever deeper into the surf, soon disappeared from my view. I courageously tried following them, but soon found myself in water up to my neck, although my toe could still touch that reassuring sandy bottom.

Atwater Beach

Suddenly a larger wave washed over my head, shocking me and causing me to lose contact with the bottom. No big deal, I thought, I'll just flail around a bit until I thrashed myself a little closer to shore.

Unable to open my eyes under water, I became quite distressed when I realized I'd lost my sense of direction—was I struggling in toward the beach or out into deeper water?

Next moment I realized that even though I was bobbing in the waves, they were coming too rapidly for me to gasp enough air, and I was suffering oxygen deprivation, which quickly graduated to intense panic. Where was that damned solid, safe, sandy bottom?

Moments later I came upon the morbid realization that I was drowning—really and truly drowning—the first feeling of mortality I'd known in my brief life, and the feeling was strong. No air! No breath! I remember discovering that I would have to scream for help, a humiliation that only happened to unfortunates in comic books and Boy Scout Manual illustrations. A few seconds later I still hadn't managed to suck in anything but water, and when I bobbed momentarily between waves, I screamed HELP! as loud as possible.

Unfortunately, one scream doesn't turn the trick for a drowning boy. It seemed like another ten seconds before my mouth emerged into air and I screamed again. Drowning! It was really happening to me, and it was terrifying. Drowning meant *death*, and I was inching toward it. Would I soon black out and sink to the bottom? Again I bobbed between waves and screamed a gasp that was silenced by a gargling sound as I slipped back beneath the surface with no precious air in my lungs.

All this impending death business is a lot for a six-year-old boy to handle. No acceptance, no resignation comes, just terror and violent struggle—when suddenly I was plucked from the water by a lifeguard. I was gasping and breathing real unencumbered air and crying, with my arms locked around the lifeguard's neck in a death grip.

The lifeguard had been trained to rescue adults in deep water. This was too easy for him—a six-year-old boy in water not much deeper than his chest.

Weeping in terrified, agonized sobs while never loosening my vise-like grip on the lifeguard's neck, I pledged repeatedly that I would never go in the water again. The lifeguard spoke to me in a reassuring, comforting voice as he waded back onto the beach, and asked me where my family was. (I would not have been allowed onto the beach without family.) I looked around and pointed toward my mother, still on her towel reading her book. He set me on my feet and I ran over to her.

"Mom! I almost drowned!" I cried.

She looked up from her book, taken aback.

"I almost drowned!" I sobbed.

"You were just fine. I was watching you," she said in even, accusing tones with a matching, measuring glare—and loud enough for nearby sunbathers to hear. I needed a hug, and all I was getting was a look like I'd done something bad. I had just been plucked from the arms of the Grim Reaper and now I was being deprived of my own mother's sympathy. She returned to her reading.

I looked around for the lifeguard to corroborate my story, but he'd disappeared. It was years before it occurred to me what the lifeguard had anticipated—my loud sobbing and pained exclamations about near-drowning would humiliate my mother publicly, possibly causing people nearby to question her competence as a mother.

I lay sobbing on my back in the sand. My mother tried to get back into the story she was reading, occasionally admonishing me for making such a big fuss over nothing. I'd just undergone the greatest trauma of my life, and my mother considered it less interesting than her book. Was I that unimportant? No more than a mild interruption between paragraphs? What if I'd actually drowned? I envisioned our Ardmore Avenue neighbors studying tomorrow's *Milwaukee Journal* with my picture on the front page:

Shorewood Boy, Age 6, Drowns.

Jerry Inglehart was pulled from Lake Michigan at Atwater Beach today after drowning in 5 feet of water.

The boy's mother, lying on the beach, engrossed in the final chapters of For Whom the Bell Tolls, *declined to be interviewed.*

Through my anguish, frustration, and tears I wondered what I could do to generate a maternal reaction more profound than if I'd just farted in front of houseguests.

Maybe I could become a big time gangster. I'd already had a little experience with crime, stealing boxes of Kellogg's Pep from the A&P to get the hero pin premiums hidden in the bottom of each box. I could practice looking like Edward G. Robinson. *Yeah, yeah!* Someday I'd drive around in a big black limousine wearing an expensive tailored suit, the lapels bristling with Kellogg's Pep pins, and a Tommy gun slung casually over my arm. That would get her attention.

What about politics? I could make speeches on the radio like FDR. *We have nothing to fear but fear itself!* Piece of cake. Mom would like that. Trouble was I knew nothing about politics and cared less.

A music career maybe? People already listened when I sang. It would be a cinch to expand my repertoire beyond "Casey Would Waltz" and "The Old Gray Mare." Maybe I could add some pop and show tunes. I had blue eyes like Sinatra. *Do-be-do-be-do...*

Or how about playing an instrument? I'd had some experience with a tambourine in kindergarten. What about violin? I'd practice hard and become another Jascha Heifitz. Mom would eat it up. My son, the concertmaster.

I momentarily considered stand-up comedy. Jack Benny made it look so simple. Timing is everything. Even if I wasn't

Jewish, Mom had had the foresight to have me circumcised. I could change my name.

After ten or fifteen minutes, my crying abated.

I had a plan.

I would pursue a life in the performing arts.

I decided to postpone my final choice of fields until another time. I'd had quite enough for one day.

*

In second grade I was placed in the homeroom of Mrs. Forler who was nearing sixty, and had learned to survive Milwaukee Public Schools by ignoring certain irritants such as me. It was a fairly quiet year.

Third grade more than made up for the lull when I was assigned to the homeroom of Miss Collins, a woman with the temper of a rabid dog. She lashed out at everyone, which made her invective toward me seem a little more bearable. No one could suck up to Miss Collins because she hadn't published a darling little children's book. She seemed well over 30 years old at the time and was possibly desperate over her marital status. Years later, after Lithium, Valium, Prozac, and other chemical anxiety controls were perfected, I thought of how these drugs could have calmed Miss Collins and softened my harsh third grade experience.

Bracing for another traumatic year in fourth grade, I was pleasantly delighted to find myself in the homeroom of the school's music teacher. Not Miss Tuhill. She had left the school system, possibly to have children of her own. Her replacement was a calm, sweet lady named Miss LaKundt who loved me without reservation because I loved her music without limit. (I was clearly a hit with those music teachers.) When Miss LaKundt taught the class simple two-part harmony I was thrilled—absolutely amazed that we could all sing harmony. I was the first to learn all those old racist 19th Century Stephen Foster songs, like "Old Black Joe" and "Camptown Races."

When she discussed George Gershwin and Wolfgang Mozart she made these dead genius composers come to life before my eager eyes. She saw that I had a fine ear and talent for music. She encouraged me to study an instrument, so I took up violin. She had a special conference with my mother, suggesting record albums to buy for me. I was Miss LaKundt's special musical prodigy, and she enjoyed teaching me.

*

One of the pleasures I gain from writing this story is in revisiting events that have since fallen into the pages of history, but which I witnessed firsthand. I can't pass up a "period" film like *Seabiscuit* or *Road to Perdition* that shows streets and dress styles that I clearly remember, automobiles I rode in, hospital rooms and doctors' offices I visited. I feel a part of these historic depictions.

Here is a sampling of my treasured historic memories:

Our telephone on Frederick Avenue in Milwaukee would confuse most modern-day Americans. It had no dial. How did you make a call? Very simple. You lifted the earpiece off the mount (it was one of those old "candlestick" phones) and listened until a female operator at the central switching office came on the line and asked "Number please?" You couldn't see the operator, but she was speaking to you through a black horn that funneled her voice to a microphone she wore on her chest. You gave her the number you were calling and she connected you with a quarter-inch telephone jack on a switchboard before her, then rang the distant phone.

Our phone was in our front hallway, sitting in a "telephone nook"—a little arched enclosure in the wall, tall enough for a candlestick phone. The ringer wasn't part of the phone, it was in a wall-mounted box below the nook. No one had ever heard of anything as luxurious as a residential extension phone in the mid-1940s. Each household that had phone service got only one phone, so the instrument had to be centrally located in the home and the ringer bell loud enough to be heard everywhere in the house. Today's callers normally hang up after three rings with no answer, but in the 1940s, ten rings was the standard wait, during which time Mom in the basement could finish feeding that bed sheet through the wringer on her washing machine, then dash upstairs to pick up the phone on the eighth or ninth ring.

Most homes had a "party line" in which six or eight homes shared the same phone line. The operator ringing your home would make the phone ring with a special code so you'd know that the call was for you and not a neighbor—but of course, any incoming call would bring several neighbors to the phone to listen in quietly on your conversation. For many, this eavesdropping was the only excitement in life, other than the mid-day live radio dramas like *The Romance of Helen Trent* or *Portia Faces Life*, collectively called "soap operas" because soap manufacturers filled the commercial breaks of these daytime dramas with messages touting bath soap, laundry soap, and soap for washing dishes. The primary audiences for these mushy daytime dramas were housewives whose apparent missions in life were getting things clean. And the sales figures from the soap advertisers hinted that this may have been true.

I saw the tail end of an era when vehicular traffic in American cities was horse-drawn. By 1940 cars and trucks had pretty much replaced carriages and wagons, but walking down a Milwaukee street in 1940, sooner or later you'd see a pile of horse turds. This was because the junk wagons and the milk wagons were still horse-drawn. Many families owned a car to transport Dad to work each day, but the two-car family was unheard of, so Mom shopped at a nearby food store almost daily, traveling on foot, carrying paper bags of groceries home in her arms or in a shopping cart. Because milk was heavy, the dairies delivered it directly to homes with a fleet of milk wagons that were all horse-drawn in 1940. The wagons were light and creaky and were always dripping water from the blocks of ice used to keep the milk cold. And those old draft horses knew their milk routes as well as the driver, who would emerge from a delivery, hop on the wagon and simply make a clucking sound to the horse. The beast would obediently start up and stop at the next house on the route.

World War II came to a sudden end in August, 1945. Bother Bill, who had a paper route in Shorewood, was alerted to keep an ear to the radio. As soon as he heard that the Japanese had surrendered, he was to report to his newspaper distribution station, because the *Milwaukee Journal* would have an extra edition ready for immediate distribution.

When the news of the unconditional surrender echoed around the world, there was dancing and cheering in the streets of Shorewood. People truly believed that there would never be another war—our atomic bomb would secure peace forever. Our troops would be home soon. Wartime prosperity would fund a new era of everlasting peace.

I came across Brother Bill, selling his newspapers in Shorewood. The Extra Edition was four pages, with a bold, black front-page headline:

WAR ENDED!
TRUMAN TELLS NATION
EXTRA

There was a brief news article, and a stock photo of General MacArthur pointing authoritatively at a map, together with several news items related to the Japanese surrender.

Most people were buying the newspapers as souvenirs. Bill gave me three copies to sell, telling me, "The cover price is a nickel, but everybody's been paying me a dime. After you sell them, pay me twelve cents and keep the rest."

By 6 P.M. that afternoon I'd sold all three copies. Everyone paid me ten cents a copy. I had thirty cents, an unbelievable fortune, most of which belonged to me.

Then I had a stroke of luck—I ran into Brother Bill again, on Capitol Drive in front of Thompson's Drug Store, selling the newspapers to motorists stopping at a traffic light. I held out a dime and a nickel to pay him for the newspapers I'd sold. He gave me three cents change—and three more newspapers to sell!

The sky was darkening. I had no thought of going home to dinner—I was in business. I crossed the street and hollered out to the passing motorists, "EXTRA, EXTRA, READ ALL ABOUT IT," just like newsboys in the movies. Two of the papers sold quickly for ten cents each. I now had thirty-eight cents in my pocket, and one newspaper left. A man yelled down to me from the window of an apartment building—"Boy! Upstairs!"

Entering the building I met the man on the stairway. He held out a nickel and took the newspaper. I said, "People are paying me a dime." He glared down at me contemptuously. A seven-year-old war profiteer! He said, "Look, here's the nickel, and here's the newspaper. Which one do you want?" Silly question. The newspaper had a street value of ten cents. To his amazement I took the newspaper and left the building. Within five minutes I'd sold it for a dime. I went home for a late dinner, wealthier than I'd ever been in my life.

My next entrepreneurial experiment was running a shoeshine stand. The marketing was considerably more difficult—schlepping my equipment down Capitol Drive, soliciting passersby. On a good day I might earn fifteen cents, but most days I had to settle for less, sometimes only a nickel. It gave me greater appreciation for the windfall profits of war, especially if you're on the winning side.

Atwater Beach

Afterward I started a messenger service, but got only one client, Mrs. Clark, a benevolent old lady living across the street who hired me to go to the grocery store for a package of noodles. On the way back from the store I began tossing her noodle package in the air, and eventually dropped it. The cellophane bag broke, carpeting the sidewalk with yellow elbow macaroni, forcing my messenger service into insolvency and failure.

I didn't start another business for twenty-six years. That one failed too.

The excitement of the election of 1948 infected me. Once every four years my parents could go to the polls and vote, and the results of their votes would unfold through the night on the radio, determining who would be the nation's next leader. Since my mother was a young liberal, somewhat radical and personally involved in many social movements, she invariably voted Democrat, while my father, a businessman, never deviated from the Republican line. The election results resolved a household conflict as well as a national one. And Mom, faithfully voting for Roosevelt, had four consecutive wins in her column: 1932, 1936, 1940 and 1944.

Looking forward to the Truman-Dewey conflict of 1948, no serious person questioned that Thomas E. Dewey would become our next president. I resolved to stay up as late as my parents would allow, and follow the election returns.

On the chilly November afternoon of Election Day 1948, I went to Weinicke Hardware Store and purchased (for about a nickel) 100 feet of wrapping paper, which the clerk pulled off of a huge roll mounted on a cast-iron reel at the end of the wrapping counter. He re-rolled it for me and tied it with string from a string cone mounted overhead and fed through a ceiling-mounted eyelet down to the wrapping counter.

At home I stationed myself in front of a wide coffee table near our radio. (Some of our neighbors had TV, but our family wouldn't buy one for another two years.) I placed the 100-foot paper roll on the carpet in front of me, unrolling it over the coffee table and down the other side. As each election return was broadcast, I recorded it on the wrapping paper, each entry identified by the time on the clock. I intended to record these broadcast results until the winner was announced, or until my mother sent me up to bed. I wish I had that roll of wrapping paper today, to show to my children, nephews, and nieces. Here's why:

Many of my entries recorded the prediction of a machine called an "electronic brain" for want of a description that people could understand. The radio announcers also called it "the Univac Machine." CBS was using it in an attempt to predict the election outcome based on fragmentary early returns applied to the known voting history in each precinct, ward, and county. It was the first time a computer had been used to predict an election.

Very early in the evening, the Univac Machine projected a win by the incumbent Harry S. Truman. The commentators attributed this prediction error to the untested newness of the electronic brain. The programmers monkeyed around with their machine until, later in the night, they got it to predict a win by Dewey, which everyone expected.

About this time my mother sent me up to bed. I had school tomorrow.

Next morning, the famous first edition of the *Chicago Tribune* contained the best-remembered error in the history of journalism with the headline…

DEWEY DEFEATS TRUMAN

I wish I still had that roll of wrapping paper.

Another notable historic episode occurred in September 1955 when my friend Doug Buck and I left for college. Railroads had revolutionized travel throughout the world beginning in the 1850s. They created a unified United States from coast to coast. An entrepreneur named George Pullman began building luxury railroad cars with parlors, dining rooms, upper and lower berths, even drawing rooms and bedroom suites with private showers, washbasins, and toilets that emptied directly onto the tracks. Combined with the impact of rail travel, Pullman was soon employing an entire town full of workers and managers on Chicago's South Side, appropriately called Pullman, Illinois. By the end of the 1940s, some of the most prestigious travel options were the luxurious "crack" express trains traveling from San Francisco to Los Angeles to Chicago to New York to Washington, D.C.

Doug and I had purchased Pullman upper berths to sleep our way overnight to college in Pittsburgh, just like in the F. Scott Fitzgerald stories. We boarded our Pennsylvania Railroad Pullman car at Union Station in Chicago, had a drink in the bar using our falsified identity cards, and then retired to our upper berths. The porter brought a ladder for us to climb into our individual berths, then closed the green curtains.

There I was, lying on my back fully dressed in a coffin-size compartment without a window. A berth passenger needed to slip out of his or her clothes and drop them into a net hammock hanging just overhead. If he or she wanted to bathe or shave or pee, it necessitated putting on a robe to climb down—or to ring for the porter to bring the ladder back. In the morning the passenger would fetch yesterday's clothes out of that hammock and wiggle back into them while still lying in the berth with the curtains closed. Mind you, 1955 was the tail end of an era when Americans, like most Europeans, bathed just once a week. If you were traveling on business, that gabardine suit would probably look pretty wrinkled after a few nights. And this was first class travel!

That night was my first and last time traveling Pullman.

In 1990 I visited a railway museum in Galveston, Texas, and toured a Pullman double berth car—the exact same model Doug and I had traveled in to our freshman year of college.

There in the museum car were the ladders, the curtains, the clothes hammocks, the little dim lights you switched on and off. My experience was now sufficiently historic to be shown in a museum.

My last historic comparison is impressive only to those who are keenly familiar with exact dates in the whirlwind history of computer sciences.

In 1979 I visited my brother Ron in Ann Arbor. Ron was eager to show us the latest rage at the University of Michigan— a computer game called Star Trek, which some buff had transported from The University of California in Berkeley and installed on Michigan's Amdahl mainframe.

Ron told me that if I could rent one of those old telex terminals with a modem (you tucked the phone receiver into an acoustic cradle on the terminal) he could give me a local phone number in Chicago that would connect me to the University of Michigan mainframe so I could play Star Trek at home. I did, for hours. And I never got a phone bill for long-distance charges. I was on the Internet when it was still a Cold War tool to link our military with the technology accomplishments of the major university think tanks.

Check it out, folks—I was on the Internet in 1979!

But back to the chronology. I left off in 1947...

Chapter 3

Dr. Rahn's Role

By 1944 my father had been promoted to manage the Walgreen Company drugstore at 3rd and Wisconsin Avenues in Milwaukee. At the time it was the largest drugstore in Wisconsin. Under his tireless leadership the store was both profitable and growing, so by 1946 Walgreen management in Chicago had pegged Dad for promotion to district management.

    The top brass at Walgreens' Chicago headquarters considered Dad for districts in Denver and Dallas, then discarded both in favor of Chicago's Loop North District incorporating all Walgreen stores from Madison Avenue in downtown Chicago to the Illinois-Wisconsin state line. In late 1946 Dad began managing that district, commuting weekly from Milwaukee and living during the week in an apartment hotel in Chicago's Uptown District. On weekends and in his spare time, he and Mom investigated the real estate market for a place to move their young family.

    Mother was acquainted with Dr. Grant Rahn, the principal of Shorewood High School in Milwaukee where my brother Bill was a freshman and brother Ron was in junior high school. Mom respected Dr. Rahn as an educator. She invited Dr. Rahn and his wife to dinner and asked him which public schools in the Chicago area were best. Without hesitation, Dr. Rahn answered, "New Trier Township. Eighty-six percent of New Trier graduates go on to college."

As far as my mother was concerned, regardless of real estate costs or taxes, we would move to New Trier Township.

The Shorewood area where we'd lived for six years was upscale for Milwaukee. The families on our block included three physicians and a few entrepreneurs. But sprinkled liberally among these small Shorewood houses and bungalows were plenty of German immigrant blue-collar families. And behind our house, on several blocks of vacant land along Wilson Avenue, a developer had hastily slapped together block after block of new, inexpensive three-story walkup apartments to accommodate the droves of new families of recent military veterans returning home to raise a Baby Boom Generation.

New Trier Township on Chicago's North Shore includes four upscale villages—Wilmette, Kenilworth, Winnetka, and Glencoe. The homes were considerably larger than those in Shorewood, built on much bigger lots, with cars in the driveways that were decidedly more costly.

After much house hunting, soul searching, and budget stretching, my father purchased a house in Glencoe, a village with a stable mixture of old Jewish and Protestant blueblood wealth. The house Dad bought was a bargain because of its condition—a tattered 60-year-old white Victorian frame house. It had an old circa 1900 cast-iron kitchen sink on legs that Dad replaced with a budget-priced Montgomery Ward sink and kitchen cabinets. The furnace in the basement was fired by coal like an old steamboat. Once each winter day (twice during cold spells) we'd shovel coal from a coal bin into the furnace stoker.

We moved to Glencoe in May of 1947. In September Brother Bill entered New Trier High School as a sophomore, and Ron and I entered Glencoe Central School, right across the street from our new house.

I immediately perceived that Glencoe schools were better than the school I'd attended in Shorewood. The teachers seemed a little sharper, and my classmates were clearly an intellectual step or two above my old chums in Shorewood.

New Trier Township was our legacy from Dr. Rahn. He had provided a bit of advice that would shape our lives permanently. We were now living shoulder to shoulder with families in a decidedly different league, both socially and intellectually. For the next eight years I would be steeped in the mindset of this community, one of the most privileged in the U.S.

Meanwhile, the academic problems I had suffered with in Shorewood followed me south to Glencoe. Miss Swan, my fifth grade teacher, was really quite brilliant and inspiring as she told my class about ancient Egypt and Greece. She read us stories from the *Iliad* and the *Odyssey*. But after a few weeks of my wisecracks and grandstanding, she detested me without reservation.

In sixth grade, Mrs. Montgomery often addressed the entire class on the subject of Jerry Inglehart, and how disruptive he was. When I was elected by the class to be our homeroom's representative to the student council, she lectured seriously, quietly, and intently for an entire hour on the drawbacks of having a person like me as the representative of the entire room in student council. As she closed her sermon, she called for a new class vote. My election was reconfirmed. Glencoe kids couldn't be dictated to.

Afterward, Mrs. Montgomery spoke with my parents and encouraged them to transfer me to a military school. My parents couldn't be dictated to either.

There was one other aspect of grammar school that plagued me. I was not competent in sports. Perhaps that's an understatement. I was simply a sports misfit. I was unable to throw or catch a ball. And in most suburban grade schools of the 1940s and 1950s, this was a rather unforgivable shortcoming.

My eldest brother Bill, who was quite proficient at sports, endeavored to help me by playing catch with me, and coaching my batting at the sandlot games we played in the field behind our house in Shorewood. Bill showed me defensive strategies when carrying a football. I remember him helping me with boxing when I was 7 or 8, coaching me while lowering himself to my height by kneeling. Later in high school he helped me with wrestling. Sadly, Brother Bill's efforts were wasted, like trying to teach a one-armed boy to use a bow and arrow.

The grammar school coach in Shorewood had been a man named Diedrich. I first encountered him in the fall of 1944, when the Allied ground troops were entering Germany and I was entering second grade. As the nation learned the gruesome facts about Hitler, I learned some facts about Coach Diedrich. There were disturbing similarities. In Coach Diedrich's mind, there were certain humans that were unfit and intolerable, including Gypsies, homosexuals, and boys not good in sports. Coach Diedrich dealt with my physical incompetence by drawing attention to my shortcomings and humiliating me in front of the other boys.

One day, two boys were having a disagreement on the playground after school. I have no idea what they were fighting about, but one was in third grade, and a head taller than the other, a second grader. I saw the bigger boy push the smaller one, who responded by shouting and pushing back. They had a standoff, but kept screaming at each other.

Coach Diedrich appeared on the scene and said to the boys, "You want to fight? Okay, let's have a fight." I realized that Coach Diedrich did not want to see what the disagreement was about, he just wanted to see a fight.

By now a large group of kids had gathered. Coach Diedrich organized the bystanders into a circle around the combatants. Then he took the eyeglasses from the younger boy and told the two boys to start fighting. There was a little circling and feinting, then the bigger boy, with a longer reach, landed a solid right fist on his opponent's nose. The smaller boy immediately sank to his knees and began crying. Coach Diedrich stepped into the ring like a referee, and said to the younger boy, "Have you had enough?" The kid nodded.

What Diedrich said next puzzled me: "You admit you were wrong?" The little kid, realizing the coach would allow the battle to resume if he did not agree, at first hesitated. Coach Diedrich repeated, louder: *"You admit you were wrong?"* The kid nodded and Coach Diedrich gave him back his eyeglasses.

I was nearby, and was tempted to lift the sleeve of Coach Diedrich's t-shirt to see if there was an "SS" tattooed there.

In Glencoe the coach was Joe Brady, and although he was less crude than Diedrich, he seemed to follow the same philosophy—boys no good in sports had no place in society. On the playing field Joe Brady never allowed one of my failings to go unnoticed by the rest of the class. For four years, from fourth to eighth grade, I was the last boy to be chosen for any team. I batted last and played right field. In basketball my teammates preferred that I remain down court at the defensive end, in order that I wouldn't get in the way when my team had the ball.

*

My father's parents lived in a cottage on the bank of the Wolf River in Winneconne, Wisconsin, a dozen miles west of Oshkosh. We'd visit there at least once a year.

That cottage on the river fascinated me. When we three brothers slept over in Winneconne, Grandma would make up beds on the porch swing, on the old brown plush living room sofa, and on the floor. I remember the smell of bedding—cozy, woolen, feathery smells of blankets, linens, and pillows being tossed down from the attic by Dad and Grandpa. The enclosed porch where I slept smelled of old magazines, the living room smelled of Grandpa's Half-and-Half pipe mixture, and the middle bedroom was always slightly fragrant from Grandma's perfume bottles and atomizers.

Upstairs was a musty attic full of a lifetime's worth of curios—a mounted deer head, boxes of old photos, and three or four collections of merchandise samples that my father had sold as a store lobby huckster during the early years of the Depression. There were thirty boxes of fountain pens from about 1931. And some costume jewelry samples called "Madagascar Gems."

The mudroom off the kitchen had an old water pump that turned on automatically when the reservoir tank was empty. It scared the hell out of me. I'd been warned sharply by Grandma never, *never* to go near that pump—it had exposed belts and pulleys that could tear off an arm. The electric motor looked like it had the face of a bulldog, snarling to keep me away as the pump churned noisily.

In the kitchen was a cookie jar full of very stale gingersnaps. And there was Grandpa's gun cabinet where he stored his shotgun and rifle. Here the aromas were more serious—gun oil, and the ripe banana smell of Hoppe's No. 9 Powder Solvent. I'd often watched Grandpa, Dad, and Brother Bill clean up their guns in this kitchen after a day of duck hunting on the river. There, as a very small boy I learned a rite of passage that had begun when I got my first toy gun and my father impressed on me that I was *never* to point a toy gun at anyone, because in an Inglehart household some of the guns were real and all of the ammunition was live.

I remember the lonely, sad call of loons and mourning doves in an early November dawn at Winneconne. Down at the boathouse on the riverbank, I could smell a pungent odor of fish guts and scales. Inside the boathouse was a wet slip for Grandpa's 12-foot fishing boat with its little five-horsepower Johnson outboard. It was raised out of the wet slip on rope loops attached to reels that you'd turn to raise or lower the boat. It was usually dark inside the boathouse but the sun would shine on the water outside and reflect up into dancing sunbeams inside on the boathouse roof where Grandpa hung his bamboo fishing poles. Stored in the back were several burlap sacks full

Dr. Rahn's Role

of wooden duck decoys—not those fancy decorative carved masterpieces you see in overpriced antique stores. These were real *working* decoys with round bottoms and anchors on strings that Grandpa had probably purchased by the dozen from a Wards catalog. Many of them had dimples in the wood from having been hit by birdshot.

And there were three wooden skiffs—charming little riverboats that looked like something out of a pastoral 19th century French etching by Jean Francois Millet. To a young boy, those skiffs represented *freedom!* I was not allowed to take the motorboat out, but at a very early age I was permitted to launch a skiff and be gone all day, rowing upriver into Lake Poygan, downriver toward Lake *Butte des Morts*, in and out of the long slough leading to the Wiezner farm or through Scots Bay, a nesting haven for ducks surrounded by a hundred old 1920s auto bodies sunk into the water as an artificial reef to protect the stands of wild rice in the bay.

In the autumn of 1948 Dad took me duck hunting for the first time. At age eleven I was still too young to shoot a shotgun, so I was along just as an observer. In the pre-dawn darkness Dad and Brother Bill equipped two skiffs with their guns, plenty of shells, bags of decoys, and rolls of rice stalks knotted together like a mat so they could be unrolled and mounted around the boat gunnels as blinds. We towed the loaded skiffs behind the motorboat to Scots Bay where we anchored the motorboat and boarded the skiffs—one for Bill and one for Dad with me seated just behind him. We poled the skiffs into the wild rice marsh, put out the decoys, and waited for dawn while sipping the hot black coffee Grandma had fixed for our thermos bottles.

Every now and then a flock would appear as the first dim rays of dawn washed across the sky. A formation of wild mallards or canvasbacks would carefully circle above our decoys, lured by the soft quacking of Dad's duck call. Closer—closer—lower—and suddenly the quiet was split by the sharp, shoulder-thudding blasts from Dad's and Bill's guns. The pungent smell of exploded powder momentarily spiced the moist autumn smell of the rice marsh.

For me the hunt was another rite of passage. Like the Indians that lived along this river for thousands of years and taught their skills of survival from generation to generation, I was learning a skill being passed down to me through at least five generations from pioneer settlers in Wisconsin who hunted in order to feed their families. It was much more than a sport—I was sharing in the work of a harvest. It was like a James Fennimore Cooper novel, except that I was in it!

*

Nowadays there are elegant labels for children's learning deficiencies, such as *Attention Deficit Disorder*. Back in the 1940s and 50s, there was just one label—"poor student." By seventh grade I began to understand the reasons for my academic shortcomings. Since first grade I had been bored with everything about school except music. To combat boredom I had developed an ability to turn my mind away from my surroundings and retreat into an inner world where I saw and heard nothing but my own thoughts—which were rather imaginative and fun. I mentally designed space vehicles and mapped out science-fiction adventures. I imagined myself in a submarine, or hiking through the English countryside, or fighting in the foxholes of the war. And when a teacher interrupted my daydreams to ask me a question, I didn't know what the subject was, much less the answer. When the class was given instructions to do something, I had no idea what the instructions were, and was somewhat amazed that everyone else in the class *did* know. I was a poor student because I simply had other things on my mind.

To further relieve my boredom when I ran out of my private thoughts, I would make attempts to draw attention to myself, mostly by being disruptive. By seventh grade I had developed an appreciation for puns that I continue to enjoy to this day. My antics got a lot of laughs from my classmates and scowls or punishment from the teachers. Since my audience was strictly the kids, I tried to come up with humor that would pass over the heads of the teachers, but would be understood by the kids. How could a teacher punish me if she couldn't understand what had happened? I recall once at Christmastime when we were all singing "Joy to the World," I sang "Goy to the World" which elicited chuckles from the Jewish kids who constituted about a third of my classmates.

I remember when our eighth grade music teacher, Miss Calvi, started us on "Coming 'Round the Mountain." After we sang the first verse she encouraged the students to remember other verses. Palmer White sang *She'll be driving six white horses when she comes*, and the class joined in. Then Susie Horberg piped up with *And we'll all go to meet her when she comes*. The next verse was initiated by Babs Johnson who sang, *We'll have chicken and dumplings when she comes....*

At the end of Babs' verse I sang, *She'll be gasping and moaning when she comes....* This brought immediate snickers from the more street-wise kids. Miss Calvi stopped playing the piano, a little confused. Perhaps at age 60 she didn't understand the pun, but she could hear the giggling. Maybe she simply didn't want to address the topic. She considered for a moment, then said, "Let's sing the Erie Canal song," and re-attacked the piano keys. *I've got a mule and her name is Sal....*

A teacher's job is to teach, and to do that she has to maintain order. But I hadn't come to school for an education, I'd come for an audience. I was at permanent odds with my teachers who were constantly fighting me for the class's attention.

My little sister Jane grew up to be a primary school teacher. When she described the problems she would occasionally have with class disrupters like I had been, I told her of my sad grade school history and record, and how important it was to be patient and understanding with those little brats who were keeping her from doing her job. She took me very seriously. I visited her class a year or so ago, and was amazed at the rapport she had with all her students. But it may have been a hard lesson for her. I remember years when she told me, "This has been a very difficult term, I had *three* Jerry Ingleharts." Or, "This was a *great* year! I had *no* Jerry Ingleharts!"

Because of this, I now realize that if I'd had sister Jane as my first grade teacher, she might have inspired me to learn. My academic history, and my childhood, might have been vastly different.

*

I'd attempted to learn to play violin in fourth grade and piano in fifth. Despite my love for music, both instruments required learning to read music. That meant *studying*, and that was too much like school. I gave up on both instruments.

In seventh grade my friend Penn Brown pulled out his ukulele and taught me to play "Frankie and Johnny." Hey, this was a snap! Four notes tuned the uke: D—G—B—E. "My—dog—has—fleas." Four easy chords, C, F, D7 and G7, and I was performing. *No studying!* I saved my paper route money and bought my own ukulele. Brother Bill taught me the words to "Mississippi Mud" and I figured out the extra chords myself. Two more paychecks and I had enough for a cheap plywood guitar. Another friend, Pete Jones, taught me the guitar chords for "Ragtime Cowboy Joe" in the key of G. Now I could play in *two* keys. Soon I was adding new songs, chords, and keys to my repertoire every few days. *I was now a musician.*

*

My seventh grade homeroom adviser was mild-mannered Ernie Bonhivert, the science teacher. This was supposed to have been a two-year homeroom assignment, through to the end of junior high school. But after a semester Mr. Bonhivert gave up on me and arranged for me to be transferred to the homeroom of

Dr. Rahn's Role

Miss Collins—not the Miss Collins who had temper tantrums in third grade in Shorewood—this new Miss Collins had taken a course or two in psychology and was considered better qualified to handle me.

In fact, Miss Collins saw in me an opportunity. If she documented my case, it might help her earn a graduate degree in psychology.

By this time in my life I was well focused on my Atwater Beach resolution to go into the performing arts. My universe became the theater. Threshold Players, the local community theater organization, cast me as a Victorian schoolboy in the play *Life with Mother*. Two other kids in that cast were William Christopher who, as an adult, would become the Padre in the *M*A*S*H* TV series, and Cal Brown who, as an adult, would become my brother-in-law. Later I played a role for Threshold in the play *Born Yesterday*. People paid to see me! I was almost a professional!

As eighth grade entered its final semester in February 1951, my greatest theatrical triumph was approaching. I was to play my guitar, sing a sea chantey, and dance a hornpipe in the Eighth Grade Operetta, *H.M.S. Pinafore*. Me! A featured attraction in my nineteenth century British sailor's uniform before all my classmates (on stage) and their families (in the audience). My great hour of triumph was close at hand.

A day before the opening night of my big performance, I wandered after school into the main auditorium to sit and gaze at the ship's deck set for *Pinafore*, on the same stage where I'd performed for Threshold Players. Here my theatrical career was launching. Just one day to go!

I went on stage and looked out over the auditorium with its high balcony and spotlight booth above in back. I wandered around the *Pinafore* set, then went backstage and looked at the huge Frankenstein-like light control panel with its eighteen dimmer controls. I stared up into the high fly gallery.

The fire curtain caught my eye. It was a huge green asbestos curtain hanging in the front of the fly gallery. I'd never seen it lowered.

Here by my hand was the counterbalance trunk and the control wire. I tugged. The fire curtain creaked and groaned and nudged downward on its rusty tracks. Another tug and the massive old asbestos firewall, with a texture of elephant skin, sank clumsily to the stage.

Now the stage area was rather dark. I reached for the "up" cable and tugged it. Nothing happened. I tugged harder. Nothing. I jumped and grabbed and hung on with all my weight. That old curtain must have weighed over a thousand pounds. And the counterbalance weights were stuck. In terror, I grabbed my winter jacket and fled the theater.

All evening I worried about that damned fire curtain. If I couldn't raise it, *Pinafore* would have to be cancelled. All my rehearsals would have been in vain! My theatrical talents would go unheralded!

Finally about 7 P.M. I left home and walked down the chilly streets in the February darkness and sneaked into the auditorium. I re-examined the curtain counterbalance system—nothing seemed wrong, it was simply old and suffering from disuse. I tried coaxing the curtain up as I watched the cables and counterweights. Nothing worked. In despair I left the theater—and was seen crossing the playground by the night janitor.

Next morning was Friday. I decided to skip library class for one last try at that fire curtain. As I entered the auditorium I saw to my incredible relief that the curtain had been raised!

At the close of my last class of the day, Miss Collins detained me in the hall, took me into her classroom, and closed the door. The janitor who'd recognized me the night before had gone into the auditorium to investigate and discovered the fire curtain down. He'd called in others and they'd worked most of the night getting the curtain back up. In the morning they reported me.

Dr. Rahn's Role

Miss Collins had been on my case for 18 months. She theorized that I had broken into the auditorium in the dead of night to sabotage my class's major triumph, the Operetta. It was a classic case of social revenge for all the humiliation I'd suffered due to dropping those fly balls in right field. Given time I might make her famous by becoming a notable anti-social headliner—a terrorist or perhaps a Unabomer.

In the empty classroom there was excited intensity in Miss Collins' eyes as she questioned me:

"What were you doing in the auditorium last night?"

"I came to try to get the fire curtain up."

A frown darted across her face. "You mean you came to put the fire curtain *down*?"

"No, Miss Collins, I put the fire curtain down yesterday right after school. Last night I was trying to get the fire curtain *up*."

Miss Collins now looked crestfallen. "You put the fire curtain down yesterday, right after school?"

"Yes."

"And you broke in last night to try to get it back up?"

"I didn't break in. I've been here four years, I know how to get in without breaking anything."

A pause. Then, "Are you certain you didn't break in last night to perform additional sabotage?"

"What do you mean?"

"Can you prove that you put the fire curtain down yesterday right after school, and not last night?"

"I've already admitted I did it. What difference does it make *when* I did it?"

The disappointment in her face was now intense, bordering on grief. I'd just torched her Master's Thesis.

Miss Collins and I arrived at an unspoken truce without victory. Thirteen weeks later I was allowed to graduate to New Trier High School, where my adventures and misdemeanors would advance to a higher level.

Chapter 4

In Search of Sharon Bates

I remember a couple of notable new movies I saw during the summer of 1951—*The African Queen*, in which the two scenes involving mosquitoes and leeches traumatized me so severely I nearly left the theater—and *An American in Paris* which provided me with a travel fantasy for years to come. I virtually lived in that movie shoulder to shoulder with Gene Kelly and Oscar Levant, we three penniless American artists making it in Europe's most fabulous, romantic capital, with parties every night and romance with skinny Leslie Caron, dancing with her along the River Seine.

I attended summer school at New Trier. Correction...I attended for about four weeks, then dropped out to accompany my family to Green Lake, Wisconsin, in July, where my father rented a lakefront cottage with two bedrooms, a Kelvinator refrigerator and a flush toilet for $40 a week. Most of the cottages in that stretch of the lake had iceboxes and outhouses in 1951. In the following decades all of these primitive but charming old cottages would be replaced by elegant summer homes. Today you couldn't touch one of them for less than a half-million dollars.

In Search of Sharon Bates

If I had been a responsible little 13-year-old, my parents might have allowed me to stay home alone and attend *all* of summer school. After the two weeks at Green Lake I returned to summer school, so far behind in all the courses, I had to take them all over again in the fall.

In September I showed up in my advisory room at New Trier High School for the start of the fall term as a freshman. Brother Ron was a seasoned senior, a big wheel, involved in the High School variety show called *Lagniappe*, and the Feature Editor of the high school newspaper, *The New Trier News*.

Ron encouraged me to test out my writing skills and submit some creative material to him for possible publication in *The News*. I wrote a piece about the frustration of an incoming freshman overwhelmed by such a big school. I tried to make it funny. Ron opted to publish it, and even got the senior class cartoonist, Eileen Connagan, to provide an illustration. Ron also gave me a byline. Jerry Inglehart was now a published author.

My mother saved that first article. She died last year. I found the article among her things and re-read it. I immediately crumpled it up and threw it away. Even for a thirteen-year-old, it was an unforgivably bad attempt at humor. The only reason it got published was nepotism. Perhaps big brother Ron realized that my grammar-school-ravaged ego was in need of healing and building.

Ron had a regular column in *The News* which he wrote in a Robert Benchley style, under the byline "Ringle." (R. Inglehart, get it?) His stuff was really funny.

I submitted another bit of creative humor and asked Ron to give me the byline of "Jingle." After two more articles, my writing still wasn't very funny, but the byline stuck. I'm still "Jingle" to many of my high school friends. Also to the State of Illinois, which issued me license plate JINGLE in the 1970s.

By November of my freshman year, some of my high school friends were passing me pages of their own attempts at creative writing, asking if I could use my influence to get them published in *The New Trier News*. And my freshman English teacher was giving me top grades, because I was writing for *The News*. Those high grades in English got me into an advanced sophomore English class a year later—a class for which I was unprepared. It was a college-level English course, which fascinated me in spite of my consistently poor grades.

Wait! Wait! Another event stands out in my memory, even though readers, especially female readers, will read it and say I should have been ashamed of myself. It happened like this:

The New Trier school day was divided into ten class periods, which placed students into their various required classes and electives. Lunch was the only time during the day when students didn't have to account for their whereabouts. The remaining class periods, not taken up by classes or lunch, were assigned to study halls in order to keep tabs on each student so he or she wouldn't be off smoking cigarettes or raising hell.

If you had something to study in the study hall, you did. If not, you read. Or slept. In this 40-minute period of boredom you might be inspired to scratch your initials on the study hall desktop with a pen or a key. You might even scratch a note.

Since up to ten students might sit at your study hall desk in the course of a day, one of the more common notes scratched on the desks was *"WHO SITS HERE?"*

One day during my eighth period study hall with nothing better to do, I scratched a brief, anonymous response to a *"Who sits here?"* I have no recollection as to what I wrote, but the next day there was a follow-up note, inquiring as to my gender.

I responded by drawing a circle with an arrow—the male sex symbol.

On the following day there was a brief response revealing that my correspondent was female—and a curious female at that. She made a guarded inquiry that was borderline sexy. I think she wanted to know if I'd ever given a hickey.

I used the whole period to craft a response that I hoped would feed and excite her curiosity. In ten words or less.

The next day, my dialogue-mate scratched another question to me that suggested that she was not only curious about my sexual experience, but was even pretending to be fairly experienced herself. This girl had some pretty racy fantasies. I had no idea at the time that fifty years later there would be an Internet with chat rooms where people could drop in unidentified and join conversations, often using the shield of anonymity to trot out a few of their private sexual fantasies, hoping to discover someone else out there experiencing similar mental dramas—or whether someone might have a few new ideas to help enhance the fantasy. In 1951 no such platform existed, other than these brief comments carved onto study hall desktops and bathroom walls.

I composed a response to my pen pal that I knew would further inflame her.

On that particular day I forgot a book under the study hall desk. Missing it during my ninth period class, I returned to the study hall to retrieve it. And there, scratched beneath my inflammatory eighth period comment was a very kinky reply.

So my correspondent occupied the desk during ninth period! Now my curiosity became overwhelming. I decided to try to find out who she was.

Next day after crafting my equally provocative response to her kinky one, I hung around just outside the study hall at the end of eighth period.

A young girl I didn't know but had seen once or twice before, entered and sat down at my desk. She immediately began studying my response. A trio of her female friends seated nearby gathered around her desk to evaluate the latest dirt. Titter, titter, giggle, giggle.

She was short, a little over five feet, skinny, with small breasts, and a Mediterranean face, thin nose, high cheeks, black hair in a flattering short Italian haircut. Her most interesting feature was her eyes—dark, shapely brows, a mysterious faraway look that turned mischievous when she smiled or laughed, which was often. She usually wore a cashmere sweater, and probably had a drawer full of them at home. This over a tailored wool dress or wraparound—costly stuff. White socks and penny loafers—the Winnetka Girl look. Attractive, but not so much as to be constantly self-involved, like many of the really cute girls at New Trier. Just good looking. She'd get asked to dance.

The very next morning during a class change I was in a hallway having a discussion with Joe Arnold, a fellow freshman, when I saw my study hall pen pal walking to her next class with a friend. I asked Joe, "Who is that girl, the one talking to the redhead?"

"That's Sharon Bates, from Wilmette. She's in our class," Joe replied. I'd expected a more European-sounding name to match her Mediterranean appearance.

Sharon's next desktop communiqué inquired whether I'd ever "done it" on the beach.

I used her first name in my response: *"Never around here, Sharon. Too chilly at night, but Jamaica's fun."*

When I returned to the study hall next day, our entire dialogue—twelve entries—had been laboriously obliterated with ballpoint pen. Not one pen, but three—as she destroyed one by scraping it on the varnished wood, she borrowed others of different colors, probably from the trio of girlfriends, until every last word—even the initial *"WHO SITS HERE?"* was blacked out, blued out, or greened out.

Beneath her extensive obliterations I scratched, *"SHARON, DID I SAY SOMETHING WRONG?"*

Next day she had brought some sort of a blade to study hall—a penknife, perhaps, or a nail file, which she used to remove the varnish and part of the wooden desktop, in case someone might find a way of wiping or dissolving her ballpoint editing to read our incriminating dialogue.

Here I let the matter drop, although I found it difficult to restrain my amusement during that study hall period. What a phenomenal reaction! But since it would be just as easy for

Sharon to identify me the same way I had identified her, I abandoned the chat room.

I did, however, write the incident up for *The New Trier News,* and submitted my write-up to Brother Ron for publication. He refused to publish this one until I cleaned it up. By the time I got it tamed down it was no longer interesting. At age thirteen I hadn't yet learned how to simply *imply* details, allowing the reader to fill in the spicy stuff from his or her own experience or imagination, as I have done here. Had I accomplished this, Ron would have published the account. Sharon, reading it, would have identified me by my byline, and perhaps been pleased to see that I didn't use her real name.

Neither then nor now.

*

New Trier may be the most elite public high school in the country. Rarely a decade passed when New Trier was not the focus of an article in a national magazine such as *Life*—often the cover story. North Shore bluebloods consistently approved school referendums and bond issues, providing a wealthy school district that could fund anything and bid for the best teachers in the country. Those teachers vied for an opportunity to teach at a school where kids were eager to learn. As a result, North Shore parents felt little need to send their kids to private prep schools like their aristocratic counterparts in New England. At New Trier the kids bonded with other North Shore kids, many of who provided all the later-in-life contacts needed for success—although maybe not quite to the extent of such private Eastern schools as Groton and Exeter.

The key thing I remember from growing up on the North Shore is that all of us at New Trier seemed to regard ourselves as having been born with silver spoons in our mouths. Our parents were successful in life, and we would also be expected to succeed. Most of us were a little terrified that maybe we might not be quite as successful as our parents.

There have been a number of notable New Trier grads. I can think of a few off the top of my head: our movie stars included Rock Hudson, Charleton Heston, Ann-Margret, and Bruce Dern. In politics, U.S. Senator Charles Percy was in the Class of '37. Secretary of Defense Donald Rumsfeld graduated with my brother Bill in 1950. In TV news, Walter Jacobson was my classmate, and White House Correspondent Ann Compton was a close friend of my sister Jane who graduated in 1964. There must certainly be many more who I can't think of, or don't know of. Cork Walgreen graduated a year ahead of me, but unlike the others I've mentioned who were self-made, Cork *inherited* the presidency of Walgreens, already a national chain the day he was born.

The school had been started in 1901 in a classic four-story red brick building with a seven-story clock tower and elegantly carved limestone window frames that made the building look like an Eastern private school. As the North Shore communities grew, the school was added to in a haphazard fashion, unified only by the fact that every added building was of red brick, matching the original tower building. By mid-century the campus included several additional classroom wings, a library that had a second floor jogging track because it had once been a gym, an auditorium, a lunchroom big enough to be fancied up for monthly dances, an almost-Olympic-size swimming pool, and several other gyms including one large enough to house our massive Christmas concerts as well as commencement exercises for classes of 700. There was a huge music building (three out of every five students were either in the band or orchestra, or singing in the choruses and opera groups), and an industrial arts building. The industrial arts building may have been a miscalculation—very few New Trier students were likely to enter careers in industrial arts.

When I arrived in 1951, this conglomeration of ivy-covered red brick could cause any freshman to get lost. Passing from class to class frequently involved walking down mysterious tunnels and passageways, and often going outside, a real burden when the temperature dropped below zero and your coat was in a locker in some other building. And there was the confusion of new construction as additional floors were added to existing buildings in preparation for the first of the baby boomers that would begin high school in 1959. The original 1901 prep-school-like main building and clock tower were slated for demolition in the summer of 1954, to be replaced by a vast new structure to accommodate the Baby Boom Generation. The summer before my senior year that old building, full of Old World character but hopelessly outdated after just 50 years, was demolished, together with the auditorium and that old library with the second floor jogging track, leaving us to stumble over brick rubble while moving from class to class. The new main building, the theater, and the library, all built after I'd entered college, were decidedly institutional and commonplace—New Trier lost its classic charm. Today it looks like any other public high school complex in America. Only the reputation and quality of education remain.

Because of my anemic grammar school grades, I'd been assigned to second track classes as a freshman—Civics instead of History, General Science instead of Physics. Even so I generated only a C average. I completed my freshman year with very disappointing grades, except in English.

Athletics at New Trier never earned its participants the leadership status they'd enjoyed in grammar school. The jocks did run in somewhat elite circles and wore their letter sweaters on assigned days, but in a school where everyone was working toward college admission, the athletes were no longer the unquestioned social leaders.

New social groups were needed in a student body so large. The new groups centered around special interests. There were the self-proclaimed outcasts who dressed in black leather, wore boots, and let their hair grow long. We called them "hoods," rhyming with "moods," short for hoodlums. There were intellectual groups, debating groups, sports groups, and such. My special interests were music and drama, two social subgroups into which I was entrenched by the middle of my sophomore year.

Coming out of a ho-hum freshman year into the summer of 1952, I felt a strong urge, at age fourteen, to establish an identity for myself—the standard adolescent identity crisis common to young people who find themselves adrift somewhere between childhood and adulthood. In the privacy of my bedroom, a look into the mirror above my dresser revealed a young boy struggling with acne, his hair slicked with Alberto VO-5 and combed carefully into a greasy wave. I was too old to be riding a bicycle and too young to drive a car. I wanted to prowl around late at night all summer long, hoping to experiment with such forbidden things as sex and beer, but my parents expected me to be home by nine, in bed by ten. Who was I, anyway?

Unfortunately for me, the tobacco industry had made the first step rather easy. If I started smoking I would look older, cooler, and be more of an individual. If I could suavely draw a Chesterfield out of the pack rolled up in the sleeve of my t-shirt, and tap the end against my thumbnail, then tuck the cigarette into the side of my lip, cup a lighted match around the end and draw in the smoke, snap the light off the match with a hand thrust and flick it aside, I would be someone to be reckoned with. I could direct my gaze or glare at someone while allowing the cigarette smoke to snake up my face and over one closed eye. The movies were loaded with sexy, mature, super-masculine cigarette etiquette to guide me.

There was one major problem to overcome—inhaling the smoke. It made me dizzy and sick, and sometimes I would vomit, which was not cool at all. If only it were possible to pull off the image without inhaling the smoke—but the cigarette industry had joined forces with the movie industry to convince the Western world that smokers who didn't inhale that nicotine-fortified smoke were sissies.

The tobacco marketers were careful to hide the fact that their products were little more than nicotine-delivery devices. Nicotine addiction created devoted customers. Cigarette ads sold the addiction through an image of glamour, maturity, and worldliness—which, they knew, was quite irresistible to their prime market—young teenage boys and girls.

So I had to learn to inhale. I had to become fully addicted. I had to become a real customer.

It didn't take too many packs of Chesterfields to turn me into a devotee during those early summer nights in June 1952. Soon I could puff away and inhale with anyone. I was a big boy now.

And I would continue to be a big boy until I was in my early fifties. The tobacco marketers gave me a sense of maturity, and I gave them my undying financial support for four decades, beginning when a pack of Chesterfields cost 21 cents.

And there was the Whizzer bike, a product targeted to boys who were too young to drive cars. State laws continued to be ambivalent as to whether you had to be a licensed driver to drive a motorized bicycle. Taking advantage of this legal vagueness I often borrowed Whizzer bikes owned by friends—at first to drive around the block on the sidewalk, later to drive on the highways to distant towns, zipping along at 45 to 50 miles an hour, the wind in my slick hair. This was traveling!

Two buddies of mine graduated themselves from Whizzer bikes to the legendary Harley Davidson 125, a real motorcycle, albeit small—a three-horsepower two-stroke engine, top speed of maybe sixty. I borrowed them occasionally, feeling very mature and cool, slowing down when I passed a young girl on the sidewalk, making sure a cigarette was dangling from the corner of my mouth.

Each year my family's vacation in Green Lake was a high point in my summer, when I could hang out with my cousin

Pete Huelster and our three buddies, Bill Blask, Don Wahlen, and Joey Stramp.

Before leaving for Green Lake in 1952, I had wanted to purchase a 22-caliber revolver to take along—a very macho tool which my buddies and I could fire in the sand pit on the hill above the lake. The gun was priced at $30 at a sports shop in Highland Park. I figured that for the drive to the lake I could hide it under the car seat where my parents wouldn't see it. I'd earned a little money caddying at Skokie Country Club in Glencoe. I hitchhiked up to the Highland Park Walgreens to ask the black porter there, a former coworker of mine, to take the $30 and buy the gun for me, since the store wouldn't sell it to a fourteen-year-old kid. The porter had the common sense to refuse, so I took the $30 cash with me to Green Lake to fund purchases of gasoline for my father's outboard. I spent a lot of time tooling around the lake in a primitive, heavy, homemade flat bottom rowboat that was included with the rent of our cottage. Powered by the five-horsepower outboard it could get up to maybe four miles per hour. It took me a full two hours to navigate the length of the lake.

Also, I think this was the summer I wrote *The Green Lake Story,* a fantasy scrawled out in ballpoint pen on dozens of pages of school notebook paper. The cast of characters in my novel included myself, my cousin, and our three Green Lake buddies—the Green Lake Rat Pack. In my fiction the five of us drank a lot of booze, which of course we were too young to purchase, although in reality I had somehow gotten my hands on a fifth of Gordon's gin that particular summer. The bottle—equal to today's 750-milliliter containers—lasted the Rat Pack the entire two weeks. Also in my fiction, the Rat Pack was talented at seducing several of the attractive girls attending the various summer camps around the lake. We simply got them sauced on our supply of unrefrigerated gin, and they became amorous. Since all of us were virgins, and the movies in the 1950s never got any more sexually explicit than closed-mouth kissing, my narratives of coupling with camp girls were pretty vague and sketchy. Usually I'd end a chapter when one of the girls shrugged out of her bathing suit top.

I think we'd read that teenage kids in big cities were into marijuana and pep pills. In my fantasy novel, the Green Lake Rat Pack spent a lot of time earning big money by distributing pot and drugs. None of us had ever seen the stuff and had no idea how to get it in our safe suburban school districts, but in *The Green Lake Story* we were moving illicit drugs all over southern Wisconsin, usually on Harley Davidson motorcycles.

The other members of the Rat Pack thoroughly enjoyed reading my episodes as I cranked them out. They liked the idea of earning big bucks distributing narcotics, seeing themselves high on warm gin, and seducing lovely, tanned suburban camp girls every afternoon before having to report home for dinner.

By the end of the two weeks I realized I had about 200 pages of literature that could get us all into major trouble if it ever found its way into the hands of our parents, so I decided to dispose of it permanently. I took the boat a mile offshore, out to the deepest part of the lake, where my map said I was floating in 280 feet of water. In what I considered a dramatic and fitting finale to my story, I cast the 200-odd pages onto the waters. I hadn't considered that notebook paper floats, so I spent the next two hours gathering the soggy pages of my first novel from the waves and tearing each page four times into sixteen pieces, hopefully too small for the ballpoint pen scrawling to make much sense when the pieces washed ashore.

Returning home to Glencoe toward the end of July, I had five or six weeks to kill in lovely summer weather. Let's see...the legendary Broadway show *South Pacific* closed at the Shubert Theater downtown, and the soon-to-be-legendary *Guys and Dolls* opened in its place. I had yet to see a professional theatrical production in a legitimate theater.

I think I spent a lot of time at the Glencoe Movie Theater. That year I saw two films that became classics: *High Noon* with

Gary Cooper, and *Singin' in the Rain* with Gene Kelly, who had been my Paris roommate the previous summer in *An American in Paris*. I also saw another Parisian adventure, *Moulin Rouge,* starring Jose Ferrer, set in late 19th century Paris. I enjoyed dropping back in time to exotic Paris of the Victorian years, and I was thrilled to watch my buddy Henri Toulouse-Lautrec create amazing impressionist posters. With a few quick strokes of his pencil he could immortalize a woman passing on a Paris boulevard, capturing the sexy sway of her long skirt that gathered tightly around her lithe waist. Henri and I did a lot of partying together in Paris that summer. We were always welcomed and given a good table at the Moulin Rouge where we swilled cognac all night. But as a roommate, he was much too morose and suicidal, unlike Levant and Kelly, my Paris roommates of the previous year, who just had fun singing, dancing, and partying all over town.

This was the year I lost confidence in the Academy of Motion Picture Arts and Sciences. It honored and applauded two underwhelming, forgettable musicals. *With a Song in My Heart*, the story of vocalist Jane Frohman, received five nominations and one Oscar. *The Greatest Show on Earth*, a big budget bummer about the Ringling Brothers Circus starring Betty Hutton and Jimmy Stewart, received three nominations and two Oscars, including Best Picture, while its director, Cecil B. DeMille, was honored with the Thalberg Memorial Award.

The Academy hardly even recognized *Singin' in the Rain*, which soon became a classic. *Singin' in the Rain* garnered two skimpy nominations—supporting actress and musical score—and no Oscar at all.

I was ready for my sophomore year, when my theatrical experiences would move from the audience to the stage.

Chapter 5

Discovering Show Biz

Starting in 1952 I made several lifelong friendships. Jack Waterman and I were studying Latin, and in true prep school fashion we decided to address each other as *Socius,* Latin for comrade.

In November I found a musical soul mate in Doug Buck who was in my Minors II-S class where North Shore boys were taught how to replace broken windowpanes and frayed lamp cord wires. Doug and I discovered that we both played guitar, so he invited me and my guitar to his Wilmette home one Saturday. Soon we were performing as a duo in class and church variety shows.

Jack, Doug, and I became a triumvirate, spending a lot of time together and addressing each other as *Socius.* Walt Oldendorf, Doug's lifelong friend from Wilmette schools, joined the clique the same year, and we were four.

My new friends seemed to enjoy my hyper imagination and willingness to abandon the rules. I had a way of creating adventures. Jack Waterman had a car, adding wheels and distance to our weekend scenarios which we dubbed "*Socius* Pilgrimages." On one such pilgrimage we drove out to the

Mississippi River, a geographic boundary previously crossed only by Jack. En route we dined on canned pork and beans heated over a campfire using the T-shape tire iron as a grill.

There were several pilgrimages to Green Lake where we tested our tolerance for hard liquor drunk in conjunction with unrefrigerated beer—room temperature boilermakers. On one Green Lake pilgrimage we camped out on a remote wooded peninsula called Sugar Loaf with tents, a case of beer and my .22-caliber rifle with which we plinked at our empty beer bottles. Today that once-lonely Sugar Loaf peninsula is lined with million-dollar residences.

*

October 14 1952 was my fifteenth birthday. My parents, responding to my enthusiasm for theater, took me to see *Guys and Dolls* at the elegant old Shubert Theater in the Loop. The Shubert, built in 1910, was one of only four legitimate theaters in Chicago. The interior was Edwardian splendor. The audience area was tall rather than deep, with three balconies and some box seats on the sides like an 18th century European opera theater. No seat in the house was very far from the stage. Like so many of the legitimate theaters from the early part of the century, it was an intimate theater where your seat was comfortably close to the actors and musicians.

Sadly, within a few decades legitimate theater would gravitate toward massive, costly productions like *Phantom of the Opera* and *Les Miserables* where the seat you bought as the "best available" might be the distance of a football field away from the stage and the entire cast would be connected to a huge sound system with wireless mikes. Such extravaganzas could never pay for themselves in the cozy, Shubert-size theaters that had made audiences feel almost as if they were *part* of shows like *The Pajama Game* and *My Fair Lady*.

From the middle of the first balcony I witnessed my first professional theater production. The mystery of theater settled

Discovering Show Biz

into my veins as the house lights dimmed and the orchestra began the overture. Then the main curtain lifted to reveal Damon Runyon's stylistic Broadway Avenue, the theatrical capital of America. The colorful gangland characters ran through their bright opening choreography, then three gamblers in pinstripe suits and loud shirts, ties, and snap-brim hats, lined up facing the audience. I'd been listening to the original cast recording of *Guys 'n' Dolls* for over a year—I knew every song by heart. It was all I could do to restrain myself from standing up in my balcony seat and singing along. *"I got the horse right here, his name is Paul Revere..."*

I pulled out a quarter to remove the opera glasses from the vending box on the back of the seat in front of me. I closely, meticulously admired the sets and costumes. I scanned the light masts on either side of the stage, mounted with huge black spots and floods, their beams colored by a rainbow of tinted gelatin filters. I examined the light bank mounted on the front of the mezzanine. I admired the spotlight activity from the booth high above me in back. I peered as far backstage into the wings as I could from my balcony seat. Here in the magic of theater, a show producer could create any fantasy world he wanted.

And the show itself! Such polished acting and dancing, such professional vocals, such a masterful little orchestra. This wasn't Threshold Players—this was the big league!

In the second act, Adelaide and the Hot Box chorus girls perform *"Take Back Your Mink."* The eight chorus girls lined up behind Adelaide, dressed in evening gowns and mink coats. After Adelaide's verse, the tempo picks up as the chorus goes into their song and dance routine. *"Take back your mink...."* A cloud of mink coats was tossed onto the apron just in front of the footlights. *"Take back your pearls...."* Eight ropes of pearls landed on top of the pile of fur. *"Take back the gown...."* What was I seeing? Eight evening gowns flew through the air, leaving eight nicely stacked chorus girls dancing in their *bras and panties!!!* Hey, this wasn't Minsky's Burlesque on State Street! This was the Shubert Theater! How could they get away with this? Never having seen a lady in her underwear before in my life I grabbed the opera glasses for a meticulous, up-close examination. Tits and ass, right here at a legitimate, respected Chicago theater. I never saw my mother frowning or heard my father chuckle from their seats beside me. Broadway sure beat the movies. At least it did in 1952.

*

Up to this point in my life, my exposure to the world of theater consisted of having been cast in two Threshold Players plays and one eighth grade operetta, coupled with this magical peek into professional theater at the Shubert, where I was a thrilled and mystified observer rather than a participant. Later that year I put together a comedy skit with two classmates, Carl Schultz and Joe Arnold, which we auditioned for *Lagniappe*, the big annual New Trier student variety show—but our skit didn't make the cut—although Joe would direct *Lagniappe* two years later.

But seven months later, in May of 1953, theater opened its doors to me and I dived in.

That spring Suzy Klein, a talented graduating senior who had starred in several New Trier drama productions, took it upon herself to write, produce and direct a musical comedy show that spoofed Chicago's wealthy Morton Salt family. She titled her show *When it Rains*, and peppered the cast with several New Trier drama regulars.

Her script called for four news reporters who would happen upon a major news break, and sing "Sitting on Top of the World" as a quartet. Suzy had heard that I'd started a barbershop quartet with J. D. Helms, Dave Arey, and Walt Farnham. She cast all four of us as her singing news reporters. Eventually Sue Goldberg, who directed the show's chorus, included me in her chorus line.

In June my brother Ron came home from his freshman year at Harvard, and encouraged me to join a student-run summer

Discovering Show Biz

theater group called Lake Shore Players. The group had been founded in 1950 or '51 by a group of New Trier students. The founders had tapped talent from both New Trier and Highland Park high schools, possibly due to common friendships arising out of North Shore Congregation of Israel, the large, influential North Shore synagogue. Ron had been active in Lake Shore Players during the 1952 season.

By 1953 Lake Shore Players was under the amazingly capable leadership of Ron's former classmate, Paul Burkhardt, who'd been very active in New Trier drama, and had directed *Lagniappe*. Under Burkhardt, Lake Shore Players in 1953 thrived and grew to nearly a hundred active participants. Thinking back on Burkhardt's astounding talent for organization during the three years he headed the theater group, it amazes me that he never went into business management. By contrast his career was quite convoluted. He first became manager of an independent movie theater in Chicago, then a candy store operator in Winnetka, then a butler. Paul finally became a rather distinguished educator in the North Shore public school system.

Lake Shore Players' major production for the 1953 season was *The Admirable Crichton*, a James M. Barrie play about a group of Edwardian English aristocrats shipwrecked on a South Pacific island. Burkhardt secured Danny Scheinfeld, another former *Lagniappe* director, to direct *Crichton*.

When Brother Ron invited me to become involved, *Crichton* was already cast with himself in the lead role, and rehearsals were underway at The Community House in Winnetka. I showed up one afternoon and was quickly caught up in the excitement of set building, rehearsals, and the fun and clever friends I was making at the parties that took place every night after rehearsals. We had homes in five suburbs from which to choose for our parties, and if all doors were closed we could generally count on partying aboard someone's father's yacht docked in Wilmette Harbor. Those parties were critical to our bonding and intellectual exchanges as young adults, as well as to the spawning of several intense romances.

Almost immediately I involved my *Socius* buddies in Lake Shore Players—Doug, who was attending summer school at New Trier, and Jack, whose father employed us both in summer jobs at his company, Waterman Engineering Company in Evanston, where we assembled and tested hydraulic valves. In the evenings after early dinners we all went to Lake Shore Players for set building, rehearsals, and parties. The parties usually lasted well into the night every summer evening, leaving us somewhat fatigued at the start of each work or school day, but drawing on the tireless energy of youth we somehow kept going, returning each evening to the Lake Shore Players rehearsals and parties.

It was a busy and exhausting summer filled with a lifetime of exciting experiences and memories. I have no idea how Burkhardt managed the financing for these activities—*Crichton* required extensive costumes—but with only minor support from membership dues, together with paid advertising in our play programs and free use of the Winnetka Community House auditorium, he somehow carried it off.

Burkhardt was also a clever manager of incentives. He organized three levels of membership: Active, Associate, and Charter, based on the amount of participation and enthusiasm. Membership awards and advancements were made at our regular meetings.

After *Crichton* we staged a set of three one-act plays, called the Workshop Productions. We lifted a couple of acts from Steinbeck's play, *Of Mice and Men*, in which, in addition to my technical theater responsibilities, I had a small acting role. Brother Ron took his second starring role of the season in a one-act play called *The Boor*.

Marshall Berman, who later became a professional photographer, produced a homemade 16-millimeter twelve-minute horror film during two summer weekends, casting Lake

Shore Players members in the various roles. The film plot revolved around a monster in ghoulish makeup who emerged from a coffin floating in Skokie Lagoons (just west of Glencoe). Marty Tippens and Gloria Strohmeier were cast as necking lovers whom the monster attacks in Marty's parked car. Doug Buck and I played cops that came to investigate. Subsequent to firing a 12-gauge round into the monster with my father's Winchester shotgun (you can't kill a thing that's already dead) I succumbed to the monster's bite which, quite predictably, caused all victims to become monsters themselves. The final scenes showed Marty, Gloria, Doug, and me wandering across the misty moors of Skokie Lagoons in monster makeup, following the victorious monster to his lagoon-side coffin.

Berman's horror film was produced solely to be shown at the final Lake Shore Players party of the season, giving some indication of how important the parties were to Lake Shore Players participants.

That final party of the year, like so many Lake Shore Players and New Trier parties, took place at the home of Marty Tippens—a house bordering the Indian Hill Country Club golf course that was huge enough to accommodate parties of any size. Marty's maternal grandfather had earned his place in history as inventor of the comptometer, a mechanical adding device that played a major role in clerical offices for nearly a century until electronic calculators from Texas Instruments made it obsolete in the 1960s. Meanwhile, a century of comptometer sales provided profits to fund three generations succeeding the inventor, and to purchase that huge old Indian Hill mansion. I remember Marty's English Tudor house with incredible fondness, not only as the site for many of our parties, but as a place where we often held rehearsals. On one rare occasion during the summer of '53 or '54, Jack Waterman and I had been out drinking beer or bourbon and had decided we were both a little too sauced to go home, so we went into the huge Tippens backyard to sleep off the booze. As dawn lit the sky, the Tippens maid, Rachel, recognized us and came out to ask us what we wanted for breakfast.

Lake Shore Players was more than just a theatrical experience with social opportunities for friendship, romance, and lots of parties. There was a feeling among the participants that we were a very select, special group of people, all of us quite creative and bright in our lofty intellectual party conversations. We enjoyed a camaraderie nurtured by the joys of young adulthood coupled with a unique feeling of expectation among us—we were struggling for an identity for our generation, some banner under which we would make our impact on history.

We envied the mystique of the "Lost Generation" of Gertrude Stein's Paris salon between the wars. That group had spawned such classics as *The Great Gatsby* and *The Sun Also Rises*—banners that underscored a major departure in thinking, writing, and art. We wanted an identity like that for ourselves.

There were a few signposts here and there that we tested as places to hang our identity. Jack Kerouac had published *On the Road* in 1950 and *The Subterraneans* in 1953. Hey, we thought—maybe we're Bohemians! If that were true, we'd need to fudge and nudge the facts here and there. We all lived privileged and protected lifestyles in our comfy North Shore homes furnished traditionally by Broyhill and Drexel, or with pricey English antiques from the Caledonian Market in Winnetka. How might we make that fit into something a little more outrageous, like the San Francisco apartments of Kerouac's free-spirited Haight-Ashbury group? Truly we were all freethinkers—we simply lacked the sling chairs and lava lamps.

Actually, our own 1950s identity was right under our noses—we just wouldn't recognize or understand it for several years. It peeked out at us from the pages of J. D. Salinger's novel *Catcher in the Rye,* and from scenes in Elia Kazan's film *Streetcar Named Desire*—both works suggesting that heroes could be less than heroic, yet be heroes nevertheless. Holden Caulfield and Stanley Kowalski weren't like Billy Batson or John Wayne—no, they were *flawed* heroes—but wasn't that what life was really like?

Streetcar and *Catcher* were just two years old during that summer of 1953. And more classics of this genre were in the works—*On the Waterfront*, *Franny* and *Zooey*, and *Rebel Without a Cause*. These masterpieces were every bit as unique for our time as Hemmingway and Fitzgerald had been in their time. Tennessee Williams, Elia Kazan, and Salinger may never have tippled together in a Paris salon, but nonetheless they, and others, were shaping the messages that defined our generation.

Of course, Kazan's place in history would be tarnished by his betrayals in the McCarthy hearings. But then, what could be more typical of the 1950s than Cold War paranoia? Communism was spreading steadily, successfully across the world through Asia, Africa, even the Caribbean. We'd fought one absurd war to stop Communism in South Korea, and we were getting ever more deeply involved in another conflict to halt Communism in Vietnam. Economic growth in the U.S.S.R. was exceeding that of the U.S. In 1957 we'd watch a Soviet satellite sail over our heads once every 45 minutes. The Soviet Premier would soon declare to the Western world, "We will bury you!"—and it looked like maybe they could. Was Communism going to take over America and destroy our freedom and our comfortable lifestyle? Senator McCarthy insisted it was already happening.

Would someone somewhere make a Strangelovian goof and annihilate us all?

And therein lay our identity—"The Cold War Generation"—an uneasy period of international uncertainty and instability lasting not one generation but two, from 1946 to 1991, with the 1962 Cuban Missile Crisis at its epicenter, when the world came frighteningly close to nuclear annihilation.

The Cold War Generation. Perhaps not as romantic-sounding as *The Lost Generation*. Nonetheless, that's who we were. And heroes like Holden Caulfield, Stanley Kowalski, and James Dean, themselves as uncertain, uneasy and unstable as the times we lived in, seemed to fit right in.

*

During the summer of 1953 I fine-tuned my appreciation for that ancient brew, beer. Actually I'd been experimenting with booze ever since the night I graduated from eighth grade, when I loaded myself with some of my father's Fleischmann's Blended Whiskey, earning myself a monumental hangover that had me puking my guts out most of the following day.

By 1953 my buddies and I were ready for some serious experimentation with social drinking. We drank on beaches in summer, in parked cars at night, and at parties when parents were either absent or indulgent.

The only real problem for us was having a regular, reliable access to intoxicants when we wanted them. At the time, all those upscale North Shore suburbs from Evanston to Highland Park were dry. This meant that the kids too young to drive were limited to nipping out of their parents' liquor cabinets and replacing the missing liquor with water—which worked fine until Dad began investigating why his bourbon looked a little pale and his Manhattans had no kick.

To buy beer, wine, or liquor, one had to travel to the towns just to the west of the lakeside communities. Skokie Highway was the borderline between safe and sin. There was a thriving establishment on the west side of Skokie Highway at Lake Cook Road called Pat Patterson's. Pat had a big bar and a huge package goods store.

In 1953 it was still quite legal and acceptable for a tavern owner to refuse to serve blacks in his bar. So the blacks drove their cars into Pat Patterson's massive parking lot, bought package goods at his store, then sat in their cars to drink.

We discovered that we could walk up to a car of boozing blacks, give them money, and ask them to go into Pat

Patterson's package goods store to buy us a bottle of gin or a six pack of Miller. *And they never turned us down.* They bought our booze and gave us back all the change from our two or three bucks. They never seemed to be looking for a tip.

And our party would begin.

On two or three occasions we couldn't find a car full of blacks in front of Pat Patterson's, so we asked whites to buy our booze. But whites always turned us down flat. To get our booze we needed partners in disenfranchisement—blacks. Pat Patterson rejected them for their race, and us for our age.

Late that summer my brother Ron and I, together with Ron's friend Howie Edmonds from Harvard, headed up for an evening of drinking in Highwood, Illinois, which was the first wet suburb north of the Chicago city limits. Highwood's taverns serviced nearby Fort Sheridan, a military base that is now closed. Howie gave me an Iowa Liquor Permit that he'd happened upon. I forget whose name was on the permit but whoever he was, he was twenty-two. I used the permit for about a year. It amused me that, at age 15, I could apparently pass as 22.

Actually, I didn't need the Iowa Liquor Permit that night in Highwood. We wandered into a tavern called My Place, across from the railroad station. It was the perfect watering hole for a military base—cheap and slummy, and big and loud enough for all your boozing buddies. On weekends hookers would come up from the city to work the G.I.s in My Place. And if a G.I. happened to be under the age of 21, he quickly discovered that the proprietors, by some arrangement with the police or city council, never bothered to check anybody's age. I was 16 at the time and was served whatever I liked without question.

What a discovery! I was soon herding my school buddies up to drink fests at My Place where we would be served even if we walked in with schoolbooks. We could even buy a pint or half-pint of whiskey to go.

The following year a friend of mine, Jim Parker, also born in 1937, showed me the ultimate fake I.D. solution. When he had filled out his driver's license application, he'd written the stem of the "7" in 1937 vertically, rather than slanted. At the time, your actual driver's license was a photostat of the application you filled out yourself. There was no mug shot. The only thing that identified the license as yours was your age, height, weight, and your hair, eye, and skin color.

In study hall, Parker took out his photostat license with the hand-written vertical-looking seven and used a soft dark pencil to blank out the top of the seven, matching it perfectly to the dark photostat background color. He made the seven look like a one. If he was born in 1931 he could buy booze.

I got a duplicate driver's license application and did the same thing. I'd been passing for twenty-two ever since I'd gotten that Iowa Liquor Permit.

When Doug Buck and I got to college in the fall of 1955, we'd had two years' experience with drinking. We were appalled to discover that most college freshmen were drinking beer for the first time in their lives. The first wet fraternity parties yielded washrooms splattered with vomit. Doug and I and most of the boys and girls of our over-privileged North Shore suburbs were more than two years ahead of our age group in our ability to hold liquor.

But, for the most part, at age fifteen or sixteen in 1953, we were all still virgins. I resolved to correct this shortcoming in myself by year's end.

Chapter 6

Trying to Undo Gloria

My involvement with Marshall Berman's horror film sparked in me an intense interest for the female co-star, Gloria Strohmeier. We saw a lot of each other during the Lake Shore Players summer season. Entering my junior year at New Trier (Gloria was a senior at Highland Park High School) I was determined to keep my romance with Gloria alive, despite our separation in different communities and school districts.

Gloria was a daughter of the upper class establishment. Her father was a wealthy attorney who owned a large, lovely frame house on a shaded residential street in Highland Park. Gloria was one of the few girls I knew who actually "came out" into society—her parents threw an elegant, catered debut party for her at the beginning of the 1953 "social season."

By the mid 1950s, the formal coming-out party had evolved into one of the dying gasps of a social class system that began sinking with the Titanic. The tradition probably survived a little longer on the East Coast, or even in Lake Forest, Illinois, where members of a more rigidly structured upper class still clung to these ancient aristocratic traditions that helped to define them as members of an elite group. Most of the children of these crusty families attended exclusive private schools. But in the North

Shore suburbs south of Lake Forest, many of the daughters of wealthy families attended public schools like New Trier, and were reluctant to participate in social events that might exclude some of their closest but lesser-born high school friends. In this respect I suppose New Trier was something of a melting pot. I never thought of it that way before.

I checked Amy Vanderbilt's guide for the proper way to structure a response to a formal invitation. I decided not to rent formalwear for the event, and arrived at the Strohmeier house in a herringbone suit. I was met by a doorman who ushered me into an attendant in white tie formalwear standing at the head of the reception line. This attendant bent toward me, asked me for my name in a whisper, and tilted his ear for me to whisper back. He then stood tall and addressed the roomful of guests in a forceful, authoritative Oxford baritone: "Mr. Jerry Inglehart." Gloria's mother and father greeted me. Gloria extended her hand to me and said with a hint of Eliza Doolittle in her voice, "How kind of you to come."

My informal meetings with Gloria involved a great deal of hitchhiking to Highland Park, plus several rides on the interurban electric train. Gloria, a high school senior, had her driver's license and unlimited access to her parents' Buick. I wouldn't reach driving age until my 16th birthday in October. So Gloria drove us everywhere. It was difficult for me to be a macho male with my debutante date when I was sitting in the passenger seat.

Gloria was more than cute. She was elegant, privileged, pampered, spoiled, and self-involved.

And as I realized on reflection many years later, Gloria was desperately anxious to rid herself of her virginity that autumn.

How could I know this at age sixteen? Actually, I didn't realize it until a few years later, when I was able to compare Gloria's response to necking with the reaction of other women to climactic sex. Gloria's moans and cries were very similar, as she gasped my name over and over again—and we were only

Trying to Undo Gloria

kissing! Gloria at eighteen was like a soft, fragrant peach, ripe for her transition to womanhood.

The only obstacle was that neither Gloria nor I were certain just how to accomplish this in the light of the rigid moral rules governing meetings between North Shore boys and girls in 1953. First of all, no matter how much Gloria wished to get laid, she could never say so to any boy. For her to put such desires into words could set off a chain reaction of male rumor and braggadocio that would quickly cast her as one of those "loose" girls. Her status as a debutante would be destroyed.

Mid-century moral rules set out a narrow, confusing formula by which Gloria and I could achieve her deflowering without damaging her reputation. We were permitted to "neck," and Lord knows, we did! But moving beyond this threshold of excitement required progress to occur according to a pattern that would allow Gloria to claim later, "I don't know what came over me!" Pre-planning was out of the question.

This meant that for us to move to a higher stage of petting, we'd have to do it "inadvertently." A casual brush of two enthusiastic bodies progressing in an unintentional manner. No premeditation.

The Maidenform Company had created a major obstacle for us: a nearly impenetrable bra with a formidable clasp. If Maidenform had invented a bra with some sort of a Velcro clasp that could be nudged apart in the heat of passion, Gloria and I could advance to the next step honorably. Unfortunately, there was that damned clasp, which, I was convinced, had been designed by a nun. We boys without older sisters couldn't very well search our mothers' underwear drawers for a much needed education. Furthermore, if a boy placed his eager fingers on the offending clasp in an effort to liberate those two heavenly, soft, fleshy bodies from their cotton prisons, he was getting dangerously close to crossing the border into premeditation.

Of course, there was a far more accessible and dynamic "hot button" on a woman's anatomy that some of us boys had heard about. It was supposed to be many times more effective in melting a young virgin's inhibitions. But no research materials in any of the libraries on the North Shore (I know—I checked them all) revealed this hot button's exact anatomical location, much less what it looked, felt, or tasted like, or even how to correctly pronounce its name, much less what you did to make it work once you found it, or how its size, shape and response level might differ from one female to another.

As Gloria and I groped and struggled with the mystery of her sexuality, Dr. Alfred Kinsey's landmark book on female sexual behavior was just being published and reviewed, but it would be a long time before a copy of the controversial bestseller would reach North Shore booksellers or the Glencoe Public Library. The U.S. Congress immediately responded to the study by cutting the funding for Dr. Kinsey's research.

Besides, any boy bold enough to attempt his own study of female sexuality by reaching "down there" would cause his well-bred adolescent petting partner to gasp, jump to her feet, and demand to be taken home. Meanwhile, unbeknownst to us opportunistic males of 1953, panty hose would become widely accepted in response to the introduction of the mini skirt in 1959, and the clitoral window-of-opportunity would slam shut.

Then there was the question of the condom. Few of us had ever advanced far enough down lover's lane to need one.

But if my luck with Gloria ever proceeded that far, exactly how, I wondered, could I sneak out that condom and unroll it over my eager masculinity? The mere sight of the thing would throw a passionate female adolescent into a fit: "Why, you were *planning* this! You *schemed to seduce* me tonight, you perverted *cad!*" And she would snatch her panties off the automobile floor, pull down her skirt, slam the car door in anger, and head for a pay phone to call her father, using the dimes wedged into her penny loafers that were there for just such an emergency.

The whole 1950s North Shore teen seduction had to appear unplanned, the unforeseen result of a fit of passionate adolescent true love that had started innocently enough,

Trying to Undo Gloria

but..."Well, Daddy, we just didn't know what got into us. I know better now. It'll never happen again." For a North Shore girl of the 1950s to lose her virginity without loss of her reputation, she would have to risk an accidental pregnancy as well.

One day while hitchhiking north to meet with Gloria, I hit on a scheme that might have overcome this barrier. That weekend I secured a condom (we still called them "rubbers" in 1953) from a vending machine in a filling station. I had to go clear to Highwood, near the Fort Sheridan military base—no gas station on the North Shore dared to install such a machine, for sanitary or any other reasons.

I figured that if I stuck the rubber in my wallet, the leather would eventually conform to the shape of the condom and reveal its circular outline. After enough occasions of pulling the wallet out to pay for movie tickets or Cokes, Gloria might notice the circular embossing. Actually, since Gloria was kind of naïve, I might have to leave the wallet out on a soda fountain table after paying for Cokes, until Gloria noticed the circle and asked what it was. I'd then feign surprise that Gloria didn't know, and tell her what it was, explaining that every responsible man always carried a rubber to protect himself against the risk of disease. By casting the little commodity as an item of health, forethought, maturity, and responsibility, I might be able to nurse it out of the category of evil, pre-planned seduction. Then if I succeeded in my plans to excite Gloria past the point of no return, she wouldn't be surprised about the rubber because she'd have known I had one handy all along. Hopefully, Gloria would not take the matter up with her mother. The key issue was to be prepared like a good Boy Scout to protect Gloria from an unplanned semester in Europe.

Unfortunately, my mother noticed the circular embossing in my wallet before Gloria did. And that was the end of that.

So like most of the other young studs in 1953, I was left struggling with the question of how to unclasp that diabolical

Maidenform bra in a way that looked like it had just popped open by itself.

Within a few months Gloria graduated from High School with her virginity intact.

A year later, I did too.

*

I was eager to continue my theatrical pursuits at New Trier. I was determined that one day I'd become a theatrical producer. I studied books about stage management and joined the high school stage and lighting crews.

Throughout the fall and winter, my *Socius* buddies and I were involved in the building of sets for several New Trier plays. We called ourselves the Socius Scenic Artists. I designed a Socius Scenic Artists logo and made a stencil of it, which we stenciled on the backs of all the sets we built.

In January, the four of us became involved in building the sets for *Lagniappe*, the highly popular annual student variety show that played to sold-out houses in the spring. My *Socius* brothers and I contributed quite a bit to that production, helping to design the sets and plan scene change logistics, and managing the fly gallery during the performances.

We watched each rehearsal from the fly gallery catwalk. One of the acts involved a comedy skit during which an actor pointed his finger skyward and pretended to shoot a gun, as the drummer in the orchestra beat out a rat-tat-tat. As the four of us watched the show from the catwalk, I decided it would be hilarious if, after this pretend shooting, we would drop a goose onto the stage from the fly gallery. To execute the gag, we should have looked around for a plush toy goose to drop, but I thought the gag would be funnier if we dropped a real goose, feathers and all.

The following day was Saturday. In the morning Jack Waterman and I went out to a poultry farm west of Wilmette and purchased a large, handsome white goose weighing about twelve pounds. All we had to do was kill it. Supposedly birds are butchered by decapitation, but our gag called for a dead goose to drop from the sky with its head intact.

My friend Joe Arnold owned an antique .22 caliber single-shot gambler's pistol that he lent to me. I purchased a box of cartridges from a sport shop and went down to the school's scene shop, where our goose, tethered to a water pipe, was waiting.

If you leave a goose alone for a few hours, as we had, the goose will defecate, as it had. Our goose had deposited several pasty green goose turds within the limited vicinity of his tether.

I grabbed his beak in my left fist and raised it. With my right hand I cocked Joe's pistol, fired a bullet through the goose's chin—and got a sudden and violent lesson in waterfowl mortality. I'd shot a few ducks out of the sky along the Wolf River in Wisconsin. Those birds had simply collapsed and fell obligingly to earth, as I expected this goose to do. But when a bird is shot through the *brain,* it flops around madly in a wild dance of death. The goose's batting wings hammered my left arm, causing me to lose my grip on his beak. He shed copious amounts of blood. For nearly a minute I watched helplessly as our fine white goose thrashed around in his own crimson blood and green feces. When he finally settled down, I realized the wisdom of using a cute plush *toy* goose for our sight gag. Had we dropped the corpse of this huge, bloody, badly mangled, turd-fouled goose onto the stage during a *Lagniappe* performance, half of the girls in the chorus would have screamed or passed out.

I didn't have the stomach to clean up the mess I'd made. I wrapped our dead goose in newspaper, threw him in the back of Jack's car and returned the gun to Joe Arnold.

That Sunday, Jack's mother invited Doug, Walt and me to a roast goose dinner. *She'd cooked our goose!* The creature that I'd made ugly and repugnant in the scene shop, Mrs. Waterman had converted to a thing of beauty once again, roasted golden brown, providing an extraordinarily juicy, tender and tasty feast which she served with savory, nutty dressing, gravy, mashed potatoes, and tart cranberry sauce. Our *Socius* goose dinner was a scene out of Charles Dickens.

My own goose got cooked on Monday afternoon, when I was called into the office of Mr. Kahler, Dean of Men, to explain the mess in the scene shop.

"What caused all that blood and fecal matter in the scene shop?"

"A goose."

"A *goose?* Why did you have a goose down there?"

Dean Kahler looked somewhat like Nikita Khrushchev, but his huge physique, threatening scowl, and gruff voice were greatly diminished by his inability to look anyone directly in the eyes. He looked just above my head. Occasionally during this interrogation I looked over my shoulder to see what he kept staring at.

"We thought we'd use a goose for a sight gag in the show."

"Who is *we?*"

I wouldn't implicate by *Socius* brothers. "Did I say *we?* I meant *me.*"

"Why all that blood?"

"We needed a dead goose, so I shot it."

"You shot it? How?"

"With a pistol."

"You had a pistol in school? Where did you get a pistol?"

I didn't want to implicate Joe Arnold either. The interview with Mr. Kahler continued for perhaps another half hour, when he possibly tired of glaring at the wall over my head. I expected some sort of disciplinary action, but he simply dismissed me with an above-my-head scowl. I don't think the 1954 New Trier Student Handbook addressed either geese or guns in school.

We abandoned the sight gag entirely. It had caused too much grief. No goose, real or toy, would fall to the stage during *Lagniappe '54*.

Trying to Undo Gloria

The following autumn, Doug Buck and I were tapped to design and build the sets for *Lagniappe '55*. The episode with the goose had either been forgotten or forgiven.

*

For spring vacation Doug Buck and I went tent camping with Marty Tippens in Brown County State Park in southern Indiana. Driving along one of the park's back roads in Marty's Buick Roadmaster convertible, we found a brook of crystal clear running water. We waded across the brook and found a lovely valley hidden between wooded hills. We carried our equipment across the brook and set up our camp in that pristine little valley.

Our camping trip was both delightful and hilarious. Marty, who was planning on becoming a professional actor, was nonstop comedy—he sprinkled every one of his anecdotes with convincing impersonations—Irishmen, Italians, hillbillies, and mental retards. We'd buy a couple of six-packs of beer and a little brandy, go back to our private campsite and drink and joke over our campfire. When the sun set and darkness covered the valley in a cyclorama of brilliant stars, we were alone with nature, laughing and joking well into each night.

After a couple of nights I suggested that we drive into the nearby town of Nashville, Indiana, to try to find a brothel. None of the three of us had ever been in a whorehouse before. But the adventure seemed worth it to my buddies—as long as I was the one who made the necessary inquiries. That night, after querying bartenders in several small towns in southern Indiana, we concluded what should have been obvious to us at the onset—small towns don't normally have cathouses. When we finally abandoned our search for sexual gratification and adventure, it was too late to wend our way back to our remote campsite, so we stopped for the night at a tourist court with cabins.

I remember that tourist court with nostalgia. The 1940s and 50s were the heyday of tourist courts on major highways. Today they're long gone, replaced by motel chains. One might occasionally find a *former* tourist court still standing today, either abandoned or converted to other uses along one of the old federal highways—but our 1954 lodging was a real tourist cabin where the three of us sat with the bugs and bad mattresses and drank our six-pack and eventually went to sleep, thinking we'd simply found cheap lodgings (three boys, three dollars,) never realizing we were experiencing a small piece of what was soon to become historic Americana, along with roadside Burma Shave signs.

Probably the most memorable two events of my junior year were my first serious romances—Gloria, beginning in autumn and ending at a Lake Shore Players Christmas party in 1953—then Kathy Sommer, who I met in April of 1954.

I think Kathy was attracted to my music. She became aware of me one Saturday night when a bunch of us and our dates headed up to Wauconda, a town in northern Illinois farmland. My date that night was a girl who enhanced her excellent figure with a slinky knit dress. I can't remember her name, although I recall vividly every curve of her body beneath that sexy green dress. Kathy was with Jack Waterman that night. Someone in our group knew of a cottage on a lake belonging to parents of a friend who had lent him a key in order that we could take our girlfriends there. I never did locate the cottage, but most of the group I was traveling with found a roadhouse where the bartender wasn't checking IDs very carefully. There was a house guitar. I sang and played folk songs and led the group in song. Kathy thought my music was pretty impressive.

Another thing appealed to Kathy—she thought I looked a little like Marlon Brando, her favorite heart-throb movie star. I exploited the similarity a couple of weeks later when I invited Kathy to go with me to the Masque Ball, a costume dance sponsored by one of the New Trier clubs. Doug, Marty, and I had seen Brando's classic motorcycle movie, *The Wild One* during our trip to Brown County. I convinced four of my friends that we should show up at the Masque Ball dressed as Brando's motorcycle outlaw gang. There were five of us—Jack and Doug, plus two of my barbershop quartet partners, Dave Arey and Walt Farnham, and me. We each secured black leather motorcycle jackets and painted the backs of the jackets with the now-famous skull-and-cross-piston-connecting-rod logo of the movie's Black Rebels Motorcycle Club. We used temporary tempera paint that could be washed off of the jackets after the party. And we borrowed other accessories which none of us owned—motorcycle boots and motorcycle caps. I added to my image with a pair of long sideburns of theatrical crepe hair, applied with spirit gum. In my bedroom mirror I perfected Brando's sexy, distant, uninvolved, superior gaze. I got Brando's nasal tenor down pat. The dangling cigarette helped. With the addition of sunglasses and jeans, I looked quite disreputable. All five of our dates dressed as hooker-slutty as their North Shore wardrobes would allow, which wasn't much. Mostly they used tight pants, form-fitting sweaters, a lot of heavy makeup and eye shadow.

As the ten of us sauntered into the costume ball, someone was doing a stand-up comedy skit on stage. The comedian stopped in mid-sentence and stared at us. The crowd turned to follow his stare. We were the showstoppers. For several minutes, until friends began to recognize us, the crowd assumed that some out-of-town motorcycle gang was crashing their party.

Perhaps I did look a little like Brando. The effect on Kathy that night was astonishing. I was the sexiest thing in sideburns.

I was accustomed to being the most daring and outrageous individual in my crowd. I could be counted on to dream up the most dangerous and exotic activities. And Kathy was a relatively straight-laced Catholic girl from a good North Shore family. She'd even attended private schools.

Nonetheless, as early spring dissolved into early summer, Kathy's clique of girl friends threw me a few curve balls for which I was quite unprepared.

The first of these was Candy Fuller who had been Dave Arey's date at the Masque Ball. As I got to know her I discovered that behind her initial appearance as a quiet and soft-spoken little goody two-shoes was a schoolgirl in an adult relationship with a man in his mid twenties. Her date with Dave Arey had been strictly for appearance, to keep her parents unaware of her real boyfriend, John Gavin, who happened to be the older brother of one of my classmates. I assumed Candy and John were sleeping together, reasoning that a man of 25 or 26 was not likely to be dating an eighteen-year-old girl unless she was delivering her part of an adult relationship. This age difference was way out of sync with the standards for North Shore girls in 1954.

A month later I learned that Candy's relationship was not unique in Kathy's clique.

Prom Night was approaching—that romantic formal event destined to be remembered for life. This was the one night of the year when many parents reluctantly allowed their eager teenage sons and daughters to stay out all night, hoping that their daughters would return at dawn sleepy but with virtue still intact. A handful of senior class girls were planning their graduation to womanhood that night. But the overwhelming majority of the class would have to settle for a night of wishful thinking—breaking of a few rules without breaking into adulthood.

In the afternoon before the prom when I went to pick up my tuxedo, Kathy asked me if I would be willing, prior to picking her up for the dance, to pick up Patricia Chambers, one of her classmates. My mission was to pretend to be Pat's date. I would then drive Pat from her home to the door of her real date, Rex Petersen, a friend and contemporary of John Gavin. This would keep Pat's parents unaware that their daughter would be spending prom night with a man seven years older than her.

Trying to Undo Gloria

Although both of these older men dressed in tuxedos that night to compliment their dates' formal wear, neither man showed up at the prom, where they would have stood out as not belonging to either the student body or the faculty. That would have generated a scandal.

But the prom was simply window dressing that night. We didn't stay long. About 10 P.M. Kathy and I left the dance with Candy and Pat, joining John and Rex outside, to drive downtown to Chicago in their cars—where we were somehow admitted to a jazz nightclub on Grand Avenue. I had my false I.D., but it was not needed—John and Rex apparently knew the nightclub owners or managers. We drank and listened to live Dixieland jazz for a couple of hours. This was all pretty exciting to me. I was sixteen years old and sitting in a rented tux in a jazz nightclub drinking cocktails. Usually I was the kid my friends relied upon to get them a bottle of gin or a six-pack of beer, or take them to that funky, sweaty bar called My Place in Highwood. But I had no fancy downtown jazz nightclubs in my repertoire of evils. I was somewhat humbled to discover that forbidden things I didn't have the connections or *chutzpah* to pull off, were lurking right before my eyes.

About 1 A.M. our party returned to John and Rex's cars and drove to a place called the Silver Cloud on Milwaukee Avenue. It featured a gay stage show. This fast lane was starting to get a little too speedy for me. But the show was pretty funny.

I thought about that night for a long time. *What were Kathy and I doing in that crowd?*
But the real shocker was yet to come.
Kathy's closest friend was a willowy girl with a rather plain face named Joan Tatman. Whereas my clique at New Trier was the drama crowd, Kathy and Joan were both part of the art clique.

Joan never seemed to have a date. I attributed this to her mousy appearance and the somewhat sloppy way she always dressed. Also, she didn't seem to care that she never had a date.

It turned out that she had been sleeping for over a year with Alvin Sargent Clinton, a middle-aged married man with a son in my class at New Trier.

Clinton was on the faculty of the Northwestern University School of Drama. At age 42 he was tall, thin, prematurely gray, and rather handsome—what James Dean might have looked like had he lived that long. Clinton directed plays for several of the North Shore Community Theaters. He'd directed me in two plays for Threshold Players in Glencoe, so I'd already known him for four years.

Somehow Clinton had managed to establish himself firmly in the New Trier Drama clique. This was important to him—Mr. Clinton had a fondness for girls in their teens. Joan Tatman had not been Mr. Clinton's first choice for a high-school-age mistress. Nor even his second. When Brother Ron returned home from Harvard for the summer, I mentioned the Clinton-Tatman relationship to him. Ron informed me that Mr. Clinton had unsuccessfully solicited not one, but two of his New Trier classmates during his senior year. I never knew how many other New Trier girls Mr. Clinton may have approached—or even become involved with down through the years. These three were simply the ones Ron and I knew about.

But then, we in the drama and art crowds prided ourselves in being Bohemian. Free thinkers. Advocates of free love. We thought that Joan's relationship with Mr. Clinton was pretty neat. We nearly idolized it. We protected them. We took pride in being among the apparently select few who knew their secret. One of our friends even lent Mr. Clinton her house keys when her family was away for a vacation.

I write this today from the perspective of a parent and grandparent. It's true that just a few years later The Pill would initiate a sexual revolution that my sons would share in, making my comparatively pedestrian high school experiences seem tame and laughable. But we children of the early 1950s, in our incredible naivety, were protecting Mr. Clinton with our silence, and supporting him with our house keys.

Trying to Undo Gloria

Perhaps my sons learned of similar indiscretions during their high school careers a generation later. Thank God I had sons, not daughters. Had I had a daughter at New Trier in the early fifties, I would have had Mr. Clinton placed behind bars.

But at the time, I was impressed. I even respected Clinton—he was one of my favorite theatrical directors, and my personal drama coach the following year, when he was somewhat instrumental in getting me accepted at Carnegie-Mellon University. More on this later.

*

When Brother Ron came home from Harvard in late May, our relationship turned from one of siblings to close friends—a relationship that lasts to this day. A year earlier Ron was inviting me to become involved with his friends in Lake Shore Players. Now I was inviting Ron to become part of my group. I introduced him to the crowd that gathered around Kathy's place. I took him to a beer breakfast party, which started at dawn in Skokie Lagoons on a school day. Ron even dated Candy Fuller a couple of times, until he saw that she was far too neurotic to be any fun.

School closed in early June—the start of the summer during which the older New Trier school buildings were to be torn down to make room for newer, larger buildings. The Speedway Wrecking Company began preparations for demolition of the beautiful old clock tower building that had stood proudly since 1901, giving this public school the Old World appearance of an English prep school. The demolition team began by stripping the building of its doors, windows, pipes, drinking fountains, sinks and toilets. The remaining skeleton would be demolished with a wrecking ball.

I wanted a souvenir of that elegant old building which had been photographed so often for national magazine articles. Speedway Wrecking Company was selling all the old plumbing fixtures, but I didn't think a drinking fountain or washstand would make an impressive souvenir, although Lake Shore Players did purchase a toilet and presented it to Marshall Berman for his birthday in July.

High atop the peaked clock tower I saw what I wanted—the copper lightning rod that had stood sentinel over the school for over half a century.

Since the building no longer had any doors, entry was rather easy. I rented a huge bolt cutter and bought some heavy manila rope. One evening in late June, just at dusk, my *Socius* brothers and I used flashlights to guide our way through the gloomy deserted hallways and up the stairways where we'd so often filed between classes along with hundreds of other students.

On the fourth floor we found the entrance to the clock tower—a door long kept permanently locked, but now a mere threshold leading to a stairway few students had ever seen. There was an unused classroom on the fifth floor. Ladder rungs were mounted into one wall, leading up to a ceiling trapdoor. This trapdoor led us out into the open air archways of what the original architect must have planned as a bell tower. Hundreds of pigeons cooed their greeting to us from the rafters overhead. The floor was thickly coated with fifty years of guano.

A tall permanent wooden ladder rose up to an opening in the floor of the next level, which was the base of the four-sided pyramid structure of the steep tower roof. Here our flashlights pierced the windowless darkness of the inside of the roof pyramid. In the center of the area a single permanent ladder led up perhaps eighteen feet to an opening near the top of the pyramid. Doug and Jack stayed at the base of this ladder while Walt and I climbed to the opening. I climbed through it and stood on the outside ledge. Just above me was the massive green copper cap of the pyramid, with the lightning rod standing like a medieval pike above it, and connected to a thick copper grounding cable that led down one of the hips of the pyramid and out of sight over the roof's edge.

Trying to Undo Gloria

I tied the manila rope around my waist and handed the line to Walt, standing inside at the top of the ladder. He tied the rope to the ladder, to stop my fall if I slipped. I grabbed the copper roof cap and climbed onto it, wrapping my legs around it. Walt passed me the bolt cutter.

I must have wrestled with that old copper rod for ten minutes. I thought it would be so easy to snip through it, but all I did was bend it. I should have brought a hacksaw instead of a bolt cutter.

I gave up and we all climbed back to ground level. In the following days, Speedway Wrecking's demolition ball leveled the tower. My fellow New Trier alums may care to reexamine their 1955 yearbook pictures of the old brick clock tower dramatically falling to the wrecker's ball—and notice that the lightning rod, which had stood proudly erect for over half a century, is bent severely to the east, as I left it.

The Lake Shore Players summer season started off with all the enthusiasm of the previous year—except that we'd apparently worn out our welcome at The Community House in Winnetka. Paul Burkhardt and Marshall Berman somehow managed to get permission to use the Glencoe Central School auditorium for our major production, *Happy Birthday* by Anita Loos. For the second straight season, Brother Ron was cast in the lead role of our major production, playing opposite Suzy Klein.

I was now the technical director of Lake Shore Players, responsible for costumes, props, lighting, set design, and construction. I designed and built a *Happy Birthday* set representing a neighborhood tavern in Oakland, California.

One of the new members of Lake Shore Players that year was Alan Solomon—a grotesque-looking, fat Highland Park boy with incredible charisma and a remarkable comic personality. He was cast as Mr. Nanino in *Happy Birthday,* and was often the life of our endless parties with his effeminate manner and fast-talking Jewish humor. Alan was seriously considering a career as a professional theatrical producer, and his family had the money to make his dream come true. Four years later, in 1958, Alan (who by then had changed his name to Alan Carr) produced Tennessee Williams' *Suddenly Last Summer* at the Civic Theater in Chicago, followed by *The Girls in 509* starring Imogene Coca. A couple of years later he produced his *opus magnum*—the fantastically successful Broadway musical *Grease,* as well as the film starring John Travolta and Olivia Newton-John.

Toward the end of the summer of 1954 Paul Burkhardt demonstrated his ability to reward hard work. I'd put in a lot of long hours as technical director, so Paul invented a new annual award— "Most Valuable Contribution of the Year." He bought a plaque from a trophy shop and had my name engraved on a plate for the year 1954. At our final party of the season, Burkhardt presented it to me as the first annual recipient.

My whirlwind romance with Kathy was approaching a major barrier. Her father, Al Sommer, who was head of the Chicago office of McCann Erickson Advertising, was being transferred to New York. Their house on Lake Street in Glencoe was sold. The family moved to Greenwich, Connecticut. Kathy moved in with Linda Sutton, a girlfriend in Winnetka, to mark time during the last two weeks before she was to leave for her freshman year at the University of Colorado in Boulder. I took her downtown to catch her Burlington-Northern train at Union Station. As the train pulled out, the beginning of a separation between Kathy and me began. It lasted nearly two years and spanned three continents.

But my most memorable high school year lay just ahead.

Chapter 7

The Nashville Jail

My new relationship with Kathy Sommer influenced me deeply. When she left me for the University of Colorado she took my loyalty with her—I would not be dating other girls. Furthermore, I reasoned, if I was to have an adult relationship with a woman, I'd have to begin applying myself to my first order of business—getting into college. I became a serious student. And to my total amazement, I found it remarkably easy to get top grades. I made honor roll. After eleven years of deplorable scholarship, I was suddenly an honor student.

*

Encyclopedia Britannica Films filled an interesting niche in the American education scheme. Every few weeks a schoolteacher would feel the need for a respite from the daily grind of teaching, so she'd order a film from the Encyclopedia Britannica Films Catalog, allowing her a period of welcome rest in the teachers' lounge while the class watched an "educational" film.

Encyclopedia Britannica was masterful at coming up with movie titles that would appeal to a teachers' sense of enhancing the education of her students while she slipped out for a cigarette. Once such title—*Learning to Study*—was irresistible. It was produced in October 1954 and was such a hit in their film catalog that it stayed there for seventeen years throughout the 1960s, long after the mid-1950s clothing and hair styles of the student actors had become hopelessly outdated, causing audiences of grammar and high school kids to chuckle, then laugh outright, and finally whoop and guffaw and roll in the aisles.

But that magical title, *Learning to Study*, kept it active with schools across the nation. And it couldn't be remade—Encyclopedia Britannica had sold its Wilmette, Illinois, production facilities in about 1962.

On the advice of Marty Tippens I had auditioned for a role in *Learning to Study*. I was cast in a lead role as a high school amateur radio operator whose hobby was usurping his study time. I had greasy hair combed into a high front wave and slicked back into a circa 1950s Duck's Ass haircut. Using my new honor roll status as leverage, I convinced my mother to let me take a week off from school to be in the film.

Encyclopedia Britannica Films was not Hollywood. We were filming in 16 millimeter, not thirty-five. The actors weren't Screen Actors' Guild. But in 1954 Encyclopedia Britannica Films' production capabilities were far more professional than anything I'd been involved with up to that time. The sound stage was good, the camera was mounted on crab dolly—and it was often pointed at me, with a boom operator holding a microphone above my head. In my crackly teenage voice I recited my lines and acted my part.

In 1971 when I was 33 years old, I rented the film to show to my two young sons. They got a kick out of seeing their dad as a mid-50s teenage film star with a James Dean haircut. They invited their friends to a second showing so they all could snicker and giggle together.

The following year I decided to buy a print of the film to keep in a vault for my grandchildren, if any. But I'd missed my

The Nashville Jail

chance. In late 1971 Encyclopedia Britannica retired the film and tossed out all the prints, including the negatives. If any of my readers happen to know a little old retirement-age teacher still surviving in today's public school system, she may have a scratchy old print of *Learning to Study* tucked away for her occasional cigarette breaks. Please contact my publisher and let me know. *I'll pay anything for that print.*

*

Theater was now my obsession in life. I played a key role on the New Trier stage crew. Doug Buck, himself now infected with theater after two seasons of Lake Shore Players, tried out for two plays and got the lead roles in both. I took a small acting role in one of the plays. Jack Waterman and I both served on the drama club board.

I consulted with my high school drama teacher, Miss Gahagen, for her recommendations on schools where I could pursue a career in technical theater to prepare myself to become a producer. She suggested four schools—The University of Iowa, Chicago's Goodman Theater, Dennison University in Ohio, and Carnegie-Mellon in Pittsburgh, which was called Carnegie Institute of Technology at the time because their major thrust was engineering. But they also had an excellent Fine Arts college with a world-class drama department.

Goodman Theater was out of the question because I'd be living at home. For years I'd been looking forward to living in a city away from my mother, in a dorm room with a door that had a lock to which my mother did not have a key.

Iowa just didn't inspire me. It was right in the middle of the Corn Belt, which I regarded as culturally deprived.

I filled out applications to Carnegie Tech and Dennison. I didn't see much hope for Dennison. It's a church-sponsored school, requiring a letter of recommendation from my pastor. Never having had a strongly religious upbringing, I had no pastor and admitted as much in my Dennison application. Or maybe I just tossed the application aside.

In early December I inquired of Doug Buck if he'd made any decisions about college. He hadn't. When I'd met him two years earlier he'd been planning to become an archeologist or anthropologist—and I'm sure that with his intelligence and attention to detail he would have been successful at either. It's easy to imagine the handsome Doug puffing away on his pipe, his studious eyes peering through his glasses at some petrified bones in the Olduvai Gorge of East Africa. *Professor Douglas Buck discovers Lucy's forefather.*

But Doug's exposure to theater had muddied the waters for him. He loved theater. I filled out Doug's application to Carnegie Tech. I think I even mailed it for him.

And thinking back over the years today, Doug is one of only four of my many Lake Shore Players cohorts who went on to lifelong careers in theater. The other three were Alan Carr, Marty Tippens, and Judy Rieger, who'd directed me in *Of Mice and Men,* and co-starred with me in *Learning to Study*, the 1954 Encyclopedia Britannica Films.

Beginning in late November, Doug Buck and I began designing the stage sets for *Lagniappe* 1955. Because the New Trier auditorium had been torn down over the previous summer, *Lagniappe '55* would be produced at the Glencoe Central School Auditorium, where I'd lowered the fire curtain and had a run-in with Miss Collins four years earlier. Glencoe Central Auditorium was familiar turf to me—and a far better theater than the old New Trier Auditorium. But it had no workshop for building sets. So Doug and I set out to find some sort of warehouse, shop, or barn where we could build our *Lagniappe* sets.

A Winnetka clothing merchant, Abe Fell, was very supportive of New Trier students, because he sold plenty of student wardrobes and rented virtually all the tuxedos for our four annual formal events. Abe Fell owned an empty store in downtown Winnetka. He told us we could use it—for a couple of complimentary tickets to *Lagniappe*. We moved in with our lumber, muslin, stage hardware, paint, brushes, and saws and began building.

I was now a Big Man On Campus, just like my brother Ron had been three years earlier. I was a senior, on honor roll, and playing a key role in *Lagniappe*.

Lagniappe activity intensified as the spring semester began and the performance date neared. We'd finished building the sets, and had them trucked from the Fell store to Glencoe Central Auditorium. Next we had to assemble and paint them.

To me, nothing on earth was more important than *Lagniappe*. My obsession began to undermine my first semester resolution to be an honor student. I was reverting back to my old habits of not studying. What was more important—the show or my classes? I wanted to be a theatrical producer, and *Lagniappe* was theater!

One Monday morning on a chilly March day, I left my house to hitchhike to school. But the previous night I'd thought of a few additional touches that could improve the *Lagniappe* sets, so I stopped by the auditorium stage door. I never got to school that day—I spent the whole day working on the sets.

I did the same thing on Tuesday. Then Wednesday. And again on Thursday. I'd cut nearly an entire week of classes.

On Friday morning my advisor called my mother, asking where I'd been all week. She had a pretty good idea. At eleven A.M. my mother walked in the stage door and confronted me.

I quickly left to return to my classes. During the day the faculty advisor for *Lagniappe* called me into his office. I was kicked out of the show. *I was no longer a part of Lagniappe!*

Well, it didn't make too much difference. My work on *Lagniappe* was done. The sets were designed, built, and painted. Our crew knew how to change them. The show was in its last days of rehearsals. The programs were printed showing Doug Buck and me as the designers of those sets. The only thing that could be taken away from me now was the treasured camaraderie with the *Lagniappe* Company. So although I was technically no longer a part of *Lagniappe,* at the end of the final night's performance I sneaked in the stage door. I was on stage for the curtain call, together with the show's cast, crew, and directors.

Then I attended the *Lagniappe* cast party, one of the most prestigious private student parties of the year.

*

Doug Buck and I had had a whole year to talk about our spring 1954 Brown County camping experience. We'd reminisced about the lovely private valley we'd found there, accessible only by crossing a stream. We'd camped, cooked, tippled, and enjoyed the magnificent sunsets and dawns of the southern Indiana hills from that beautiful valley. And in the months that followed, we'd embellished our stories of our hikes in the park, visiting the bars in the nearby rural towns, and searching for a whorehouse. By March, Jack Waterman, Walt Oldendorf, and I had decided to pack up our camping equipment during spring vacation to try to find that private valley.

During February, my letter correspondence with Kathy Sommer at the University of Colorado had evolved into a major disagreement between us. We'd called our romance off. We were both dating others. But on the eve of my departure to Brown County, Kathy showed up unannounced in Glencoe, on her way back East for spring vacation. Since she'd taken the time to visit me, I decided to call off my camping trip. So I bid my *Socius* buddies good-bye as they headed south without me. I told them I might join them, depending on how things progressed with Kathy.

After three days Kathy left for New York, so I explored means of getting myself down to Brown County to join my camping *Socius* buddies. Brother Ron had an old black pre-war Chevy sedan that Paul Burkhardt had sold him. Paul had

The Nashville Jail

purchased it in Palo Alto, California, and driven it back to Chicago. I figured if that old Chevy could cross the Continental Divide, it ought to be able to make it to Southern Indiana. Ron agreed to lend me the Chevy since our parents were out of town, and he'd have access to the family Buick.

I arrived in Brown County late at night and cruised through the hilly back roads of the park checking all the campsites. I could find neither the hidden valley nor my camping buddies.

After midnight I parked the car by one of the entrance gates and went to sleep in the back seat.

In the morning I was awakened by an Indiana state policeman who asked for identification. I reached for my wallet—and discovered I'd left it at home. I was driving without a license.

The officer arrested me and escorted me to the back seat of his patrol car. I was driven to Nashville, Indiana, where I was fingerprinted, photographed, and booked for driving without a license—and having a *concealed weapon!* In those days before pop-top beer cans I carried a beer can opener in my pocket. The cop decided to fortify his case against me by calling the can opener a "concealed weapon."

Then I was escorted to a jail cell and locked up.

Had I known that Nashville, Indiana, was the Midwest's Gulag Archipelago, I might have recommended an alternative campsite to my friends. Here I was, in a jail cell with a bunk, a washstand, a toilet, and a window looking out on the junky gift and souvenir shops and galleries of this little Indiana colony for wannabe artists.

Then it occurred to me that a new drama was unfolding, with me as the central character—I was having a Brown County experience that would make last year's search for a whorehouse seem minor league. That previous spring we'd never made it into a brothel, but now I was in a *jail*, charged with possession of a *concealed can opener!*

The most upsetting thing about involuntary confinement is that your keepers have almost total control over you. I could lie down; I could nap; I could pace about six feet in one direction and three feet in the other; I could wash my hands; I could drink water from the tap; I could pee; I could look out the window. I could talk to myself, or even sing to myself. Beyond these few things my freedom was nonexistent.

Most irritating of all, I hadn't been told when, and under what circumstances, my confinement would end. And, it occurred to me after an hour, that I had a right to make a phone call—a right which hadn't been offered to me.

I think I'd been locked up at about 8 A.M. Sometime around noon an inner door opened and a man with a metal tray of greasy food appeared in front of my cell door. He reached down to slide the food tray through a slot at the bottom of the door, sort of like feeding a dog in a kennel. I'd never had a meal served to me on the floor.

I said, "I believe I have the right to use a telephone."

The man paused, looked at me, and said, "Okay." He unlocked the cell door. I stepped out over my greasy, uneaten lunch tray. He led me to a payphone outside on the street.

"Why," I asked this bureaucrat, "am I being held?"

"Driving a car without a driver's license."

"That's it?"

"That's it." I guess they'd decided that the can opener wouldn't hold up as a weapon in any court of law, even in front of their own Brown County judge. I'd been searched prior to being locked up, and the few dollars I had probably wouldn't cover the fine and court costs for driving without a license, but I wasn't hearing anything about a vagrancy charge.

Mostly, I think the Brown County authorities were simply bored. The tourist season in Brown County wouldn't start for another two to three months, and they were probably just looking for something to amuse themselves.

"But I have a driver's license," I replied.

"It has to be in your immediate possession."

"When will I be released?"

"Whenever you can get the money for the fine and court costs."

"How much money?"

"Oh, thirty to forty dollars."

I dialed the operator and asked to place a collect call to the Walgreen headquarters on Peterson Avenue in Chicago where my father worked. This would be touchy. My father was sufficiently well known at the headquarters for the Walgreen operator to accept the charges when I identified myself. But I had to present my case in a way that wouldn't embarrass my father.

I knew my father was traveling that week, and I had to get someone at Walgreens to tell me where I could reach him. I was connected to one of my father's colleagues—I can't recall the name—and he gave me the number of a Walgreen store somewhere in Iowa where Dad was that day. I asked the operator to place another collect call to that store, person-to-person to Mr. G. A. Inglehart, so the store would accept the charges.

When they got my father on the line I felt relieved. And very ashamed. But Dad was entirely sympathetic and nonjudgmental. I guess he remembered his own youth. He dropped whatever he was doing to find a Western Union office and wire me some money.

Since Nashville, Indiana, had no telegraph office, the wire had to be sent to a telegraph office in Bloomington, Indiana. The Sheriff of Brown County drove me to Bloomington to pick up the money. On the way back he stopped by a house in Nashville to pick up the County's only judge, an ancient, wobbly old man who needed help walking. He'd been sleeping when the Sheriff arrived.

I think the fine was six or seven dollars. Court costs ran it up to thirty-eight dollars.

I paid my fine. Then I asked where my car was. "You can't drive without a license. You'll have to go home and get your license before we'll release the car to you."

The Sheriff drove me all the way back to Bloomington to get on a Greyhound bus to go home and get my driver's license. The bus was a local and took all night to get to downtown Chicago. About 5 A.M. I boarded a commuter train that would take me to Glencoe. I found my driver's license and headed back on the train and bus to Bloomington, where I hitchhiked to Nashville, arriving about 10 P.M. I got Ron's old Chevy.

I drove all night, stopping along Highway 41 about 30 miles south of Gary, Indiana, to climb into the back seat for a nap.

When I woke up and climbed back into the driver's seat, it was Easter Sunday—the last day of one very complicated spring vacation.

*

A few weeks later I made a date with a young blonde classmate named Charlotte Hawkins, to see *The King and I* at the Shubert Theater. The seats I'd secured were in the last row of the top balcony, right next to the spotlight booth.

During intermission I wandered into the spotlight booth and began chatting with the union lighting technicians. They operated a bank of three of those old smoky carbon arc lights with chimneys. As the house lights dimmed for the second act, they let me stay in the booth with them. When they weren't too busy I picked their brains on the finer points of working a spotlight booth. I got to watch all three technicians swing into action for the complicated Uncle Tom ballet in Act Two

After the show I apologized to Charlotte for leaving her sitting all alone in the balcony.

*

Doug Buck and I both received letters from Carnegie Tech College of Fine Arts. The Drama Department invited us to attend on-campus pre-admission evaluations in May. Applicants

The Nashville Jail

who wished to major in acting were asked to prepare two acting monologues—one serious, one comic. Since Doug and I were applying as technical theater majors, we were required to prepare only one acting monologue. It surprised us that the school wanted technical theater majors to prepare any acting monologues at all. But because this school's entire drama department was oriented toward acting, they wanted at least one monologue from all applicants.

I memorized the closing speech from the final act of Tennessee Williams's *Glass Menagerie*, spoken by the character Tom Wingfield, son of the faded southern rose, Amanda, a character Williams patterned after his own mother. Tom spoke the monologue directly to the audience from the fire escape outside his family's humble St. Louis apartment. *"I didn't go to the moon, I went much farther..."*

Then I developed some serious stage fright. Wow! I'm no actor! How can I go before a panel of professional actors in a drama school, and pretend to act?

I decided to try acting like an actor. I couldn't do Tom as Marlon Brando—too cool. Or Gary Cooper—too suave. Wait! There was a New Trier grad named Dave O'Brien. He'd landed lots of leading roles in New Trier plays, even a lead in the New Trier opera. By 1954 O'Brien was acting professionally at Tenthouse Summer Theater in Highland Park. He had a supercilious way about him. He exuded self-confidence and superiority.

I began rehearsing my monologue—not as Tom Wingfield in *Glass Menagerie*, but as Dave O'Brien playing Tom Wingfield in *Glass Menagerie*—a very self-confident, superior Tom. When I thought I had it right, I looked up Mr. Clinton, the drama coach, to evaluate my monologue. He sat down before me in a studio theater. I began strutting back and forth on that fire escape like Napoleon. I was using a cigarette as a prop, pretty much like Bogart.

I finished the monologue and looked to Mr. Clinton for comment. He asked me, "What is Tom thinking out there on that fire escape?"

"Well...about his sister, Laura, who he'd abandoned." Tennessee Williams had patterned Laura after his own sister, who, like Laura, was crippled.

"How does he feel about Laura?"

"Well, he loves Laura. He feels responsible for her. He'd tried to protect Laura, and he had one big chance to do it, but he botched it so badly, he just ran away from her, from his family, from St. Louis."

"He felt guilty?"

"Very."

"What else?"

"Well, failure."

"What else?"

"He's lost in the world. He can't escape his guilt. He can't find any peace. He ran out on Laura, but the memory of Laura continues to follow him and haunt him."

"Do the scene for me again, Jerry...but this time, let me see a Tom's who's lost, and guilty, and running—a Tom who feels he's failed. A Tom who can't escape the image of his sister Laura."

What Mr. Clinton had just said made so much sense. Suddenly the scene and the character were very easy for me. I didn't strut—in fact, I never took a single step. I looked off into the distance at some lonely street in a lonely, seedy part of a strange city. I saw Laura with her glass toys. I felt very sad, I felt terrible—*but the scene felt great.*

"Much better," said Mr. Clinton when I finished. "Now you've got a Tom I can sympathize with."

And I got my first acting lesson.

That May, Doug Buck and I boarded a Greyhound bus for Pittsburgh and the admission tests and interviews at Tech. We crossed through Indiana and Ohio to Pennsylvania. I'd never been east of Indiana and now I was in an eastern state for the first time. Pittsburgh, in the foothills of the Allegheny Mountains, had steep hills. I'd never seen foothills, much less mountains. Having lived 17 years in the flat Midwest, I felt a little claustrophobic about all those hills closing around me in Pittsburgh.

In the Studio Theater at Carnegie Tech, eighty or ninety student candidates were gathered. Mary Morris, the drama teacher, addressed us—Mary Morris, a legend, a former actress, the actress for whom Eugene O'Neill had written *Desire Under the Elms*, a woman who'd had a child by O'Neill.

This wasn't Lake Shore Players. This was the major league. In the course of a few short years this department would spawn such notable actors and directors as William Ball, Josef Sommer, and Holly Hunter. Martha Henry, the future Shakespearian star of Stratford, Ontario, was seated in the auditorium with me, waiting to audition.

Mary Morris asked the assembled candidates who would like to be first to do the monologues. Because I was anxious to proceed on to the interviews with the technical theater instructors, I volunteered. I walked up the steps to the stage, created my fire escape in my mind, leaned against the proscenium arch, lit my cigarette, and did my Tom.

When I finished, I looked down at Mary Morris. She paused three or four beats, and then asked me, "And what did you prepare for your comic monologue, Mr. Inglehart?"

"I only prepared one monologue—I'm a technical major."

"Well," said Mary Morris, "I expect that in four years we can do something about *that!*" I left the theater to go to my other interviews.

The following September, as a student at Tech, I discovered that I'd caused something of a panic with my monologue. Most of those student candidates in the studio theater were applying as acting majors. They were justifiably nervous. They needed to get up and perform well enough to be admitted to this outstanding drama school.

I'd stood up and did my Tom Wingfield. I'm told I did an impressive job, leaving many of them even more intimidated. How could they follow *that?*

Then I announced that I was a technical theater candidate—and some of them felt for a few moments that they'd gotten in over their heads. If the *technical* majors were this good at acting, how good would the *acting* majors be?

Mr. Clinton still stands out in my memory as a middle-aged lecher, a married man who was sleeping with a high school classmate of mine.

But, despite my dreary high school transcript, Mr. Clinton helped to get me into a very good college.

My moment of fame on the studio theater stage even earned me a couple of "groupies" among the female acting majors when I showed up on campus for Rush Week that autumn. One was a dramatic, mysterious blonde named Janet Young who quietly shadowed me for an entire year. The other was a perky, cute Greek actress named Kris Fourgis who cornered me after dark in an alcove of the Fine Arts building, where we spent some pleasant minutes necking and such. Kris seemed to glory in her conquest of the legendary Tom Wingfield actor her very first day on campus.

*

The new leaves on the North Shore trees came out. The grass became lush green. Letters of acceptance to Carnegie Tech arrived for both Doug Buck and me—Doug because he had an outstanding scholastic record, and me because of my Tom Wingfield monologue, possibly coupled with my honor roll status during the first semester of my senior year. It was fortunate that the Tech Admissions Office would never see my second semester grades—I was about to flunk two subjects and pull the lowest grade point average in my scholastic history.

The Nashville Jail

Doug and I applied as roommates to share a dorm room in Scobell Hall—the cheapest dorm on campus. In four months I would leave home to live in a different city, in a different region of the country, in a different life. I'd be out from under the supervision of my judgmental mother. I'd be a big time college man—an adult! I could hardly wait.

We had Echoes Day at New Trier, when all the students got their *New Trier Echoes* yearbooks, plus an afternoon off to get them autographed by friends.

Then came graduation—for us senior men, the fourth occasion of the school year to rent a tuxedo from Abe Fell—this time with a white summer jacket. Each of the 300 or so graduating senior girls was given a bouquet of 18 long stem roses, one for each year of her age. This was a tradition and an extravagance that the nostalgic township had supported for years, and may still to this day. It looked pretty to see all those girls in their white formal gowns, the lovely crimson long stem roses on their left arms, their right hands tucked into the arms of freshly bathed and shaven senior class males in white dinner jackets, walking down the aisle in step to Elgar's *Pomp and Circumstance*. I can never hear that piece without getting a little choked up. New Trier had been a marvelous experience for me.

The next day I returned my tux. And based on my grades, I probably should have returned my diploma as well.

*

Kathy dropped out of the University of Colorado in about May. As "punishment" for abandoning her college career, her father banished her and her sister Jane, a dropout from Mills College, to a year of exile in Paris, France. Or at least that's what I believed for many years. Later, as an adult, I realized a more likely truth—her father probably figured that if Kathy wasn't in college in Colorado, she might wander off to the North Shore to visit me again. She might even marry me. In his mind, any alternative was preferable to having Jerry Inglehart as a son-in-law. So he sent Kathy and her sister to Paris for a year. My on-again-off-again romance would have to wait.

It was time to launch the 1955 Lake Shore Players season. Paul Burkhardt lined up a Chicago radio D.J. to direct Tennessee Williams's *Summer and Smoke*. Tryouts were held in June. The lead role went to—who else?—Brother Ron.

By now Lake Shore Players was losing some of its momentum along with some of its membership. As a smaller group we needed to produce plays with smaller casts.

As a student-run group, we had a tendency to act irresponsibly, both financially and socially. We'd worn out our welcome at The Winnetka Community House after the 1953 season, and after 1954, Central School in Glencoe no longer wanted us back. Paul Burkhardt lined up a small auditorium at Stolp School in Wilmette for 1955.

Everyone tended to show up thirty to forty-five minutes late for rehearsals. After three weeks the exasperated director finally quit. Burkhardt took over as director. But the key ingredient—the nightly parties—went off smoothly. In July we pulled off a very respectable performance of the Tennessee Williams classic at Stolp School, and went on to the Workshop production, *The Silver Cord*, a play about two adult sons of an overly controlling mother. Ron shared top billing with Bill Heiser, another old Lake Shore Players regular.

The charter members who had been holding the group together were now considerably older. It would be Paul Burkhardt's last season with Lake Shore Players. At the last meeting of the year, I was promoted from Technical Director to Producer, replacing Burkhardt as the top executive of Lake Shore Players for the future 1956 season.

*

The Nashville Jail

Sometime during the summer of 1955 I went downtown to Chicago. The Prudential Building had just been completed—the newest and tallest building in Chicago—the first major building to be built in Chicago since the Board of Trade building in 1934. The hog butcher to the world, a dead city since the Depression, was starting to flex its big shoulders again.

I wanted to see what Chicago looked like from its newest pinnacle. At the top floor observatory there was a fancy cocktail lounge. Might as well get a sky-high drink, I thought to myself. Sitting down at the bar of this high and impressive architectural summit with my phony driver's license, I ordered a Manhattan and began to gaze out over the Illinois Central tracks, the south Loop, Grant Park, Buckingham Fountain, the lakeshore, and the museums.

The bartender delivered my Manhattan—and some future shock. One dollar! My bill for one cocktail was one dollar! Never in my life had I paid more than sixty-five cents for a cocktail—maybe seventy cents once. But a whole dollar!

I took out a five-dollar bill, which the bartender took and returned with my second future shock in ten minutes time—he laid down three one-dollar bills and four quarters. Did that bastard really think I was going to tip him a *whole quarter?* A twenty-five-percent tip? I was so incensed, I told him I didn't need all that change. He took the quarters and returned with another dollar bill. I left him a dime.

Today I've become sympathetic toward hard-working waitresses, waiters and bartenders, many of whom are really out-of-work actors, actresses, dancers, and opera singers. My wife and I both tip big—never less than 20%—sometimes 25%.

The trouble is, whenever we get lousy service we tip just 15%, thinking of it as an insult and a reprimand. Our servers never understand. They think 15% is just fine.

But now a whole new city, and a new series of discoveries and shocks, awaited me five hundred miles to the East.

Chapter 8

Marlon and Me

Doug Buck and I stepped down from the Pennsylvania Railroad Pullman car at Pittsburgh's Central Station rather early on a sunny September morning in 1955. We claimed our footlockers from baggage, together with my guitar and Doug's portable phonograph, and headed to the front of the station to catch a cab—something neither of us had ever done before.

We arrived at Scobell Hall, found our assigned room unlocked, and hauled our footlockers inside. We plugged in Doug's phonograph. I put on Puccini's *La Boheme*, which seemed very appropriate—if we were to be living in a loft (well, actually it was a first-floor dorm room) and if we were now, in fact, *in theater*, we'd better start shedding the vestiges of our privileged North Shore upbringing and start acting like artists. Perhaps Puccini's story of Parisian Bohemian writers and artists of the 1890s would help set the scene on our first day.

A new city. A new school. A new crowd of people—my first real exposure to young adults who hadn't grown up in New Trier Township. I was somewhat overwhelmed. There were new groups and cliques to be discovered and formed.

Throughout the summer we'd been receiving long, *handwritten* letters from members of Tech's dozen or so fraternities, extolling the virtues of their organizations. Now, before we'd even had a chance to unpack our clothes, the fraternity reps began calling at our dorm room to invite us to lunch or dinner at their various houses.

I was impressed. It's nice to be rushed, whether by a fraternity, or a prospective employer, or a club. It didn't occur to me that if we became fraternity members, we'd be spending a good part of each summer handwriting long letters to incoming freshmen, and shortening our summers by one week for the mandatory participation in Rush Week.

I'd wanted to pledge a fraternity primarily because it was a collegiate thing to do, and I wanted the total college experience. During Rush Week, when you decided which fraternities you felt comfortable with, you would attend their fraternity house meals and parties regularly, hoping they would notice you, vote on you, and give you a bid to join. If they did, a couple of the fraternity brothers would single you out on your next visit, take you to a private room, and invite you to pledge their fraternity. Then they'd take nearly an hour to run through a very carefully scripted sales pitch on the virtues of their fraternity, hoping to convince you to join. Good fraternities needed to make just a couple of dozen bids to fill a pledge class of about 15. The less popular fraternities might have to issue a hundred bids.

I liked the brothers at Kappa Sigma and Pi Kappa Alpha, and got bids from both houses. A third bid, from Beta Sigma Rho, arrived in my mail after Rush Week. Doug and I pledged Pi Kappa Alpha. And to increase our commitment to fraternity life, we moved from the dorm into the Pi Kappa Alpha house, a magnificent structure on Morewood Avenue. It had once been the residential castle of some Pittsburgh magnate. It had about 20 bedrooms and a fourth-floor ballroom. But like all fraternity houses, its interior splendor had suffered since its days as an upper-class home. The walls were bare, the woodwork and moldings were chipped, and the furniture was Salvation Army. But that's okay for a bunch of college males who need it mostly for sleeping, studying, partying, and playing bridge. Doug and I and another drama student, Tom Casker, moved into a large second floor bedroom.

There were fraternity parties every Friday and Saturday. One of the late fall parties was a costume ball. Since I'd had tremendous success 18 months earlier with my Marlon Brando *Wild One* costume, I decided to re-create it. I borrowed a black leather jacket and used tempera paint to make the Black Rebels skull-and-cross-piston-connecting-rods logo on the back. I borrowed a motorcycle cap, motorcycle boots and sunglasses, and applied theatrical hair sideburns to my cheeks.

I didn't have a date for that party. I just had the costume. And the Brando drawl. And the look. I sauntered across the fraternity barroom floor with a bottle of beer in one hand, a cigarette in the other, and a faraway expression on my face.

One of the most gorgeous female drama students was a long-haired blond sophomore beauty with a classic model's figure. Her name was Martha Poor. I'd seen her around the campus and had drooled over her physical perfection. She had an innocently sexy face, a soft, sensuous alto voice, and perfectly smooth complexion like a Swedish model.

Apparently Marlon Brando was one of Martha's fantasies. And once again, I seemed to be an irresistibly close copy. In an upstairs hallway of the fraternity house she approached me and purred into my ear, "Black Rebels? What are you rebelling against?"

"What have you got?" I drawled in a dreamy, slightly distant Brando tenor that exuded pure animal musk. During previous steamy dating situations with other young girls, I knew that this fraternity house contained no closet, corner, cul-de-sac, or cranny where a passionate young couple could find privacy to work out their fantasies without one of the brothers happening unexpectedly on the scene. It was too cold outdoors to retreat to a shadowy secluded spot in a park. This upstairs hallway offered as much privacy as we would get. Looking through my dark aviator sunglasses, I focused my casual Brando gaze on Martha's pretty brown eyes. Martha drew closer and began nibbling my earlobe, then thrusting her thirsty little tongue into my ear as she nudged me down onto a hall chair. The scent of her silky, fragrant hair aroused me so much I was having difficulty sustaining my sexy Brando cool. Martha unzipped my black leather jacket and snuggled her firm, perfect breasts against my t-shirt. Sitting on my lap I felt her hips moving slightly, subtly, driving me crazy. I'm pretty certain Martha was not sufficiently experienced with sex to understand what would one day become known as the lap dance—I think she was simply very excited and rolling with her passion.

I knew that if I were to ask her to slip away with me to a room at the Webster Hall Hotel, she'd have agreed. And if I'd had ten dollars to pay for the room, I'd have asked her. Come Monday I would no longer be in possession of my borrowed Brando motorcycle cap, jacket, boots, and sunglasses, and the fuzzy crepe hair sideburns would be in the trash. Would Martha even recognize me when she saw me on campus? By evening's end, lovely Martha had become just one more missed opportunity of my inexperienced youth.

*

Many of our fellow drama students were from the East. Most had seen shows on Broadway in New York. For theater students, there was a certain snobbishness about New York City, the capital of American live theater. Anything west of the Hudson River was considered "the hinterlands." And I was from the Midwest—a little outpost called Chicago, way off where farmers raised corn and there were still a few Indian reservations. I'd never been further east than where I was standing. I was trying to figure out how to hide my immense provinciality from my more worldly drama classmates. How could I disguise the fact that I'd never been in New York City in my life? Never boarded a New York subway? Never walked down Broadway or seen a Broadway show?

I began reading *The New Yorker* and *The New York Times*. I read up on Damon Runyon, carefully memorizing all the Manhattan street names and restaurants. I got a map of Manhattan to plot each important location—Broadway, Times Square, Park Avenue, Lindy's and Sardi's restaurants, the Algonquin Hotel.

At our frequent trips to The Greeks, which was the pivotal campus restaurant and bar, I tried drinking Scotch because it was an East Coast drink. I tried it straight, on the rocks, with water, soda, even ginger ale. I hated that smoky taste, it made me gag. So I tried rye, another East Coast staple. Then Canadian. One Saturday evening at the Greeks, after several attempts to scarf down these snobbish East Coast whiskeys, while in a daze of mid-level intoxication, I said to my friends, "Shit! *Dammit!* I'm a Midwesterner! I was born in Milwaukee! I live in the city of Carl Sandburg. We butcher hogs! I've got big shoulders and I'm proud of it! *Bartender! Bring me a goddamn shot and a beer!"*

It was an important realization for me. *I gotta be me!* Whoever that was.

By December I'd learned another valuable social lesson in this new pool of non-North Shore people. The student body at Tech consisted of two basically incompatible groups. On the one hand there was a huge number of engineering students who wore side holsters for their slide rules—all very serious and mathematically gifted, with straight faces, close-cropped hair, and very little sense of humor. Complimenting them were the Margaret Morrison College girls—home economics majors who came to Tech to secure their futures by marrying engineers.

Into this rather homogenous, stable group was a smattering of us noticeably different drama students with our decidedly longer hair, occasional beards (considered totally outrageous in 1955), somewhat more outlandish clothes, and remarkably non-conformist attitudes.

Socially, it was like trying to mix oil and water. I was in a fraternity full of serious engineering students. We had little in common. In early December I de-pledged, moved out of the fraternity house and back to Scobell Hall.

I was still somewhat devoted to Kathy Sommer who I hadn't seen since April. She was in Paris with her sister. We wrote infrequently. I had no idea when I'd see her again. Her father had now been transferred to the McCann-Erickson office in Caracas, Venezuela, and was in South America arranging to move his family there. Possibly he figured the move would further protect him from the threat of having Jerry Inglehart as a son-in-law.

I decided I wanted to visit the Sommer family in Greenwich for Thanksgiving. Although Kathy and Jane were in France, and Al Sommer was in Venezuela, I was anxious to continue bonding with the rest of her family. Two brothers—Dave and Rick, and two sisters—Connie and little Mary, had been an important part of my social life during the summer of 1954 when Brother Ron and I and many of our Lake Shore Players friends had hung around the Sommer house in Glencoe.

So I wrangled an invitation to Greenwich for Thanksgiving.

Doug Buck asked me if he could come along. Of course he could! And when Jack Waterman at Harvard got wind of it, he decided to come, too. Then Paul Burkhardt, who was living in Cambridge, Massachusetts at the time, decided to come to Greenwich too. Paul had dropped out of Stanford University because he wanted to be near his girlfriend, Betsy Alderman, who was attending Smith College. Paul arrived in Cambridge and slept on sofas in the Harvard dorm rooms of various friends, including Howie Edmonds' and Jack Waterman's. Paul was not a student at Harvard, but he began attending whatever classes interested him. In the spring he tried out for the Harvard Hasty Pudding Show and got cast as the female lead. (Harvard wouldn't be co-ed for several more years.)

As I understand it, a week before the Hasty Pudding show was scheduled to open, someone tipped off the club that Paul Burkhardt was not a Harvard student. He couldn't be in the show. So in 1956, for the first time in over a century, The Hasty Pudding Show didn't open.

Doug and I got a ride with an eastbound student to Jersey City where, late in the evening of the Wednesday before Thanksgiving, Jack Waterman picked us up. We drove to Greenwich, Connecticut, and invaded Al Sommer's huge old white frame house on Bruce Park Drive. We spent the entire holiday weekend. We drove up to Yale and visited Walt Farnham there. I'd never been on the Atlantic Coast. I walked along the sea enjoying the sights and smells of salt water. I explored tidewater pools where I found the skeletons of horseshoe crabs. This was the ocean, just like in the musical *Carousel.*

*

The Tech drama department was a no-nonsense serious theater school. While freshmen in other colleges were studying English, Western Civilization, and Science, we drama students were taking courses like Stage Movement (ballet, actually), Voice and Speech, Theatrical Makeup, and Stagecraft.

The one concession to a liberal education was a course called Thought and Expression. It was actually Freshman English Lit, renamed to appeal to drama students. It was also the most inspiring college course I would ever take, and was taught by a successful novelist, Gladys Schmitt, who'd had a number of best-sellers in the late 40s and early 50s, including *David the King,* a historic novel about the biblical King David. Gladys made English Literature come alive as few could, possibly because she was one of its most prolific contributors. From Gladys I got insights into Shakespeare, T. S. Elliot, Hemmingway, Fitzgerald, and others that I'll always cherish.

A major part of the teaching experience of a school of drama is its stage productions. Ours began the first week of the term and continued nonstop throughout the year. One of the most time-consuming involvements for freshman was stage crew. After a day of classes we'd spend most of the evening building sets, painting sets, changing sets during performances, or striking sets to begin new sets for another performance. The sophomores served on lighting crew. All drama students would be involved with acting roles or crew duties until 10 P.M. or so. Theater is a nocturnal profession, and so was our curriculum.

What totally blew me away that first month at Tech was the professionalism. The closest I'd ever come to theater of this caliber was being backstage momentarily at the Shubert, Harris, or Erlanger Theaters in Chicago when I would sneak in through the stage door after the final curtain to examine the sets, the lighting, and the backstage technicalities. My experience with Threshold Players, *Lagniappe*, New Trier drama, and Lake Shore Players was beginning to seem very pedestrian. These students at Tech knew how to *act*, and within weeks I was participating in some outstanding performances. The sets we were building were highly imaginative. Backstage, above stage, and in the lighting galleries I was immersed in professional techniques and secrets I'd never known. There was a constant air of excitement as talented students, hoping to carve careers in theater, did their utmost to measure up.

My guitar-playing skills (still rare in 1955) were called upon from the start. I was needed to play the part of The Dreamer, a guitar-playing Latino, in *Camino Real* by Tennessee Williams, which was the second main stage production of the year. Never mind that I was a production major—I could play guitar. I was given a role any freshman acting major might have sold his mother for.

Camino Real ran for twelve performances. After the last night I looked around for evidence of a cast party. From the very start of my theatrical experience, cast parties had been part and parcel of theater. Threshold Players always had them after the last performance. So did all the New Trier plays and operas, including *Lagniappe*, which was the end-all of high school parties. And Lake Shore Players had been an endless series of parties.

The final curtain came down on *Camino Real* and the cast and crew simply went home. They had classes to prepare for. Next day the crews began striking the sets and lighting. This was the world of professional theater, where a party might occur after an *opening* performance, in Sardi's or some other Broadway theatrical bar where the cast and the director would drink the night away waiting for the reviews to come out in the morning papers, hoping to see if everyone was going to be employed for a while. And when a show closed, it was because it had run its course and lost its audience draw. Not exactly a reason to party.

The third major play was a very imaginative adaptation of Andre Gide's book, *Lafcadio's Adventures*, written by our faculty playwriting instructor, and starring William Ball. Technically, it was the most ambitious production of the year, involving a stage with turntables, interesting rear-screen projections, and more than a dozen scenic backdrops and cut outs, all of them raised and lowered from the fly gallery above the stage. This was back in the days when sets and backdrops were lifted or dropped on lines counterbalanced with sandbags. Doug Buck and I, together with Tom Casker and a new friend of ours, Gordon Smith, ran the fly gallery for *Lafcadio* from the elevated catwalk just offstage.

One thinks of stage crews mostly in terms of sitting around, waiting for the curtain to go down so they can execute a scene change backstage. In *Lafcadio*, the scenes changed so often, they took place in full audience view. Up in the fly gallery we were part of the show. We raised and lowered the sets in and out of view by hand, tugging on the lines to bring the sandbags down, thus lifting one set into the fly gallery as the stage turntables rotated furniture and props into view for the next scene. Then we sailed the new set down to the stage. The four of us spent every night for nearly two weeks up on the fly gallery catwalk, trimming the sets and balancing them by adding or removing sand, then working out our choreography for perfect scene changes. It was thrilling to do scene changes that were a part of the live performance.

Tech acting graduates were rarely headed for Hollywood or Broadway—they tended to fill the casts of the serious classical repertory theatres. Martha Henry in my class became one of the most noteworthy Shakespearean actresses in Stratford, Ontario. William Ball became producer-director of a highly lauded repertoire theater. My friend Nicholas Martin went to Stratford, Connecticut, and I saw him last in a production with Josef Sommer in Ann Arbor, Michigan. Joe Sommer, who was in both *Camino Real* and *Lafcadio*, has had dozens of supporting roles in motion pictures, including the police detective in *Witness* with Harrison Ford. The biggest Tech success story of all time was Holly Hunter, who attended the school years after me.

For the acting majors, the most important production of each year was the annual Shakespeare play. We produced *Antony and Cleopatra* during my year at Tech. We created a set with an "inner above" stage like the Elizabethan Globe Theater. Tech's shining powerhouse of acting talent brought Cleopatra's Egypt alive for twelve exciting performances. Sally Breskin, one of the senior class's most capable actresses, created an elegant, regal Cleopatra. Ron Goldswig did a cocky, scheming Octavius Caesar. Even some of the show's secondary performances were quite memorable—Byron Rengland played the ancient soothsayer, wobbling on stage aided by a long staff pole, his all-seeing eyes piercing the assembled Egyptians and Romans. At the end of the play, Cleopatra is imprisoned, and a strange, mystical man played by Ray Bevilaqua smuggles a poison serpent into her cell for her suicide. I'll never forget the red-eyed Bevilaqua with his scraggly beard, chanting to Cleopatra, *"I wish you the joy o' the worm."*

For the final production of the year, an Englishman named Peter Bucknell directed a thoroughly hilarious production of Moliere's *Hypochondriac*. I didn't appreciate Moliere until I saw Bucknell's production. The audience was rolling in the aisles.

*

Dormitory living was boring and confining. I wanted an apartment with a living area and a place to study. After Christmas break I looked in the classified columns and found an ad for a seven-room furnished house on a side street called Mawhinney Street in Oakland, right behind the Carnegie Museum. Mawhinney was a funky one-block street lined with century-old Victorian row houses that had seen better days. Number 3 was the middle four stories of a row house containing three homes. All the interior walls were crooked and the floors were uneven. The entire place was furnished with castoffs from Good Will. The top floor had a large firetrap bedroom. There were two bedrooms and a bath on the third floor. The second floor had an entrance from the street plus a front bedroom, and a living room. The first floor included a rather large kitchen plus a storage room with a water heater. Several rats lived in the storage room. There was no furnace, no central heating—each room had a fireplace with gas radiants made of baked clay or ceramic.

The landlady wanted $90 a month. This was unbelievably good. Six students could split the rent six ways, spending $15 per month each, share the gas and electric bills, and have a kitchen and communal living room, all at a price lower than dormitory living.

I told my friend Tom Dennis about it. Tom, an acting major, was married, living with his wife in an apartment, and looking for something cheaper. They could occupy the master bedroom on the second floor. Classmates Gordon Smith and Jon DeHart agreed to share the large firetrap bedroom on the top floor. Nicholas Martin took the bedroom downstairs beside the entrance, and I took the second floor bedroom that was partitioned off from the only bathroom. The wall between my bedroom and the bathroom was very thin. From my room I couldn't avoid hearing the bowel, bladder, and bathing habits of everyone living there.

I was first to move in and spend a night at 3 Mawhinney. On a Friday night I brought some bed sheets, a blanket, and a pillow, together with a Revere Ware pan I'd borrowed from Barbara Dennis, and some silverware I'd filched from the school cafeteria. I bought half a dozen eggs, half a pound of bacon, and a loaf of bread.

Upstairs in my cozy little bedroom I lit the gas burner in my Victorian fireplace and made up my bed. I fell asleep watching the flames dance against the ceramic radiants of the gas burner. In the morning I cooked my own Saturday breakfast in my very own, my very first kitchen!

I wanted to decorate my bedroom. I had three ideas, and ended up using them all: on one wall I pasted up burlap cloth. I painted the fireplace wall black. The other two walls I papered with historic newspapers that I'd been collecting for several years, including the *Chicago Tribune* "Eisenhower Wins" front page from November 1952. I applied a dozen coats of shellac to the newspapers to make them look old and yellowish.

I would have invited Doug Buck to join our commune, but he was still a pledge living at the Pi Kappa Alpha house. For him, semester break would be Hell Week. I did not envy him. I took a Greyhound bus home to Glencoe while Doug stayed in Pittsburgh.

When I returned to 3 Mawhinney after the semester break, Doug showed up looking very depressed. The absurdities of Hell Week had made him totally disillusioned with the fraternity, and he'd de-pledged. Doug is no quitter. He took his commitments seriously. I had quit the fraternity after a few weeks. He'd hung in for a whole semester. Doug graduated from Tech after four years. I left after one year. Doug eventually spent his entire professional career in theater. I backed out the following year.

*

I planned to go to New York over spring vacation, to see some Broadway shows. *My Fair Lady* had opened in the fall of 1955, but obtaining tickets to that incredible sell-out was hopeless. I ordered a cheap high balcony seat to a show at the Cort Theater. I don't recall what show was playing there, but I still have the cancelled check for four dollars.

Then my poverty caught up with me. I couldn't scrape together enough funds for the New York trip. Broadway would have to wait, and my Manhattan images from *Guys and Dolls* would have to tide me over until a more solvent time in my life.

*

About this time I decided that Carnegie Tech Department of Drama was too oriented toward acting majors to serve my career ambitions. I wanted to be a producer, and that aspect of theater was business. I needed to take some hard-nose business courses like accounting and marketing. Maybe what I needed was an M.B.A., which Tech didn't offer.

My grades at Tech had been quite good. I was offered a scholarship for my sophomore year. I also applied to Northwestern University and was accepted. Northwestern could offer more of the courses I felt I needed.

In late May, I would be bidding farewell to Tech, to 3 Mawhinney, to Pittsburgh, and to some of the most memorable months of my life.

Prior to my departure, though, I had to complete my final exams. My English Lit course with Gladys Schmitt would bring a top grade for certain. In the stagecraft course I could get A's without even attending the classes. Voice and Speech simply required me to make a voice recording significantly superior to the one I'd made on entering Tech in September. The course in theatrical makeup was a certain grade of B. In the acting course I was way outclassed by the acting majors, but I could count on a C. And the scene design course was my specialty—an A for certain.

The one exam I feared was Stage Movement. Earlier I'd mentioned that this course was actually ballet, taught by a wire of a woman with a head of hair like a Brillo pad. Her name (and this is her real name) was Cecil Kitkat, an English lady of about 60 who could touch her face to her shins without bending her knees—something I hadn't been able to do since I was eight years old.

During a previous class, students had been required to demonstrate their stage movement capabilities by moving about the stage as if they were riding a huge bicycle. I watched my actor friends do this with ease, banking on turns, accelerating on straight-aways, their leotarded legs pumping, their ballet-slippered feet pit-a-patting smoothly around the stage. I was not at this school to learn how to act—I was a technical major. I couldn't achieve the method-acting magic of pedaling along a bike path. I couldn't even fit into tights—I wore jeans to class.

Cecil called on me to perform.

I stood on stage, extended my arms to my imaginary handlebars, and began pit-a-patting partway around the stage, then suddenly stopping, dismounting, looking down at my bike after less than a single circuit of the stage.

"What's the problem, Mr. Inglehart?" boomed Cecil's Oxford English voice. (She'd come to be as impatient with my disruptions as had my grammar school teachers.)

"It's that front tire, Cecil. Flat."

"Oh, get on with the exercise, Mr. Inglehart!"

"On that tire? I might fall."

"*Ride,* Mr. Inglehart, *ride!*"

By now I was getting the titters and snickers from my classmates that enabled me to proceed with dignity. I spread my arms to my imaginary bicycle handlebars, remounted, and began pit-a-patting around the stage. "I'm going to ruin that rim, Cecil."

"Mr. Inglehart, *please!*"

For the final exam I was to begin center stage, my expression and body language conveying euphoric happiness. This was to melt slowly into abject grief, and finally, to victory. I was expected to use at least 70% of the stage area for this exercise. I could take up to five minutes.

No matter how many shots and beers I downed at The Greeks, I had no idea how I could make a funny parody out of this exam.

On exam day, when Cecil called me up, I performed miserably, unable to wait until the end of my inadequate interpretation when I could get off the stage and get the hell out of there. I used no more than ten percent of the stage. *I want to be a producer, Cecil, not an actor! Am I asking you to be Cecil B. DeMille?*

She donated me a barely passing grade.

Since her course was actually the equivalent of Phys Ed, my miserable grade didn't make much difference.

I went back to my room at 3 Mawhinney and set my alarm clock for two hours before dawn.

*

At 4 A.M. on a dark but clear early June morning I left 3 Mawhinney with $2.50 in cash and a small zipper bag with a change of underwear, a toothbrush, a razor and a stick of deodorant. Doug Buck would be leaving for Chicago later in the week—he now had a car, and had agreed to take my guitar, footlocker, and books to Chicago.

Jack Waterman had classes at Harvard for four more days. I planned to hitchhike to Cambridge and hang around Harvard while Jack finished his exams. Then we'd drive home together via the stretch of Ontario between Niagara Falls and Detroit.

On Forbes Avenue, a block from our funky Mawhinney Street commune, I hopped on an eastbound trolley and rode it to the end of the line, where I stuck out my thumb for a ride. It was still dark. Before a quarter hour had passed I had a ride not only to the Pennsylvania Turnpike, but east all the way to Harrisburg.

There I wasted four hours trying unsuccessfully to get a ride on the turnpike ramp. Perhaps the drivers thought it was illegal to pick up hitchhikers on a turnpike. Finally I gave up and hiked over to nearby U. S. Highway 22 and got a ride from a salesman who took me all the way to New York City via the George Washington Bridge, where he dropped me off just north of Harlem.

I was in the city of my dreams for the first time—the legendary Manhattan Island. Of course I was nowhere near Broadway—this was 180th Street, then an Irish neighborhood. I found a Western Union office. It was nearly 6 P.M.; I'd never make Boston that day as I had hoped, and meals had diminished my funds to less than a dollar. I'd have to ask Jack to wire me some money.

The girl in the telegraph office was Irish, blonde, plain, skinny, and sweet. In her native brogue she gave me the telegraph office address to relay to Jack for my wire. I went to a pay phone to call Jack collect for a small financial transfusion.

I now had forty cents left, so I went into a nearby bar crowded with joking Irishmen, and bought a beer, which I nursed for the two hours it took for my wire to arrive. When I got my cash (maybe five dollars, maybe ten, I don't recall) I followed the sweet Irish lass's directions to the Broadway subway and took it to Grand Central Station. I had now ridden a subway in the Big Apple.

The next New Haven train to Boston wouldn't leave until 1:15 A.M. I had another three hours to kill. For a dime I locked my zipper bag in a train station locker, wandered out onto Park Avenue, then headed west looking for the legendary streets I'd seen in *Guys and Dolls*. I eventually found Broadway, but couldn't locate Lindy's restaurant where Damon Runyon had held court for so many years and eaten so much of their famous cheesecake.

On the New Haven train I promptly fell asleep in my coach seat. It was a local and would take the rest of the night to get to Boston.

Following Jack's instructions I got a Boston subway to Harvard Square and found his dorm—Wigglesworth Hall—at about 7A.M.

I love the East Coast. It has a sense of history that's missing in the Midwest. The streets, shops, and townhouses have a cozy, colonial atmosphere. In Boston I can imagine the presence of Pilgrims, 18th century politicians, and Revolutionary War soldiers with muskets. I walked around Cambridge and ate with Jack at the Harvard Union where, just two years earlier, Brother Ron had dined during his stint there.

Three days later, about 5 P.M., Jack finished up his exams and packed, and we headed west on U.S. Highway 20 across Massachusetts. The following morning as dawn broke, we were looking out on the Niagara Canadian falls. For the first time in my life I was outside the United States. Gasoline was expensive and was sold in Imperial gallons. I got a kick out of paying for it in Canadian dollars. I kept a $1.00 Canadian bill as a souvenir, and have it to this day. On the backside of the bill is a picture of a long, flat, boring Ontario two-lane prairie highway that looks exactly like the highway Jack and I drove across that province in 1956. This currency no longer exists—Canada retired the $1.00 bill decades ago.

We spent that night with the family of Jim Parker, a New Trier friend who had moved to Detroit. In the morning we drove east to Port Clinton, Ohio, and took a ferry to South Bass Island in Lake Erie, where we found the Sommer family cottage. A front door key was hidden in a coffee can beneath the steps. We entered and spent the night in the cottage, being careful next morning to cover all evidence of our unauthorized visit. We arrived home in Chicago the following day.

*

Marlon and Me

At the close of the 1955 Lake Shore Players season I was looking forward to being the producer and top dog of the group for the summer of 1956. I'd planned to produce *The Male Animal* by James Thurber as our main-stage production.

But by November of my freshman year at Carnegie Tech I began having second thoughts about leading Lake Shore Players. It was amateur theater, like Threshold Players. Now I'd been to the mountaintop, involved in professional theater, working side by side with students for whom theater would be a vocation, not just a summer social event.

I just couldn't fathom coming home to a theatrical party group in a grammar school auditorium where rehearsals started an hour late and broke up when everybody wanted to party.

Paul Burkhardt wasn't around to fill the gap—he had a job at Hinsdale Summer Theater in the western suburbs. Brother Ron, the group's lead actor, was no longer involved either. At tryouts for *The Male Animal* I saw that we didn't have enough participants to cast the play, much less to fund it.

This theater group had played a profound role in my happy high school years, and had helped to steer me and my friend Doug Buck into professional theater. But in late June of 1956, Lake Shore Players, under my leadership, dissolved due to lack of interest.

*

That summer both Paul Burkhardt and Doug Buck were employed at Hinsdale Summer Theater. Unlike Music Theater in Highland Park which staged popular Broadway hit musicals and cast Broadway stars in the lead roles, filling out the casts with local talent, Hinsdale Summer Theater booked entire pre-cast shows, most of which were dramas headlined by known stars such as Vincent Price and Charleton Heston.

I visited Doug and Paul in Hinsdale several times that summer, and got a peek at a few shows starring once-famous talent. I remember a show there starring Chico Marx of the

Marx Brothers. Another starred Bert Lahr who had just completed *Waiting for Godot* on Broadway that June. During that visit Doug and I were passing through the dressing room right after final curtain. It was amusing to see the Cowardly Lion in his underwear.

Another show starred Joan Blondell, the eternal supporting actress who'd been in dozens of Warner Brothers films and been nominated once for an Oscar. After that show, Joan Blondell and the entire cast and company were invited to the Gaslight Club on Rush Street in Chicago, because the club owner wanted publicity photos of Blondell in his establishment.

I tagged along for the free drinks and food.

The Gaslight Club was huge, with rooms for cocktails and other rooms for dining. The décor was turn-of-the-century, apparently inspired by Carl Sandburg's descriptions of ladies of the night who stood under Chicago's gas streetlamps, luring the newly arrived country boys. The waitresses were lovely, shapely young "Gaslight Girls" dressed in scanty, revealing costumes like hookers in a turn-of-the-century mining town barroom. Above the bar, a huge sign in 19th-Century gold letters proclaimed, "Work is the Curse of the Drinking Class." The patrons were young, successful Chicagoans who would, in a later day, be known as "Yuppies." Doug and I recognized one of them—Ron Mays, the tenor who had sung Nanki Poo in *The Mikado* at New Trier in 1954. We said hello. Ron boasted that The Gaslight Club was his home away from home.

Afterward Doug and I were part of a small group that accompanied Blondell to a nearby bar on Chicago Avenue for a nightcap. In most of her movie roles Joan had played blond bimbos. Her level of conversation in the bar suggested she may have been type cast. She had a pretty smile, though.

I attended a Music Theater production of *Finian's Rainbow* in Highland Park. Sue Goldberg, one of the old Lake Shore Players regulars, was in the chorus. I saw Paul Burkhardt in the audience and said hello to him during intermission. Paul had a date with Sue Goldberg after the show. They were going to a party of theater people at Gibby's, a theatrical bar located right next to the Shubert Theater on Monroe Street in Chicago's Loop.

I showed up at the party. The bar was filled with some of the finest talent in the Chicago musical theater community. A piano player played requests. Professional singers and dancers seated at the tables would stand and sing on request.

I heard an absolutely splendid rendition of "Two Ladies in de Shade of de Banana Tree" from *House of Flowers,* sung by a young, lanky black whose calypso body was as loose and lyrical as his delivery. Another fellow sang "Brush Up Your Shakespeare." Then a baritone stood up and sang the title song from *Oklahoma!* except that he pronounced it "Oyklahoma" and sang it in a minor key with a lot of vocal wavering like a cantor in a synagogue. His hilarious lyrics, peppered with Yiddish, questioned why a pair of fine Jews like Rogers and Hammerstein would write a show about rowdy, gun-toting cowboys and their *shiksa* girlfriends on a godforsaken prairie 400 miles from the nearest delicatessen. The song's famous final phrase, "Oklahoma! O.K!" he sang in a wavering chant, "Oyklahoma! Oy vey!"

Then a very good Stubby Kaye imitator stood up to sing "Sit Down You're Rocking the Boat," which is Nicely Nicely Johnson's confession and testimony from *Guys and Dolls.*

That musical number requires complex vocal support and fills from a full mixed chorus of Broadway gamblers and Salvation Army staff, singing along with Nicely Nicely Johnson's testimony. No sweat! The barroom guests, from their seats at the bar or at tables, happened to constitute a very large, very talented chorus of professional musical comedy singers—and they came in right on cue, in harmony...*including me!* From listening repeatedly to the original cast recordings, I knew the words, the melodies, the fills, the choruses, and the harmonies—and at Gibby's bar I was singing in a professional chorus of *Guys and Dolls!*

"And I said to myself sit down…"
Said to myself sit dow—ow—ow—n
"Sit down you're rockin' the boat"
Sit down!

I wasn't sitting. I was standing. Smiling. Singing. In seventh heaven.

*

A few weeks later I was at a stag party with some buddies in Glencoe. We were all getting pretty drunk. Someone mentioned the frustrating absence of girls at our party. Someone else said, "Hell, let's all go to a whorehouse and get laid."

My whore was a girl named Peggy, a southern Illinois brunette with an appealing Ohio River Valley drawl. I selected her from a field of eight candidates offering themselves in the living room of that particular brothel in Kankakee, Illinois. Peggy escorted me to her room. Her face was somewhat commonplace but her open, rather compassionate expression was calming to me. I was especially attracted to her perfect Playboy bunny curves revealed through her work garment—a sort of fancy, sexy one-piece bathing suit thing with a zipper down the back that she could slip into and out of quickly. I tried to imagine what she might look like in a prom dress. She was about 22. I was 18. I offered her five dollars which she accepted after her brief but experienced paramedical examination of my penis.

I chuckle every time I think about Peggy. She must have sensed the nature of my prom night fantasy, and spiced the start of our encounter with a pretense of naughty adventure. Her playacting was rather exciting. Sadly, five dollars didn't allow her much time to play out the entire prom night scenario—which wouldn't have worked for very long anyway, since it would have required me to assume a dominant male role in a gentle seduction drama in which she'd pretend to be a hesitant virgin, and I was finding it impossible to stick to my Brando routine with no pants on. We rapidly progressed to the point where it was quite obvious that the only virgin in the room was me. Peggy slipped calmly into the driver's seat in order to stick to her quickie time schedule. "Now push, Honey...thaaaaat's right."

*

The previous March, Kathy Sommer had left Europe with her sister Jane and returned to her family, now living in Caracas, Venezuela. She wrote me in August, informing me that she was engaged to marry a Chilean who worked for her father at the McCann-Erickson office in Caracas, and she was coming with her sister Jane to spend autumn on the North Shore.

Why, I wondered, would this girl, now engaged to a Chilean in Venezuela, be planning to spend autumn in my neighborhood? Silly question. I was still too young and naïve to see the answer. So, apparently, was the Chilean.

Kathy and her sister arrived in early September. Kathy had a fancy engagement ring with three large emeralds. I helped the sisters find an apartment in Evanston.

When I'd last dated Kathy, I was a high school junior. Now I'd had a year of college and I'd been to New York City. In order to impress Kathy with my urbanity, I decided to take her to the Gaslight Club on Rush Street in Chicago. A valet at the door took my car and we followed another couple into the club. We sat down at the bar beneath the huge Victorian sign reading, "Work is the Curse of the Drinking Class." I ordered drinks. The bartender asked to see my key.

"My God," I said, "is this a key club?" On my previous visit I'd been with the Hinsdale Summer Theater people and Joan Blondell. We'd all been ushered in as guests of the club's owner. I glanced around the room nervously, hoping that Ron Mays, a Gaslight regular, would be there to rescue me.

Kathy and I had to leave the club. Kathy was embarrassed and livid with rage. I was humiliated, having been disgraced when I was trying to be so impressive. My anger was further fueled by Kathy's lashing out at me in my moment of vulnerability. Back in the car we yelled at each other and fought like a pair of cats. I took her home. She told me she didn't want to see me anymore.

*

My year of precious residential privacy in Pittsburgh was over. I was living again in my parents' house in Glencoe. As the school year started I'd awake each morning at 7 A.M., bathe, dress, and head for the commuter train to get to my Northwestern University School of Speech classes in Evanston. My course load included English, Play Directing, German, plus Accounting, a business school course that I tucked into my curriculum in an effort to create a major that didn't really exist—Bachelor of Theatrical Production—partly fine arts, partly hard-nosed business administration.

Even before the start of classes I'd become involved with an independent group of Northwestern students that was producing a musical variety show called *Broadway and Basin Street*. We hoped to sell productions of the show to fund-raising groups. The group had asked Paul Burkhardt to be their business manager. He declined, but recommended me.

Broadway and Basin Street might have become an outstanding musical production. We certainly didn't lack for talent. The chorus and dancers were superb and the choreography was charming. Our two leads were Nancy Dussault and Ron Houseman, both of whom I'd met at the songfest in Gibby's bar a month earlier. Ron and Nancy subsequently went on to careers in TV. But our producer-director, Bill Sheffler was incredibly disorganized. Soon we'd run up several bills we couldn't pay.

Broadway and Basin Street folded in November.

Marlon and Me

In October at Northwestern I was cast in the role of the Arab in William Saroyan's *The Time of Your Life,* a Speech School main stage production directed by faculty member Bob Schneiderman. By that time I'd noticed that the Northwestern Speech School's quality of faculty instruction as well as the acting talents of the students were both significantly lower than what I'd known at Carnegie Tech. Northwestern's faculty included a legendary old acting instructress named Alvina Kraus. Her main claim to fame seemed to have been that she'd coached such actors as Patricia Neal, Cloris Leachman, and Charleton Heston when they were at Northwestern. Alvina Kraus was a "method acting" advocate. The students held Kraus up as a goddess. In spite of her track record with three famous actors, I didn't think she was in the same league with Alan Fletcher or Mary Morris, the acting teachers at Carnegie Tech.

*

The *Socius* brotherhood decided to get together for Thanksgiving dinner in Pittsburgh. Doug Buck then lived at 3 Mawhinney Street, where we could have our dinner. Jack Waterman would drive from Boston. Waldo, at Stanford, was too far away. I boarded a DC6 at Midway, the world's busiest airport at that time. That flight to Pittsburgh was the first of over a thousand flights I'd take on commercial airliners in forthcoming decades.

Doug and Jack prepared our Thanksgiving turkey. Since I was somewhat helpless in the kitchen, my contribution consisted of a gallon of red wine. By dinner's end we were all pretty drunk. I described my experience with Peggy in the whorehouse in Kankakee. The story apparently appealed to my inebriated *Socius* buddies. We jumped in Jack's car and headed to Steubenville, Ohio, a town we'd heard had whorehouses.

My whore, a young woman named Beth, had none of Peggy's sense of adventure or romance. Beth performed her service much like a librarian checking out a book. She was little more than a cylinder for my piston—I might have achieved more drama with my own hand.

But the real drama of this event wasn't Beth, it was the setting—the Steubenville, Ohio, red light district, and its remarkable contrast to the one I'd visited in Kankakee the previous July. The Kankakee whorehouse had been above a tavern. Its front window had a huge sign proclaiming the place "OFF LIMITS TO MILITARY." It was on a lighted street in a retail district with lots of foot traffic. Inside, you declared your intention to the bartender who then directed you to a door in back that he unlocked from behind the bar with a solenoid switch.

I'd hoped to see a small jazz combo playing Dixieland like in old New Orleans. Or at least a piano player. Instead we were greeted at the top of the stairs by a tough-looking old madam who demanded to see proof that we were 21. When she glanced at my Iowa Liquor Permit she said, "Did you borrow that from your daddy?"

Beyond this checkpoint we were welcome to go into the parlor and pick out a girl from the eight flashy, scantily-dressed women of the night seated or standing there. A couple of the women were young and somewhat appealing, like Peggy. Others were older and faded, dependent on heavy makeup and push-up bras to market themselves.

By contrast to Kankakee, Steubenville was as different as a Starbucks is from a sleazy waterfront bar in a movie. Or perhaps in Marseilles. We arrived on a dark riverfront street lined with dreary run-down turn-of-the-century factory workers' houses built right to the edge of the sidewalk. The house facades were sided with tarpaper or asphalt shingles. High overhead was a steel highway bridge crossing the Ohio River to the West Virginia panhandle. The bridge lights filtered down to the street. They provided the only illumination.

We parked the car and headed down this decrepit riverfront street. All of the houses looked abandoned—there were no lights in any of the windows. We wondered if we'd been misdirected to a deserted neighborhood.

Then we noticed some movement behind one of the windows. In the dim lights from the bridge high above, we saw a woman in the dark window dressed in a short red negligee, smiling with painted lips, motioning with her hands for us to come closer, directing us around the corner to a side entrance. We watched her, smiled back, then noticed movement in a dark window of the house next door. There we saw a woman in nothing but her underwear, smiling and making provocative gestures. Across the street a warehouse door opened slightly to reveal another female solicitor with a head of bleached blond hair dressed in a coat against the cold November air. "Hey, boys!" she quietly called to us in a breathy voice.

Years later I'd recall every detail of this sordid yet colorful riverfront scene. I'd never witnessed anything like it, and I wanted to remember it in case I ever needed to design a theatrical set depicting this depraved street.

In 1956 a whore in Kankakee cost five dollars for a quickie. The Steubenville whores charged only three dollars.

You get what you pay for. Peggy was a better lay.

Doug waited in the car.

My experience with professional women ended that night in Steubenville. My next visit to a whorehouse wouldn't occur until the late 1990s when Christie and I visited two outstanding brothel museums—one in Ketchikan, Alaska, on our trip to the Arctic Circle, and the other in Butte, Montana en route to visit Sandy and Walt Oldendorf. The one in Butte is quite remarkable, and worth going out of one's way to see—a true-to-life depiction of a popular but little-known piece of Americana in this old mining town. My hat is off to the founder and curator—he did an amazing job of creating a museum out of a once-popular three-story brothel that had been closed and deserted for over thirty years. He gained valuable insights by interviewing several women who had worked there in the past as prostitutes. Our young tour guide in this museum was quite knowledgeable—one can well imagine the torrent of questions she was asked by both the men and women on her tour.

*

By mid-December I hadn't spoken with Kathy for three months, but I was still quite serious about her. Apparently she was still engaged to the Chilean, but she hadn't left Evanston. She was working at Slenderella, a reducing salon on Davis Street. Her sister Jane sold handbags at Marshall Fields.

One evening at closing time I waited in a borrowed car just down the block from Slenderella. Kathy came out with a coworker. I stepped out of the car and called to her. She looked in my direction, then spoke a word or two to the coworker, who proceeded on down the street alone as Kathy walked over to me. I guess Kathy was still interested in me, or she wouldn't have dismissed her friend when I called her name.

We started seeing each other again. Within a few weeks we agreed to get married the second week in June. Sister Jane flew to California to be with a guy she'd met and hoped to marry. Kathy moved into a smaller room with a shared bath in a house at Ridge and Greenleaf Streets in Evanston.

By the start of my second quarter at Northwestern in January, college began to seem irrelevant to me. I was studying less and attending fewer classes. My grades deteriorated. If I was to be a married man, I didn't want to be a student, I wanted to be in a *career*.

I got the name of the General Manager of Hinsdale Summer Theater from Paul Burkhardt. I sent him a resume, naming both Paul and Doug Buck as references, since they'd both worked for him. I phoned him three days later to inquire about employment opportunities. He'd read my resume and was impressed. He needed an assistant. "How old are you, Jerry?"

I'd often lied about my age to buy liquor, but I didn't think I could lie to a prospective employer. "I'm nineteen," I said. There was a pause on the line. Then he said, "Jerry, I'm afraid you're too young for the job. If I sent you to O'Hare to pick up one of our stars, you couldn't even buy her a drink."

*

I decided that as soon as Kathy and I got married, we'd move to Pittsburgh, where I knew more people in theater. Maybe I could get my career started there.

Pittsburgh? This must sound strange to today's Chicagoans who take pride in their city as the second capital of theater in the United States. Isn't Chicago home to such cutting-edge theaters as Steppenwolf, Briar Street, Apollo, The Second City, and the Lyric Opera? Didn't Chicago theaters launch the careers of Alan Alda, John Cusak, Alan Arkin, Bill Murray, Mike Nichols and many others?

Yes, that's theater in Chicago *today*. But none of those theaters existed in 1957 when Chicago was a theatrical wasteland, offering virtually no opportunities for a wannabe producer like me.

Of course, the horizons in professional theater weren't any better in Pittsburgh, either. New York and Hollywood were the places to get started. But my only contacts with professional theater were in Pittsburgh, and I hoped those contacts would help me launch my career. Kathy and I could live cheaply at 3 Mawhinney Street. Manhattan Island was so costly it terrified me. With no money, I could envision Kathy and me homeless in New York, sleeping on a bench in Central Park.

One morning just before Easter I got on the commuter train to Evanston where I was scheduled to take a final exam at Cahn Auditorium. I was unprepared, and had little hope of passing. Wouldn't an incomplete be better than a failing grade?

I walked past Cahn Auditorium and became a college dropout—a heavy decision made in the ten minutes it took me to walk five blocks. At the time it seemed like a smart move—a positive step toward my future career.

In reality, I was lost. And in a matter of weeks I would learn just how lost I'd become, and wonder how long it would take for me to recover my sense of direction.

ACT I

SCENE 2

PLACE: Working class neighborhoods in Pittsburgh, Chicago, and Rockford, Illinois

TIME: Spring 1957 to spring 1971

Chapter 9

Missed Cues

There was an employment agency operating out of a seedy little office above Chandler's Stationery Store in Evanston. The agent there found me a job as a transit clerk, clearing checks at First National Bank of Evanston. There I began my life as a breadwinner—I would hold full-time jobs without interruption for the next 41 years. Both Kathy and I were now working in downtown Evanston. We met for lunch every day at Coolie's Cupboard, a large Evanston tearoom where I'd worked earlier that year as a waiter.

One day at Coolie's in early May Kathy informed me that she was a couple of weeks late with her period. We immediately moved our wedding date from mid-June to May 17, less then two weeks away.

After lunch I walked over to the nearby Methodist church and talked to a pastor there, Rev. Dr. Harold A. Bosley. I explained to Dr. Bosley that I was planning an elopement because my fiancée's parents were not likely to approve of our wedding, much less sponsor it—or even attend it. Dr. Bosley agreed to perform the service in his church's chapel.

I informed my parents that Kathy and I would be eloping on May 17. Mom would not hear of such a plan. She and Dad arranged to augment our wedding plans with flowers and an organist, and paid for a small reception dinner at the Orrington, a downtown Evanston hotel near the Methodist chapel.

I consulted with an obstetrician who informed me that it was too early for Kathy to have a rabbit test, which was the only reliable pregnancy test at the time. Maybe Kathy was pregnant, and maybe not. We were taking no chances.

Kathy wrote to her parents in Caracas to inform them of our wedding plans. On May 10th Kathy received a letter from her father informing her that if she would postpone marrying me, he'd buy her a new car. They'd be coming to America for a vacation in August at their cottage on South Bass Island in Lake Erie, and would further discuss the subject of marriage with her at that time. Kathy had not divulged to anyone but me that she still hadn't had her period.

Jack Waterman flew in from Boston to be my best man. Kathy wanted her maid of honor to be her sister Connie, who was attending Trinity, a Catholic college in the East. Connie's Mother Superior permitted her to attend the wedding as long as she did not participate in the service, since it was not in a Catholic church. Mary Beth Potts, a friend of Kathy's from high school, agreed to stand up for Kathy in place of Connie.

On May 16th, the day before the wedding, Al Sommer wired his daughter from Caracas. *"Kathy, please don't disappoint us."* Kathy's sister Connie was present when Kathy got the telegram. I was amazed at Connie's reaction. She assumed that Kathy, without question, would now call off the wedding. Al Sommer had always enjoyed total veto power in his family. It had never occurred to him—or to Sister Connie—that third parties such as myself might someday have greater influence over his children than he had.

My mother invited her friends to a bridal shower for Kathy in Glencoe on the morning of the wedding.

Missed Cues

Ron flew in from basic training at Fort Leonard Wood. He lent me his car, an old Hudson, to get us to Pittsburgh after the wedding. All of our worldly possessions fit in that car's trunk.

We had a lovely, informal ceremony and reception dinner. My mother hired a high school kid to take photos. We spent our wedding night at The Palmer House, that venerable, elegant old hotel in downtown Chicago. The Palmer House sent a huge fruit and snack platter to our room.

In the morning we had breakfast in bed.

Then we dressed, checked out, got into Brother Ron's old green Hudson and left for Pittsburgh, arriving late that afternoon. The only thing of value in the trunk of Ron's Hudson—Mrs. Waterman's gift of a set of sterling silverware—was missing when we arrived. The parking attendants in the Palmer House garage had overheard Kathy mention to someone that we'd just been married. Weddings meant gifts. Like sterling silver.

*

Arriving in Pittsburgh I immediately applied to the Pittsburgh Playhouse for any kind of theatrical production position they might offer. They had no openings.

Next I talked with Grace Price, owner of a Children's Theater that employed my former classmate, Tom Dennis. Grace Price offered me a job for $35 a week. This would be a strain for us, even with the low $30 per month rent at 3 Mawhinney Street. A week later Grace Price called and said she'd have to reduce her offer to $25 a week.

With that phone call, my hope of a theatrical career, which I'd dreamed of and planned for, came to an end. In the course of just two months I'd dropped out of both college and theater—two decisions that would alter the course of my life. If I'd had money, Kathy and I might have pulled up stakes and gone to New York, where theater opportunities were more plentiful. But money, or the lack of it, now ruled my life. In the next three weeks I sold two pints of blood for $10 each.

There was good money to be earned at the steel mill. United States Steel ran the nation's largest mill in nearby Homestead, Pennsylvania, a grim mill town where the steel workers lived in tiny frame houses sided with asphalt singles. These dreary homes stood shoulder to shoulder on 25-foot lots in endless rows like the ranks of a defeated army. The windows were sooty and grimy and the streets underfoot were gritty from the filthy smoke belching forth from the steel mill stacks 24 hours a day. The sun rarely broke through the gloomy haze over Homestead. This was a "company" town with a single employer.

I got a job as a general laborer. My new boss was a second generation Greek named "Lefty" Koulous, a rough middle-aged fellow with a sixth grade education. Lefty looked up from my personnel paperwork. "Says here you've got two years of college," he said.

"Yes."

"What are you doin' here?" he asked. College had never been an option for Lefty or anyone else in the labor gang. And I thought Lefty would be suspicions of anyone who'd attended college. Lefty caught me off guard. He encouraged me to somehow get back into college and get a degree.

Lefty assigned a big black man to walk me around the mill on a first-day orientation, and to take me to the company store to buy a pair of the mandatory steel-toe boots. Six dollars would be deducted from my first paycheck for the boots. My yellow hard hat was issued without charge. By noon we were in a locker room. The black man lay down on a bench and slept for the rest of the day.

Each day at the mill was pretty much like every other day. The laborers—all of them black except me—would meet at the General Labor Shack at 8 A.M. We'd wait for directions from Lefty as to where we'd work that day. After ten minutes or so Lefty would mumble a few instructions. Lefty could speak

Missed Cues

Ebonics. Following Lefty's instructions we'd go to the tool shed and load the tools needed for the day—sometimes shovels and picks, sometimes jackhammers—onto a truck. We'd then climb into a wagon with benches inside and be towed by a tractor for ten or fifteen minutes through the massive steel mill complex to wherever we were to work that day.

I'd grown up in a quiet suburb. Now I was working in a steel mill, which is like working in hell. There's enough intense heat there to melt massive amounts of scrap metal into hot, soupy lava. Huge blast furnaces belch like dragons. Everywhere you are surrounded by deafening noise and danger. Giant overhead cranes hoist great ladles full of tons of molten metal. The molten metal pours into ingot molds. Flatbed train cars grind slowly along their tracks loaded with red-hot ingots standing ten feet high. The hot ingots get crunched between rollers that flatten them into sheets.

If these mill workers went to a bar after work for a shot and a beer followed by an argument and a fight, it was all just another part of a day in hell—a life filled with dirt, noise, heat, and violence.

Intensive safety measures were a part of every workday. They were also a part of union featherbedding. At the mere sight of an approaching train or crane, the labor gang would immediately stop working, drop their tools, move away, and sit down.

On the more interesting days my gang would work at the endless job of replacing the inside linings of various furnaces after they'd cooled down for several days. With jackhammers we'd break up the old lining and haul the pieces away. Then we'd cut open boxes of Ramtight, the material for the new lining, and hammer it into place. Some days we worked inside the open hearths, other days we climbed down into idle pit furnaces that, even after days of cooling, were still so hot we had to work in shifts, fifteen minutes in the pit, fifteen minutes up top cooling off.

I began to understand the meaning of hopelessness among unskilled laborers. Conversations in the labor gang before work and at lunch tended to focus on the numbers racket, a gambling game in which anyone could dream up a number and bet a few cents on it. Random numbers appeared in each daily newspaper. If your number came up you might win a couple hundred dollars. If you could manage to bet a dollar or two and your number came up, maybe you could quit the mill and buy a liquor store. But mostly you bet a few cents that, day after day, you lost.

The numbers racket was run by organized crime, because transactions were in cash and profits were not only huge but went unreported. For these laborers at the bottom rung of the economic scale, the numbers represented the only hope they'd ever have in a life with no future. Everywhere were young and old men alike, all earning about the same money, all doing the same work in a filthy, noisy mill in a sad, decrepit town, breathing polluted air. The treadmill would end only with permanent injury or retirement at age 65. Nothing else changed. But for these hundreds of mill workers, the numbers game represented a possible light at the end of the tunnel.

I could identify with this. My ray of hope was somewhere on Manhattan Island. But I was no longer a hopeful theatrical producer—I was an unskilled laborer in a hellhole called Homestead, Pennsylvania.

This was a union job in a union town, so the money was outstanding for unskilled labor—just over a hundred dollars a week. It put food on the table today, but held no hope for tomorrow.

I quit after three weeks. If my dream for a life in theater was smashed, I'd just have to build a future some other way. I took a job as a transit clerk in a downtown Pittsburgh bank, clearing checks for $250 a month.

Kathy was disappointed. As long as I was working in the steel mill I was really still in theater, just between jobs, like the actors and opera singers who worked as waiters and waitresses.

But if I held a job in a bank, it meant that Kathy was married to a lowly bank clerk.

*

In June Kathy went to see Dr. Irving, an obstetrician. Dr. Irving confirmed that Kathy was pregnant. The baby would be due the third week in January. When Kathy told me I gave her a proud grin, a big bear hug, and a dozen or so kisses. We were going to be parents!

We wrote to our own parents: *"You're going to be grandparents, and the baby will arrive a little early!"*

August came. Kathy began to show. Gordon Smith and his new wife Gayle, both of them acting majors at Tech, showed up at 3 Mawhinney. Gayle was pregnant, maybe a week or two further along than Kathy. Gordon and Gayle introduced us to a book called *Childbirth Without Fear* by a British obstetrician. It explained the birthing technique that later came to be called Lamaze. It explained how to get through childbirth naturally, without anesthesia. Most important, Lamaze involved me with the pregnancy. Together we rehearsed Kathy's breathing and muscular control. I massaged her back. I learned to identify and understand the three stages of labor. We were pioneers. In 1957 fathers were expected to wait in the fathers' waiting room and know nothing about anything. Little did we know that within a couple of decades Lamaze would be the rage, and by 1975 there would be Lamaze classes offered at every hospital. A father's participation in both the Lamaze classes as well as the birth itself would come to be considered so mandatory that even single pregnant women would often choose Lamaze partners from among their friends.

In 1957 Dr. Irving simply informed me that there was no possible way McGee Hospital would allow a father into a delivery room. If I wanted, I could work with my wife in the labor room, but when she went into delivery I would be ushered into the fathers' room. I asked if I could alter this rule with some sort of donation to the hospital. He said, "Don't attempt to bribe anyone at McGee." (McGee, within a couple of decades, became the leading obstetrics hospital in the country. Today they'd probably be embarrassed over their rigid paternal rules of 1957.)

*

Our happiness over the prospect of parenthood was diminished by two conflicts. One was mine, the other was Kathy's.

I was struggling with the consequences of the bad decisions I'd made over the past few months, and the fact that I'd painted myself into a corner. I'd dropped out of college. I'd gotten Kathy pregnant when I couldn't afford to support a family, financially or emotionally. And I'd moved us to Pittsburgh in pursuit of a dream that had turned into a puff of smoke. This last disappointment intensified when Doug Buck and the other Tech students returned to college in September. The Tech students would all soon have college degrees and promising futures to look forward to. I'd shared that expectation once. Now I was just a white collar bank clerk earning $250 a month, barely making ends meet.

Meanwhile, Kathy was feeling extremely uncomfortable living with these theater people at 3 Mawhinney Street. In this house just one year earlier I'd created a charming but humble little dramatics commune where we students could exercise our cleverness with impromptu vignettes acted out around the dinner table each evening. But theater people are often as vindictive as they are clever—egotistical, brusque and tactless. They tend to act superior to people like Kathy who are not in the arts. Kathy was pregnant, she was young and unsure of herself, she was not an actress, and she often felt the subtle barbs of disdain from this witty but hypercritical group of theater people.

Missed Cues

Some old friends of the Sommer family lived nearby in an elegant Pittsburgh neighborhood. Joe Hague, who was Jane Sommer's godfather, owned a vintage Oakland mansion where he lived with his wife Ginger and their six children.

Joe called Kathy and said he'd like to come by to visit us. We thought he'd be coming to welcome us to the Oakland district of Pittsburgh. Kathy prepared coffee and baked some teacakes.

Joe knocked on the door of 3 Mawhinney. Kathy welcomed him in. He got as far as the living room, then said, "I just wanted to say hello," and backed out the door.

Kathy was surprised and upset that Joe Hague didn't stay for a visit. What we didn't know is that Joe had been sent by Al Sommer to check up on his pregnant daughter's living conditions. Joe reported back to Al that Kathy was living in squalor, in a slum.

A day later Kathy's mother Kim phoned to say that she would come to visit in two days. She would stay not with us but with the Hagues.

Kim entered the house and looked around, said a few words, then retreated to the Hagues.

Kathy and I were invited to dinner at the Hagues the following evening. At dinner, Kim announced that she had found an apartment for us in Pittsburgh, and Al would be paying the rent for a while. I was flabbergasted. Kim hadn't even consulted us about finding another place for us to live.

Apparently Al Sommer figured that if he couldn't get rid of me, perhaps he could neutralize me by controlling my life, starting with a rent subsidy. And I was not about to become indebted to a man who I knew detested me.

To Kim's shock and amazement, I told her "Thanks, we already have a place to live." It had never even occurred to her that we'd turn down Al's offer to rescue their daughter from the house that Joe Hague had described as substandard.

Kim turned to her daughter. She probably figured that if Kathy could put pressure on me, maybe I'd cave in. To my relief, Kathy said "No thanks, Mom...we're doing just fine."

Had Kathy said anything different, it probably would have been the beginning of the end of our marriage.

But Kathy had said *"No thanks, Mom...we're doing just fine."* She was willing to stand by me, even in a house full of drama students who looked down on her.

I may not have had many prospects for the future. But, by God, I had a loyal wife.

Kim Sommer spent the remaining day of her stay visiting with Kathy at 3 Mawhinney and imparting some of her experience with six babies—how to keep the baby warm while bathing it in front of the gas fireplace, how to bundle the baby up at bedtime.

A week later, Allied Van Lines arrived with a shipment from Kim and Al in Greenwich. It was the cradle in which all six of the Sommer children had slept as babies—a charming old-fashioned rocking cradle that Al himself had built out of a large oaken barrel. Kathy painted it blue and decorated it with cloth lining and bedclothes and a big ribbon bow.

*

In the late afternoon of January 30th Kathy went into labor and we began our Lamaze exercises. Her water broke at 11:30 P.M. I rushed her to McGee. They prepped her, removed her wedding ring and wristwatch and gave them to me. We worked Lamaze for several hours together, until she was wheeled into delivery.

In the early dawn I found a florist shop. I could see a clerk working inside. I hammered on the door and got her to sell me some flowers in a box with a ribbon. I fastened Kathy's wedding ring in the knot. On a card I wrote "I love you both."

Missed Cues

James Almon Inglehart made a big entry that morning, weighing in at an ounce less than ten pounds. Fortunately for him, Kathy was physically equipped to deliver such a large child. I saw my son before he'd been bathed, when his body was still covered with splotches of blood from the delivery.

I took Kathy home on February 3rd. Jamie had been in the immaculate care of the hospital nursery for four days. I was somewhat intimidated when they actually handed our infant to us, to take to our funky commune home in our old 1947 DeSoto automobile that I'd purchased for $65.

The following Saturday Kathy needed to shop for groceries. I drove my little family to the supermarket, and then told Kathy I was going to take a walk with Jamie while she shopped.

Ten pounds may make a big newborn, but it's nonetheless a tiny package. And little babies, when they have no spit-up on their Dr. Dentons or poop in their diapers, have a very endearing fragrance of powder and baby oil. My son looked up at me, totally helpless, totally trusting and curious as I bundled him in his blanket against the mild February chill.

I remember that walk so clearly—the old Oakland row houses, the bleak February sky, the light little bundle in my arms, head resting on my shoulder. This is my boy. I'm a daddy now.

The Army was drafting married men, but not fathers. I rushed to send a copy of Jamie's birth certificate to my draft board in Evanston, Illinois. I also enclosed a cigar.

*

There's a little footnote to include here. When Kathy's mother died in the early 70s, a document emerged showing Kim and Al's wedding date. Kathy recalled that her parents had never celebrated their wedding anniversary. And we discovered why.

Kim and Al were married on May 17th, the same date Kathy and I were married.

"When is your sister Jane's birthday?" I asked Kathy.

"January 30th—a day before Jamie's."

"Well, I'll be damned—they did the same thing we did!"

On her wedding day, Kim Sommer had been one day *more* pregnant than my wife was on our wedding day! It amazed me that Al could have been so unsympathetic, and so blind to the reality of our situation, having experienced it all himself.

*

By mid-February I was fed up with Pittsburgh. The town represented a career failure for me. And the theater people at 3 Mawhinney made my wife feel uncomfortable in her own home.

Just before our wedding day my father had asked me, "Do you think you'd ever be interested in the drug business?" As Director of Personnel for Walgreens, he could help me. In late January I called him from Pittsburgh and told him I'd like to move back to Chicago and start working for Walgreens. I knew that I would never make Walgreens my career, but I'd have to tough it out a few years, in deference to my father's position as Director of Personnel. After that, if I found myself in a reasonably stable financial condition, perhaps I could think about building a new dream.

Rent in Chicago would be higher than the $30 a month we were paying at 3 Mawhinney Street. We had friends who lived in a small apartment on Agatite Street near the Chicago lakefront, who were paying $87.50 a month rent. But my wages in Chicago would be higher, too. Walgreens would start me at $310 a month for forty hours. And since Walgreen store personnel worked six days a week (all at straight pay) I'd get about $372 a month—roughly $300 take-home after taxes, Social Security, and health insurance. And when I sold blood to the Evanston Hospital, I'd get $5 a pint more than the Pittsburgh blood bank paid.

Most important, we'd have the security of my parents at 660 Grove Street, Glencoe. If we ran out of food money, Kathy and I and our little baby would be welcome to be fed for a weekend in Glencoe.

I packed our things into our DeSoto.

I packed my wife and six-week-old son into a Douglas DC7 aircraft at Greater Pittsburgh airport.

In this way I closed the Pittsburgh chapter of my life. My son was born but my dream was dead. And I wasn't even 21 years old.

Chapter 10

Wrong Show

This chapter and the one following it were difficult for me to write. They describe a time when economic circumstances forced me into two roles for which I was unsuited—at Walgreens and Sears. I turned in a pair of second-rate performances, and didn't manage to get my act together until 1967, nine years later.

I condensed the two chapters down to about 21 pages, and even considered deleting them from the book. But pulling nine years out of a sixty-year history makes for a chronology that looks like a smile with two missing front teeth. The good news is that I survived those years, and even learned from them. Here are the condensed details.

*

In February 1958, Dad's Assistant Director of Personnel, Tom Baima, hired me as a Walgreen Store Management Trainee, which is a glorified title for an entry level position. I started as an assistant stockman at a new Walgreen store that was being opened near Clark and Foster Streets in Chicago.

Wrong Show

I moved my family into a small walkup apartment in a relatively safe working class neighborhood near Chicago's Uptown area where our living expenses would be quite low. I worked the standard Walgreens 6-day, 48-hour week. Our rent was less than $90 a month. Our entertainment consisted of a six-pack of beer on weekends and an occasional movie. Even so, the $69 in my weekly pay envelope never seemed to last. Unexpected expenses, like new brakes for the DeSoto, would pop up and we'd be short of money. Every three months or so I'd have to hit up my father for a $50 loan. I was always checking the want ads for part-time opportunities.

One such opportunity in the *Tribune* "guaranteed" a hundred dollars a week. I phoned and was granted an interview downtown in an office in the old Mystic Theater Building on Monroe Street, which housed the Shubert Theater. In the "interview" I was seated in a meeting room with seventy other applicants. A pitch man walked in and explained to us that he had quit a very promising job earning $20,000 a year to come to work here at Colliers Encyclopedia because he'd seen the W-2 form of his boss at Colliers. Now he claimed he could drop $200 a night on Rush Street and think nothing of it. Best of all, he explained, we applicants wouldn't be *selling* Colliers Encyclopedias; we'd be *giving them away free*. But the "guarantee" of $100 a week wouldn't take effect until we'd proven we could "sell."

This contradiction, coupled with the high-pressure pitch, was just too fishy for me. I felt certain I was going to have to buy something in order to try to earn something. I sympathized with all the desperate kids seated in this room who'd take the bait and sign up—I didn't stay long enough to find out what they'd have to do or buy or sacrifice in order to qualify as Colliers Encyclopedia salesmen.

I heard about another part-time job opportunity from a friend named Donald Mathis, who later married Mary Sommer and became my brother-in-law. Mathis had a friend named Art Diamond. (The name alone should have tipped me off.) Art

Diamond worked for a company called Record of the Week Club, which gave subscribers a free hi-fi phonograph if they signed up to buy one $4 record each week for a year. Donald said Art Diamond was earning some serious money. I contacted Diamond and met him at the Record of the Week Club sales office on the South Side. I trusted him because he was a friend of a friend.

That night Diamond told me I had "qualified" for a sales sample kit consisting of a portable hi-fi phonograph and 20 records. Diamond had me sign a "receipt" for it. Even though my dad had told me never to sign anything I hadn't read, I didn't read what I'd signed until I got home. I had just been sold a hi-fi and twenty cheap closeout records worth about ten cents each—all for $80. I'd even signed a wage assignment guaranteeing payment. I'd been suckered. And by a friend of a friend. Now I was deeper in dept than ever.

I never did manage to sell a Record of the Week subscription. In 1958, stereo phonographs were making hi-fi obsolete.

In August I had an unexpected preview of my future career in advertising. It happened like this:

Every week each Walgreen store was given a promotional tape recording to play on the store's sound system Thursdays through Sundays. The tapes had narrated spiels about the sale items featured that week, interspersed with music.

The narrations on the tapes were unprofessional, characterless, and dull. "Remember folks, during our big Back-to-School celebration we're featuring notebook paper, four packs for a dollar, and packs of twenty pencils for just 99 cents. And don't forget to buy vitamins to keep your little back-to-school youngsters healthy and on their toes. And this week Walgreens ice cream is five pints for just a dollar. For better health, for better living, your dollar buys more at Walgreens."

Then the tape would cut to some worn-out public-domain instrumental music played by a few Musicians' Union dropouts.

Wrong Show

"Sweet Sue." "Yes, We Have No Bananas." "Clementine." I think the tapes even featured a few old Stephen Foster tunes performed on an electric organ. God, were those tapes terrible! They grated on my sensibilities. Was I really working for a company that played such trash in its business environment?

One day I mailed in a Walgreen Suggestion Form proposing that Walgreens either improve the tapes or discontinue them as a benefit to store employees who had to listen to them for four days. (Even at age 21 I still hadn't learned the rudiments of tact.)

A week later I got a call from Walgreens Purchasing Department at headquarters, where a couple of assistant buyers were assigned the weekly task of throwing the tapes together in their spare time. I had hoped my suggestion would be offensive enough to be noticed. But because my name was Inglehart, it was taken quite seriously. I should have signed a false name.

The assistant buyers would be preparing next week's tape the following Tuesday, and they invited me in to Walgreen headquarters on Peterson Avenue to make suggestions.

Well, Jer, I thought to myself, *you got what you deserved.* I spent that Thursday thinking what an ass I would probably make of myself in the production meeting with the buyers.

Then I thought, why not just write and produce a tape, and bring it along? Brother Ron was in the army, doing information work at nearby Ft. Sheridan. He worked with professional sound recording equipment. I called him explaining the hole I'd just dug for myself at work. With our mutual experience in theater, combined with a government recording studio, could he help me redeem myself? Of course we could. "Take the train to Ft. Sheridan Friday after work. I'll meet you at the station."

I created a script describing the coming week's loss leaders in a logical, conversational sequence. Then I had Kathy write a script for cosmetics, drawing on tips from a recent women's magazine. Next I wrote a *Dragnet* script in clipped dialogue in which cop Joe Friday and his sidekick work out the logic of all the Back-to-School values.

Finally I selected music cuts from my record collection. That was the easy part. I chose an instrumental of "The Jet Song" from *West Side Story*. And another instrumental from *Kismet*. Music to shop by. Contemporary. Upbeat. Fun to hear.

In the Ft. Sheridan studio on Friday evening, Ron and Kathy both did very professional, pleasing deliveries of the two monologues. Ron and I did the *Dragnet* dialogue together. Then we edited several music cuts into the tape. We came up with a tape I felt proud to take to the Walgreens production meeting.

I played it for Dad in Glencoe that weekend. He suggested I come to headquarters Monday morning so we could present it to R. G. Schmitt, Director of Store Operations. This would have the effect of preempting the purchasing department.

Schmitt thought the tape was good. He arranged for my tape to be played at two Chicagoland stores on a test basis—my store on North Clark Street, and the Old Orchard store in Skokie. Schmitt wanted me and the Old Orchard store manager to report to him a week later on public reaction to the tape.

I watched the shoppers carefully as my tape played.

What I learned was that when people come into a store to shop, they're there to look, not to listen. They wander down the aisles, pick up some toothpaste, maybe some shampoo, and see if there are any interesting values or sale items. They come as shoppers, not as an audience. They're oriented toward products and signs, and the newspaper coupons they may have clipped. The recorded messages on the store speaker system, whether good or bad, are ignored.

In a brief but thoughtful and respectful letter to Mr. Schmitt I explained my findings and supporting opinions. Possibly the Old Orchard store manager reported similar findings, because two weeks later, Walgreens discontinued the tapes. So my first encounter with the dramatic world of advertising proved to be of no value to me, although it saved my employer a few bucks.

*

Wrong Show

I was beginning to associate my financial frustration with having become a college dropout. Gail Winston, an old friend from Lake Shore Players, showed me a catalog for Northwestern University Evening Divisions. I realized that if I worked part-time toward a college degree I'd no longer be a college dropout. I'd be a *degree candidate!* In the fall of 1958 Northwestern University Evening Divisions admitted me, but on a probation basis because of my poor grades the previous year. I was allowed to take two courses.

I began an uninterrupted nine-year cycle of evening classes at Northwestern that would eventually put me into the Northwestern graduating class of 1967.

*

In October our District Manager, Bob Telfer, called me in to the district office. He was promoting me to Merchandise Manager at a larger store at Harlem and Irving. I got a very nice raise. Little did I know what lay ahead for me.

When I arrived at the Harlem-Irving store, my new boss, store manager Bill Terrill, was on vacation. There was a merchandise manager already there—a fellow named Bill Donaldson. "You're the Merchandise Manager?" I asked him.

"Yes."

"Forgive me if I'm a little confused—Mr. Telfer sent me here as Merchandise Manager. Are there supposed to be two of us?"

"Mr. Terrill told me you were coming here as an assistant stockman."

"Not according to his boss, Mr. Telfer."

"Well, our boss, Mr. Terrill, will be back in a week—I guess we'll just have to see what he knows. Meanwhile, he told me before he left that you're an assistant stockman, and until he says differently, maybe you should work in the stock room."

A week later Bill Terrill returned and called me into his office. "What makes you think you're a merchandise manager?"

"I didn't say I'm a merchandise manager...your boss, Mr. Telfer said I'm a merchandise manager."

"I'm going to meet with your father about this."

Apparently Terrill felt he was being victimized by nepotism, which was rampant in the Walgreen Company at the time. Bill Terrill felt I was probably an unqualified son of a headquarters executive that was being rammed down his throat. Terrill met with my father at headquarters to protest.

Dad told me later that he'd explained to Terrill that I had served eight months in the store on Foster Street where, according to reports from my store manager and district manager, I'd shown outstanding performance in several capacities, and was worthy of promotion. When Terrill left this meeting, Dad was under the impression that he'd changed Terrill's mind about me.

Instead, Terrill started a storewide vendetta against me in an attempt to get me to quit. He criticized me openly and often in front of other store personnel. He got the key store people to attempt to find fault with my work whenever possible. In a matter of weeks I felt like the goose with a bald neck because every other goose in the gaggle had pecked his feathers off.

I couldn't accept the idea that there was a formal, sanctioned vendetta against me. It sounded too paranoid. That was what crazy people told their psychiatrists. "They're all against me!" I didn't dare tell my father about this. He was convinced he'd changed Terrill's mind about me. And my financial situation prevented me from simply walking away from this mess. I had a family at home. So six days a week, week after week, I was doomed to enter, on a daily basis, a torturous and humiliating persecution drama that reminded me of one of those paranoid dream sequences in an Ingmar Bergman film.

We were going into the important Christmas season, when we did 25% of our annual sales volume in a four-week period. There was lots of work to do, setting the store for Christmas merchandise and keeping everything stocked during days of heavy traffic and volume. In 1958 at Walgreens, store employees who hoped someday to advance to store management positions were expected to put in lots of extra hours at no pay between Thanksgiving and Christmas. We would all come in at 9 A.M. and work until closing at 10 P.M., including our days off. I was putting in over 80 hours a week, and attending two night school classes at Northwestern as well. After my night classes I'd return to work. All these extra hours I put in for free—no extra pay beyond 48 hours straight time.

I had part of Christmas morning at home with my family, but at 10 A.M. on Christmas Day I had to be back at the store. Hour-for-hour, store sales on Christmas Day were the highest of the year.

Then we started the huge job of re-setting the store—taking down the extra Christmas displays, packing away the unsold holiday stock, and re-merchandising for January. I could identify with my dad as a young father, working seven days a week for Walgreens during the Depression.

The vendetta by the key employees never let up through the holidays and beyond. I'd come home totally defeated and depressed. The vendetta had such a negative impact on me that it was destroying my marriage as well. My life was in shambles. In February Kathy and I began seeing a marriage counselor.

In March the vendetta at work suddenly stopped. One day I came in to work and discovered that I was being accepted as one of the team.

Shortly afterward, Terrill left to join another retail drug firm, taking with him one of my coworkers named Frank Sobin. Just before departing, Sobin, privately admitted to me that Bill Terrill had personally and officially organized the vendetta, directing his key employees to find fault with everything I did in order to try to get me to quit. So the vendetta had not been a figment of my imagination.

Then in March Terrill called the vendetta off, telling the key employees, "Let's face it—this Inglehart is really good."

Frank Sobin said everyone involved was amazed that I hadn't quit—and that I had been able to tough it out all those months. Surprisingly, he added, "I don't know what you're doing here at Walgreens, Jerry. You're no loser."

I felt like a war veteran.

*

The decade of the 1960s dawned. In January no one could have predicted the massive social changes looming on the horizon because they were still embryonic. Eisenhower was still president. In November I voted for JFK in the presidential elections.

In April 1960 I was transferred to a Walgreen store in Park Ridge, as Assistant Manager. By Christmas of 1960 my income was sufficient to take a great deal of the stress out of living. Two years earlier I'd moved my family from the little apartment in Uptown to a larger one on Winthrop Street, just north of Foster Avenue, in a building where Jack and Judy Harris, two high school friends of ours, lived. Judy had been the star of *Lagniappe* in 1954, and had married Jack, a high school friend of Kathy's who was now studying at the Chicago Art Institute.

The new feel-good era of self-appeasement was resulting in a lot of divorces. Jack and Judy's close friends in the apartment across the hall from them divorced in February. Jack and Judy followed suit a month or so later.

After a personal crisis, Kathy and I separated for a few weeks during the summer of 1959. But by autumn we seemed to have worked our marital problems out. I felt more confident in the strength of our marriage. A year later, around Christmas of 1960 I felt, for the first time since moving to Chicago, that my marriage to Kathy would last. We planned to move to Evanston.

We also planned another child.

Chapter 11

Miscast

We found a pleasant third floor one-bedroom walkup apartment on Elmwood Street in Evanston in the spring of 1961. It had a sun porch in front and windows looking south onto a park. The apartment was only 800 square feet but seemed a little bigger because it was bathed in sunlight from the south exposure windows. We moved in on May 1st.

*

About midnight on the night of November 18th Kathy woke me. She'd been in labor for a few hours and thought it was time to head for Evanston hospital. We left Jamie with neighbors downstairs.

The birthing experience at Evanston Hospital was far more personal than what Kathy had experienced in the McGee Hospital baby factory four years earlier. We did the Lamaze exercises again until Kathy went in to deliver at about 6:30 A.M. Just as in Pittsburgh, fathers were excluded from the delivery room.

I went to the cafeteria for an early breakfast. In the quiet of the empty cafeteria I ate my scrambled eggs, drank my coffee and looked out the window. It was a magical morning—the first snowfall of winter, and a heavy one that blanketed the gardens outside the window with 18 inches of virgin snow. There was a nurse dormitory across the courtyard and I watched a few nurses in their capes hurrying along the freshly shoveled walk to their assignments. The deep white snow created a peaceful silence. I saw the sky lighten with the first hint of dawn on a new day—the first day in the life of my second son. I sipped my coffee and thought, *What a magnificent morning to be born!*

Chris beat out his brother by one ounce, weighing in at exactly ten pounds.

*

Al Sommer was transferred from Venezuela back to New York. In September I packed my small family into our little 1958 Volkswagen Beetle and we headed for Greenwich, Connecticut, to visit Kathy's family in their massive colonial house on Bruce Park Drive with its endless bedrooms and secret stairways connecting the kitchen with the servants' quarters. They'd owned it for eight years. My last visit had been Thanksgiving 1955 when I was a freshman at Carnegie Tech

I spent a lot of time in my beloved Manhattan, the city of dreams for me, once because of Broadway, and now because I wanted to get into advertising. Madison Avenue in Manhattan was the address of many of the world's biggest and finest advertising agencies, and therefore the advertising capital of the world, with fancy, costly glass-enclosed offices looking out on the East River. Here advertising campaigns were created that changed the nation's buying patterns—often changing preferences, lifestyles, and ideals in the process.

But it would be several months before I would see the interior of any of these great commercial edifices.

Breakfast at Tiffany's with Audrey Hepburn was released that year, providing me with a new set of visual images of

Manhattan, far more realistic than the stylized scenes from *Guys and Dolls*. My second day in Manhattan I found Tiffany's, and looked around to see where Holly Golightly had bought her coffee and doughnuts to eat in front of the bullet-proof, jewel-laden Tiffany windows.

The third day Kathy and I toured the island, following highlights on a map Jack Waterman had marked up for us. We took a cab to the Metropolitan Museum, walked down Fifth Avenue, had tea at the Plaza Hotel, walked through Central Park, and then took a subway to Greenwich Village.

The next day I took Jamie with me and did a photo tour of Jamie on the Brooklyn Bridge, Jamie looking out at the United States Line passenger ships in their Hudson River slips, Jamie near the George Washington Bridge looking down at the famous Little Red Lighthouse.

*

I still felt I was in an economic trap. Our annual two-week vacations consisted of low-cost trips to Put-in-Bay, Green Lake, or other places where we could stay rent-free in property owned by parents. We couldn't consider travel beyond the range of our family Volkswagen.

This frustration was underscored deeply in the summer of 1962, when Brother Ron, recently returned from Europe, lent me his copy of *Europe on $5 a Day* by Arthur Frommer. Frommer had been a G.I. stationed in Germany after the war, and he'd learned how to travel cheaply in economical post-war Europe, staying in the lodgings and eating at the restaurants frequented by Europeans, rather than the pricey American hotels. Ron had used the book as a guide for two European trips.

God, how I longed to see Europe! London, Munich, Vienna, Rome—Europe in 1962 was such a bargain for the traveler who followed Frommer's guide. There were chapters on each fabulous European city, with details on lodgings costing $2 or less per night, and places where you could dine for $1.25, get lunch for 75 cents and breakfast for a quarter, leaving you change for trolleys and museum admissions. *Yes! Yes!* Kathy and I could easily afford that for two weeks. We could park the kids with grandparents and travel on a Eurail Pass from Frankfurt to Amsterdam to Brussels to Paris, following Frommer's little bible. *Yes!*

Actually, no. These were the years before airline deregulation. *Getting* to Europe in 1962 cost four times as much as *being* in Europe for two weeks. The cheapest airfare from Chicago to London was $250 per person, $500 for a couple. And on what I earned, we could never allocate that much for a vacation. The alternative was to book passage on a freight ship for $50 or so, but the crossing could take up to two weeks in each direction. That was fine for students and teachers who had the entire summer off—my annual vacation lasted only two weeks.

Frommer's book was a wish book. Europe would have to wait. In the meantime, we would have to limit our vacation plans to those places where we could drive our Volkswagen Beetle, stay in free lodgings, and return in sixteen days. And that didn't include London, Amsterdam or Rome. It didn't even include San Francisco.

*

I was searching for my exit from Walgreens. My job there seemed to be the epitome of life without meaning. Six days a week I'd stock, inventory, and merchandise thousands of items that were trivial to me, from shoe polish to fungicide to nail clippers. The idea of advancing to the position of store manager seemed as uninspiring as the men like Bill Terrill who were store managers, and presumably my role models. Two Walgreen store managers I'd known had already been fired for stealing. I'd seen a few district managers and they, too, were an unimpressive lot. I'd met only one regional supervisor, a man

Miscast

named Harold Yousi, who seemed to be a complete jerk. Walgreens' top management in the Chicago headquarters was apparently rife with nepotism. And from more than one of our suppliers I was hearing that the buyers at headquarters insisted on bribes, just like Congressmen.

In the back of my mind I saw a Northwestern Bachelor's Degree as an escape hatch. I'd been a college dropout, but now I was getting mostly A's, and never lower than a B. Night by night, course by course, semester by semester I was working my way down a path leading to graduation. But that degree from the hallowed halls of the Harvard of the Midwest appeared to be about five years distant. I couldn't wait that long to leave Walgreens. I'd put in almost five years there, and I felt I was worthy of an honorable discharge.

I wanted to enter the world of advertising, a glamorous life working with film directors, actors, and jingle writers. It was creative work that required creative people—writers and art directors and producers. I was creative. And the ad agencies were in tall, prestigious office buildings downtown on North Michigan Avenue, lining streets that were busy, urbane, and full of beautiful people. I'd occasionally get to downtown Chicago to see a show, or to shop, or take Kathy to a fancy dinner for our anniversary. The idea of working down there inspired me. It had sights and sounds I never saw on my dreary commutes to Walgreen stores in middle-class Chicago suburbs.

I added several advertising courses to my Northwestern curriculum that autumn.

In August of 1962 I began a letter campaign to get interviews at Chicago ad agencies. My first interview was at Foote, Cone & Belding. I bought a conservative summer weight suit for the interview—the first suit I'd bought since before I was married.

By late September I'd managed to get twelve or so interviews. From the creative directors I learned that nobody gets a job as an ad agency copywriter until he's had some experience as a writer. "Go to Sears, Fields, Wards, any retailer, any catalog house. They'll hire you. Write retail copy. Get your feet wet." This sounded like good advice. Many top creative people in advertising started out writing retail copy.

I visited the offices of the Spiegel Catalog on the South Side, where I was offered a job as a copywriter on my first interview. But the job involved a pay cut from what I was earning at Walgreens. Still it was a necessary career step.

I told my father that I'd be giving notice at Walgreens on October 1st. He wasn't disturbed about me leaving Walgreens, he'd always anticipated that. He was concerned about my going to Spiegel's, a less-than-first-rate retailer. But he had an acquaintance in the personnel department of Sears.

Dad lined up an interview for me at Sears where I was offered a position as the retail copywriter for Coldspot appliances, working at their headquarters on the West Side. The job paid $550 a month—more than the Spiegel offer but less than my Walgreens salary—I'd still be taking a 15% pay cut. But at last I'd be working with a typewriter instead of a box cutter. I would write copy that would be printed. I'd have an office—well, not looking out on Michigan Avenue; in fact, it had no window at all, because the Sears Retail Advertising Department was in a basement.

But I was finally back on track.

*

My plan was to stay at Sears for nine months, then take my ad proofs and return to Michigan Avenue for more ad agency interviews.

It wasn't a bad plan. I wish I'd followed it. But a personal conflict emerged and blocked my plan. It came in the form of a job offer from the Sears Coldspot Appliance National Sales Department. They offered me a job as a retail assistant.

Sears is a retailing giant that exists on the buying and selling of merchandise. Therefore the big bucks are in the purchasing and sales departments, not in retail advertising. A

Miscast

job in sales wasn't the creative future I'd hoped for. It was a sales position. But an entry-level job with the Coldspot National Sales Department could lead to promotions into jobs where men were earning large incomes—inside a corporate giant that also offered a lot of job security.

At age 25 I was a man with heavy personal responsibilities—a family of four that demanded a secure income. More money meant more future. So I shelved my plan to prepare myself for a career in a creative field. I took the Coldspot sales job instead.

At first I was put to work supervising the copywriter who replaced me in the advertising department. This led to preparing sales bulletins and brochures. Coldspot followed the strategy of the auto industry in Detroit—each calendar year required a whole new line of products. Not that the previous year's line was outmoded—but a new product line meant new things to talk about in sales meetings.

It also meant new photography, new brochures, and new sales manuals. I could handle that. The National Sales Manager suggested a slide film for training. I put one together that was sort of "a day in the life of a wife with her refrigerator." I used a lot of music cuts. I cast a very cute model as the housewife and spent a week working on photos of her in the Sears in-house photo studio. I spent another couple of days working on the sound track in the Sears in-house sound studio. I called the film *Red Roses* because the final music cut I used was *Red Roses for a Blue Lady,* a popular Bert Kaemfert instrumental. I unveiled my film to my sales department. They were very impressed. They'd never had a sales tool as exciting or professional—something they could use for knockout sales meeting openers around the country.

Sears' National Advertising Agency was Ogilvy & Mather in New York, regarded then as one of the top creative ad agencies in the country. Ogilvy & Mather was doing some remarkable national ads that personalized Sears. The campaign started with a beautiful ad showing a 14-year-old girl in her slip looking a little apprehensive because her mother was taking her to Sears for her first bra.

Now Ogilvy was planning a Coldspot refrigerator ad to run nationally in *Life Magazine*. It was easy to do an endearing ad about a little girl and her first bra. How, they wondered, do you do something soft and warm and fuzzy with a refrigerator? My slide film, *Red Roses* had done it. The Ogilvy account executive visited our department. My sales manager showed him *Red Roses*. The account executive told my boss that he wanted the Ogilvy creative team in New York to see the film, and they'd pay to fly me and my slide film there.

Could it be? Me and my slide film flying to the Big Apple? On a jet plane? First class? To Madison Avenue? To the legendary offices of Ogilvy & Mather?

I fantasized that the Ogilvy Account Executive, having seen my gloriously creative sales film, wanted to pirate me away from Sears to work as a copywriter or producer for Ogilvy in New York. It was like when a pretty girl smiles at you in a bar, and your imagination says she's trying to get you into bed with her. But all she did was smile at you in a bar.

The Ogilvy creative team gathered in a conference room in their modern, glass Manhattan tower. There before me were what must have been the finest copywriters, art directors, and producers in the world because they were employed by the most creative ad agency on earth. And they were young people in their mid twenties, like me.

I didn't bother with an introduction. I was sure my amazing slide film would speak for itself. I called for the lights to dim and started my show. Six minutes of "a day in the life of a housewife and her refrigerator."

At the end, when the lights came up, there were a few questions from these fabled copywriters and producers. Then I was thanked and ushered out. Would my job interview and offer come next? Nope—I was taken to lunch by a low-level junior

Miscast

account executive assigned to take low-level client representatives to lunch, and then flag them a cab to LaGuardia. Maybe another time.

In 1965 Sears came out with a top-of-the-line refrigerator we called the Coldspot Supermart. My sales manager suggested another sales film. I wrote and produced one based on the Paul Harvey News and Commentary format, and hired Paul Harvey to narrate it. It took me three weeks to film. By the time I was finished I'd hired at least a dozen professional models and actresses and had used my wife, both of my kids and my father as extras. As sales films go, this was an outstanding one. Paul Harvey is a masterful pitchman, and the film was hard-hitting and convincing as a training vehicle.

*

Sears actually had its own in-house motion picture producer—an elderly, dramatic fellow with a white South African upbringing and an elegant British accent. His name was Frank Cellier. Whenever a merchandise department decided that their sales training would benefit from a movie (which was rare), Cellier would be involved to price it out, write a script, then rent the cameras, dollies, microphones, recorders, and lights. He would hire a film crew, and if needed, a sound stage.

Cellier heard about my film, *Red Roses*, and arranged to see it privately with his staff, which consisted of one female editor who doubled as a gofer.

Coming out of the showing, Cellier congratulated me and said, "My department appreciates creativity of this quality."

That comment made me feel like Tom Sawyer, lost for days in McDougal's cave, finally seeing a tiny glimmer of sunlight. Cellier was near retirement age. Could I possibly be transferred to his staff, there to become the future producer of Sears training films? Cellier's comment was nothing short of an invitation to apply. I immediately said, "When can we discuss this further?"

Cellier invited me to his office the following day. There he reciprocated by showing me what he apparently considered his finest work—a training film called *Every Inch a Lady,* showing Sears window trimmers how to select a tasteful outfit for a female window mannequin.

At the end of the film, the mannequin comes alive in the window.

Cellier's assistant turned on the lights. Cellier turned to me and said, "Did you catch the Freudian implication?" Controlling an urge to giggle, and somehow managing to keep a serious face, I nodded "yes."

It would not be difficult to improve on this man's work. It would mean waiting a few years for him to retire, then doing whatever I could to stretch my creativity to overcome the limits of small budgets, non-union actors, 16-millimeter filming, and editing on his old Moviola machine. Eventually I'd produce a few blockbuster training films. Then I'd go to California and land a job as a Hollywood director. In retrospect, this wasn't an unrealistic dream—unbeknownst to me, in 1966 a young director of industrial films would land a job as a Hollywood feature film director. Within five years his directing credits would include *M*A*S*H* and *McCabe and Mrs. Miller.* His name was Robert Altman.

Frank Cellier spent nearly an hour with me, evaluating his directorial role in *Every Inch a Lady* as we might have examined Mike Nichols's direction of *Who's Afraid of Virginia Woolf?* Cellier probably hoped the meeting would end on that note, but I was there for a job offer, so I asked for it.

Cellier paused. He knew my question was coming, and was prepared for it. "The reason my department at Sears has lasted for as long as it has," he explained in his educated English voice, "is because I have resisted the temptation to expand it. It's just me and my editor. And I intend to keep it that way."

No job offer.

Miscast

1966 dawned with a new creative opportunity. The Coldspot Sales Manager came up with a new scheme to sell more Coldspot freezers—by selling frozen boil-in-bag entrees! These entrees were new on the market and seemed to offer an unexplored niche—a busy working wife could put together a fairly decent meal for her family in a few minutes with little more than clean plates and boiling water. The Sales Manager said, "If I have to sell food to sell more freezers, I'll do it."

I asked him if he'd like to see a training film on the subject. He nodded yes. If Cellier wouldn't hire me, I'd have to work around him.

So instead of a slide film, I wrote a movie scenario in which an Ann Margaret look-alike arrives home after a busy day as a successful trial attorney. She seduces her Woody Allen spouse with boil-in-the-bag magic every night for weeks.

My Woody Allen film never got past the scenario stage.

*

In a little over two years, I'd put together some excellent Coldspot brochures and training manuals, plus two outstanding training films. But that wasn't really my job. My job was to work directly with retail salesmen in the field. But I had difficulty talking to the field men. I'd never sold a refrigerator in my life. How could I manage sales meetings, telling salesmen and sales managers how succeed at something that I'd never done myself?

And dealing with salesmen required skills at one-on-one communications, which had always been my weak suit. I was a showman who needed an audience. I usually felt uneasy in one-on-one situations. Without a script to follow I never seemed to know what to say.

My boss finally realized this. I could put together excellent training films, but I couldn't talk authoritatively to the field men—not even on the phone. I could never manage one of his sales territories. I was unpromotable.

I received a lateral promotion to another department. In July of 1966 I became an assistant buyer of floor coverings.

In September 1966 I began my final semester at Northwestern. For nine years I'd never received a grade lower than B. I was invited to join Alpha Sigma Lambda, a scholastic honor society.

I turned 29 in October. I'd get my degree before age 30!

My last final exam took place in Wiebolt Hall on the Chicago campus of Northwestern University in mid-January 1967. My new boss wished me luck as I left work that day. A major snowstorm was starting as I headed downtown on the Eisenhower Expressway.

Kathy took the subway downtown to meet me at Wiebolt Hall after the exam, for a little victory celebration. We trudged through deep snow to the East Inn Rathskeller on Superior Street. We had the place to ourselves—the storm kept people at home.

On our way home driving north on the Outer Drive, the snow got deeper with every mile until traffic was down to one lane of deep tire ruts. At Foster Street the car ahead of me got stuck and I couldn't get around it. We sat in the car for about an hour waiting for help that never came. I attempted to mount chains on the rear wheels, but I was dressed in a business suit and had no overshoes. The wind was fierce and cold. The snow was nearly waist deep. After three attempts I gave up, too cold to continue. We abandoned the car and struggled through the wind and snow across Lincoln Park to catch the elevated train.

At the same time, a far more devastating storm was developing—one that would blow me right out of my job.

Chapter 12

Awakening from the New Trier Dream

In May 1967 I moved my family to a bungalow on 16th Street in Wilmette. Kathy was tired of life in an apartment and wanted a place with a lawn and a garden.

Wilmette was the start of a difficult time for our nine-year-old son Jamie, who began experiencing in Wilmette what my brother Ron and I had discovered in Milwaukee and Glencoe: for Wilmette boys, your social status was directly related to your proficiency at sports. And Jamie was as ineffective at sports as Ron and I had been. Having been through the same ordeal myself, I was very concerned. Jamie's self-confidence was being undermined.

Summer school offered a sports club, and we enrolled Jamie, thinking he might pick up a few pointers on how to bat and field a baseball. I certainly wasn't equipped to teach him myself. But the sports club consisted of little sports jocks, and Jamie wasn't one of them. Every day he was sentenced to go to sports club and demonstrate his shortcomings to all his peers. The ridicule built. Jamie was becoming like that goose with no feathers on his neck. I can't remember whether Kathy and I pulled him out of the club or decided it might be better for him to try to tough it out.

We were in Wilmette only five months—a bad time for Jamie.

And for me.

During all those years of anticipating my degree I'd somehow thought I'd receive the certificate immediately after I completed all my requirements in January 1967. I wanted to promptly photocopy it and present copies to my boss at Sears and to the Sears Personnel Department.

As it turned out, I would not get the sheepskin until June, when I'd graduate in a cap and gown with the rest of the Class of 1967. So I asked the university registrar to send a letter to the Sears Personnel Department indicating that I'd completed my degree requirements and would receive my degree in June. I wanted Sears to know *immediately* that the college dropout they'd hired in 1962 had now graduated with honors.

After a few days I received a memo from Personnel congratulating me, and informing me that the Northwestern letter would be placed in my personnel file.

I'm not certain what I had expected, but I'd had nearly a decade to ponder it. Somehow I'd come to attribute all of my financial struggles and career shortcomings to my having dropped out of college, which had downgraded me to a far less employable category. The American Dream for North Shore kids included a promising career upon completion of college, like those enjoyed by many of my high school classmates who were working for employers with impressive names like Merrill Lynch and Bell Labs. All those fine, lofty companies would actually *seek you out,* sending representatives to your college campus during your senior year to interview and recruit you, promising you a substantial starting salary, an office with a telephone, your name on the door, and a private secretary. In a few years you'd become a vice president and move to a fancy corner office with a view. By the time you were 30, you'd own a Mercedes Benz and a house in Winnetka, just like your dad's.

Every week, three semesters a year for nine years I'd hungrily sought that pot of gold at the end of my rainbow, as I studied my textbooks, attended those downtown night classes, and earned top grades, always thinking, *One day I'll get my degree. I'll have corrected my life's greatest mistake. One day I'll qualify for my place among my high school peers.*

And now I had my coveted degree—plus a memo saying that Sears had put a notation in my personnel file. Nothing else changed. The days after my final exams were exactly like the days before.

I can draw a parallel here.

The ten years between 1954 and 1964 were years of great promise for the future of blacks in America. In the 1954 *Brown v. Board of Education* case, the U.S. Supreme Court replaced the old "separate but equal" education laws with equal education for blacks. School bussing began. During that ten-year span, white Americans gradually seemed to become more aware of the condition of blacks in their country. Many whites became sympathetic. Several thousand whites marched in protests, or sat in with blacks at segregated lunch counters in the South, or worked in Mississippi to register blacks to vote. Equality for blacks was becoming a popular cause among an ever-increasing number of whites.

In 1964 President Lyndon Johnson pushed the Civil Rights Act through a very reluctant Congress.

That Act appeared to be the dawn of a new era in race relations. Federal law now assured blacks voting rights. It gave blacks access to public accommodations. It guaranteed them equal education opportunities. It assured them that they could live wherever they wanted. It legislated equal employment opportunities and equal access to jobs and contracts in federally assisted programs.

It appeared as if racial discrimination had *ended!* The highest legislative body in the nation had made it *illegal!* United States law said that black men and women could now eat in white restaurants, live in white neighborhoods, apply for white jobs, and send their children to white schools! Their equality was now a *federal law!*

Blacks all over America sang and danced in the streets.

Then in the months that followed, blacks saw that many schools in the South were becoming private. Restaurants were becoming clubs. In California the voters passed Proposition 14 to block the fair housing components of the Civil Rights Act.

Worst of all, blacks awoke each morning and returned to the same demeaning jobs they had always held. They hadn't become stockbrokers or vice presidents—they were still sweeping floors and scrubbing lavatories. They still lived in the same decrepit ghetto homes where they had always lived.

The law seemed to have changed nothing. And their disappointment was intense. The federal government had legislated racial inequality out of existence, but nothing had happened.

Something did happen, of course—in the Watts section of Los Angeles, starting on August 11, 1965. Disappointment turned to rage, and rage turned to flames, rioting and looting. *Burn, Baby, Burn!* More race riots soon followed in Newark, Detroit, and other cities.

I can sympathize with that rage, because in the months following my completion of requirements for a degree from Northwestern University, my disappointment fueled a similar rage in me that heated up and finally boiled over. I had worked toward my own dream of equality through nine years of night school classes, all the time reciting my mantra: *One day I'll have my degree, and my financial misery and humiliation will end.*

As winter faded and the trees began budding, I thought about all the mistakes of my life which I thought the degree

Awakening from the New Trier Dream

would correct—having started out as a laborer in a steel mill, then working as a bank clerk clearing checks, then as a stockman in a drugstore, ultimately living in a rented Wilmette bungalow, driving a compact Ford purchased on a used car lot, and earning a paltry $9,000 a year on the eve of my 30th birthday. Each class, each exam, each high grade would one day erase all those errors as I struggled toward my place, shoulder-to-shoulder with all those successful New Trier kids who had graduated with me and gone on to college.

Had I somehow believed, through all those years, that Sears would make me a vice president when I got my degree?

Years later I would finally come to accept my studies at Northwestern for exactly what they were—a marvelous expansion of my intellectual horizons.

But in the spring of 1967 I saw that, while the degree had gained nothing for my career, it had caused me to lose something very precious to me—*my excuse for failure*. The loss of that excuse was the most bitter part of the pill I was swallowing. I harbored a nagging suspicion that I had squandered nine years on an empty dream.

How could I have been so naïve, for so many years?

My disappointment began to poison my attitude toward my job and my relationships with my coworkers. *Burn, Baby, Burn!*

My boss, Sam Mallery, tried his best to deal with me, but after nine months he threw in the towel. In October I was sent to the Personnel Department to be given my walking papers. I asked if I could be transferred to Frank Cellier's motion picture department. The personnel manager informed me that when Frank Cellier retired, his department would be folded.

And I hadn't been sent to the Personnel Department to be transferred. I was being fired.

My pay would continue for four more weeks.

I signed a statement acknowledging that I would never again be eligible for employment by Sears.

Now my situation was far worse. Not only was I *not* standing shoulder-to-shoulder with my New Trier classmates, I was standing shoulder-to-shoulder with bums, derelicts, drunkards, dope addicts, thieves, and other such "unemployables." In 1967 we were still close to the generation of the Great Depression—a devastating economic struggle that taught our fathers to get a job and stick with it faithfully for an entire career, as my dad had done. And large, safe employers like Sears *never* fired anyone in the 1960s, except for stealing. People who got fired were not to be trusted or associated with.

Fired?
The word wasn't even in my lexicon. Sure, I'd been in the school principal's office a few times. I'd been kicked out of *Lagniappe*. And I'd been locked in a jail cell in Indiana. But nothing—absolutely nothing in my life compared with the humiliation I felt at being fired. I could never admit this to my parents or friends—I didn't even admit it to my wife, although she easily put two and two together.

I even tried to hide the fact from myself, in order to protect my wounded ego and to allow the hurt to ease a bit—but my depression hung on me like a shroud, following me everywhere I went, finally climbing into bed with me to destroy my sleep.

I'd heard that some men would retreat upon being fired. They'd take a vacation, bringing their depression with them to a beach or an island or a cottage. I might have done this myself, were it not for a book I heard about somewhere—maybe a review in *Time* or *Newsweek*. The book was *Executive Jobs Unlimited* by Carl Boll. It was written for executive-level people who had recently been fired. Kroch's bookstore on Wabash Avenue said the book was out of stock. But they had a copy of the book sitting in their display window! I went to the window area, found the access door for the window trimming team, opened it, and like a drowning man swimming toward a floating log, in full view of the crowds on Wabash Avenue, I climbed across all the window displays and grabbed that book.

Awakening from the New Trier Dream

The book was helpful from the author's first paragraph. Carl Boll assumed I'd just been fired, and knew exactly how desperate I felt. He told me to forget about taking a vacation, that I now had a new job, a vital job, a sales job, and perhaps the most important job of my life. In a matter of a few days I had to learn how to sell *myself*. And Boll had some great ideas. I've never forgotten his lessons.

"The job seeker," Boll wrote, "is expected to mail out resumes by the thousands. The employer expects to receive resumes by the thousands. But people who do the *expected* don't get noticed. So you must now do the *unexpected*.

"You're going to write a letter. Your resume won't be attached. If the prospective employer sees a resume enclosed, he'll lapse into the expected and read it—and ignore your letter.

"But if you can capture his attention in the first paragraph—in four sentences or less—he'll read your letter.

"And if he likes your letter, he'll agree to see you when you call him a day or two later.

"You may never have to show your resume. A resume is fixed like writing in stone. Once it's written you can't change it in a meeting. But if you can walk in and *control* the meeting, you can discover what the interviewer seeks—and then tailor your experience to fit his needs so well, it'll look like you've spent your whole career getting ready for the job he has to offer.

"How can you control the meeting? By asking the interviewer what kind of experience he seeks for this job. Get him talking about something he's familiar with—the job—rather than something he's NOT familiar with—namely, YOU.

"But first, he's got to read your letter.

"So let's start thinking about that brief opening paragraph."

Boll's strategy was to have a showstopper for an opening sentence. The more unusual, the more outrageous the opening sentence, the more likely it would be to jar the reader into awareness of you, so he'll read on. One accountant that Boll had counseled had audited books primarily for public institutions—

including a federal prison. His opening sentence was impossible to ignore: "I've been in Sing Sing Prison seven times…"

Since beginning this narrative I've searched my files, my memorabilia, my bookshelf. I can't find my copy of Boll's *Executive Jobs Unlimited*, I've lent it out so often. Copies of my broadcast letters are tucked inside the book's front cover, wherever it may be. And the opening paragraphs of those letters, which I can't remember, must have been dynamite, because my broadcast letter landed me more job interviews than I could handle. I soon had two job offers as product manager, plus three ad agency jobs to choose from.

But I'm getting ahead of myself. This road to victory was paved with a few major disappointments. So—back to the start of my job search:

First, there was an ad I saw in the business section of the Sunday newspaper: *How to Be Fired Successfully*. That phrase would stop anybody in my position. I phoned.

"Are you married?"

"Yes."

"You have to bring your wife."

"My wife works. She can't come." I smelled a rat. Somewhere I'd heard that high-pressure sales situations often involved trying to open a wedge between a reluctant prospect and his wife, then using a two-against-one approach to wear the prospect down.

"Can she take time off?"

"Out of the question." They agreed to see me, without my wife, the following week.

I walked into their reception room in downtown Chicago five minutes before my appointment time. The receptionist told me to have a seat, then gave me a loose-leaf binder. It took me fifteen minutes to get through it—a heavy-duty sales pitch, emphasizing the probable depth of my despair and this company's remarkable track record in placing people. As I closed the binder, right on cue, the receptionist picked up her phone and said "Mr. Inglehart is ready."

She escorted me into the office of a gentleman behind a desk who pretended to be very busy with papers in front of him, but took time to stand up, smile a manufactured smile, introduce himself and extend his hand. More rat smell. I'd had enough experience with theater to recognize a phony show of pretending to be busy.

I said, "Do you have job interviews to send me to?"

"We haven't decided whether we want you for a client yet."

Powerful rat smell. After exposing me to that binder in the reception room with its emotional appeal and high-pressure sales pitch, they wanted me to think that *they* would choose whether or not to serve *me*, rather than the other way around. They hoped I'd beg them, and pay any fee they asked. Fortunately for me and sadly for Mr. *How to Be Fired Successfully,* a week had passed since my first call to them. In that week I'd already had good feedback from my broadcast letter. I was no longer sufficiently desperate for their strategy to succeed.

I stood up. "If you decide you want me for a client, you have my phone number. Call me with interview appointments." And I left. Once again I'd discovered that there were always parasites waiting to exploit anyone who felt he was at the end of his rope. I never discovered what their program consisted of, or how much it would have cost me. But I'd learned how to identify the smell of rats.

The first of three fields I considered was the industrial film field. I hoped to use my Coldspot film script to land a job as a writer of industrial films, which would eventually catapult me to a job as a Hollywood screenwriter where I would someday redeem myself on nationwide television as the recipient of an Academy Award.

Every letter I sent out to film studios landed me an interview. That was because the industrial film industry in Chicago was just as desperate as I was.

Academy Films on Oak Street was my first interview. I soon ascertained that Academy Films consisted of one man who had invested in a 16 millimeter Ariflex camera and managed to pay for a small office on a month-to-month basis. He was not only the marketing director for his "studio" (he beat the bushes by calling at any building with a smokestack) but he was also the writer, casting director, film director, cinematographer, and editor. I asked him if he edited on a Moviola or the newer, more sophisticated Kem machines. He said he edited on a table with a pair of rewinds. He took me into his projection room and showed me a film he'd recently produced for Mogen David Wines in Chicago. I could see that his creative level was in a league with Frank Cellier of Sears. He finally admitted that he couldn't afford to hire me, but if I could go out and find a client and sell him on a film, he'd be happy to work with me.

There were three larger studios I interviewed at before abandoning the field of industrial motion pictures, which seemed to be a pathway to oblivion, not to an Academy Award. One studio was Wilding Films, working out of an old studio building on Argyle Street in Chicago. The second studio had a major production facility on West Washington Street where Oprah Winfrey today produces her TV show. The third was a studio in Detroit that had a sales office in Chicago.

None of these four film studios exist today.

The second field I pursued was product management. A product manager works for a manufacturer and assumes responsibility for a given product. He works with suppliers, customers, and advertising agencies. Here my Sears background made more sense. In a matter of a couple of weeks I had completed four successful interviews at Wilson Meats in the Prudential Building. They made me a nice job offer as a product manager for Wilson Bacon. About the same time I was also offered a product manager position with Trailmobile, the truck trailer people. I turned both offers down because by then I could see that I was close to landing a job as an advertising copywriter, which I felt was better suited to my creative capabilities, and would put me back on the track from which I'd self-derailed four years earlier.

I was getting lots of interviews at advertising agencies, mostly in downtown Chicago. Between interviews I'd be in downtown building lobbies pumping coins into pay phones to line up other interviews. At one point I was familiar with every bank of pay phones in every office building from the Prudential to the Playboy. Some were far better suited to my needs because there were three or four phones in a row, allowing me to wait on hold on one phone while placing a call on another. The best phone banks had a wide shelf running beneath all the phones for me to lay out and shuffle my notes and letters.

My "pay phone strategy" was to tell the prospective employer that I was calling from the lobby of his building. It was the only way to get in to see some of the busiest agency creative directors, who could rarely find time in their crowded schedules to set aside a block of minutes to interview a job applicant. But I might just luck out and catch one of these executives between meetings or projects or thoughts, in a natural but unplanned break in his day. "You're downstairs now?" "Yes." "Well, come on up, I'll see you for a couple of minutes." It happened a lot.

I got in to see a lot of the big shops with major national package goods accounts: Kenyon & Eckert. Burnett. Foote, Cone & Belding. Needham Louis & Brorby. In these interviews I discovered that the best thing I had going for me was my hard-hitting broadcast letter. Without it I would never have seen what it looked like inside these big, high, glitzy offices with impressive views of the city and the lake. There I would set up my slide show projectors and launch into *Red Roses*. If I was lucky I'd get my interviewer to sit through part of the Paul Harvey film. More often than not, the creative director, or whoever was interviewing me, would hold up his hand three minutes into *Red Roses,* signaling me to stop the show.

"Have you done any TV?"

"This is as close as I've come to TV. I was hoping..."

"Look, Jerry, we don't do slide films here. We do TV commercials. How much are you earning now?"

"Eleven thousand." (I included my annual Sears Profit Sharing contribution.)

"We start entry-level copywriters here at about eight thousand. How old are you?"

"Umm...twenty nine." I'd just turned thirty.

"Beginning copywriters generally start at about age 22."

End of interview.

The next category of ad agency was smaller shops that had established themselves as "creative hot shops" like Rink Wells, Rosenthal, and Hurvis, Binzer & Churchill. They were a phenomenon of the sixties, years when the economy was expanding rapidly. Many businesses were enjoying profitable years. As a result, the stuffy advertising of the fifties came to be considered old hat. To overcome consumer lethargy in an economy where everyone had plenty to spend, many companies gravitated to outrageous headlines and show-stopping commercials. The revolution had been started with the success of Volkswagen advertising that was as un-Detroit as could be. William Bernbach was the Godfather of creativity at Doyle Dane Bernbach in New York. His ads called the Volkswagen everything from a pregnant roller skate to a beetle. "It's ugly but it gets you there." Referring to New York City, Bernbach boasted, "We sold a Nazi car in a Jewish town!"

Red Roses didn't fly in the creative shops either.

The last category of ad agency wanted and needed me—the out-of-town agencies. I had two interviews lined up—one was with Biddle, an agricultural agency in the rolling Illinois Corn Belt north of Springfield. The other was with Hollingsworth, a tired old-line shop operating out of a very old office building in Rockford, Illinois.

The heart of the advertising industry was in downtown New York, downtown Chicago, and downtown Los Angeles, with major outposts in Detroit and Minneapolis to serve the automobile and food products industries. Everywhere else in the country was considered the hinterlands. This was because the lion's share of the package goods advertising budget is for broadcast media, which depends on daily access to film studios, actors, directors, sound studios and editing studios, all of which are clustered in downtown New York, Chicago, or L.A. If an ad agency isn't close to the heart of one of these advertising capitals, it can't easily produce high-quality broadcast advertising. So the out-of-town agencies serve mostly local industrial advertisers who distrust big city agencies with their fancy offices and high costs.

Another difference between the major (package goods) agencies in big cities and the out-of-town shops was the job description of the person who contacted the clients. In package goods agencies, contact was handled by account executives who talked and dressed as businessmen. The creative staff was kept out of view of the client, primarily because the copywriters and art directors who created the broadcast advertising often dressed in outrageous bellbottoms and wild floral-pattern shirts, with long hair that sometimes smelled of marijuana.

By contrast, most out-of-town agencies used the old "copy-contact" system in which the man who talks to the client is also the man who writes the ad copy. The ability to write imaginative headlines and ad copy requires certain qualities that salesmen rarely have. Consequently, most of the creative ideas and copy coming out of copy-contact account executives is pretty dull.

This posed a dilemma for the out-of-town shops in the mid-1960s because their industrial clients were seeing a lot of exciting creativity in package goods advertising, and wondering whether their own advertising might benefit from it. How can a little out-of-town shop with its straight-laced copy-contact account executives respond to this need? How can they create something they don't even understand?

In walks Jerry Inglehart with a portfolio of bright, exciting appliance brochures and training manuals, and two very imaginative slide films—just about as creative as anything they know how to recognize—but I'm wearing a pin stripe suit, and I have a decent haircut. Could this be for real? They'd never produced any brochures or manuals this imaginative, polished, or professional, and they wouldn't know where to begin if they needed a slide show. They were simply blown away.

Hollingsworth had several industrial clients. The biggest was National Lock, a manufacturer of door hardware. National Lock was demanding more creativity in its advertising.

Mr. Hollingsworth thought, *Maybe I was the answer.* But he wondered if I'd "fit in." He was about sixty years old and politically slightly to the right of John Birch. He was reluctant to make the decision on his own, so he had me talk to his three key account executives.

Then he decided to have me come back for a second meeting with Merritt Yale, the Marketing Director for National Lock. Yale sat quietly as I went through my Coldspot literature, then swung into the slide films. Paul Harvey closed with *For Sears Coldspot...Paul Harvey...Good Day!* Merritt Yale spoke his first words of the meeting: "Holly, we need this man. I urge you to hire him." He got up and left.

Hollingsworth was still reluctant. If only I could have been a good-ol' boy from Rockford or some other rural community. Finally he resorted to his conservative religious ideology and asked me, "Jerry, do you believe in God?"

Hollingsworth offered me $14,000. I told him I needed four days to consider his offer. I had two more interviews lined up.

The next day I was offered a job with Biddle in Bloomington, Illinois. I turned it down. I didn't want to write ads for feeds, fertilizer, and tractors.

Awakening from the New Trier Dream

The following day I had a late interview at a small Chicago consumer agency named Burlingame Grossman. Their account list was small, but it was all package goods accounts. This was the job I wanted. Package goods advertising. In a downtown agency.

After showing the literature and slide shows to a tired, spaced-out creative director, he said, "I like your stuff. I can use you." I was quietly ecstatic.

"I have two people here that I need to get rid of." I kept quiet. He began talking generally about what he wanted to do with his department. And then he pointed out that my first order of business would be to fire two members of his staff. "Is that okay?" I nodded. "Okay…you start Monday."

I packed up my stuff and walked across the street to a bar where I ordered a double Manhattan. My head was in deep turmoil. My first order of business would be to fire two people I'd never met. He was hiring me to do his dirty work.

It took another double Manhattan for me to see that once I'd done what he didn't want to do himself, my usefulness to him would probably end, and I'd be back on the street. I wouldn't even have time to write and produce a TV commercial. I wanted this job, but not under these circumstances. I walked to the door of the bar. The bartender called me back. In my daze I'd forgotten to pay.

No team wants to punt. But when it's fourth down with six yards to go, you just do it. For me, Rockford was a punt.

Next day I called Mr. Hollingsworth and accepted his offer.

Chapter 13

Will it Play in Rockford?

The following Sunday night I checked into a room at the Rockford YMCA. On Monday I started working at Hollingsworth. After a week I signed a lease on a three-bedroom house. On a sub-zero day in mid-December, 1967, I moved my family to Rockford.

Rockford was about 100,000 people in 1967. I'd never lived in a small town. I immediately noticed that a town this size lacked the urban anonymity that I was accustomed to. In Chicago, people disappear into the crowd. But in Rockford, at any time, on any street, a coworker or a neighbor might recognize you. The moment I left my house in the morning, I was conscious that I was constantly among people who might know me. This is why crime in a small town is minimal. Your wife is safer from rapists. Your kids are safer from pedophiles. Your car is safe on the street. You can leave your house unlocked. Burglars, thieves, and perverts realize they will be identified as strangers in any neighborhood. People will note their appearance and license plate number. It's sort of like "Mr. Rogers Neighborhood."

But, despite all its faults, I happen to enjoy urban anonymity. A big city gives you *privacy*.

Will it Play in Rockford?

People in small towns seem to feel that neighborliness is not only nice, it's vital. Small town people tend to stick their noses into your business to be sure you're okay, that you conform. You must be white, Christian, Republican, and heterosexual. If you're not, you're cause for suspicion. This public enforcement of values reminded me of *Middletown*, the revealing study of Muncie, Indiana by sociologist Robert Lynd. *Middletown* made my skin crawl. I'd studied it briefly at Northwestern, never expecting that one day I'd be living it.

Rockford employers seemed to feel entitled to examine the personal affairs of their employees. Mr. Hollingsworth's asking me if I believed in God should have been the tip-off. But the following corporate invasion of privacy made me cringe:

A large Rockford corporation had some local bank presidents serving on its board of directors. Their banks controlled a big share of the personal banking business in town. I was told that these bank presidents would periodically download the personal banking records of all of the employees of that corporation, and turn them over to the company's Personnel Department. Employees who, in the opinion of management, were not setting aside enough of their income in savings would be called in for a review of their personal finances, and would be advised to spend less and save more. It was a highly illegal practice of course. Big people in small towns can bend the rules, I guess. Your only recourse was to move your accounts to an out-of-town bank—which would raise a few eyebrows.

The very first week at Hollingsworth I had visits *at my office* from pastors of the local churches, inquiring if my family had joined a Christian church in Rockford, and if not, when we would. Then they'd proceed to sell me on their own parishes. I couldn't tell them that I didn't believe in any god or gods, Christian, pagan or otherwise. (I'd lied to Mr. Hollingsworth in my interview.)

My employer and my neighbors would *require* my family to join a church. So we did. And because I had some experience with music I was soon cornered into joining the church choir as well. After the third week I missed a choir rehearsal, and was informed next day that while I was absent, the choir had elected me their president. So now I not only had to attend church, I had to sing in the choir, and I had to learn *Roberts Rules of Order* so I could preside over choir meetings.

Soon my coworkers informed me that I would eventually be required to join a "service club" like Elks or Moose or Shriners—clubs that thrive in little towns.

On another occasion I was asked to join a religious discussion group. An old fellow named Ezra Swenson, who was a friend of our church pastor, initiated the group and involved me and three others. The topic of discussion we were to pursue was how to get more young people to become active in church programs.

I asked, "What does the church offer young people?"

"Why, lots of things. Youth Fellowship for one." Old Ezra clearly thought that Christianity was an end in itself.

"But what are young people looking for these days?" At 30 I was the youngest person in the meeting—by about half.

"Well, you should know. You're a young person. That's why you're here."

"Look at the TV news. Look at *Time* magazine. This is turning out to be a revolutionary decade. Young people today are a lot different than they were when I was growing up in the fifties. They want to participate in the big changes they see around them. They want social equality. They want an end to the war in Vietnam. They want to go down to Mississippi and help register blacks to vote."

Ezra looked at me suspiciously. "Not Rockford's young people," he retorted indignantly.

If I made an enemy of old Ezra, at least I got myself out of that discussion group. If there were any subsequent meetings, I was not invited. They sure didn't want a bunch of liberals and peace mongers marching around in Rockford, trying to integrate their country club.

Will it Play in Rockford?

Perhaps old Ezra typified Rockford, where conformity is critical and individuality is suspect, reminding me of when Mr. Hollingsworth introduced a health plan at his agency. The health plan required that all participants purchase a whole life insurance policy. I told him that I preferred term life insurance. He said, "Term life builds no cash value. You're just poking money down a rat hole. With whole life you build cash value."

I went back to my office and made a chart. The first column listed the monthly whole life insurance premiums for a $10,000 policy. My next two columns totaled the cumulative premiums paid in, and the policy's cash value accumulated through time. Beside these columns I entered a column showing the accumulated annual premiums for a term life policy of $10,000, which of course was a lot cheaper. In a last column I showed the difference between the two premiums, which I placed in a theoretical passbook savings account earning 5% interest. The chart showed that, for any given year, the term-plus-premium-savings built an annual balance in the passbook account that was always greater than the cash value of the whole life policy.

I took the chart into Mr. Hollingsworth. "What's this?" he asked.

"It shows why I prefer term life insurance over whole life. Term insurance gives me the $10,000 protection, and the savings in premiums in the passbook amount to more cash value than the whole life policy offers."

He squinted at the figures, then looked up. "But term life doesn't build cash value," he said.

"No, it doesn't, but the passbook savings do. You get more cash value."

He looked down at the figures again, then looked up at me angrily. "You're a damned fool, Jerry. With term life you get *no* cash value. You're simply poking money down a rat hole!"

"But..." I started.

He thrust the chart back at me. "Don't tell me. *I know! Whole life is better!"*

Suddenly I realized that I was offending a man who had been buying whole life policies for at least forty years. I took the chart back to my office, quickly filled out the whole life application and returned it to Mr. Hollingsworth.

In Rockford there were certain things you simply did not question, including Christianity, the Republican Party, and whole life insurance.

The Hollingsworth account executives involved me in every one of the agency's new business presentations, in which I showed *Red Roses* and the Paul Harvey film to prospective clients as a means of demonstrating the high level of creativity at Hollingsworth and Associates.

I wondered whether it would be possible for me to produce ads for National Lock that were so imaginative, they'd get me a job at a consumer ad agency. Within five months I'd made some major breakthroughs with the National Lock ads in trade magazines like *Hardware Age, Chain Store Age,* and *Progressive Grocer.* These magazines all conducted research on their ads, measuring how many readers had noted various ads, read the ads, understood the ads. To encourage the advertisers, they'd present award plaques for the winners. My National Lock ads were winning them all. The flood of plaques was becoming a joke at Hollingsworth.

That summer an ultra-conservative industrialist from Peoria named John Altorfer threw his hat into the primary race for Governor of Illinois, running against Richard Ogilvie. His politics were just far enough to the right to appeal to Hollingsworth, who committed a week of my time to support Altorfer through local advertising coordination and publicity support. Altorfer had an upcoming media trip to Rockford.

Altorfer's advance man was a pudgy, high-voiced, fast-talking guy that seemed like some sort of a con man and reminded me a little of James Cagney in *Mister Roberts.* My evaluation proved right. In a meeting with two of the three

Will it Play in Rockford?

anchormen on Rockford TV news stations, the advance man said he wanted to buy us all a drink. He took us to a downtown bar called Jacks or Better. After the first round of drinks the advance man said to me, "Jerry, how about another round?" I had a hunch that the bastard intended to stick me with the tab for all the drinks, which of course he did.

At one point I was driving in a convoy with the Altorfer campaign group from the Rockford airport to a TV station. I was driving a Hollingsworth company car—a big black Mercury sedan. I had a black Borsalino hat over my short-sided haircut, plus sunglasses and a black cashmere overcoat. I saw myself on TV that night, climbing out of my black sedan and falling in step behind Altorfer like a secret service man. My God, was that me? Five years later, during the Watergate scandal, *Newsweek Magazine* ran a cover photo of Haldeman and Erlichman, looking quite guilty, evasive, and conspiratorial in their sunglasses, black Borsalinos and black overcoats, almost like a scene out of *The Godfather*. I thought, *They look just like I did in that Rockford TV footage!*

Every week I'd work at packing my "parachute"—my portfolio of ads to get me out of Rockford.

I wrote a broadcast letter to send to New York advertising agencies, and arranged a one-week vacation in New York for late August 1968. I didn't want the New York ad agencies to know that I lived and worked in a little town called Rockford, somewhere out there beyond the Hudson River. My brother-in-law Dave Sommer lived in Manhattan, and Dave agreed to let me use his address for my mailing campaign. I packaged up my broadcast letters and sent them to Dave, to be mailed in Manhattan so they'd have a New York City postmark.

A few days after Dave mailed my letters to the New York ad agencies, I started calling him every night to find out if I was getting responses. Apparently I had written another powerful letter because lots of New York shops wanted me to call to set up appointments. Each workday at noon I'd rush home to spend the lunch hour making follow-up phone calls to New York to set up appointments and to try to get through to those shops that had not responded.

I arrived at LaGuardia on Saturday, August 24th to begin a full week of interviews.

One of my most valuable interviews just happened, by luck, to be my first—Monday morning August 26, 1968. I was interviewed by a copy supervisor who was probably five years my junior.

I handed him my binder. He opened it to the first page, which was an ad for one of Hollingsworth's smaller accounts—a manufacturer of foundry equipment. I'd had it photographed in a Rockford foundry, a hot, sweaty, violent place that reminded me of the Pittsburgh steel mill, except that instead of pouring giant ingots they were pouring castings in sand. The ad photo showed a sweaty foundry worker in a t-shirt, setting up my client's product—a "foundry flask" which holds the casting pattern as the worker packs and hammers the fine moist sand around the pattern. The photo angle was very dramatic. Somehow I'd gotten a Rockford photographer to capture the action, the sweat, even the heat and noise of the foundry in that photo, and I was proud of it.

The kid looked up from the proof and said, "What's this?"

I explained.

"But we're a package goods agency."

"I know."

"So why are you showing me this ad?"

This kid really wanted to help me. I'm not sure why. He went through every ad in my binder. Then he said "Look, you've got to get rid of the binder. You never want to show everything you've got. You want to be able to tailor your presentation to the accounts they have at the shop where you're interviewing.

"Next, select your *third best* ad sample, and have it loose in some sort of portfolio where you can pull it out first. Place the

Will it Play in Rockford?

sample in front of your interviewer and wait. Don't say a word. Don't explain. Consumer advertising has to be self-explanatory. If it doesn't have immediate impact, it's no good.

"When the interviewer looks up at you, if he asks a question, you answer it. If he doesn't, you reach into your portfolio and pull out another sample.

"After about eight or ten samples, pull out your *second best* sample and put it in front of him. And *stop*. No more samples. At this point he's either interested or he isn't. If he isn't, he'll thank you and you can leave—no job offer there. If he's interested, he'll look down at your portfolio and say, 'What else have you got in there?'

"Then you pull out your *best sample,* your tie breaker, your award winner. Now you've got him thinking, *if this is an ad he wasn't even going to bother to show me, everything in that portfolio must be incredible.* But now you turn off the supply. You talk about what sort of writer they're looking for. You talk about the clients they have. You *do not* pull out another ad. You leave your best ad sitting on top of the stack in front of him as you discuss a possible offer. If necessary, you reach for the stack and put it back in your portfolio, like you've got another appointment."

(Did this young man ever read Carl Boll's *Executive Jobs Unlimited,* I wondered.)

"And Jerry..." he said, holding up my broadcast letter. "You signed this thing 'G.G.Inglehart.' That's a banker's signature. You're a writer. Sign your name 'Jerry Inglehart.'"

It all made such marvelous sense. In an art supply store I bought a zipper portfolio with carrying handles. I pulled my binder apart and slipped the proof sheets into the portfolio.

At the end of my week in Manhattan I'd interviewed at over a dozen shops, including some of the creative "hots" like Wells, Rich, Greene and Smith Greenland where advertising history was being created. I also recall a couple of interviews at large shops doing more pedestrian work for major clients. I remember one creative director explaining to me the strategy behind their campaign line, "*Dirt can't hide from intensified Tide.*"

The New York trip got me no job offers—but it provided me with a hell of a fine education on how to prepare myself for consumer advertising, and how to interview at package goods ad agencies when I was ready.

I got another significant piece of advice from a sympathetic creative director at Tatham, Laird & Kudner. He said, "Look, the question you have to answer, for yourself and for this business is, can you write consumer advertising? Here's what you should do: dream up snappy headlines for any products you like. Jot them down. Keep them in a folder. Show me a folder full of scraps of paper and pieces of napkins with really promising headlines. I'll read them."

So I didn't really need ad samples. I simply needed good ideas.

I started a notebook for jotting down ideas. I called it The File.

I thought of ChapStick, a product I'd used all my life. On the plane back from New York I jotted down: ChapStick: *Crack a smile without cracking a lip.*

Into The File.

Shortly afterward, Coca Cola launched their famous television campaign showing a bunch of young people of all nationalities holding Cokes on a hilltop in Italy, and singing:

> *I'd like to teach the world to sing
> in perfect harmony.
> I'd like to buy the world a Coke,
> and keep it company.*

This was back when bank credit cards were just emerging and threatening the granddaddy of credit cards, American

Express. But the American Express card was still the only one you could use worldwide.

I jotted down: Billboard visual—a huge picture of an American Express credit card.

Headline: *Like to buy the world a Coke?*

Into The File.

Back in Rockford I returned to the grind of turning out great industrial ads. And I continued to pack my parachute. The File grew larger with each bright addition. Occasionally I'd get out of bed at night and add to it. Just as often, I'd pull a scrap of paper out and toss it. It was important to have a lot of good ideas in The File, but it was equally important to have no weak or poor ideas, suggesting that I might not understand the difference between the two.

By January The File included television campaigns for Harley Davidson motorcycles and Miller beer, and a provocative print ad for Northwestern University Evening Divisions. I'd even expanded my ChapStick "Crack a Smile" idea into a clever TV campaign featuring Pat Paulson, that eternally straight-faced, non-smiling comedian.

I took my notes and scraps of paper from The File to Roland Wade, a friend and former neighbor in Evanston. Roland was an art director for Washington National Insurance Company. I paid him to design professional layouts and storyboards for all my ideas. The File became my new portfolio.

I was pretty comfortable in my role as account executive for National Lock. I could come and go as I pleased. At the same time I was sending broadcast letters to consumer ad agencies in Chicago and making follow-up calls, either from home or from phone booths in downtown Rockford.

I'd line up appointments in Chicago for the end of the day—4:30 or 5 P.M. At 3 P.M. I'd tell the Hollingworth receptionist that I was headed for National Lock. I'd hit Interstate 90 east of town with The File in the back seat. I could get to downtown Chicago in about ninety minutes. The speed limit at the time was 70, but since I knew all the speed traps I could generally average 85 or 90 until I got into the metro area. I'd fly down the Ohio Street spur to Michigan Avenue—I knew the location of every parking garage near the Avenue.

This went on throughout the rest of the winter. Some interviews were promising, others were a waste of time. One was actually fraudulent—at Post-Keyes-Gardner the creative director looked at my stuff and said, "Can you be here Friday at 2 P.M.? We may need you for the Monroe Shock Absorbers account."

I'd be anywhere he wanted me to be at 2 P.M. on Friday. I'd call in sick. Funny...I didn't think Post-Keyes-Gardner had Monroe Shocks.

I showed up in his office on Friday. His receptionist directed me to a conference room. This was it! I was going to be interviewed by the top agency brass! They were serious about hiring me!

I sat down in the conference room. There were about twelve people. The creative director nodded to me from three chairs down.

An account executive started a presentation. I was confused. Then I realized that four of the people at the conference table were from the Monroe Auto Supplies Company. This meeting wasn't about me—it was a new business presentation! They didn't even *have* the Monroe account!

They got to the creative presentation. The creative director stood up and introduced the creative team he had selected for the Monroe Auto Supplies account—introducing an art director sitting beside me, and me, Jerry Inglehart, the writer. Then he introduced and ran their TV sample reel.

So I'd been called all the way in from Rockford, Illinois, simply as a warm body to fill a chair in a new business presentation, making it look like this shop was already staffed for an account it didn't even have. My fee? The prospect of a job. *Maybe.* No promises.

Will it Play in Rockford?

Post-Keyes-Gardner didn't get the account. So I didn't get a job offer.

In late April I interviewed with a small shop called Lillienfeld, in the LaSalle-Wacker Building. Lillienfeld's biggest account was ReaLemon Lemon Juice. They also had F&F Cough Drops, Jays Potato Chips, Strongheart Dog Food, Sparkle Glass Cleaner, WBBM Newsradio 78, Montgomery Wards Chicago Group, and National Food Stores—all consumer accounts, most requiring broadcast advertising.

They had only two writers, one of which they'd just lost to Leo Burnett.

I stuck to The File.

I got the job.

Years later it occurred to me that if I'd started The File in 1958, it might have cut a very unproductive and painful decade out of my life—ten years that I'd spent chasing puffs of smoke in a long, pointless, and frustrating chase that took me to Pittsburgh, through the hallowed halls of Northwestern University, to Walgreens, to Sears, and finally to Rockford, Illinois.

Back in Rockford I packed up my family and headed east on Interstate 90, never once looking in the rearview mirror. The future was starting to look really interesting.

Chapter 14

Setting it to Music

Kathy and I found a nice, affordable little brick house with four small upstairs bedrooms on Greenleaf Street in Evanston. I had fifteen hundred dollars from my Sears Pension Plan. Brother Bill and a friend, Remi Clignet each lent me $2,500 for sixty months, allowing me to come up with the necessary 20% down payment. In May 1969 we moved in.

I now faced a pair of financial threats. I was employed in consumer advertising, a business with a notorious reputation for losing clients almost as fast as it gained them. Package goods ad agencies could lose a significant share of their billings in a single meeting. The staffers supporting that business would have pink slips by the end of the day.

And as a homeowner I had a real estate investment that could be taken from me through a foreclosure.

I phoned the Illinois Department of Employment Security to find out what my weekly unemployment benefits would be if I was fired, and how long the payments would last. Then I sat down and charted my minimal expenses—mortgage, utilities, food, insurance, medical. I figured I could hold off my charge card creditors for a while—they could destroy my credit rating but they couldn't take away our house. I calculated exactly how many weeks I could survive financially on unemployment. If we held onto our paid-for car and avoided any extravagances, I calculated I could be on the street for maybe eleven or twelve weeks without risking a foreclosure.

*

Almost immediately I wrote my first television commercial at Lillienfeld—and one that ran nationally at that. The agency had bought a schedule for ReaLemon on *The Joey Bishop Show,* a national nightly talk show in competition with Johnny Carson's *Tonight Show.* I wrote a sixty-second monologue that Lillienfeld produced starring a rather young Chicago actor named Byrne Piven. This was before Piven founded the Piven Theater Workshop in Evanston, where the Cusak family received its first theatrical training, including older sister Joan and subsequently her famous brother John Cusak—who later cast Piven's son Jeremy in many of his films, starting with *Say Anything* in 1989, then moving on to *The Grifters, Serendipity,* and a major supporting role in *Runaway Jury.* Although I used Jeremy's father in dozens of commercials (he became a regular member of the Inglehart Acting Troop of actors and actress I hired regularly in coming years,) I never hired Jeremy, or for that matter, either of the Cusaks.

I was a scant thirty days into my career as a consumer products copywriter when my Piven commercial for ReaLemon ran on national TV. I could go home and watch one of my own commercials on network TV, just like those elite writers on Madison Avenue in New York.

Sadly, the commercial was taped rather than filmed, to save money. You couldn't interview at another ad agency with a 2-inch network videotape. So I was still without the necessary 16 millimeter film "sample reel."

Lillienfeld produced one filmed commercial each year for ReaLemon and another for F&F Cough Drops. The agency had done some outstanding commercials for both clients, and although the shop had never won a trade award, the previous year's ReaLemon commercial had been selected by *Advertising Age Magazine* as one of the year's 100 best TV commercials.

Lillienfeld needed a storyboard for a new commercial for F&F Cough Drops. I'd come up with an idea that I discussed with Mel Grant, my copy chief. It involved a guy going to his car in a parking lot late on a chilly winter night. He is coughing from a persistent winter cold. A hold-up man comes up behind him, pretending to have a gun in his pocket. "Stick 'em up!" the hold-up man demands. But his victim can't stop coughing. "Hey, man, control yourself." "I can't help it—my throat." "Try one of these." The hold-up man nervously takes out a box of F&F Cough Drops and hands it to his victim, who removes a lozenge and puts it on his tongue as the announcer says, "To soothe an irritated throat, reach for handy F&F Throat Lozenges." The hold-up man says, "Makes your throat feel better, hey?" "Much...thanks...HELP! HELP!" The hold-up man beats a hasty retreat as we hear a police whistle. Cut to product box in the man's hand.

Grant loved the idea.

The account executive for F&F called a meeting in Ann Coyle's office. Ann was the Lillienfeld creative director. "The client wants to see a storyboard for a new TV commercial by Friday," he said.

"We can't make a storyboard this week," said Ann. "Our art director is on vacation."

"Wait," said Grant. "We have a commercial. We don't need a storyboard. Here, we'll act it for you. Jerry, go ahead. I'll be the hold-up guy."

I started coughing. Grant came up behind me. "Stick 'em up!" When we'd run through our 30-second act, the account executive asked if we couldn't make Polaroid photos of what we'd just acted out and paste the pictures into a storyboard for the client.

Setting it to Music

By Friday we had our storyboard of Polaroid snapshots, filmed in the parking lot behind our office. The client approved it.

Ed Auxer, the agency producer, got bids from several studios. The winner was GTR, a small, relatively new Chicago studio run by a young man named Gerald T. Rogers. Together, Rogers and Auxer cast the commercial and set up a late September shoot date for after sunset in a parking lot behind CBS's Chicago studios on McClurg Court. It was my first location shoot. Jerry Rogers had bid an incredibly low $5,000 to cast, shoot, and edit my commercial because he wanted it on his own sample reel. But even at that low price, the only compromise he made was to shoot in 16 millimeter rather than 35. He hired a bus for the cast, crew, and client to sit in and keep warm against a rather chilly evening. Chicago is a union town, so he had a union cameraman who, of course, had an assistant cameraman. There was a soundman with a Nagra recorder. And a couple of grips and gaffers. I was thrilled to be at my first shoot.

I finally had a commercial reel with one 30-second TV commercial—and a very good one at that, one I was proud to include on all my sample reels for the balance of my advertising career.

Next I dreamed up a new commercial for ReaLemon, in which a lady was preparing a fancy, romantic, candlelit dinner for a devoted husband (or possibly a boyfriend, or maybe even a lover while the husband is out-of-town on business—I left that up to the audience to decide). This lovely lady was, of course, using ReaLemon for the fish course, the salad, and the iced tea.

One of my underlying talents was music. I wrote a musical soundtrack employing a flowing, romantic folk melody in the style of Joni Mitchell, who was very hot in 1969. At the time I was taking a class in advanced guitar at the legendary Old Town School of Folk Music on Armitage Avenue. I knew just about everyone there, including the professionals, as well as the professionally hopeful—including a young blonde vocalist with a sweet Joni Mitchell voice. I hired her privately for a minimal demo fee to come up to the Lillienfeld offices on a Saturday morning and sing a demo of my new ReaLemon song over my guitar accompaniment. I recorded us on the agency's semi-professional recording equipment. I played a series of arpeggios to give the jingle the ethereal, flowing style of Joni Mitchell to enhance the visuals of the lady preparing a romantic dinner.

On Monday I went to Sears headquarters where I had an old buddy and coworker in the Sears sound studio who had worked with me on the sound track for *Red Roses*. I had him record me doubling up the guitar track with some melodic arpeggios in a higher register. I was pretty pleased with what I'd created.

Tuesday I played my new ReaLemon demo sound track for three of the people in the Lillienfeld creative department, including Mel Grant, our copy supervisor; George Schneiderman, our art director; and the creative director, Ann Coyle. They were all delighted. They'd never had anyone on staff who understood music well enough to be able to produce a polished in-house demo music track.

I suggested that an ordinary storyboard might make the presentation to the client a little too static. To convey the feeling of this romantic commercial I proposed instead that we shoot stills with a model. There was a new type of slide projector out that could dissolve from one visual to the next, and I knew where to borrow one. Schneiderman, the art director, agreed. At the end of that week he hired Denny Witt, a photographer, who hired a beautiful, wispy-looking blond Austrian model named Laurie Nolan. Laurie slipped into a diaphanous white evening dress, and we filmed my storyboard.

The agency's broadcast producer, Ed Auxer, had been out on vacation that week. He returned the following Monday and reviewed my board and music track. I could see Auxer doing a slow burn. I had produced a demo sound track. That was HIS job. We'd produced a motion storyboard. That was HIS job too. We'd usurped his role for one of the major Lillienfeld productions of the year. I now represented a threat to our agency producer.

Auxer said that, as in-house demos go, my music track was pretty good but wouldn't do for client presentation. He'd have to have it arranged and recorded professionally. I didn't want Ed Auxer to redo my demo track. Musically, I knew exactly what I wanted. My music track had charm because it was simple, ethereal and folksy, like Joni Mitchell. I didn't want it redone and glitzed up by one of Ed Auxer's studio guitar players.

Ed asked me for a "lead sheet" (hoping I wouldn't know what a lead sheet was) that he could show to a music producer of his choice. I said I'd have his lead sheet in the morning.

I happened to know that very few studio guitar musicians could read music. They'd all learned their trade informally, in basement recreation rooms, not at the Julliard School of Music. They relied on the chord notations above the melody line on the staff, and interpreted the delivery any way they felt appropriate.

So I sat down with score paper and *wrote out every note of my arpeggios*, for both guitar tracks—two strings of flowing, rapid arpeggios—about 24 notes to the bar for each of the two guitar lines, with four key changes.

Next day Auxer looked at my score paper and knew he was in trouble. He'd asked me for a lead sheet and I'd given him finished music—music he couldn't expect a studio guitar player to be able read or perform.

And I'd just made an enemy. But I didn't care. I would be out the door soon anyhow.

*

I never knew what became of my sexy little ReaLemon commercial. By October I had a portfolio consisting of the ever-growing contents of The File, as well as my TV sample reel containing the F&F "Hold Up" commercial. My radio samples included a number of never-produced comedy scripts, including one for Sparkle Glass Cleaner based on Charles Dickens' *Great Expectations* in which Estella begins removing the draperies from Miss Haversham's windows to let sunlight into the house, only to discover that the windows are filthy with twenty years of accumulated grime, which she cleans up with Sparkle Glass Cleaner. Another was a ReaLemon in-house demo track for an animated TV commercial of the Mad Tea Party in *Alice in Wonderland*, in which the Mad Hatter serves Alice her tea with ReaLemon Lemon Juice.

My print samples were sparse, but that didn't matter much since most consumer ad agency billings were in broadcast. I had a pair of ads for WBBM Newsradio 78, one of which was for some sort of help line they sponsored. It showed a young black female in a small, shabby urban apartment. George Schneiderman had photographed it in a run-down building on North LaSalle. It had been a whorehouse for a while, and then had been broken up into tiny welfare apartments. (A dozen years later when I was divorced and looking for a condo, I came close to buying a very elegant, yuppie unit in a renovated building on LaSalle Street. In one of the bedrooms I recognized the location where George had photographed our black welfare mother for my WBBM ad.)

I'd been quietly interviewing at the larger, as well as the hotter shops in Chicago. I kept my portfolio in a downtown bank vault and would often quietly slip out of the office for an interview.

J. Walter Thompson, the country's largest shop, had interviewed me twice and appeared to be ready to make an offer. I'd also interviewed at the Chicago office of Young & Rubicam, the world's second largest ad agency. One day the creative director of Y&R called me for a lunch interview. I'd come to work that morning in jeans, so I rushed out to Marshall Fields to buy a pair of gray dress slacks and a blue blazer, both

Setting it to Music

of which fit pretty well without tailoring. I added a dress shirt and tie and was ready for my interview.

Bill Lacey, the Young & Rubicam creative director, and Dave Fullerton, the copy chief, bought me lunch at the restaurant on the top floor of the United Building at State and Wacker, where Y&R was located at the time.

They offered me $16,000. I accepted on the spot.

Bingo! I'd made it to the major league.

Chapter 15

Playing in the Majors

1969 was a very intense year in American pop culture. *Rolling Stone Magazine* was just one year old. In San Francisco several cutting-edge rock groups were redefining pop music. The Woodstock Rock Festival in August became the ultimate cultural statement of an era typified by young people high on pot, acid, and protests. The war in Vietnam provided a meaningful agenda for a rapidly growing counter-culture.

So much was going on in places like San Francisco, Oakland, Woodstock, and Grant Park in Chicago that the students of Northwestern University in Evanston began feeling left out. So early one morning they tore down a century-old wrought iron fence surrounding the campus and dumped the sections in the middle of Sheridan Road, a main arterial road that was loaded with rush hour commuters. Then the students stood back to try to figure out what statement they had just made, if any. It seemed right for the times.

I was teaching guitar at the Old Town School of Folk Music. At our after-class gatherings at the Fifth Peg Pub, anyone with guts and talent could get up and sing. Some who stood up included John Prine and Steve Goodman. I saw Odetta in there once.

Playing in the Majors

My sideburns and hair were becoming longer, and my clothing choices more outrageous. I recall buying a Tom Jones shirt at an Evanston head shop that autumn—a very eighteenth-century garment with wide flowing sleeves, lace-up front and sexy narrow tapering waist—I had to lose ten pounds immediately in order to fit into it. Outrageous? Not for 1969, when one of my coworkers once came to work dressed in a Superman outfit.

One Friday I acquired a nickel bag of marijuana from a Y&R coworker. That night Kathy and I tested out our first "high," which was a bad trip for me: I was a block from our porch when the passage of time came to a halt inside my resin-saturated brain, and I thought I'd never be able to reach home.

*

Moving from the non-creative environment of Rockford, where all advertising was intensely dull, to Y&R, where the magnificent juices of creativity flowed through the air every day, reminded me of my theatrical transition from the amateurism of Lake Shore Players to the professional excellence of the drama department at Carnegie Tech. Of course, I'd been five months at Lillienfeld, which was considerably more creative than Hollingsworth, but nowhere near as imaginative as Y&R.

I'd been hired to write for four Y&R Chicago office accounts: U.S. Navy Recruitment, Armour Meats (ham, turkey, pork sausage, and new products), Scotchgard Fabric Treatment, and International Harvester Trucks (today the company is called Navistar).

At the beginning of my third week at Young & Rubicam, three of the agency's eight copywriters were fired. I'd been hired as a part of this major reshuffling.

I started to work on a very appealing and challenging project—eight Navy recruitment commercials, all of them musical, just my bag. Each was tailored to a different branch of Navy service—nurse recruitment, Waves, general enlistment, nuclear power, Naval Reserves and such.

The first one I tackled was directed toward male college graduates, attracting them to flight officer training. My lyrics were inspired in part by a very hot rock group called The Band. Their music had been used in the film *Easy Rider*. One song in the movie soundtrack, "The Weight," impressed me. Using the same lyric format, I created a flight training commercial:

> *Poundin' streets, knock on doors,*
> *You went lookin' for a place to work.*
> *The Man with a grin sez "Come on in,*
> *Gonna start you as a clerk.*
> *Steel desk and a pencil,*
> *You get a phone in a year or two.*
> *Gotta start out small 'til you learn it all*
> *And we know what you can do."*

I wrote an announcer script to come in over an instrumental bridge: "You just spent four years getting a college degree. Now's no time to be starting at the bottom..." The announcer appealed to young men to consider Navy flight training.

Bob Carney, our agency producer, hired a Chicago composer, Dick Boyell, to write and arrange the music for all eight of my commercials. We booked a studio for a week. The sessions took place at a small, state-of-the-art sound studio on Ontario Street that had the latest 16-track recording equipment.

For "Poundin' Streets," Boyell hired two guitarist-vocalists. One was Jim Post, who went on in later years to write and perform one-man shows in Chicago including a marvelous two-act Mark Twain monologue and a delightful monologue about 19th century Illinois settlers, which he called *Galena Rose: How Whiskey Won the West*.

The other musician-singer was none other than Steve Goodman, a discovery of Boyell's. Goodman was still unknown, although he'd already written "City of New Orleans" and was performing it regularly as part of his act at The Earl of Old Town Pub on Wells Street.

Post sang lead. Goodman sang harmony on the last phrase. The duo's brilliant guitar playing was backed up by Boyell's keyboard, plus drums, and electric bass—the standard studio combo. This was in the days before synthesizers replaced most studio musicians.

It was exhilarating to watch and hear my music commercials come to life from behind the control booth window of the sound studio.

Here's a poignant side-note on the music business: a few weeks later I returned to the studio to download some copies of "Poundin' Streets." And there on the tape index was "City of New Orleans!" Apparently Boyell had kept Goodman and the musicians at the studio after my session to lay down a track of his own arrangement of "City of New Orleans"—he even brought in a string section. To save money he'd laid the track on my Navy master tape.

I'd heard Goodman perform the song quite brilliantly at Earl of Old Town Pub, accompanied only by his own guitar. Boyell's arrangement with a full studio combo and strings was thrilling! I downloaded a copy for myself—the first studio recording ever produced of that song.

Boyell had recognized a great song. In the coming weeks he sent tapes of the recording to every record company in America and England. None of them bought it. But shortly afterward, Arlo Guthrie came through town, heard Goodman sing the song at The Earl of Old Town, liked it, and recorded it himself. The rest, of course, is history. "City of New Orleans" was one of Guthrie's biggest hits. Within a year at least a dozen popular vocalists had recorded it, including Johnny Cash, John Prine, Joan Baez, Willy Nelson, and Judy Collins. A few years later it was used for a Western Electric TV commercial.

But Dick Boyell had been the first to discover that song—and he never made a penny from it. His arrangement of "City of

New Orleans" is bright, driving, and happy. I occasionally take it out and listen to it, and remember how the song slipped through Dick Boyell's fingers.

The following night we recorded my Navy Waves commercial, directed at female enlistment candidates. Dionne Warwick was a hot vocalist at the time, and I wanted something romantic and lyrical in Warwick's style, to lure girls out of humdrum office jobs into more exciting careers in the Navy with lots of young guys and world travel. My lyrics were:

> *Hey, Girl in the nine-to-five world*
> *Full of desks that you dust*
> *and calls that you place,*
> *Memos to type*
> *and mistakes to erase.*
> *Except for a ration*
> *Of two weeks' vacation*
> *Will all your tomorrows*
> *Be nine-to-five hours?*

(At this point in the song, I inserted an instrumental passage with an announcer voice-over to sell the girls on joining the Navy.)

> *Take a look at yourself*
> *and the world that you live in.*
> *There's something better for you.*
> *The Navy.*

The previous night, while working on "Poundin' Streets" with Goodman and Post, I'd made some musical suggestions to Dick Boyell. My suggestions rubbed our music producer, Bob Carney, the wrong way. Tonight as we worked on "Girl in the Nine-to-Five World" I interrupted Boyell again to suggest a change in a musical phrase. Once again, I was interfering with

Bob Carney's authority. The music was HIS job. Carney stood up and slammed his hand down on the control panel. "Your job is writing lyrics and copy. That's ALL!"

For the second time in less than a year I'd managed to offend an agency producer.

And my struggle with Bob Carney was just beginning.

I was assigned to write a series of eight five-minute radio programs to be distributed to stations nationwide, to be run as public service pieces. The programs were called *Red, White, and Navy Blue,* and featured the music of the U.S. Navy Dance Band. Sadly, the dance band sounded like something out of the forties, and didn't measure up to the standards set by Tommy Dorsey and Glenn Miller. The previous writer on the account, who'd been fired, had cranked out the preceding series of eight shows quite unimaginatively: intro theme—announcer intro—announcer introduces band piece—band piece plays—insert Navy commercial—another band piece—segue to closing theme and out at 300 seconds. Not exactly *Prairie Home Companion.* I could see why the writer had been fired.

The music of the Navy Dance Band made the U.S. Navy seem very outdated. To overcome that image I decided to create some announcer scripts to replace the second band number. I studied the two-hundred-year history of the U.S. Navy, and there were some fascinating tidbits there—the story of navy grog, the story of John Paul Jones, the first submarines under the polar ice cap, the amazing feeling of flying a helicopter and leaping over buildings in a single bound. For each program I carefully wrote out a separate monologue theme for the announcer, sometimes weaving my musical commercials into the theme by looping the music to provide a longer bridge for the announcer monologue.

Bob Carney was supposed to produce the radio programs, but he had no feel for what I was trying to accomplish. In the studio sessions he got so fed up with my interruptions and comments, he got up and walked off. Eventually he stopped showing up at the recording sessions.

Meanwhile, I was coming to be recognized as the agency's authority on music. When other writers wanted to explore jingle development for a commercial, they would often come to me for guidance.

*

As the writer for International Harvester trucks I was invited, along with the art director Mel Lain and three of the agency's account services staff, to an unveiling of the Transtar 5000, the newest International Harvester truck—a massive tractor designed to pull the heaviest long-haul semi-trailers. The unveiling took place at International's test track in Ft. Wayne, Indiana. Most of the guests were truck fleet owners.

We all attended a presentation, then stepped out to the tarmac of the test track where International had its Transtar mounted with a fully-loaded tanker trailer. Parked beside it were the three major competing trucks—a White Freightliner, a Peterbilt, and a Kenworth, all brought in for comparison to the Transtar.

The fleet owners, all experienced truck drivers, looked at the trucks, looked under the hoods at the engines, then, one-by-one, climbed into the cabs to test drive them around the track, a two mile oval—about the size of the Indianapolis Speedway.

After an hour, most of the fleet owners had driven all four trucks and had had most of their questions answered by the International product manager.

I figured, Well, if I'm going to write about the Transtar, I should probably learn as much as I can about it. I climbed the four steps up into the cab and closed the door. I was at least six feet off the ground in a cab with almost as many dials and gauges as an airplane cockpit, but the cab was four times larger than a cockpit. The largest trucks I'd ever driven before were those I'd rented to haul theatrical sets for Lake Shore Players.

The engine was idling. I pushed in the clutch, consulted the chart for the positions of the five forward gears, slipped into

Playing in the Majors

low and gunned the huge engine. The two vertical exhaust stacks roared like a pair of dragons, puffing black diesel smoke skyward. Easing the clutch out I felt the entire tractor hump upward as the tons and tons of liquid in the tanker behind me reluctantly surrendered their awesome inertia. Pulling onto the oval, checking carefully to see how far ahead I was of the other three trucks, I slipped into second gear. At twenty miles an hour I shifted carefully into third. By fifth gear I was soaring down the track's backstretch at about 65 miles an hour. I glanced down at the switch on the gear shift lever that controlled the rear axle splitter. I'd read about those splitters. I flipped the switch, then eased my foot off of the accelerator until I felt the rear axle klunk reassuringly into its cruising gear.

Despite its incredible mass, the rig handled nicely. I swung around the end of the oval and passed the tarmac. Two of the agency account executives looked up at me.

A few minutes later, on my second pass of the tarmac, I noticed that all of the agency people were staring up at me.

Toward the end of the final lap I nudged the trailer brake lever on the steering column until I felt it drag slightly. Then I began decelerating, downshifting both the axle and the transmission. I pulled slowly off the oval onto the tarmac, stopped, set the brake, left the engine running and climbed down from the cab.

I noticed that the agency account executive staff seemed a little distraught. Were they upset with me? Why, I wondered? I'd handled that rig just fine.

I found out later that on my first pass of the tarmac, one of them had looked up and said, "What the hell—is that Inglehart driving that thing?"

"Who's Inglehart?" asked the client product manager.

"He's our *copywriter*, for Christ's sake!"

"Well, he seems to know what he's doing. And that's why we brought the trucks out here."

On my second pass of the tarmac, the three account executives I saw from the cab window seemed to be looking overly concerned. Were they worried about my safety?

No—it was because if I drove that monster, they would feel pressured to do the same—something I hadn't foreseen.

After climbing down from the cab I saw the account supervisor, Doug Callahan, consulting nervously with the product manager. The manager put a hand on Doug's shoulder and led him toward the driver's side of the Transtar cab. Then he walked around the front of the truck and climbed into the passenger seat. The biggest thing Doug had ever driven was a Lincoln Town Car. Looking like a man mounting a gallows, Doug carefully began climbing the steps up to the driver's seat.

*

For Armour Star Pork Sausage I developed the *Talkin' Sausage Blues*, a piece that was never produced for Armour, although it delighted my children. It involved a "Talkin' Blues" musical format in which most of the verse is spoken over guitar accompaniment in the style of Woody Guthrie. His son Arlo used the technique in the movie *Alice's Restaurant.*

> *I was born in the country with the fields and the hay,*
> *The breakfast meal would last a boy all day.*
> *The rooster's crow would mark the start of a race,*
> *Beat my brother to the kitchen, start feedin' my face.*
> *Corn fritters...plate of grits...biscuits and gravy...*
> *Then onto the MAIN course.*

> *I'm a married man now, and live in the city,*
> *Got a sweet little wife who's lovin' and pretty*
> *But I rush off to work at the start of each day,*
> *Man, I miss the country breakfast way.*
> *Get coffee...piece of toast...run for the bus...*
> *Tummy still growlin'.*

Playing in the Majors

But on Sunday morning my wife'll choose
Armour Star Pork Sausage for my breakfast blues,
Links 'n patties in a package with a star in the middle,
Turn on the heat an' pop a few on the griddle,
Start to sizzle. Smell so good! Clear to the bedroom!
I'm shaved an' dressed an' downstairs
like a hawk swoopin' in on a stray chicken!

CHORUS, SUNG:
When somebody wants to lose
The early mornin' breakfast blues,
The tastiest links and patties are
The pure pork sausage with the Armour Star.

At the time I was teaching guitar classes at the Old Town School of Folk Music. During each of my classes, one of my students was likely to ask me what my day job was. I said I wrote jingles, then I'd swing into "Talkin' Sausage Blues" on my guitar. The class would be delighted.

When I started my own ad agency a year later, I paid to produce this jingle as a demo for my agency radio reel. I hired a square dance fiddler to saw away behind the band track, which added a nice rural touch.

Later, when I had the Partridge Meats account in Cincinnati, I rewrote "Talkin' Sausage Blues" for them. It ran in Cincinnati and Dayton.

*

Armour management was inspired by the success of Kellogg's Pop Tarts. They decided to come up with a frozen toaster snack containing meat. The resulting test product had meat fillings inside a pastry jacket. I recall three tasty varieties: hot dog and cheese, pizza and sausage, and sloppy Joe. The samples from the client's test kitchens were very plump and delicious with superb, flaky pastry and lots of meat inside. I thought it was a fine product—a mother with kids could feel a lot better about her children snacking on these meaty, nourishing morsels after school, rather than filling their bellies with the sugary jam and junk of the shelf-stable Pop Tarts.

Armour needed everything to support this new product introduction—a product name, product positioning, and TV. I suggested the name "Armour Toaster Things," and began development of a TV commercial.

I worked with art director Frank McMillan. We prepared boards for a campaign based on children's stories—Red Riding Hood bringing Armour Toaster Things to Grandma, and Snow White feeding them to her dwarfs.

I also developed a jingle for an alternate campaign idea. The previous year the Beatles had released their final album—*Abbey Road*. In that album I enjoyed the happy flippancy of "Maxwell's Silver Hammer" and decided to use the chord sequence as the basis for a jingle to introduce Armour Toaster Things. I wrote out lyrics and a fresh melody, and recorded a demo track in a sound studio, singing through a megaphone to duplicate a low-fidelity 1920s sound.

Bob Carney was once again pissed that I'd invaded his area of responsibility by writing my own music. He said my track sounded too dated. He hired a composer arrange and record a demo. The composer's track was slick and polished, and lacked the delightful spontaneity of my demo. I said so to Carney. He blew up at me in my office and stalked out, returning a few minutes later to apologize for his Irish temper.

Upstairs in marketing, it was decided that Armour Toaster Things needed to meet a price point closer to Pop Tarts, the product that had inspired the entry in the first place. I noticed that the latest product samples, pared down to fit the lower price point, were very short on meat, short on taste—in other words, terrible. They'd taken a marvelous product and virtually trashed it, trying to meet the price of a junk food product that I didn't think even fit into the same food category. Our product had *meat!* It was *frozen!* It was a healthy snack for kids! Why were they trying to position it against a shelf-stable, junk food product full of nothing but *jelly?*

I'd read the success story about Stan Freeberg's creation of the advertising for Chung King products in Minneapolis. Chung King kept compromising product quality to meet a price point. Freeberg told the client to return to the original product quality, which he felt he could sell at any price as long as it was good. He bet the company president a ride in a jinrikisha through Minneapolis—the winner of the bet would ride in the jinrikisha, the loser would pull it.

Freeberg sold Chung King at the higher price. And the photo of his client pulling him around Minneapolis in a jinrikisha made all the trade pubs.

I told the marketing people, "I think I can sell that product if you'll just forget about the damned price point and make it big and meaty and tasty, like it was in the beginning. We have something going for us that Kellogg's can never match—the name Armour. To the public, Armour means *meat!*"

I was a copywriter, not a marketing man. My comments didn't count. Armour Toaster Things soon found its place on the huge trash heap of failed food products.

*

For a Thanksgiving campaign I worked on an idea for Armour Golden Star Turkey with art director Don Zimmerman. Don was perhaps the most outrageously creative art director in the shop. It was tough to work with Don because he was so outspoken and pushy, but his ideas were good. Armour Turkey's competition was Swift's Butterball Turkey, and there was absolutely nothing about Armour Turkey that made it better, or different for that matter, from the Butterball.

I dreamed up a "First Thanksgiving" commercial in which the on-camera spokesperson is a Pilgrim, backed up by his Pilgrim wife and children, and a couple of Indians, including a weathered old chief who would nod knowingly at the Pilgrim's thoughtful, serious pitch to the camera, spoken with "thees" and "thous" like Gary Cooper as a Quaker farmer in *Friendly Persuasion*. My spokesman would sympathize with the woman. "Thy reputation as a cook and a wife goes on trial in front of thine extended family, when thy Thanksgiving turkey be placed on the table and carved. Either too dry or too raw or maybe a bit of each—lest it be an Armour self-basting Golden Star Turkey with its own thermometer that pops out when thy bird is perfect."

American Indians, especially in the environment of the year 1970, were stereotyped as a sad, poor, alcoholic minority living in abject poverty. My boss, creative director Bill Lacey, was flabbergasted that Zimmerman and I would even consider using members of this controversial group in our commercial. The project was scrapped in its entirety. We didn't produce my Armour turkey commercial.

But we did produce a commercial for Armour Golden Star Ham. The product was a canned ham—a category that had been losing market share for years. Given a choice between a *canned* ham, which was a gelatinous mass of ham chunks jammed into a pear-shape can, versus a whole *smoked* ham, either boneless or bone-in, the consumer would invariably choose the costlier smoked ham, which consequently dominated the market.

There was one unique thing about that canned ham that I decided to exploit. It was the can itself. Previously, the pear-shape can had been made of tin and was opened with a key. You emptied out the ham and tossed the can away before one of your kids cut a finger on it.

But the Armour Star ham came in a *plastic* pear-shape can with a plastic lid like a coffee can. After the can was empty it could be washed out and used as a refrigerator container. Or the kids could keep their crayons in it. I liked the idea of the value-added appeal in the package.

Playing in the Majors

I came up with the headline *"Our Can Lasts Longer"* for a print ad. Don Zimmerman prepared a layout showing four pictures beneath the headline. Frame one showed the pear-shape container being opened to reveal the tasty ham. Frame two showed the container full of leftover chicken. Frame three showed a child's hands putting crayons into the container. Frame four showed the container as an aquarium with a pool of water and a rock with a little pet turtle on it.

Bill Lacey may have been suffering from one of his many hangovers when we showed him the layout. He hated it. I was somewhat taken aback by his totally thumbs-down attitude, and began to defend the idea. He interrupted me, saying "This meeting is over."

Thinking back, maybe Lacey was right. But this was the second time in as many weeks that my work had elicited a negative response from him. Not good.

"The problem with a canned ham," explained my wife, Kathy, "is its size—five to ten pounds. You can't put one of those ugly things on a platter when you have company. For that you need a regular smoked ham that you decorate with brown sugar and cloves and pineapple chunks, and maybe make a fancy sauce out of honey or jelly. So a big canned ham is simply for economy. But the damned thing is so big, you're carving at it night after night until everyone is sick of it."

Armour had a 1.5-pound version of the product—the smallest size. I decided to position it as a single meal ham—*"The Hamlet...the Little Ham That Doesn't Last Forever."*

I worked with Art Director Steve Mull to develop a storyboard, which the client approved. My commercial was shot in New York. Neither Steve nor I were invited to attend the shoot, so our baby was born with us waiting in the fathers' room back home in Chicago. The commercial came out very well, though.

So I now had a TV sample reel that was 60-seconds long—two thirty-second commercials.

And my radio reel, with all those superb Navy commercials, was becoming awesome!

*

Ray Kroc had started the McDonald's chain in Oakbrook, Illinois, in 1954. His original agreement with franchisees required McDonald's to spend a certain percentage of sales on advertising. Kroc never dreamed how huge McDonald's sales would become. And the McDonald's ad budget was fixed by agreements dating back ten or more years.

The result was an ad budget of enormous size. As billions of hamburgers were sold, countless millions of dollars were committed to advertising.

Ray Kroc decided to change ad agencies in 1970. The finalists were Young & Rubicam, Leo Burnett, and Needham, Harper & Steers.

We at Young & Rubicam put on a good show. But Keith Reinhart's creative group at Needham won the account with the "You Deserve a Break Today" theme that was instrumental in tripling the size of the McDonald's chain in the next decade. Then Leo Burnett won the account away from Needham.

*

When advertising agencies were invented back in the late 19th century, they didn't bother to write any ethical standards, like those that existed for other professions like medicine and law. As a result, ad agencies seeking new business would openly solicit the clients of other agencies, without first being invited by the clients themselves.

We did it. All agencies did it. To some extent, working for an ad agency was like being one of those tarts I'd seen on the street in the red light district of Steubenville, Ohio, back in 1956, all gussied up in revealing clothes, leering at passing men and calling out propositions. That's the ad agency business.

Playing in the Majors

Solicitation of prospective clients didn't stop with a simple letter and a follow-up meeting. If the prospect seemed interested, the ad agency would often create a new marketing strategy, complete with creative development, sometimes even going beyond layouts and storyboards to demo commercials. All at no charge, simply in an effort to get the account signed up. The streetwalker lays down for free.

Often an advertiser with a major dollar commitment to advertising will suffer a loss of sales or market share to a clever new product, and the C.E.O. and Board of Directors will scream at the marketing vice president like a bunch of fishwives. When that happens, those whores on the street might look kind of appealing. After all, they work for free. And one of them might provide a nice, romantic respite from the tired old hag of an agency back home that can't seem to come up with an idea to regain lost market share.

It's all in pursuit of bucks. Millions of them, committed to costly network TV and national magazines.

In 1971 a new book would become the hottest piece of literature in the business world. It was *Up the Organization* by Robert Townsend, the marketing wizard who'd turned Avis Rent-a-Car around with the *We Try Harder* campaign. Townsend's book advised new marketing directors: *When you take over your new job, immediately fire the ad agency. Just on principal.* Ad agencies were always fearful of a new marketing director, who was usually called in to alter a bad situation. By firing several people, as well as the ad agency, the new marketing director could at least establish fault.

As one can imagine, there is little room for loyalty in this kind of a business environment. So if a client fired his agency in the morning, the pink slips would circulate to agency personnel the same afternoon. Disloyalty breeds disloyalty. Anyone working for a package goods ad agency had to recognize that no matter how talented he or she was, he or she could be on the street at any moment, with little or no advance warning.

I willingly entered this risky environment in 1969. Many of the writers and art directors at Young & Rubicam were single. I had a wife, two kids, and a mortgage.

In early December 1970, shortly after our failed McDonald's presentation, Dave Fullerton and Bill Lacey walked into my office and gave me two weeks' notice.

Well, I'd been there, done that. But it didn't make any difference. I took it personally. I was shocked. But I was in good company—art directors Don Zimmerman and Frank McMillan were both fired the same day.

My portfolio was ready. TV and radio reels, print ads, and those magnificent samples in The File. I was out interviewing the very next day. Mac Churchill at Hurvis, Binzer & Churchill, one of the brightest, youngest shops in town, was very impressed with my stuff. He especially responded to "Poundin' Streets." Bert Burdis also liked my work—he went on to form the famous Dick and Bert creative team with Dick Orkin. But neither Burdis nor Churchill had openings when I interviewed.

In two days I could see that I was a very hot property. After three days Todd Lief of Nader-Lief snapped me up for $18,000.

But there was a postscript to the firing of me, Don Zimmerman, and Frank McMillan that day in December 1970. Within 18 months both Dave Fullerton and Bill Lacey were fired from Young & Rubicam.

Also that year the writer who replaced me at Lillienfeld was fired, as well as the writer who replaced me at Young & Rubicam.

Revolving doors. Sooner or later I'd have to deal with that. I had too much at stake to gamble it all on those spinning doors.

Chapter 16

The Writing on the Wall

I joined Nader-Lief in mid-December 1970.
Al Nader had started this ad agency a couple of years earlier, calling it Al Nader and Associates. Al was of Syrian descent—a fast-talker, loud and argumentative. When Nader talked, his eyes seemed to be scanning quickly over your face and hands, like he was thinking you might pull a knife on him.

Nader's shop had been marketing oriented, and weak on creativity. He'd hired Bert Burdis, later of Dick and Bert fame, to try to overcome his shop's creative shortcomings, but Bert had left Nader after only a few months.

Todd Lief was an intellectual North Shore boy. He was quiet, bearded, and looked a little like Sigmund Freud. A couple of years earlier he'd started his own agency, Todd Lief and Associates. He'd won a lot of creative attention in a short time. But his agency was weak in marketing.

Nader and Lief needed each other. Their merger formed the most improbable combination of personalities imaginable. They leased about 3,000 square feet in the Playboy Building on the north end of Michigan Avenue, across from the Drake Hotel and the Oak Street Beach. Nader committed tens of thousands of dollars to leasehold improvements. He wanted his office to wow incoming clients and prospects. The reception room and front hall walls were plastered to look like flowing taffy with occasional irregular nooks and alcoves holding improbable lighted displays of weird vases. For his private office Nader took a 500-square-foot chunk of corner overlooking Lake Michigan's shoreline. From 19 stories up, anybody walking in would be transfixed by the view.

Todd Lief brought his major account, Henry Goodman Furniture, to the merger. Al brought the Chicago White Sox and Baird & Warner, an old Chicago realtor dating to 1855. Together they landed First National Bank of Highland Park, and were actively pursuing new business to justify all those costly leasehold improvements.

Nader had a way of conducting business with smoke and mirrors. He presumably had a branch office in Kansas City. What we really had was a rep on commission who lived in Kansas City and had a Nader-Lief post office box. The rep would work the streets of Kansas City, playing the ad agency streetwalker routine, calling on any advertiser and promising outstanding advertising, marketing, and creativity, all of which could be sampled for free.

One such taker was Katz, a drugstore chain in Kansas City. With my Walgreens background I certainly knew a lot about chain drugstores. Katz wanted some radio. I suggested—what else? A jingle. Todd approved my theme *"The Everything Store—That's Katz."*

By now I knew not only how to produce my own radio commercials. I hired some top Chicago acting talent for my Katz Drug scripts and signed Dick Boyell to compose my jingle. The jingle was what we called a "doughnut"—a music and lyric open and close, with an instrumental bridge for an announcer script in the middle.

I had Boyell compose a bright, fast theme. He brought in a remarkable young female vocalist he'd discovered named Joan Bateman, a girl still in high school who would cut classes to do Boyell's recording sessions. She sang the open and close—

"The Everything Store—That's Katz." I wanted a long middle doughnut because I'd written a lot of crazy little vignettes to pack into the musical bridge. I could use a lot of different voices in the commercials, because the talent union for radio and TV actors never bothered to monitor markets as small as Kansas City for use and reuse fees.

I used a bunch of ad agency staffers to record a chorus chanting *"Welcome—welcome to Katz!"* I recorded them at half-speed so that the fast playback would make them sound like a bunch of little munchkins out of *The Wizard of Oz*. Then I had the bright, innocent voice of our high-school vocalist reply, "Oh, Toto, I have a feeling we're no longer in Kansas City!"

I wrote a dialogue and cast Steve Goodman for his marvelous tenor speaking voice (it was the first time Goodman had ever shown up at a recording studio without his guitar). The other half of the dialogue was Joan Bateman, playing the part of a Katz clerk. Goodman asks the clerk for help finding vitamin drops, isopropyl alcohol, cotton balls, Nivea lotion—all the things the obstetrician tells a new dad to buy before he brings his wife home from the hospital with their new baby. The cheerful clerk knew what Goodman was going to ask for next, and even reminding him of an item he'd forgotten.

That filled out two 60-second commercials. For the third, a 30-second commercial, I had Boyell play the melody for *"Oh, Promise Me"* on the organ. The dialogue-over was:

> MINISTER: *John and Myrna, do you take this store to be your local neighborhood Katz, supplying your needs with service, selection, and value for as long as you both shall live in the neighborhood?"*
>
> GOODMAN & JOAN: *We do.*
>
> MINISTER: *Men and women of Katz, do you take John and Myrna to be your customers,*

supplying their needs with service, selection, and value for as long as they both shall live in the neighborhood?"

CHORUS OF VOICES: *We do.*

MINISTER: *I now pronounce you Katz and customers. Please place the register receipt in her bag and live happily ever after. (Next couple please.)*

    I called the campaign "Katz as Katz Can."
    Walking back to the shop with Todd, he said, "That was a good day's work." A subdued compliment, but he was very pleased. I was the first capable radio writer-producer he'd ever had on his staff. A good start in a new job.
    Katz ran the series for about six weeks, but never awarded us the account.

    The Kansas City rep came in one evening with a package of Rice's Pure Pork Sausage. He needed some creative development. Wow! I showed him how I could rewrite my *Armour Talkin' Sausage Blues* commercial, which had never been used. The client never approved it.
    That was the end of the Kansas City office of Nader-Lief.

    Sometime in February I decided to have lunch with a former coworker at Sears, a sales manager named Guy Carlisle. Kathy and I had always enjoyed Guy's company—he was a true Southern gentleman, soft-spoken, very insightful and understanding. After lunch we were talking in front of one of the headquarters buildings of Sears' West Side office complex. In my peripheral vision I saw someone stopping to look at me. Having worked there for five years once upon a time, I assumed it was another former colleague who was trying to remember my name. I turned to him and smiled.

The Writing on the Wall

To my surprise, he said "Jeez!" and turned away with a disgusted look. I turned back to Guy and said, "Who was that?"

Guy said, "Oh, I think he was just reacting to your hairdo." The Sears staff on the West Side was still dressing and cutting their hair like it was the Eisenhower years. My long haircut and full sideburns were just fine for North Michigan Avenue, but not for Sears headquarters three miles west of downtown.

In the short span of thirty months I'd changed from looking like a secret service man in my Borsalino hat, cashmere coat, sunglasses, and big black Mercury, to a hippie-looking writer, too outrageous for Sears. Oh well, I couldn't be rehired by Sears anyway.

Since working with Guy at Sears I'd suffered through some difficult years. I'd been fired twice. A few years after my lunch with Guy, I read in the *Chicago Tribune* that he and a fishing buddy had both been murdered in a Wisconsin cabin—shot to death by Guy's son, a mentally unstable ex-Marine and ex-cop. After that I felt my problems were pretty trivial by comparison.

In April, Todd Lief fired me.

I decided to rethink the direction of my career. I knew I could get rehired quickly by another shop, probably at a higher salary. But this business was too much like a game of musical chairs. It was nice to be considered a hot young writer with a reel full of bright commercials and clever jingles. But I was also a man with a young family. Sure, I was still young, but at age 33, not *that* young. As I got older, would I still be considered hot? Would I still be playing musical chairs when my kids were in college? When would the day come when the music stopped, and I didn't have a place to sit down?

There was an obvious solution—a scenario that had been played out repeatedly by the creative giants of advertising, including David Ogilvy, George Lois, and William Bernbach: *Get your hand on the tiller!* Start your own ad agency. Become the person who makes the decisions about who will stay and who will be tossed out on the street.

Brother Bill said he'd fund me. I designed a letterhead.

A week later I heard that Todd Lief was moving to Milan, Italy. Todd had occasionally mentioned that he and his wife were thinking of moving to Southern Europe. And I'd often wondered how the improbable matchup between Nader and Lief had lasted as long as it had.

Al Nader's press release told the story differently in the trade publications: *"Nader-Lief to open office in Milan, Italy. Todd Lief to head office."* Unwilling to admit he'd lost his partner, Nader had convinced Lief to allow him to send out a face-saving press release.

Now you see it, now you don't. It's a shell game.

A few years later, Nader asked me if I'd be interested in merging Inglehart and Partners with Nader-Lief. Sure, Al. And maybe a timeshare vacation home in Syria, too?

—INTERMISSION—

ACT II

SCENE 1

PLACE: The Chicago offices of Inglehart and Partners Advertising

TIME: Memorial Day 1971 to late autumn 1986

Chapter 17

Bringing Home the Bacon

Inglehart and Partners was born the day before Memorial Day 1971, when the State of Illinois issued my corporate charter.
 The Playboy Building, built in about 1926, is one of those old tower buildings with setbacks on the higher floors to allow daylight down to the streets. This architectural feature also provides smaller office spaces in the tower—something few modern office buildings have. I leased an office on the 17th floor—about 180 square feet for $125 a month. I bought some base cabinets, two side chairs, and a plain steel desk and a swivel chair. I removed the Formica tops from the desk and cabinets and replaced them with slabs of thick maple butcher block. My biggest capital investment was an IBM Executive electric typewriter. I installed a two-line phone and hired Marietta's, an answering service catering to actors and voice-overs.
 Advertising Age regularly published an important directory that would become my client prospect list—*The Red Book of Advertisers,* listing every advertiser in the country. My total assets amounted to a corporate charter, a letterhead, an office, a phone, a typewriter, two broadcast sample reels (radio and TV),

a directory of all the companies that were spending money on advertising, and a bank account with $800.

What I lacked in order to be an ad agency was an account executive—a "front man."

An advertising agency is a marriage of necessity between strange bedfellows: businessmen and creative people. The businessmen, or account executives, communicate with the advertisers. The creative people, who create the ads and commercials, communicate with the public.

Agency creative people—the writers, art directors, and producers—are a lot like those theater types I'd lived and worked with years before. They have an intensity that makes normal people uncomfortable. They tend to be inept at one-on-one relationships. Their marriages often fail. They're true performing arts people, constantly in search of an audience. Performing arts people were never intended to address people one at a time. For that they hire agents and managers.

An agency account executive, quite the opposite, is the masterful "front man," an expert in the vital one-on-one communication skills needed in private offices, in fancy restaurants, and on golf courses. He's the guy with a business degree—a cool, well-organized diplomat in a three-piece tailored pin-stripe suit who inspires client confidence—the way I didn't believe I ever could. I was always too intent on protecting the integrity of my creative work, not allowing anyone to alter or diminish it. That inflexibility had gotten me into difficulties with agency producers, creative directors, and other coworkers. It had contributed to my being fired three times. I needed to have someone standing between me and these troublesome one-on-ones.

So I felt a strong need to have a "front man."

I talked to an account executive I'd worked with at Nader-Lief. There was some interest, but no guts. Then I talked to another I'd known at Young & Rubicam. Plenty of guts, but no interest.

Bringing Home the Bacon

I was on my own. It was a lot like climbing into that International Transtar truck cab in Ft. Wayne a year earlier—I'd never driven anything like it, but if I had courage, maybe I could make it go.

I wanted to capitalize on the strongest area of my experience—radio. If possible, jingles. From the *Advertiser Red Book* I sifted out all the advertisers in the Midwest that were investing in radio advertising.

I had an idea for a new business mailing to sell my radio experience: Into a small corrugated box, about 10 inches per side, I would unroll a bunch of 2-inch-wide 16-track magnetic recording tape—about 75 feet of the stuff, rolled off the reel and dumped into the box where it would form a heap that filled the box. I'd clip the end of the magnetic tape to the top of a letter that would rest on the heap of tape. The letter margins were set so the copy block would match the two-inch width of the recording tape. It read,

> *Here's a present for you, Mr. (name.)*
>
> *Recording tape. Enough for a 60-second commercial.*
>
> *This tape is made by 3M— unquestionably the world's finest recording tape.*
>
> *Now all you need is the world's most outstanding radio commercial on this tape. One that'll win recognition, image, and sales for (your product).*

That's what we do. And if you've got a few minutes, I'd like to come by your office and play you some commercials and jingles we've created for Armour Meats, U.S. Navy, ReaLemon, and a little drug retailer in Kansas City that now has 18 stores.

Maybe you'll decide that we can put the world's best commercial on the world's finest tape. For you.

I'll call in a day or so.

*Very truly yours,
Jerry Inglehart*

    My plan was to send out about 20 tape boxes a day and begin the follow-up calls five business days after they went in the mail. I sent mailings to every radio advertiser in Chicago, generating enough interest to allow me to set up several appointments per week. I did the same mailing to radio advertisers in Milwaukee, Detroit, and St. Louis. I landed a few little bitty projects now and then.
    Since I was not a full-service ad agency with departments for marketing and media, I figured I could present Inglehart and Partners not only as an advertising agency, but also as a *creative service*. This would allow me to call on and service other ad agencies since a creative service, technically, does not compete with an advertising agency. Lots of ad agencies used creative services to supplement areas where they were weak, like broadcast or comedy writing. Some ad agencies didn't have any

creative departments at all—they farmed everything out to creative services.

An agency in the Wrigley Building hired me to do a jingle for Yorktown Shopping Center in the southwest suburbs. A fellow named John Caesar ran a one-man agency called Beverage Marketing, catering to retail liquor chains. Caesar hired me to do a series of ten-second spots for Armanetti Liquors in Chicago and a jingle for Cut Rate Kid Liquors in Anchorage, Alaska.

There was an agency on Wacker Drive named Gardner, Stein and Frank. They specialized in hotels and resorts, and kept their overhead down by using outside creative sources like me. That summer of 1971, most of the income that kept me afloat was from Gardner, Stein and Frank. I did mostly brochures and newspaper ads for them, buying my graphics from a *Playboy Magazine* art director named Vito Ramanouskas, or from a design shop on Wells Street called Blake & Weiss. I spent the summer dashing madly from client to source to client. The work from Gardner, Stein and Frank flowed in steadily and kept me hopping—a restaurant menu for Scottsland Resort in northern Illinois—a series of ads for MGM Grand Hotel, just opening in Las Vegas—a new hotel just opening across from McCormick Place in Chicago—ads for the Sazerac Lounge in New Orleans—a brochure for French Lick Resort in Indiana.

The Gardner, Stein & Frank relationship was a major exercise in deception by both me and them. On one hand, I was pretending to be a full-service creative source, when in reality I had no graphics staff whatsoever, and farmed out all my layouts and graphics. At the same time, I was pretending NOT to be an ad agency, and therefore not in competition with Gardner, Stein and Frank. Meanwhile, Gardner, Stein & Frank was pretending to be a full-service ad agency, when in fact they had no creative department at all—they outsourced all creative work to me and other creative services.

Playboy Enterprises, right in my building, had hired me for a couple of radio projects. Then Playboy decided to hire an ad agency for their Playboy Hotels and Resorts. My contact at Playboy suggested I pitch the account. Great! I had dozens of superb hotel and resort samples to show them. MGM Grand in Vegas. McCormick Inn. Scottsland Resort. French Lick resort in Indiana—all the work I'd done for Gardner, Stein & Frank.

My Gardner, Stein & Frank business suddenly stopped. I called them a few months later, looking for a project. My contact said, "Jerry, we can't use you."

"Why?"

"Mr. Gardner made a presentation to Playboy. He pulled out the MGM Grand campaign. Playboy said, 'Oh, this is Inglehart and Partners' stuff, we've already seen it.' "

Smoke and mirrors.

Gardner, Stein & Frank didn't get the Playboy Resorts account. Neither did I.

By autumn, two advertisers had hired Inglehart and Partners as their advertising agency. One was Vulcan Containers, manufacturers of plastic shipping drums for liquids. The other was 2nd Debut Cosmetics, manufacturers of a moisturizing lotion. 2nd Debut hired Inglehart and Partners to develop and place broadcast advertising. That meant I would be buying broadcast media, the bread and butter of an ad agency's income. For that, I'd need to work with an independent media buyer who could translate all those mysteries about radio markets, areas of dominant influence, and gross rating points, into a logical media buy.

I contacted Bernard Weisner, a media buyer I'd worked with at Young & Rubicam. He agreed to make my media buys on a freelance basis.

In October my wife Kathy quit her job and joined me. I added another butcher-block-topped desk, and ordered another swivel chair, phone, and typewriter. In three days she landed a client—Betty's of Winnetka, a small but growing retail chain selling clothes to young women. Kathy negotiated a monthly retainer of $800.

Inglehart and Partners now had three clients.

Bernard Weisner was buying fairly substantial media schedules for 2nd Debut. He was also putting pressure on me to hire him—which I did just before Christmas. I rented a slightly larger office in the Playboy Building—maybe 360 square feet.

But I still needed that "front man."

There was an account executive at Young & Rubicam named Frank Bloom. Frank and I had worked together on several Armour food products as well as the U.S. Navy. I had lunch with him to find out if he was interested in coming to work for me. He was impressed with the creative work I'd done for Armour, and that I wanted to go after food product accounts—his own area of expertise.

I offered him $1,000 a month and a percentage of billings for any new business we landed. He agreed. The office next to ours was vacant. We put in a door and two more desks and phones for Frank and Kathy. I hired a receptionist-secretary, Angela Terrana.

All four of us—Kathy, Bernard, Frank, and myself—were sending out new business letters and making follow-up calls. In January, Bernard got a response from John Morrell Meats, with headquarters on LaSalle Street in Chicago. Bernard, Frank, and Kathy met with Al Schneider, the marketing director for John Morrell. Later that week we made a full presentation to Morrell, showing all of my Armour Meats ads and commercials. Frank and Bernard discussed their experience in marketing and media for Armour Meats.

We were hired for two Morrell brands—Hunter Meats in St. Louis, and Rodeo Meats, with a packing plant in Kansas and fragmentary market shares in Wichita, Tulsa, Oklahoma City, and Kansas City. The combined annual budgets were only about $600,000, yielding an agency commission of less than $100,000—which meant Inglehart and Partners was a little heavy on staff and would have to continue hustling for new business. But we were now a viable advertising agency.

Al Schneider had us begin development of four TV commercials, two for each brand. For the bacon TV for both brands I came up with a campaign line *"The Bacon That's Almost as Perfect as the Egg."* The storyboard showed an egg rolling around in an animated fashion among several product packages that opened to reveal nice red strips of perfect lean bacon.

The hot dog commercials would be directed toward the youth market on kids' programs. I wanted to do a jingle. Since both product names (Hunter and Rodeo) suggested horseback riding, I dreamed up a pair of commercials in which young kids on horseback ride to a big kids' picnic of hot dogs and all the fixings that go with hot dogs. I hired Ray Tate, an accomplished studio guitarist, and president of the Old Town School of Folk Music, to lay down an instrumental demo track of my jingle.

At the client meeting in Morrell's LaSalle Street headquarters, about twelve client representatives gathered in a conference room to see our proposals for creative work. Frank ran through some marketing strategy. He was totally at ease with branded meat products and spoke convincingly, before turning the meeting over to me for the creative. I went through the bacon storyboard including my tag line and justification: Bacon goes with eggs. Eggs are always perfect. Bacon varies. Often too much fat. Hunter bacon (or Rodeo bacon) is better—more reliable—*almost as perfect as the egg*. I saw a lot of nodding of heads around the table. They seemed pretty happy with their new agency choice. Even if we were new and small—and therefore a risk for them to gamble on—we were showing them things they liked.

Next I showed them the hot dog storyboard—kids riding horses to a hot dog picnic. I told them the sound track would be a jingle. I hit the "Play" button on my portable Sony to start the instrumental demo track, and started singing the lyrics, which I had written out on a big poster for everyone to read:

Bringing Home the Bacon

There's the Hunter's horn calling every kid in town.
Watch the hungry hunters come from all around.
So listen for the horn. Follow the chase
To the great tasting hot dogs Hunter makes.
Snack time or lunch time, if you're hungry too,
Join the fun like the other kids do.
Grab a tasty Hunter hot dog,
   just for the likes of you.

Big, BIG smiles all around as I sang. Then I said, "Now, if a guy with as lousy a voice as mine has the guts to stand up in front of all you people and sing that song, you can all certainly help me sing it! C'mon!" (And the band track looped itself back to the top.)

I sang. My agency people, smiling, recognizing they had a winner, sang their hearts out. And every last one of those client people sang, whether they had good voices or were hopelessly tone deaf.

I had them hooked!

For the final hot dog TV soundtrack I hired twelve kids from the St. Luke's Church boy's choir in Evanston to sing the jingle. (When Robert Altman shot his film *The Wedding* in Lake Forest six years later, he used the same choir.)

I put the four TV commercials out for bids by production studios in both Los Angeles and Chicago and selected Walt Topel Studio on North Halsted Street, in a building that later became the Briar Street Theater. Bernard Weisner prepared a TV schedule that would start running in the five cities in April.

The outdoor hot dog commercials needed to be filmed in early March in order to make the air date. March in Chicago is still snowy and grim—I needed a location that would be lush and green. Topel selected a dude ranch outside of Dallas.

We were in Dallas for over a week, first selecting locations, then casting the kids from a local talent studio. We had a crew of four from Topel Studio in Chicago. The Topel crew hired 14 crew people from the Dallas motion picture industry, including two cameramen, two assistant cameramen, three grips, four gaffers, a stylist, and two horse wranglers. For three days we filmed kids riding horses through woods and fields and around a big picnic table full of hot dogs and picnic fixings.

Then we came home to shoot the bacon TV in Topel's studio on Halsted Street. We made the egg roll around by blowing it with an air jet. Then we went on to a week of editing and post-production.

In producing commercials, I'd learned to hire the best talent affordable, then leave them alone to do their thing. I hadn't yet learned that lesson in my dealings with my own staff. Frank Bloom, after being over-supervised and hounded by me for several months, bailed out, taking his food marketing know-how with him. Frank went to work for Jordan, Tamraz & Caruso in Chicago. They handled the John Morrell national brands, and were therefore in direct competition with me.

I replaced Frank with a young fellow named Bill Cotterill.

I also advertised for an art director, and soon hired a winner—Jerry Huyler, a fellow graduate of New Trier High School. Jerry left Foote, Cone & Belding to join us. He understood food products. He'd art directed and produced a lot of mouth-watering TV commercials for food products at Foote, Cone. Huyler was intensely creative—ideas flowed from his imagination like a waterfall. But he couldn't seem to tell the good ideas from the bad ones. I guess that was my job.

We pitched FlavorKist Bakeries in Chicago. They awarded us their Toast'em Toaster Pastries, a product imitating Kellog's Pop Tarts. Then we picked up Radio Station WBBM-FM, the local soft rock station.

Bringing Home the Bacon

As we moved into summer I moved the agency into a larger suite in The Playboy Building—a 1,500 square foot end suite with five offices and a reception room looking out on Michigan Avenue.

Al Schneider at Morrell was very disappointed with the creative ability of Jordan, Tamraz & Caruso, the agency handling the John Morrell national brands. In early 1973 Schneider asked us to develop some TV storyboards for Morrell Bacon and Morrell Ham, two of their national brands handled by Jordan, Tamraz & Caruso. At the same time Schneider assigned us two additional regional brands—Partridge Meats in Cincinnati and Dayton, and Tom Sawyer hot dogs in the Twin Cities. With these added assignments, our income from John Morrell would now amount to over $1 million annually.

By comparison, our income from our other clients amounted to peanuts. FlavorKist was running a few coupon ads in Charlotte, N.C. Betty's of Winnetka was still only earning us our $800 monthly retainer. WBBM-FM did trades with other media, which brought us no media income—just our fees for commercial development and production. Our 2nd Debut schedule on *Paul Harvey News and Commentary* ran only one commercial per week. Vulcan Containers had fired us.

About 80% of our income was from John Morrell regional brands.

Jerry Huyler and I worked up a package of five TV commercials: Morrell Bacon, Morrell Ham, Partridge Ham, Partridge Bacon, and Rodeo Ham. Al Schneider approved all five storyboards for production. Huyler was accustomed to big-budget production at Foote, Cone & Belding, and had expensive tastes. He bid the commercials out through some top-shelf studios and came to me with the list of the production studios he'd chosen. He wanted to film the Morrell Bacon in Hollywood. The storyboard was based on the rolling egg commercial I'd done the previous year for Hunter and Rodeo, but Huyler knew a Hollywood studio that could do a better job with it, including a more dramatic method of making the egg roll end over end.

For the Rodeo Ham commercial Huyler chose Filmfair in Chicago, using one of their top directors, and filming on location in Old Tucson, Arizona. For the remaining three commercials he chose a Chicago film studio. Huyler decided to cast the commercials in New York and fly the talent to Chicago for the shoot.

I was impressed with Huyler's expertise and enthusiasm. With Huyler producing our TV so professionally and capably, it was no longer necessary for me to travel to the film studios and location shoots. Huyler was much better at TV production than I was. In fact, when I was around I just made him nervous. I still hadn't learned to leave my people alone to do their jobs. I'd lost Frank Bloom due to my over-supervision. And I'd soon lose Jerry Huyler for the same reason.

Morrell had previously worked with major ad agencies, and didn't blink at our production package totaling over $120,000 for five TV commercials. I told Huyler to pack another $5,000 into the budget because I wanted to hire Slim Pickens to narrate the Rodeo Ham commercial.

Al Schneider's assistant, Tom Kincella signed our $128,000 production estimate without batting an eye.

I flew to Los Angeles to produce a radio commercial for Partridge, using a Hollywood talent I'd selected. On the flight back home I was listening to one of the music channels on the airplane headset and heard The Carpenters perform *Top of the World*. Richard Carpenter's keyboard accompaniment seemed to me to be perfect for background music for the Morrell Bacon commercial—happy, upscale, full of motion like the egg rolling around on the screen. I composed a music track based on the chord sequence of *Top of the World*. Back at the office I phoned my sound studio engineer at Universal Recording in Chicago.

"Who does keyboards like Richard Carpenter?" I asked.

Bringing Home the Bacon

"For that," he said, "you want Gregg Perry. He's out of Milwaukee."

"Gregg Perry? I met him once in the parking garage across from Universal Studios. He was carrying an electric bass. I thought he was a bass player."

"He is, but he mostly does keyboards. Here's his phone number."

Gregg did a masterful job on electric piano for my bacon music track. I congratulated him afterward. "I thought you were a bass player at first."

"Well, actually, I'm a composer-arranger."

"Really? Jingles? You compose and arrange for studio combos?"

"Also brass, woodwinds, percussion, strings, the works. I'll send you a copy of my sample reel."

It was the start of a long and fruitful working relationship with Gregg Perry.

As good as the St. Luke's Children's Choir had been the previous year on Hunter and Rodeo Hot Dogs, their lyrics were too hard to understand, and I knew I should re-track the jingle. The Jimmy Joyce Singers, a kid's vocal group in Hollywood, had recently backed up Karen Carpenter on her hit single, *Sing*. I booked the Jimmy Joyce Singers and flew to Los Angeles to record them singing the Hunter and Rodeo Hot Dog songs. The session went well, the kids sang happily and brightly.

*

In addition to John Morrell, we achieved a few other creative victories.

One of them was Speed Queen, the laundry appliance manufacturer, located in Ripon, Wisconsin. Speed Queen had been making laundry equipment for decades. Their major market position was in coin laundromats. To reach this market they had a strong sales force supported by ads in trade publication and lots of brochures, product sheets, and sales manuals. For years they'd used a small ad agency in nearby Oshkosh, Wisconsin, named Geer-Murray, that was quite capable with trade ads, product sheets and sales manuals.

But in the early 1970s, the elderly president of Geer-Murray knew that his relationship with Speed Queen was in trouble. Speed Queen wanted something he couldn't provide—advertising support for a stronger position in the consumer product arena. To accomplish this, Speed Queen had to buck heads with the giants in consumer appliances, like Whirlpool and Maytag. That required a sophisticated consumer products marketing strategy, plus aggressive advertising in consumer media, especially television—two areas that the president of Geer-Murray knew nothing about.

Speed Queen knew that if they wanted to gain any momentum in the consumer market, they would have to fire their trustworthy, hard-working little Oshkosh ad agency and move the account to one of those big, expensive consumer products ad agencies in New York or Chicago.

The president of Geer-Murray needed help to save his biggest account, and he needed it fast. I'm not sure how he got my name. Maybe he'd somehow learned that I was the son of parents who grew up in Oshkosh and attended Oshkosh High School. He needed a big league TV commercial for Speed Queen, and maybe a guy named Inglehart would be a good ol' country boy like himself. So he trusted me. He had little choice. He wanted to retire, and I soon became aware that this old fellow hoped I would help him save the Speed Queen account, then buy him out, move to Oshkosh and become the new president of Geer-Murray.

Having survived Rockford, I wasn't about to relive the small town experience.

Jerry Huyler and I dreamed up a powerful 30-second TV commercial for Speed Queen. For the announcer I selected a Hollywood actor named Simon Oakland, who'd been in many movies and TV dramas. He'd played Police Lieutenant Schrank in the movie version of *West Side Story*. He had a voice as tough and durable as a Speed Queen washer. I flew to L.A. to record him.

Meanwhile, Huyler shopped for a studio to produce his baby. He happened upon a new Chicago film studio run by Paul Roewade, a fellow I'd known as a kid in Glencoe. I used to ride Paul's Whizzer bike. Paul had grown up to become an outstanding director of TV commercials.

Speed Queen eventually moved its account to Foote, Cone & Belding in Chicago. Geer-Murray was left with nothing but its little trade accounts and product brochures. But Inglehart and Partners had another superb TV commercial on its sample reel—one that showed we were just as capable in appliances as in food products.

*

We came up with a campaign theme for our client WBBM-FM, the Soft Rock radio station in Chicago. Today the term "Soft Rock" is well known in the music field. I personally coined that term, and I can point to the WBBM-FM newspaper ad where I first used it.

We based our new campaign on the tag line, *"A Sound Track for the Story of your Life."* We sold the client an ad campaign and a jingle, for which I'd written both the lyrics and melody.

Gregg Perry had recently moved from Milwaukee to Nashville. I wanted him to arrange my jingle and play keyboards, so the Friday prior to a Monday recording session I flew Gregg Perry up from Nashville and rented an electric piano for him to work with in my office.

During a work break in our Saturday session, Gregg took out a tape of a pop song he'd arranged and recorded the prior week in Nashville. It was composed by a friend of Gregg's who was trying to break into pop songwriting down there. The song was called "To Nashville With Love."

As I listened to it, my mind was still on WBBM-FM. I said "Gregg, I'm hearing another jingle for this WBBM-FM campaign. Just a minute..." I went into another office and sat down at a typewriter. The lyrics virtually poured out of me:

FEMALE VOCAL, ALTO; CHARISMATIC, WARM:

Meet me every morning.
I'll waken you at dawn.
I'll sing to you the whole day through,
I'll set your life to song—
Songs for your happiness,
I'll cheer you when you cry
With songs you are living,
A sound track for the story of your life.
BBM-FM.

There were virtually no corrections, cross-outs, or changes on the lyric sheet I handed to Gregg. He read it. "That's really nice," he said as he switched on the electric piano. Following the chord sequence for "To Nashville with Love," he created a new melody as quickly and easily as I'd created the lyrics.

This new jingle was romantic, memorable, flowing—and considerably better than the melody for the other jingle we were working on, the one I'd written myself. It occurred to me that melodies flowed in Gregg Perry's mind the way blood flowed in his veins. In all the years I would work with Gregg after that, I'd never bother to write another melody. He could do it better and faster.

Judy Maslanka, a vocalist I knew from the Old Town School of Folk Music, sang our alto vocal with enough warmth and charisma to make you fall in love with her. Gregg coached her to sound a little like Olivia Newton-John.

For years after we lost the WBBM-FM account, they continued to use "Meet Me Every Morning" as an on-air filler.

Bringing Home the Bacon

For me it was the ultimate ego trip—to be sitting in a restaurant or coffee shop talking to somebody, hearing some soft background music, and unexpectedly hearing my own creation. Thirty whole seconds of it.

On one of our trips to St. Louis to service Hunter, we got an appointment to see the director of marketing for Downyflake Frozen Waffles at Pet, Inc. He wanted a jingle for TV.

Pet, Inc.! One of the biggest food manufacturers in the country! I agreed to do a demo jingle for Downyflake, on a speculative basis—we'd get paid only if they decided to use our work.

I went home and wrote:

Hey, Sleepyhead! Time for Downyflake.
Rise and shine and head on down to Downyflake.
Toast the morning in a tummy-warming way.
Downyflake will start you with a smile.
Let your toaster make your breakfast.
Let Downyflake make your day.

The TV visuals would complete the proposition—appetizing shots of the waffles popping out of a toaster and being spread with butter, then drenched in maple syrup.

Gregg Perry had convinced me to produce jingles in Nashville, rather than Chicago. By that time he knew all of the musicians in a town that was loaded with outstanding musical talent. Gregg came up with a wonderful Downyflake jingle.

By now I was beginning to understand that advertising is a lot like theater and movies—it takes more than outstanding talent to succeed. It takes a break—being in the right place at just the right time. Like when Arlo Guthrie came through Chicago and heard Steve Goodman sing "City of New Orleans" at the Earl of Old Town Pub. Arlo decided to record that song himself. It was a big break for Goodman.

Gregg said that on any day of any week there would be at least ten great songs echoing through the sound studios of Nashville—any one of them worthy of becoming a nationwide or worldwide hit, just hoping for a star vocalist and a bit of luck. Without such a break, the ten songs would simply fade into history, like his friend's song, "To Nashville with Love."

Our Downyflake jingle was just such a winner. Pet, Inc. could afford to spend millions running it.

Kathy, Jerry Huyler, and I flew to St. Louis to present our jingle and storyboards to the Pet Marketing Director for Downyflake. He saw that we'd produced a damned good TV jingle for him, but for reasons we'd never know he could not assign us the account. But since we'd done such good work, he didn't want to just bid us farewell. He asked us to come up with a public service campaign—some ideas for Downyflake that would be "socially redeeming."

I wish he'd just sent us away. He was wasting our time and our money. We came up with some print ads for a campaign in which some of Downyflake's profits would benefit St. Jude's Children's Hospital in Memphis, another in which Downyflake product was donated to feed ghetto kids at school, another benefiting environmental cleanup. *"We're going to clean up Lake Erie with waffles."*

But nothing ever came of it.

*

Morrell's other ad agency, our competitor Jordan, Tamraz & Caruso, handled all the John Morrell brands that had product distribution nationally. The advertising budget for the national products amounted to about a million dollars—just about equal to our billings for Hunter, Rodeo, Partridge, and Tom Sawyer.

The Morrell national brand billings were easy, highly profitable billings for Jordan, Tamraz & Caruso because one commercial for one product could be run in all Morrell markets, whereas the four regional brands we were handling each required separate marketing plans, separate product positioning, and separate creative development because all these brands had different names, and ran in eight different markets. Furthermore, we had to travel to packing plants in four different cities, while client contact for the Morrell national brands all took place on LaSalle Street, a cab ride away.

Even more burdensome was the fact that each of our markets had its own special promotions that required newspaper ad support. Hunter in St. Louis ran a very successful "Hunter Night" program each year in which the public mailed in product packages in exchange for tickets to a Cardinals home game in Busch Stadium. Partridge had an annual sweepstakes promotion in Dayton and Cincinnati. Rodeo had a promotion for tickets to the National Finals Rodeo in Oklahoma City.

In other words, we did four times the work for the same amount of income earned by Jordan, Tamraz & Caruso on the Morrell national brands.

At one point, this workload had our entire staff running ragged, meeting deadlines and client requests everywhere from Cincinnati to Arkansas City, Kansas. The pressure was incredible. In the course of six months Inglehart and Partners produced five TV commercials, six radio campaigns, and twenty-eight 1,000-line 2-color newspaper ads. Somehow Jerry Huyler and I managed to maintain our quality standards, turning out excellent creative for both print and broadcast.

Over the course of this incredibly busy spring of 1974, Al Schneider ran three new products past us, asking for creative development on all of them.

The first was a new chitterling sausage. Chitterlings are cut up hog colons, an inexpensive meat product purchased mostly by blacks. Unless you've grown up on collard greens and such, the chitterling sausage product tasted wretched to you no matter how it was spiced. The product was abandoned.

Next was a product developed by a Morrell division in Manchester, England—a fruit product for making your own jam. In England many wives would make marmalade each year when the new crop of Seville oranges shipped up from southern Europe. With the Morrell product they didn't have to wait for the arrival of the new Seville oranges—they simply bought a can of "Ma Made" concentrate and followed the directions to cook up a batch of marmalade. Or strawberry preserves. Or grape jam.

Al Schneider wanted to see if he could launch the product in the United States. Kathy and I flew to England in May to look into it. We met with Morrell's British ad agency in Manchester. Back at home I came up with the product name *"Jam That You Make"* and did some package development and product positioning.

Nothing ever came of it.

The third project was "International Favorites"—four canned meat entrees in 24-ounce cans. The only flavor I can remember is Beef Stroganoff.

We'd been trying for two years to convince Morrell to get into frozen entrees like Stouffers. It required a major investment in equipment that Morrell didn't want to make. They were more comfortable with their canned meat entrees—corned beef hash and chili. So they came up with International Favorites.

Canned meat entres—in 1974? There's not a hell of a lot you can do to improve the taste of canned meat products. They always have an overcooked, artificial taste. They sit in your mouth like a glob, with the vegetables and meat all feeling gooey and lacking in texture. That's why frozen entrees became so successful.

I swung into creative work for International Favorites. I remember my ad headline:

> *Announcing delicious new entrees in a place you'd least expect to find them—in cans!*

*

Bringing Home the Bacon

Our ultimate reward for all this good work was just over the horizon.

Al Schneider kept hinting that he might assign the entire John Morrell account to us, making us their sole advertising agency, at the beginning of the next fiscal year, on July 1. We'd already created and produced two TV commercials for Morrell brands. They were being placed by Jordan, Tamraz & Caruso. If we took the Morrell business from Jordan, Tamraz & Caruso, we'd double our billings from this client—and pick up the most profitable billings Morrell had to offer.

In early June, Al Schneider announced that he wanted the executives in the Morrell Brand packing plants in Memphis and Sioux Falls, South Dakota, to meet us. Kathy and I were flown out to a Sioux Falls meeting in the John Morrell jet prop plane, together with Al Schneider, Tom Kinsella, and others from the LaSalle Street headquarters. The meeting was to start at 9 A.M. next morning. Arrival night was social. Cocktail hour started at 5 P.M. in the hotel.

Al Schneider was a heavy drinker, and many on his staff tended to follow his lead, matching him round for round, never seeming to know when to knock it off and go to bed. I should have said goodnight at 10 P.M., to set an example. But this was client contact—socializing—bonding—the part of the ad biz where I felt least qualified and most in need of a smooth, polished "front man." I felt obligated to stay up with my client.

About 3 A.M., after ten hours of out-of-control boozing, Al decided he wanted everyone to go swimming in the hotel pool. He didn't have a bathing suit. "Who needs suits?" he said. He wanted us all to skinny dip. Al, a married man, had been hitting on our agency receptionist, Angela Terrana, for a year. I didn't want him nude in a swimming pool with my wife.

Shortly after 3 A.M. I was searching the hotel for swim trunks for my client. Finally I secured a pair of disposable swim trunks and knocked on Al Schneider's door. He answered totally nude and giggling. Moments later he passed out on his bed, far too drunk to put on the bathing trunks, much less swim.

I didn't feel like a successful ad agency president. I felt like a pimp.

Next morning all of us limped through a meeting and a plant tour, everyone severely hung over, barely functioning on four hours' sleep.

Then we flew to the Memphis plant. Fortunately the Memphis meeting was a little more controlled and civil. Perhaps our Sioux Falls hangovers were lasting into the second day.

On the flight back to Chicago, Al Schneider invited Kathy and me to his house in Palatine for dinner Saturday night.

When we showed up, it became evident that Al's wife was as serious a drinker as he was. After two rounds of drinks on their patio, our hosts didn't bother going inside to refill the drinks—they just hauled all the bottles from the bar and parked them on the patio table in front of us. After four rounds nobody bothered with mixers or ice cubes. Just straight booze. Kathy passed out in the car going home. All the way back to Evanston the road was spinning wildly before my eyes.

Next morning I had to take my visiting nephews, Mark and Michael Brown, to the airport at about 11 A.M. I woke up and drank a lot of strong black coffee.

At the airport I got my nephews on their plane back to Florida. But walking back to the parking lot, my severe hangover and my coffee nerves started ganging up on me. I'd never heard of an anxiety attack. But as I pulled the car toward the parking lot cashiers, I was hit with a sudden attack of nerves similar to a 10,000-volt shock that refused to stop. I wanted to jump out of the car and scream for help. I had no idea that the human nervous system could do this—actually short circuit itself and start sparking and exploding like an electric generator gone haywire.

I drove slowly, painfully to the hospital emergency room in Evanston. How do you tell a nurse that something's seriously wrong with you when you're not bleeding to death? I figured my life as I knew it was over. I feared I'd be a basket case, spending the rest of my life in a straight jacket. I called Kathy. "I'm at the Evanston Hospital Emergency Room. I need your help badly. When you see me, try not to be shocked—try to be strong and calm. I'm in a very bad way."

She called my doctor who had the hospital emergency room fill a prescription for Valium. "Give him one tablet," my doctor told her. "Don't give him two unless you absolutely have to."

A half-hour after Kathy found me in the emergency room and gave me a dose of Valium, my nerves started to settle down. I thanked God—I thought the anxiety would never pass. I felt as if I was returning from the living dead.

I was 36 years old then. Today I'm sixty-six. I've never had a repeat attack, but I've feared one for all thirty of those years. And for ten years after that event, I was afraid to leave my house without a little emergency container of Valium tablets in my pocket. I don't know how I ever lived through that attack—and I don't think I ever could again.

*

Al Schneider sent a memo to his boss, Morrell president Albert Paul. "Unless I hear from you otherwise, I will be assigning the advertising for all our brands to Inglehart and Partners next week."

I thought to myself, "My God, in the next year I'll probably be able to pay myself a salary of $100,000!" A hundred grand in 1974 was major bucks. The salaries of the dot-com executives in the 1990s, amounting to hundreds of millions, might make $100,000 seem trivial, but in the early 1970's, $100,000 a year was way up there in rarified air.

And I was about to do it! I'd be rich and very successful. Just three years earlier I'd been on the street.

George Lazarus at the *Chicago Tribune* got wind of the Morrell account change and phoned me at home. I told him nothing. But the following morning his column was headlined, "Morrell Brands to Inglehart."

The following Friday, the trade publication *Ad World* carried the page one headline: "MORRELL TO INGLEHART."

John Morrell is part of a set of corporations that are like a stack of Lego blocks. The Morrell name goes back many years. In the process of expansion, Morrell purchased regional packing plants such as Hunter, Partridge, and Rodeo, and kept marketing those products under their established brand names.

In 1966 a company producing milk bottle caps, headed by a man named Eli Black, bought John Morrell. Three years later Eli Black bought United Fruit Company, which had been growing bananas in Central America since about 1850. In 1944 United Fruit developed a banana cartoon character called "Chiquita Banana" patterned after a popular Latin entertainer named Carmen Miranda.

Eli Black renamed his newly merged company "United Brands." In time, it would become Chiquita Brands. Black moved the United Brands headquarters to an office on a high floor in the Pan Am Building in Manhattan.

Black generally left Albert Paul, the Morrell C.E.O., to run Morrell his own way. Black had turned a $24 million loss in 1971 into a $16 million profit in 1973.

But in early 1974 Morrell was showing red ink. So was United Brands. They seemed to be heading toward the most disastrous year in their history.

Albert Paul thought he'd better run the Inglehart and Partners assignment past his boss. Eli Black responded, "Hold off until I get there next week. I want to meet this agency."

Eli Black met with me, Kathy, and Al Schneider in the LaSalle Street headquarters of John Morrell. I told him about my experience with Armour Meats and what we'd done in the past two years for Rodeo, Hunter, Partridge, and Tom Sawyer.

Black asked me, "What do you think about International Favorites?"

Bringing Home the Bacon

If I'd been a marketing man, I'd have answered something like "Well, in today's environment with frozen entrees so popular, I'd say International Favorites is bucking a major trend, but we're working to position it *against* frozen entrees."

But I'm a creative man. My job is to take the client's product and believe in it so hard that maybe I can get the public to believe in it with me. So I said, "International Favorites could be the first product in a new trend." It was a major error—an mistake a true "front man" would never have made.

The following Friday Al Schneider called Kathy. Per Eli Black's dictate, Al was to assign ALL Morrell brands to Kenyon & Eckhardt, a major Chicago ad agency.

That included Hunter, Rodeo, Partridge, and Tom Sawyer. All of our accounts.

In one day we lost 80% of our income.

*

Running a business can be a hell of a strain—struggling to beat competition, sweating to meet payrolls and pay vendors, scratching for new business, screaming for recognition. It can result in high blood pressure. Migraines. Ulcers. Anxiety attacks.

It put me in a hospital emergency room.

And seven months later, on February 3, 1975, it put Eli Black on the sidewalk in front of his Manhattan office building.

I got off easy. I walked out of the hospital emergency room after a few hours.

But Eli Black was carried off that sidewalk in a body bag. He'd leapt to his death from the 44th floor window of his Pan Am Building office.

Not long after that Al Schneider, still a fairly young man, died of a heart attack.

Would Inglehart and Partners perish as well?—or could it recover?

Chapter 18

Rebirth

I looked at what was left of my ad agency, trying to decide whether the glass was four-fifths empty or one-fifth full. 2nd Debut had undergone reorganization and was no longer advertising. We had only three solid clients—WBBM-FM, Toast'em Toaster Pastries, and Betty's of Winnetka—hardly enough income to support myself plus a secretary.

In three years as an entrepreneur I'd learned that a business is *more* than an inanimate thing that you create with a corporate charter. Once born, a business takes on a personality—or rather, a series of split personalities. The personality your business chooses at any one time is based on how well you feed it—and the only diet a business understands is money. Profits.

If you can feed your business a healthy diet of steady profits, it will act kindly to you and support you like a quiet benefactor. If you can manage to enrich its diet with lots and lots of money, it becomes your favorite rich uncle, funding your purchase of a nice house, putting your kids through college, and providing you with a comfortable retirement. If you're incredibly lucky and your business feasts regularly on a gourmet diet in the hundreds of millions, or even billions, your

Rebirth

business can actually *immortalize* you by funding a charitable foundation in your name and paying for college libraries and dormitories that will bear your name long after you're dead.

But if you let your business miss *just one meal*—say a payroll date—it turns into a screaming infant in a high chair, pounding its tray and angrily bellowing its lungs out for its money. If you happen to miss several meals, your business becomes a monster that turns against you and schemes to destroy you, sending bill collectors to your door followed by summonses and lawsuits that soil your name and reputation, and turn your friends against you.

My baby was too big and too hungry. It needed a "money fix" right away. The bellowing infant didn't care that Inglehart and Partners had a glowing reputation for brilliant ads and bright, imaginative radio and television commercials. It only saw that its diet had suddenly been reduced by 80%.

Replacing over $1,000,000 in billings doesn't happen overnight. But the infant must be fed daily.

I immediately began reducing the payroll, sadly dismantling the lean, brilliant team I'd built so carefully over two years. I fired our marketing director, an account executive, and a secretary. Jerry Huyler smelled death and returned to a major ad agency.

Bernard Weisner, my media director, had lost his survival instinct. He'd grown soft and happy being wined and dined by his media representatives. He'd been looking forward to the coming years when he could place big network buys for John Morrell. That would mean more fancy lunches with his Old Buddy network of smiling media reps. Bernard couldn't see that survival meant saying good-bye to all those fair weather friends in media and getting out to beat the bushes for business. I had to let Bernard go in November.

Now Inglehart and Partners was almost back to its own starting line—Kathy, myself, and a secretary. Our lovely hall-end office space with its nice views of Michigan Avenue was full of empty private offices. Kathy said, "This place looks like death—we can't have client meetings here with all these empty offices." I agreed. They only served as a daily reminder of our loss. We moved into a considerably smaller office space in the Playboy Building.

Kathy started prospecting for business immediately. New business efforts were familiar turf to her—it's what had occupied most of her time when she'd joined me three years earlier. Sadly, her best efforts yielded only a dreary list of tiny new clients, mostly retailers. A bridal shop in Kenosha, Wisconsin. A housewares retailer on Clark Street. A retailer of foam rubber furniture on the South Side. In Evanston, she signed four accounts—an antique dealer, a retailer of war surplus goods, a paint and wallpaper store, and a health foods store. Pitiful little earnings that hardly justified any major effort, much less that of a creative guy accustomed to producing radio and TV commercials in New York and Hollywood, and music tracks in Nashville.

My own prospecting yielded little more than scrapings and leftovers. I got a Michigan Avenue clothing retailer. I landed an assignment to produce a radio campaign for Chicago House of Vision. One of the John Morrell pilots who'd ferried us around the country in the Morrell Beechcraft had invented a kite called "Space Spinner" and I did a TV commercial for him, insisting on prepayment.

I got an appointment with the national franchiser for Dog and Suds, an old drive-in fast-food chain that would soon go belly-up in the wake of McDonald's, Wendy's, Kentucky Fried Chicken, and Burger King. I even called on Componetrol, the company that had purchased Waterman Engineering from the family of my high school buddy, Jack Waterman.

My business had suffered a killing autumn frost, and it looked like these paltry assignments would be the only Indian summer we'd have.

Kathy and I still had our eye on the dream—landing another major food products manufacturer that would return us

Rebirth

to glory. We flew several trips to St. Louis and Minneapolis where we called on biggies like General Mills and Land o' Lakes. We got one speculative assignment from Pillsbury to promote their new Poppin' Fresh Pie Shop restaurant chain, but ended up with nothing to show for it but receipts for plane tickets, hotels, and car rentals. In less than a year, Pillsbury sold the pie shop chain—but not the Poppin' Fresh name. The buyer renamed the chain Baker's Square.

Once again Brother Bill came to my aid. His company, GC Services in Houston, had just purchased a savings and loan in Killeen, Texas, and he assigned the advertising to Inglehart and Partners. I came up with a theme, *Keep a Good Thing Growing*, and prepared a number of very nice newspaper and outdoor ads plus a jingle which I recorded with Gregg Perry in Nashville, using a young vocalist named Janie Frickie who would later land a CBS recording contract, release several albums, and become a major national figure in country and western music. I developed the Killeen Savings jingle into a series of good but low-budget TV commercials and some clever radio commercials based on people visiting the Killeen Savings money tree to watch their savings grow.

Since I never knew at the beginning of any year how much money I'd have left at year's end for Kathy's and my salaries, we would live for an entire year on advances from our expense accounts. Then on December 31st I'd see what was left, and cut two salary checks for us for the entire year, most of which would go to repay our expense account advances. December 31st became our one and only payday each year.

On December 31, 1975, I closed the books for the year with billings of a little more than $400,000 and net income of about $100,000. After reducing that by rent, payroll, and other overhead expenses there wasn't much left.

The Kenyon & Eckhardt ad agency in Chicago was still running all my John Morrell, Hunter, Rodeo, and Partridge TV commercials in 1975, so in early 1976 I sent copies of all nine of the commercials we'd produced for Morrell to *Advertising Age* magazine. The commercials were written up in the magazine's annual review of the "100 Best TV Commercials of the Year." This put Inglehart and Partners' creative in a league with the largest ad agencies in the country. I made reprints of the *Ad Age* article and sent them out to the long list of prospective clients we were pitching.

By 1978 our exhausting new business travels and presentations began to yield some solid results:

For several years I'd been talking to Hinckley & Schmitt, a bottled water company with distribution in Chicago, Milwaukee, St. Louis, New Orleans and Phoenix. They finally hired us for brochures and broadcast advertising.

Enterprise Paints, headquartered in the northwestern suburbs, hired me to support Magicolor Paints, the private brand they manufactured for Wickes Lumber. I prepared a series of color trade magazine ads and some radio commercials.

We'd called on Concorde Confections, manufacturers of the Willy Wonka Candy Bar in St. Louis. The marketing director, Chuck Perreault, asked us to do some TV storyboards for Willy Wonka. He liked our work, but was unable to hire us. Later in the year he moved to Leaf Confections in Chicago and hired us to do a TV commercial plus some radio and print ads for both consumer and trade media.

In my many travels to Texas I connected with Evans Black, a carpet manufacturer in Dallas. I would serve them for several years, providing radio and TV commercials.

On one of those Dallas trips I called on a little outfit named Autotronics, Inc., manufacturer of "The Snooper XK," a radar detection device for drivers who want to know when their speed was being electronically checked by the police. The Autotronics president sat me down in a meeting with his marketing man. In

Rebirth

frenzied phrases he explained how U.S. municipalities were ripping off the driving public with speed traps. He pulled out a book he'd self-published, showing a cover picture of a fat, sinister-looking state trooper with a vascar radar gun pointing straight at the reader. The title of the book was *AMBUSH!*

I said, "Hold on, fellows. If I present your product to the public the way you're presenting it to me, we'll not only infuriate the law enforcement authorities, we'll offend the law-abiding public as well. Let me take this home and think about it."

At my office I came up with the following 60-second script:

> ANNOUNCER: *"If you listen closely for the next sixty seconds, you may never have to pay another speeding ticket.*
>
> *"This message is about a dependable little electronic device called 'The Snooper XK.' It sits on your dash like a watchdog. The moment it detects radar, it flashes a warning and beeps,* (SOUND EFFECT: BEEP BEEP BEEP) *reminding you to check your speed. You get plenty of advance warning, whether the radar beaming device is on the roadside, in the sky, or hidden in a tree.*
>
> *"Now, if you're like most people, you drive at the proper speed anyway. But if you're human, you occasionally make a mistake. The Snooper XK tells you when you DON'T want to make a mistake.*
>
> *"So relax. Drive with the Snooper XK, and you can hear radar. (BEEP BEEP) Make no mistake about it."*

I scrolled the script up in my typewriter and read it. This was good. *Really* good. I'd taken a product shrouded in illegality and made it acceptable to the general public.

I got up and paced over to my office window, then back to my script and read it again. Not one word or phrase could be changed without diminishing it. And it was so incredibly simple! I could produce it for little more than the cost of the announcer plus a half-hour of mono recording studio time.

Autotronics approved the copy without changing a single word. All I needed now was the right voice—masculine, quiet, convincing, sympathetic, yet firm. I considered Simon Oakland who I'd used for the Speed Queen TV commercial. But reviewing my tapes of New York and Hollywood actors, I decided instead on an actor named Steve Brodie in Los Angeles. From the Autotronics office in Dallas I recorded Brodie, directing the session at a Hollywood recording studio via a phone hookup.

The folks at GC Services sent another little plum my way. They'd purchased First National Bank of Killeen which, together with Killeen Savings and Loan, gave them a near total lock on the financial life of this little town halfway between Dallas and Austin.

That called for another jingle, of course. I decided to focus on the word "First"—the first word in their name, the first thing of importance, that sort of a tie-in:

> FEMALE VOCAL:
> *The First thing is the people, working hard like you*
> *Deep in the heart of Texas, knowing what to do.*
> *We'll help to build your future,*
> *We're working on your dream.*
> *First National Bank of Killeen.*
>
> *You're on your way to somewhere,*
> *you know the reasons why,*

Rebirth

Banking on a day when there's
a rainbow in your sky.
When money makes the difference,
we're playing on your team.
First National Bank of Killeen.

CHORUS:
The First thing is to keep tomorrow
looking bright and green,
The First thing to remember,
First National of Killeen,
We're here to serve you—
BACKUP VOCALS: *Come on over!*
First National Bank of Killeen.

On the phone to Gregg Perry in Nashville, I said "These bank directors in Killeen are good ol' small town Southern boys, and they damn near worship country and western music. And these lyrics are sentimental enough for country and western. I think we can get away with a country and western treatment on this track, something we probably couldn't do with any other bank in the country."

"Do you want Janie Frickie for the vocal?" asked Gregg. "I don't think she's doing jingles anymore, her albums with CBS Records are so hot now."

"You're right, she told me that when I approached her to do a remake on my House of Vision jingle. She only did the remake because she wanted to shop at Lord and Taylor in Chicago. I had to pay her double scale, fly her to Chicago first class, put her up at the Drake, take her to dinner, even sing to her in the John Hancock building parking ramp."

(I'd wined and dined Janie in the 95th floor restaurant in the Hancock building so this country girl could look out over the entire city of Chicago. We'd talked at dinner about her music. Janie was big on love songs and most of her hits were love songs. I'd told her about the love song, "And This Is My

Beloved," from the 1953 musical, *Kismet*. It wasn't country and western by any stretch, in fact, it was based on a romantic theme by the 19th Century Russian composer, Alexander Borodin. But she loved the lyrics. I had my twelve-string guitar in the trunk of my car, so when we left the restaurant and got back to my car, I took out the twelve-string and sang the song for her. Janie has a warm, kindly Southern nature to her. I was convinced her enthusiasm over my parking ramp serenade was genuine. I was hoping I'd inspired another hit single.)

"Listen, Gregg," I said, "I want a warm, charismatic female vocal like Janie, and I'd love to have someone who can do those magnificent improvised falsetto vocal fills like Janie does, she's almost like Edie Gorme in that respect. I have someone in mind. Do you have any idea who's been doing those vocals on the Diet Rite commercials?"

"Oh, that's Florence Warner. She used to be in Nashville, but she's in New York now. She flies to Nashville a lot to do recording sessions. Hold on, I think I have her number."

I called Florence Warner in New York. Her answering machine had no voice message, just the beep. With vocal cords like hers, I suppose she had to be concerned about harassment and stalking. I left my name and number and mentioned that I'd gotten her number from Gregg Perry.

She called back next day. I asked her how much she'd want to record a jingle in Nashville. In her warm, melodic Southern voice she purred, "I'll sing for union scale plus a first class ticket to Nashville. My boyfriend lives there, so I like to get there as often as I can."

I booked her for a Friday session at Ironside Recording in Nashville. That way she could spend the weekend with her boyfriend.

I'd just booked one of the top female studio vocalists in the country—for *scale!* Sometimes it pays to be a small ad agency. She never sang for scale for the Royal Crown Corporation.

By now I'd learned to expect nothing short of greatness from Gregg Perry. I'd worked with several other composer-

Rebirth

arrangers in my career, and Gregg was by far the best. He could sit down and compose a fresh, exciting, polished melody, and score the whole band track in his head. On the plane back to Chicago I listened to my fabulous new First National jingle on my headphones about a hundred times.

By year's end in 1978 my billings had grown to over $500,000, for a gross profit of somewhere in the area of $125,000. After deducting the operating expenses, I was able to pay Kathy and myself an almost respectable amount that at least kept our mortgage payments on time. A lot of the billings were fees for the production of an assortment of radio and TV commercials for Hinckley & Schmitt, Chicagoland Aamco Transmission franchises, Evans Black carpets, and a slide show for Abbott Labs. I was also doing a lot of brochures and sales tools for Associated Life Insurance Company in Chicago.

Looking at our personal income tax situation, I saw that Kathy and I were getting hammered by the marital tax penalty—that quirk in the Internal Revenue Service tax code that penalizes married couples by taxing them more than if they were each single and paying taxes separately. The marriage penalty hits hardest for those couples, like Kathy and me, with roughly equal incomes. In April 1976 I filed separate tax returns for myself and Kathy in order to slightly reduce the marriage tax penalty.

That month I also calculated what our income tax liability would have been if Kathy and I were single, but living together—and saw that a divorce would save us enough in taxes to pay for college for our two sons. I suggested this to Kathy. I had no intention of leaving Kathy; I expected we would be together for the rest of our lives. I simply wanted to nullify that marriage license document on file in the Cook County Recorder's office that was bleeding us in marital tax penalty.

Kathy's response to my proposal was frightening. I began to understand that, despite 18 years of marriage, she had never felt certain of our marriage and always feared I would someday divorce her. She thought I was simply using the marital tax penalty as an excuse.

In the coming months we discussed with several married friends my idea of a paper divorce to nullify the marital tax penalty. Some agreed with me, others disagreed and sided with Kathy. As a postscript, I was able to look back five years later and discover that those couples that had agreed with me were still married, while those that disagreed had all gotten divorced. Apparently my suggestion seemed reasonable and practical to stable couples, and threatening to those whose marriages were shaky. It hadn't occurred to me that my own marriage was one of those in the latter group.

Beginning with the year 1976, with no hope of reducing the tax bite through a paper divorce, I took a different approach to reducing taxes. I told Kathy that I'd be paying myself ALL of the Inglehart and Partners' income for our household. She would receive no salary. Not only would this bypass the marriage penalty, it would halve our sizeable bite for Social Security tax liability as well.

Kathy objected to this strongly. She wanted her own paycheck, regardless of the taxes involved. I said, "Fine, I'll pay you all the household income, and take nothing for myself. It will have exactly the same effect in reducing tax liability." This, too, was unacceptable to Kathy. In June she quit and went to work for another ad agency.

Her departure from Inglehart and Partners soon resulted in the loss of her key account, Betty's of Winnetka. At the same time, the general manager of WBBM-FM was fired, and his replacement immediately fired Inglehart and Partners. Our total billings, so recently a bright beacon, were now reduced to the equivalent of a kerosene lantern.

I was once again a solo act, like when I'd started in 1971.

*

Rebirth

I read in *Advertising Age* that the Chicagoland Chrysler-Plymouth Dealers were seeking presentations from ad agencies. I wrote to them, sent a resume of Inglehart and Partners' experience—and got assigned for a presentation slot, together with seven other ad agencies.

For this presentation I needed a media department. Since Bernard Weisner had left, I'd been working for a couple of years with Kelly, Scott & Madison, a Chicago media buying organization. They were media experts, placing probably ten million in billings annually. They agreed to pitch the account with me.

Since losing Jerry Huyer, I'd been using independent graphics designers, mostly Mel Lain who'd been one of my coworkers at Young & Rubicam in 1970. Mel was very creative, and easy to work with. I called a strategy-planning meeting at my office with Chuck Abrams from Kelly, Scott & Madison; Mel Lain; and my assistant, Cindy Peterson, who I'd hired as a replacement for Kathy. I said I'd be willing to go all out, like a major ad agency, for a presentation that would include a jingle and storyboards. My two sub-contractors, Chuck and Mel, agreed to pull out all the stops for a major pitch. The first order of business, we agreed, was to meet with all six members of the Chrysler-Plymouth Dealers advertising committee—six individual dealership owners. We wanted to get the lay of the land.

We divided the six dealerships among us for private meetings—two for me, two for Chuck, and two for Cindy Peterson. After these meetings, the three of us planned to get together and compare notes for building a strategy.

At the end of the day of these meetings, Cindy phoned me. She was still at her luncheon meeting with one of the car dealers in the suburbs. She told me she was getting a tremendous amount of inside information from this dealer, an elderly man named Mike Hyman. Hyman proved to be the pivotal person on the advertising committee. He was in his 60's, tall and gray-haired, and had an affinity for exotic European sports cars and young blonde women. Cindy was a cute blonde with a perfect figure. She would play a major role in our landing the account. Through her, Hyman was steering Inglehart and Partners through the complex politics of the Chicagoland Chrysler-Plymouth Dealers Association.

I got my creative juices flowing. Most auto dealers in the 1970s were—and may still be to this day—a bunch of horse traders, determined to out-fox their customers, and because they did it, they assumed everyone was out to cheat them as well. Most of their advertising focused on trying to correct this negative image of themselves. You'd see a lot of advertising stressing that this or that dealer is "a real honest guy"—"a dealer you can trust."

Mostly, car dealers needed image.

I came up with a theme line, focusing not on dealer trustworthiness, but on the quality of the vehicles they sold. My hook line was *"Come on up."* I envisioned a hot air balloon that would float around the city with a banner reading *"Come on up to a Chrysler-Plymouth deal."* I contacted a hot air balloon owner and pilot who was willing to bring his balloon to our presentation at a suburban hotel, inflate it and fly the dealers around for a ride—for the cost of a couple of tanks of LP gas to fuel his burners.

I wrote a jingle:

> *You've driven many miles and*
> *   you'll travel many more,*
> *And there's something we want you to know:*
> *Your Chrysler-Plymouth dealer has*
> *   the car you're looking for,*
> *Your car for now and tomorrow.*
> *Come on up, come in and see*
> *   Chrysler-Plymouth quality.*
> *Great cars, great deals,*
> *   and a great deal more.*

Rebirth

CHORUS:
*Chicagoland Chrysler-Plymouth dealers are
Inviting you to drive a special car,
Come on up (Chrysler Plymouth!)
Come on up (Chrysler-Plymouth!)
Come on up to a Chrysler-Plymouth deal!*

Like most automobile dealership advertising, there was absolutely nothing concrete in the promise. "Quality" — "great deals" —a bunch of empty claims. But it could give the dealers the identity they needed.

In Nashville, Gregg Perry dreamed up a dynamic melody and arrangement. I booked Florence Warner to do the vocal and flew her in again, first class, from New York. Gregg was working as Dolly Parton's producer at the time, and he booked Dolly's back-up vocalists for our session.

During the same session I sandwiched in a band track for a new Toast'em Toaster Pastry jingle. I would record the vocals later in Chicago, using a chorus of kids:

*Breakfast, lunch or snack time,
Toast'em on the shelf.
Something good and tasty hot
That you can fix yourself.
Toast'em's what you call 'em,
It's also what you do.
Toast, toast, toast 'em
And you eat 'em when they're through.*

I wrote a radio script I called *"Andrew"* in which a little girl entices a little boy to come play at her house by serving him Toast'em Toaster Pastries. I had access to film director Jordan Bernstein who was a master at directing the two most difficult-to-direct elements in films: animals and children. He'd filmed all the Morris the Cat commercials, as well as my Leaf

The World is a Stage

commercial for Whoppers Malted Milk Candy. I hired Jordy to help me direct the kids for the radio dialogue. He'd never worked on radio production. In a two-hour session I learned how Jordy directed children. He'd feed them their lines one-at-a-time and parody the delivery he wanted. It was delightful to watch the kids respond to Jordy's animated, comic antics.

On the plane home from Nashville, I played the Chrysler-Plymouth track over and over on my headphones. Once again, Gregg had accomplished masterful stuff despite my rather bland lyrics. Like nearly all of our tracks, it started out simple with a subtle keyboard accompaniment, then gained momentum on the middle phrase with drums, bass and rhythm guitar, finally building to a climactic close with background vocals. Uplifting, memorable, it made you want to stand up and sing along. I could visualize the TV storyboards. I could see the hot air balloon sailing over Chicago, carrying the *"Come on up"* banners. I even dreamed up a Christmas TV commercial in which our hot air balloon pilot, sailing over the Chicago skies on a cold December night, would cross paths with Santa and his sleigh.

Cindy Peterson's dealer friend had managed to convince the ad committee to give us the closing slot on the presentation schedule. Of all eight agency presentations, Inglehart and Partners would be up last, the best possible position!

For three nights I rehearsed my presentation as if I was preparing for a Broadway opening. I'd edited my band track into a loop so it would play the jingle and sound track over and over. I ran through my presentation maybe sixteen times until I had it down perfectly.

The presentations started at 8 A.M. in a hotel conference room. Each contender was allowed one hour. By 3 P.M. my pilot had his hot air balloon inflated and bobbing on its tethers in the parking lot outside the hotel. I was ready to move my big sound system into the room at the stroke of 4 P.M.

Rebirth

I opened the presentation with a description of the "Come On Up" campaign theme, supported by the hot air balloon flights over the metropolitan area, displaying the campaign theme banner. Mel Lain opened the meeting room's window blinds to reveal the huge hot air balloon bobbing outside. Then Mel presented his storyboards for the TV commercial, generating a nice level of excitement among the dealers. I stood up and explained some of the logistics of the theme and tie-in. Then I moved into the theatrics—my jingle. Mel started the tape player. Florence Warner's glorious voice and Dolly Parton's backup vocalists belted out my lyrics over Gregg's thrilling music track. Then the band track looped into the instrumental without the vocals, as I excitedly told the dealers that the chorus of this jingle would be on every one of their commercials, both TV and radio. Every eye in the room was on me. They'd all just suffered through seven hours of boring presentations, and at last, at day's end, something thrilling was happening. I had them! I hollered over the band track, "Here comes the chorus…on the count of eight, following the build—five, six, seven, eight, (and I sang along with the band track), *Chicagoland Chrysler-Plymouth dealers are inviting you to drive a special car—Come on up!* (Dolly's back-up vocals on the sound track came in the fill—*Chrysler-Plymouth!*) *Come on up! Come on up to a Chrysler-Plymouth deal!*

"Now," I said, raising a giant lyric poster over my head as the instrumental track looped back to the start, "If a guy with as lousy a voice as mine has the guts to stand up in front of all you guys and sing that song, you can sure as hell sing along with me…five, six, seven, EIGHT! *Chicagoland Chrysler-Plymouth dealers are....*"

Since the vocal and band track were very uplifting and memorable, I wanted it to get under their skins. I wanted to make them hear it as often as I dared. What I did next, few ad men except me, with my background in music and theater, would have had the courage to do. As the band track entered its fourth loop, I said, "Now, I could see that MOST of you guys were singing, but I saw a few of you with looks on your faces like you were thinking, 'I'm too damned *cool* to sing along!' " (Laughter.) "Now I want to see *everybody* singing! Come on, this is your new theme, this is a campaign that'll give you the recognition and the traffic you've only dreamed of...five, six, seven, EIGHT! *Chicagoland Chrysler-Plymouth dealers are...*"

They were singing. They were hooked. The secretary came in with her stopwatch, showing it to the head of the advertising committee. Time up. He waved her off. We continued.

Next day Cindy Peterson had another meeting with Mike Hyman, her dealer friend. She reported back to me:

"Jerry, the ad committee never had any *intention* of changing ad agencies! The whole program of soliciting agency presentations was simply a scam, to convince the dealers that the ad committee was doing its job. They've been comfortable with their old agency for years. But the presentation by their own agency was just put them to sleep. Then you came in and blew them away with your jingle and the hot air balloon. The dealers want you to get the account. But first, the ad committee is going to have a run-off presentation between you and the old agency, to give them a chance to come up with something as good as yours."

I'd won. And yet I hadn't. But there was a significant spin in my favor. That other shop was probably just like Geer-Murray in Oshkosh—they had neither the talent nor the knowledge to create anything like what I'd created. They didn't understand jingles. Or broadcast production. Or just plain creativity. I sincerely doubted that they'd ever be able to develop anything as exciting as my jingle and the hot air balloon idea. Certainly not in two weeks.

They did come up with a spokesperson. I'm sure they searched frantically through the talent agencies for a spokesperson who would blow the socks off of the dealers—and found that good talent was far too expensive for the Chicagoland Chrysler-Plymouth dealers. They finally settled on

Barbara Eden. Personally, I'd have looked for a Telly Savalas or Karl Malden, someone forceful and convincing when talking about a tough, well-designed car built to last. But maybe the other agency understood that some of the dealers had affinities for pretty blonds. When Barbara Eden had appeared in the TV series *I Dream of Jeannie* in the mid sixties, she was thirty, fresh, and cute. In 1978 she was affordable because she was 44 years old, and a trifle faded.

Meanwhile, the *Come On Up* theme was fresh, powerful and original. And it did the job. We signed the account in September, with a monthly retainer fee of $6,500.

Shortly afterward, Cindy Peterson got a new Chrysler LeBaron convertible.

One of the top commercial filmmakers was Filmfair, with studios in both Chicago and Hollywood. I'd worked with them before. Filmfair, under Jerry Huyler's supervision, had produced our Rodeo Ham commercial in 1974. One of their best directors was George Gootsan, who worked out of their Hollywood facility, but their representative, Dave Oakes, said Gootsan was coming to Chicago and he could direct the Chrysler-Plymouth commercials. Great!

Each TV commercial was to end up with a glamour shot of the Chicago skyline, with the names of dealers flying forward from the horizon toward the camera, and disappearing off the top of the screen. The chorus of the jingle had eight bars, and I decided to show titles naming eight dealers in each commercial. It would take five separate edits of the commercial to cover all forty dealerships in Chicagoland.

I spent two weekend days scouting for the best view of the buildings of downtown Chicago, working counter-clockwise from North Lake Shore Drive. I ended up at Meigs Field, where an airport security guard drove me out to the southeast end of the tarmac of Northerly Island—and I discovered the most exciting, most perfect view of the towers of downtown Chicago, dominated by the Sears, the Standard Oil and the Hancock. As I write this, it's been just a few months since Chicago's Mayor Daley terminated Meigs Field by quietly bringing in a bunch of bulldozers at night to tear up the runways. Now Northerly Island is to become a new public park. Perhaps in a year everyone can see that impressive view of the Chicago skyline that I saw on that Sunday afternoon in October 1978. It's well worth the trip out there.

Next I learned what it was like to deal with a bunch of horse traders.

We organized a pre-production meeting of the Chrysler-Plymouth Advertising Board at Kelly, Scott & Madison. I presented Filmfair's bid of $22,000 to produce the TV commercial. The Board then asked us to step out into the hall while they conferred. What the hell was going on? Why did they have to exclude us from their discussions? We could be in there to answer any questions that might come up.

They invited us back into the conference room. The ad committee chairman said, "We'll pay you $19,000 to produce the TV commercial."

I'm not the best diplomat. I told them they couldn't negotiate a TV production price the way they niggled and jiggled the price of a new car. If they want to pay $19,000 for a commercial, they'd get a $19,000 commercial, not a $22,000 commercial.

Next, they asked why we marked things up by 17.65%, when the agency commission is 15%. I explained that it's the difference between a *commission* and an *added markup*. "If we place $10,000 with media, we earn $1,500, which is 15% of the *gross*. But if we buy a TV commercial for $10,000, we have to add a *markup* of 17.65% and bill you $11,765. We still earn 15% of the *gross* price, since 15% of $11,765 is the same as 17.65% of $10,000."

They conferred once again with us out in the hallway. Then they told us they wanted us to mark up the TV commercial by only 15%—and furthermore, they wanted us to rebate them part

Rebirth

of our media commissions so we'd earn only a 15% *markup* on media, rather than the full 15% *commission.*

I was beginning to see that this account was in trouble. The dealers were treating us the way they treated customers in their showrooms. They lived in a world of inflated prices. We didn't.

Dave Oakes and George Gootsan at Filmfair figured out how to pull $3,000 out of the TV production budget.

When I presented the invoice for $19,000 they said they wanted to cut a check that was payable *jointly* to both Inglehart and Partners and Filmfair. Apparently they were afraid I might abscond with their $19,000.

In late November I received our second $6,500 check from the dealers' association, but it had an endorsement on the back saying I was accepting it as prepayment for the TV commercial production. I deposited the check, then wrote them a letter explaining that, per the terms of our agreement, the $6,500 was a retainer against future commissions, not a prepayment.

In early December the ad committee called a meeting with us at a hotel in a western suburb. The association secretary walked in with a tape recorder, which she placed in the center of the conference table and turned on. The ad committee chairman said, into the tape recorder, "We've had some misunderstandings with Inglehart and Partners, so we're recording this session." He spoke his name and recited his social security number. All the way around the table, each man on the committee spoke his name and social security number into the tape machine. Cindy Peterson and I did the same, wondering what in the world was going on.

Then I found out. In the ensuing discussion—actually it was an interrogation—they tried to get either me or Cindy to say, on tape, that they hadn't agreed to pay us a retainer against commissions, and that the two monthly checks they'd submitted were prepayments against TV production. I got up, read into the tape recorder the clause in our contract in which they agreed to pay us a $6,500 monthly retainer against future commissions—

and headed toward the door. The committee chairman said, "You're fired, you know."

"I guessed as much," I said. "You owe me $6,500 for December. And according to the terms of our agreement, you have to give me 90 days' written notice of termination, so that'll be another $19,500 due by March 1st."

I consulted with a contract attorney. He felt that it would cost more in legal fees to sue for the $26,000 than it was worth. Maybe I had the wrong lawyer.

That Chrysler-Plymouth jingle was one of my finest commercials, and I'd been looking forward to submitting it for creative awards. But to be eligible for an award, the commercial had to have been broadcast.

The price of a single radio spot run between midnight and five A.M. on an FM station in Chicago was about $12. I bought one of these spots and ran the jingle once in late December.

Shortly after the loss of the Chrysler-Plymouth account, Cindy Peterson left Inglehart and Partners, and I lost touch with her. Two years later, Kathy called her and invited her to dinner at our home. Cindy drove up to our house in the latest model of Chrysler convertible.

In the course of our dinner conversation I asked Cindy if she'd ever seen Mike Hyman again, after we lost the account. Cindy was taken aback by my incredible naivety. "I'm still seeing him, Jerry." And it finally dawned on me why Cindy was driving that new Chrysler parked outside. I was astounded that I could be so oblivious to things that were right before my eyes. And I suddenly felt glad that I'd lost the Chrysler-Plymouth account after just 90 days.

In this wild business of tinsel, glitter, open solicitation, inflated promises, and free samples of your work, a man could become a pimp without even knowing it.

Chapter 19

"Seeking the Bubble, Reputation"

I thought to myself, what I need is some publicity. It had been three years since I'd mailed out the Ad Age reprint mentioning my Morrell TV commercials in conjunction with the 100 best commercials of 1975. And my creative output during 1978 had been pretty good. I wondered if my Snooper XK commercial could win any major industry awards. Could a simple announcer script compete with big budget national commercials out of New York? It would be a long shot. I packaged the Snooper XK and Chrysler-Plymouth commercials up with a couple of others and submitted them in the 1979 industry award circuit.

Each of these awards is patterned after the Academy Awards, with five finalists in each category, the winner in each category receiving a statuette at an awards presentation. And like the Academy Awards, which is duplicated by other festivals such as the Sundance, Cannes, Golden Globe, and Screen Actors Guild, there are several award festivals in the advertising industry. The Chicago Advertising Club sponsors the WINDY Award. The New York Ad Club offers the ANDY Award, and the New York Art Director's Club sponsors the ONE SHOW Award, both of which accept entries from all over the country. The ADDY Award begins with regional competitions, then submits the regional winners in a national competition. And there are two worldwide competitions, accepting entries from every country on Earth—the International Broadcast Awards (IBA) sponsored by the Hollywood Radio and Television Society, and the CLIO Awards. The IBA competition is particularly stiff because it has fewer categories than the others.

As May rolled around, the various sponsoring organizations informed me that I had *nine* finalists—two in the Chicago competition (The Snooper XK commercial was a finalist in two categories), plus three in New York, where the Snooper XK commercial was nominated for a ONE SHOW award plus two ANDYs. In Hollywood, the Snooper XK commercial was in the running for two CLIOs, including Best Automotive and Best Copywriting, and my Chrysler-Plymouth commercial was a finalist in two categories—Best Corporate and Best Retail Dealers commercial.

This was unbelievable. My little one-man ad agency, billing a paltry half-million dollars a year, was making a very respectable showing against some of the highest-paid creative giants in the largest ad agencies in the world, with billings in the hundreds of millions.

I was especially pleased to see the showing that my low-budget Snooper XK commercial had generated—*seven* finalists for a commercial that was little more than an announcer script. Clearly the judges on all four juries were more impressed by a good piece of copy than by production value. The automotive industry spends tens of millions producing car commercials. Imagine an announcer script commercial gaining recognition against those extravaganzas.

The presentation ceremonies would kick off with the CLIOs the first week in June. The CLIOs ran simultaneous festivals in New York and Hollywood, with the TV presentations taking place on the final afternoon. But I noticed that the presentations for radio commercials took place in New

York on Thursday afternoon, and were repeated in Hollywood on Friday morning. This offered me a chance to save myself a trip out-of-town to show up as an also-ran—providing I could get the festival committee in New York to reveal whether my Snooper XK commercial was the winner. If I was the winner I could take a red-eye flight to L.A. to receive the award in Hollywood on Friday morning.

Late that Thursday afternoon I phoned the CLIO committee in New York. "Who were the winners in the Automotive and Copywriting categories?"

"We're running a festival here, and things are very busy—could you call back on Monday, or just check the newspapers?"

"Love to—but my commercial is up for both awards, and if I'm a winner, I'll fly to Hollywood tonight for the presentation tomorrow."

"Let's see—hold on." It's very important to the festival promoters to have recipients come up to the podium for their awards. He came back on the line in a minute. "The award for Best Automotive Radio went to Autotronics, Snooper XK, Inglehart and Partners."

"Tell them I'll be there in Hollywood tomorrow morning."

It was true. I'd won the coveted CLIO.

On my flight back from Los Angeles I was bumped to first class, and there was an empty seat beside me. I placed my CLIO statuette on that seat and belted her in.

Whatever grief I'd suffered in those years at Inglehart and Partners, peer recognition of this magnitude made up for a lot of it. I'd written a sixty second commercial, produced it in half an hour, and it had won a CLIO.

*

One of the Chrysler-Plymouth ad board members was an Elmhurst dealer named Larry Roesch. Larry had a neighbor named John Adams, who happened to be the general manager of the Chicago office of McCann-Erickson, America's second largest ad agency. Adams was therefore a successor to Al Sommer, my father-in-law, who'd been McCann's Chicago General Manager twenty years earlier. Twenty years is an eternity in the world of advertising—John Adams had never heard of Al Sommer.

Larry Roesch had been impressed with the *Come On Up* theme I presented to Chrysler-Plymouth in late summer. Since his friend and neighbor John Adams was an authority on advertising, Larry played a cassette of my jingle for John.

"Who did this?" John asked.

"Inglehart and Partners in Chicago."

"Never heard of them—but this is a very good jingle. What was the campaign like?" Larry explained the *Come On Up* theme with the hot air balloon. John thought that was a powerful promotion and a pretty clever tie-in.

John Adams had another neighbor friend named Dave Bachmann. Dave had inherited his father's business—a shop in Mt. Prospect that sold and installed replacement doors and windows. Dave felt he could turn his dad's Mom-and-Pop store into a chain. He decided to simplify the name spelling to Bockman. He knew he needed a good logo, a good identity, and some advertising. Who would know more about that than his friend and neighbor, John Adams?

McCann-Erickson had a list of advertising accounts that read like the Fortune 500, including Pepsi Cola, Budget Rent-a-Car, and Amoco. They weren't structured to handle a door-and-window store in Mt. Prospect. But John remembered the Chrysler-Plymouth campaign Larry Roesch had showed him.

John Adams called me and explained about his neighbor with the door-and-window store in Mt. Prospect. Would I be interested? Of course I would. John wanted to come over and see some more of my work.

The tables seemed to be ironically reversed. Hadn't I been the kid at the pay phone with a stack of coins, doing anything I could to get in to see the Big Man in his office at the Big Agency? Now the Big Man was coming to my office.

"Seeking the Bubble, Reputation"

John was indeed a big man, with a round red face and a level of sincerity and straightforwardness I liked. I showed him a few print ads, selecting samples for hard goods rather than food. I ran my TV commercial reel for him. And I played him some radio commercials, and gave him a cassette copy of my radio sample reel.

Looking at the cassette label, he said something I'll never forget: "If we had a radio reel like this at McCann-Erickson, I could have gotten a lot more business."

"Maybe we should be working together," I replied. I'd been trying to connect with a "front man" for eight years.

"Not unless you want to move to England. In three months I'll be heading up the London office of McCann Erickson."

I took the Bockman account. I wasn't too anxious to serve another retailer, but Dave Bachmann appeared to have major plans for expansion. And he wasn't going to question my creative suggestions because John Adams had told him not to.

Dave's store didn't sell Andersen or Pella or Marvin, or any other national brand of doors and windows. He had his own private brand of Bockman replacement doors and windows, made to his specifications by an old German immigrant named Foder who had a workshop on the South Side of Chicago. Mr. Foder built doors and windows the way Rommel built tanks. And Dave, a straight-talking Christian Scientist, knew how to sell them at premium prices. While most replacement doors were comparatively flimsy and would get out-of-alignment after a few good Chicago winds and a few thrusts by a German shepherd dog, a Bockman door was tough and could take abuse.

My theme line for Bockman doors and windows was *Built to Work and Built to Last.*

I'd always been impressed with the New York actor Ed Binns. He'd been one of the *Twelve Angry Men* in the 1956 Henry Fonda version of the movie. He was one of the generals in *Patton* with George C. Scott. Subsequently he'd play the Boston archbishop being sued by the Paul Newman character in the film *The Verdict.* Binns had a folksy, gravelly voice that exuded both toughness and integrity. I booked Binns for double union scale and flew to New York with Dave Bachmann to record our first bank of Bockman radio commercials that included a script I called *Granddad,* describing the fine workmanship of doors and windows back in Grandfather's time. When Ed belted out my tag line, *"Bockman. Built to work, and built to last,"* his words had the strength and authority of both General Patton and Pope John.

For the TV commercial, Mel Lain and I designed a limbo set with a door threshold mounted with a Bockman storm door and bordered by a few outdoor evergreen trees. For my on-camera actor I hired a sincere little milquetoast fellow that I'd seen on one of Joe Sedelmaier's award-winning "Where's the Beef?" commercials. He was to walk onto my set, examine the Bockman door closely, open it, close it, check the hinges and hardware, knock it and kick it a little, then test its strength by hanging by his hands from the top of the door. At that moment a sudden wind gust, powered by an off-camera wind machine, would blow a cloud of autumn leaves across the set as the door, actor and all, would snap suddenly outward, the actor's feet swinging in the wind. Then a little boy and a big black dog would charge out through the door on the second wind thrust. A perfect demonstration commercial—TV's strongest capability.

By the end of the year, Dave Bachmann had bet his entire inheritance on his baby. He poured half a million dollars into broadcast advertising and opened three additional Bockman stores in Skokie, Downer's Grove, and West Chicago.

*

By year's end I'd taken in over $850,000 in billing. And once again I was anxious for some more peer recognition, and the publicity that might come with it. Since all award finalists are considered winners of "Merit" or "Recognition" awards, every nomination yields an award certificate. And my reception room wall had nine lovely award certificates, beautifully

"Seeking the Bubble, Reputation"

mounted in handsome, simple gold frames for all visitors and prospective clients to see. But I wanted more.

I'd had another good creative year. I felt confident about the Bockman radio and TV. Also, Hinckley & Schmitt, which in previous years had tried to micro-manage my creative output, now seemed to be willing to trust me to produce radio the way I wanted. I was very proud of two radio commercials I'd produced for them in '79. One, which I called *"Witches' Brew,"* opened with a thunderclap, a roaring wind, and a screeching cat, as a MacBeth-type cackling witch read the contents of a can of Diet Cola. *"Double double, toil and trouble...sodium saccharin, phosphoric acid, sodium benzoate preservative..."*

Over this bedlam I cast and recorded Mason Adams as the announcer. Mason is the folksy voice of Smucker's Jam. Recently he'd played the newspaper editor on the popular TV series, *The Lou Grant Show*. Mason had one of the most trustworthy voices in America.

Mason's magic voice intoned:

"There's a modern-day witches' brew made of water and chemicals. It's called the diet soft drink.

"But maybe you're a label reader, concerned about the health of your family."

WITCH: *"...use of this product may be hazardous to your health! (Cackle cackle.)"*

ADAMS: *"Maybe you've already discovered the zero-calorie drink that's as pure as it is thoroughly delicious and totally refreshing: Hinckley & Schmitt pure drinking water, delivered right to your home. So handy, you and your family probably drink a lot more pure water and a lot less pop.*

"So why not tell a dieting friend about

Hinckley & Schmitt pure water. Help him kick the chemical habit and join the pure water generation.
"After all, you are what you drink."
WITCH: *"...milligrams per fluid ounce saccharin, a non-nutritive..."*

I wrote this commercial many years before a health-conscious public would cause bottled water to outsell most brands of diet soft drinks.

Another Hinckley & Schmitt commercial I called *"30 Days."* In it I cast Jerry Kaufherr, a brilliant Chicago actor who could do a flawless imitation of Felix Unger, the delicate half of Neil Simon's *Odd Couple*. Unger stands before a judge who is sentencing him to thirty days on bread and water for some unidentified crime. Unger, in his effeminate but persuasive voice, convinces the judge to commute the sentence to 30 days on bread and Hinckley & Schmitt Pure Drinking Water.

I'd created a storyboard for a new Bockman TV commercial. This commercial would feature a cute little blond Goldilocks girl alone in her idyllic suburban house. As the chilly Chicago autumn winds come up, Goldilocks goes to lower the storm windows. One is too hard—she can't budge the panels. Another is too loose—it crashes down and frightens her. But the Bockman window is *just right*, and the little girl easily raises the screen and lowers the storm, then jumps onto her bed beside her family of three stuffed bear toys.

George Gootsan and Dave Oakes had left Filmfair to start their own film studio. I hired them for the Bockman commercial—I was their first client. Ed Binns was too masculine and gutsy to do the voice-over for the soft, gentle Goldilocks commercial. I needed a more kindly, charming, fatherly voice. I chose William Schallert, who'd been a key actor on "The Patty Duke Show," and booked him at a Hollywood studio for the afternoon of March 10, 1980. I chose that date because the International Broadcast Awards dinner was taking place in Hollywood that evening, and I'd been informed in February that my Hinckley & Schmitt campaign was up for three of the eleven radio awards.

The I.B.A. presentation was the first festival of the annual industry award circuit, and was by far the glitziest of the presentations, patterned most closely after the Academy Awards. It was a black-tie event. Tickets cost a hundred dollars per person. Each year they awarded a scant eleven radio trophies, plus another seventeen television trophies—about the same number as the Academy Awards. This allowed enough time in the presentations to have major Hollywood notables on hand to make each trophy presentation, just like the Oscars. This assured good media coverage in Los Angeles.

And, like the Academy Awards, they would not reveal names of winners ahead of time. But with three nominations, I wasn't willing to miss the presentation.

After recording William Schallert, I went to my hotel room and put on my rented tuxedo.

At the end of the evening I returned to my room, put my tux back in its garment bag and went to bed. I'd been just another also-ran, like all those Oscar nominees who show up dressed to kill, but never get to deliver their acceptance speeches.

But the 1980 awards circuit was just starting. During April I received nominations for thirteen more awards, including two ONE SHOW awards in New York. To my amazement, the Bockman and Hinckley & Schmitt radio commercials generated *six* CLIO finalists. Sadly, none of the six won me a trophy.

But I hit pay dirt in New York City that season. On June 24th I booked an afternoon session with Ed Binns in New York to record some new Bockman radio commercials, and stayed to pick up my ONE SHOW trophy at the awards ceremony that evening.

By August my reception room award wall was nearly full—seventeen handsome new gold-framed certificates to add to last year's nine, nearly tripling the display on the wall.

In late June I got a call from Renee Rockoff, a young lady who'd worked with my wife at Brand Advertising. Renee had started as a secretary at Brand, and using her incredible creative talents, had graduated to copywriter. "Do you need a writer?" she asked. Brand had let her go.

I said, "Renee, what I'm actually looking for is a receptionist-secretary. You've done that before. And I'll give you whatever writing opportunities I can. But it might be a step back for you."

"Well, let me think about it."

Apparently the chance to work in the creative environment of Inglehart and Partners, even as a secretary at first, was tempting for Renee. She joined me on July 11 and we began attacking the creative workload before us—Bockman, Hinckley & Schmitt, Leaf Confectionery, and a new assignment to create radio commercials for Hart, Schaffner & Marx, maker of men's wear.

In mid-summer I heard from Dave Bachmann that his friend John Adams was back in town. Apparently he and McCann Erickson in London had had a falling out and they'd given him a golden parachute of one year's salary. He was planning to fulfill a lifelong dream of moving with his wife to the Southwest. There he planned to purchase and run a business of some sort.

I'd been looking for my "front man" for nine years. And who could fill that role better than a former vice president and general manager of McCann Erickson Advertising, the world's second-largest ad agency?

I called John and made a luncheon appointment with him at a restaurant in Palatine. I got down to business:

"You said last year that if you'd had my creative talent working for you at McCann, you could have generated a lot more business. And I believe if I'd had your business skills and contacts working for me, I could have generated a lot more business too. Maybe we have a fit."

John looked at me and said, "Wow." He'd expected a strictly social lunch.

He said, "If I joined you I'd lose my golden parachute—the terms exclude me from re-entering advertising. But can we get together at your office? I'd like to look over your books."

That evening he sat with me in my office, looking over my billings and overhead figures for the years 1977 through 1979.

After half an hour he closed our old-fashioned ledger with its columns of pencil entries. "I'd thought there'd be more there," he said.

That comment summed up the history of my ad career. At age 42 I was a significant creative force in foods and durable goods, the winner of national and international creative awards, and still unable to generate even a paltry million dollars in billings. But couldn't John Adams, with his widespread contacts on two continents, change all that?

"Give me two days to think about this," John said.

In two days John called and said, "I've decided to move to San Diego. Thanks for your offer."

My best hope for a front man disappeared. I discussed the situation with Brother Bill that night on the phone. He said, "Jer, someday you're going to look in your mirror and realize that you've been staring at your front man for years."

In October I got a call from Gregg Perry. He was now Dolly Parton's producer and band leader, and he traveled with the show. Like many country and western personalities of that era, Dolly traveled with her band from gig to gig all over the country in an elegant European-made touring bus with a private cabin for herself and bunks in back for the band.

The bus was heading north to a weekend performance at Mill Run Theater in Niles, Illinois. In their travels Gregg had had lots of opportunities to tell Dolly about the commercials he and I had produced together over the past seven years.

Gregg wondered if I could compile a reel of the jingles he'd done with me so he could play them for Dolly and the band before the performance at Mill Run Theater. Of course I could. Gregg said to look for the big purple bus in the theater parking lot at about 6 P.M. on Friday evening. He'd also have a pair of tickets for me to see the show.

I asked Kathy if she wanted to join me, to meet Dolly Parton and see her show. She wasn't interested.

When I spliced together all my work with Gregg, I had a full twenty-minute reel, going back to our first Morrell Bacon track. We'd done Magicolor Paints for Wickes Lumber, Downyflake Frozen Waffles, Killeen Savings, Killeen First National, Chicagoland Chrysler-Plymouth, and a host of others. As I listened to Gregg's House of Vision sound track, the melodic string section passages reminded me of the work of Andrew Lloyd Weber. Gregg was a musical genius.

In the Mill Run parking lot I was welcomed into the front lounge of Dolly's purple touring bus, and found myself among friends. I'd worked with every one of these musicians and back-up vocalists. Gregg cued up my reel on the tape deck.

Dolly Parton came into the lounge and greeted me with her brilliant smile. In her folksy, charming Smoky Mountains voice she said, "Well, Mr. Inglehart, your reputation preceded you here—we've heard so much about your work with Gregg, and we're all looking forward to hearing it."

For the next twenty minutes Dolly and her band oohed and aahed over every one of our tracks.

Sitting alone that night in a front row seat at Mill Run Theater I discovered something about myself and my fragile ego. It was nice to receive some of the highest praise on earth—*but not alone.* I'd attended that ONE SHOW ceremony in New York alone—as I walked up to the podium that night in New

York to receive my trophy, there was no one at my table sharing my moment of triumph—no wife, no colleague, no sons, no friends. And somehow that mattered very much to me. I needed to have someone smiling proudly at my few moments of glory as I returned to my table. Sitting alone, that glory seemed hollow and empty. That night at Mill Run Theater in Niles, Dolly Parton dedicated one of her opening songs to me, and smiled her thousand-watt smile at me from the stage. Video crews from the local NBC and CBS affiliates were in the back of the theater recording the start of the show for news coverage, and they filmed Dolly's touching little dedication to me.

And I sat alone. A born performer—with no audience.

As January 1981 rolled around, Renee and I had our plates pretty full. Our typewriters were clicking out copy for Hinckley & Schmitt, who wanted a whole new creative campaign for 1981. Leaf Confectionery needed an ad campaign supporting Ronnie Williams, a Rodeo star who they had just signed as the spokesman for their Chaw bubble gum, a product that Leaf packaged in a round can like snuff, to allow little boys the masculine rush of pulling out a snuff-like can and grabbing a pinch of bubble gum.

In April I flew to Florida to record some radio commercials with Jack Nicklaus for Hart, Schaffner & Marx. I hired a Miami sound engineer to bring in professional location equipment, and we recorded Nicklaus in his Palm Beach home. From there I flew to Ft. Worth to meet the rodeo star Ronnie Williams and get some stills of him on his ranch. Comparing Ronnie Williams's humble Texas ranch with what I'd just seen at the elegant Nicklaus home in Palm Beach, I would advise any budding young athlete to pursue golf rather than rodeo.

The 1981 award circuit nominations came out. I was up for a single CLIO and two IBAs. And I was up for *eight* ANDY awards from the New York Advertising Club. One was for Hinckley & Schmitt Radio, two for the Hart, Schaffner & Marx, and *five* for Bockman. I was determined to attend that ANDY presentation in New York on June 3rd.

But not alone.

Kathy and I were close to divorce. We no longer lived under the same roof.

I'd recently run into a friend of a friend—a rather interesting lesbian named Jake something-or-other whom I'd met at a gathering in Chicago. She lived in Manhattan. I phoned her. She was available to accompany me to the New York Advertising Club festival.

That night turned out to be one of the wildest nights of my life.

I met Jake at the mid-town Manhattan hotel where the awards ceremony took place. My Bockman *Granddad* commercial won an ANDY. I returned to my table with my ANDY statuette. Jake smiled proudly for me. I was on a high that Jake and I intensified with a few snorts of cocaine in a dark corner of the hotel lobby. I'd experimented with cocaine prior to this evening, finding that it delivered a euphoria that made me feel ready to take on the world. It also tended to keep me awake all night. It had the same effect on Jake.

After the presentation, Jake wanted to meet briefly with a business partner of hers in an apartment a block away from the hotel. At his apartment Jake's partner tried to sell me a bulletproof vest, a product line he was marketing. I let him know that I was willing to take my chances with stray urban bullets.

Jake was also a co-owner of "The Zoo" which was one of those Manhattan sex clubs that admitted women free and charged men fifty dollars. Jake had some business to attend to at The Zoo that night.

The Zoo was in a basement on Broadway south of Times Square. Singles entered the club, removed all their clothing and receive a percale bed sheet to wrap in like a toga, for their entrance into the dimly lit "Zoo." There was a dark central lounge where they could sit and order drinks while choosing sex partners. Then they took their partners into the shadowy Zoo cages to engage in sex, in partial view of the lounge.

While waiting for Jake I talked with the doorman, who turned out to be a musician. He was impressed that I was an ANDY-winning producer of jingles, hoping I might need a clarinet player like himself. I told him that I produced all my music tracks in Nashville.

After half an hour the doorman apparently remembered his duties as a host and said to me, "By the way, if there's a lady in there you'd like to be with, you can enter free as Jake's guest."

I didn't want to be so undiplomatic as to say that none of those female patrons in there interested me in the least, so I simply said, "It's not exactly my style."

He nodded knowingly, and I realized he assumed I was gay, like Jake. But it was as good an excuse as any—I had no desire to drape myself in a bed sheet to go in and pet one of those horny animals in Jake's Zoo.

About 2 A.M. Jake emerged from her office in the back of The Zoo and took me to one of her favorite nightspots—a transvestite show bar where Jake knew several of the cross-dressed patrons. We watched the stage show, including an act by a rather fetching man in drag doing an animated, effeminate rendition of "I Enjoy Being a Girl" from *Flower Drum Song*.

About 4 A.M. Jake and I had breakfast at an all-night diner. Jake, in her masculine way, proved to be quite an interesting young lady. And quite attractive, too.

In the cab back to my hotel, Jake decided to pick my brains. "Traffic has fallen off at The Zoo this year. I'm thinking we might need a new theme. Maybe a different name. Got any ideas?"

"Um...how about City City Bang Bang?"

A smile darted across her face. "No..."

"I'm probably the wrong person to ask."

"Probably."

Jake dropped me at the New York Hilton.

In the wee small hours of the morning, with a faint tinge of dawn starting to light the sky over Manhattan, I walked down Sixth Avenue a half block, feeling a bit like Sky Masterson in *Guys and Dolls*. I'd booked a guaranteed room at this hotel and would be billed $150 whether I used it or not. But after such a strange night in Never-Never Land—this weird, multi-dimensional island to which I'd hitchhiked over half a lifetime ago—I was feeling a pressing need to return to the comforting, mundane reality of Chicago where I might still be able to get in part of an honest day's work. The effects of the cocaine had worn off, leaving me totally exhausted, but I could sleep just as well on an airplane as in a room at the Hilton. I raised my arm to flag one of the cabs flying down Sixth Avenue and headed for LaGuardia Airport. I boarded a 6 A.M. American flight back to Chicago with my ANDY statue. Arriving in my office about 8 A.M. I closed the door, put my ANDY on the desk, and slept on my sofa until noon.

Waking from my sofa unbathed, unshaven, rumpled, teeth unbrushed, I looked at my cherished new ANDY statue on my desk. I'd need to have a Lucite display case built for the reception room to hold all my award statues—already my ONE SHOW trophy had been stolen right out of the reception room. Who would want a trophy with my name engraved on it? Adding this year's harvest of award certificates, my gold-framed certificate wall would now need to turn the corner in the reception area and begin occupying another wall. Meanwhile, looking at my ANDY's cold, pupil-less stainless steel eyes, I tried to decide if he should stare directly at the door, demanding attention from anyone entering my private office. No, too presentational. Something subtler. Maybe a profile, with him looking contemplatively out the window at the Michigan Avenue skyline. I moved a few desktop papers to reposition him.

Then I noticed one of Renee's scripts that I hadn't seen before. Renee had spent a lot of time coming up with ideas for the new Hinckley & Schmitt campaign. She regularly placed scripts atop the jumble of chaotic disorder on my desk.

The script in my hand was titled *"WATER LILIES."* Had she written it yesterday? It read:

> RAG-TIME MUSIC TRACK.
> ANNOUNCER OVER MUSIC: *"The Hinckley and Schmitt Water Lilies!"*
>
> ANDREWS SISTERS VOCAL:
> *I love pure water,*
> *Clear as can be.*
> *There ain't no water*
> *As healthy for me.*
>
> *No salt or chlorine,*
> *Drink up and keep fit.*
> *There's nothing hiding*
> *In Hinckley and Schmitt.*
>
> *Get some pure water,*
> *Pick up the phone.*
> *You'll love pure water*
> *Delivered at home.*
>
> *Once you have tried it*
> *You won't want to quit,*
> *Oh, so delicious!*
> *Hinckley and Schmitt.*
>
> ANNOUNCER OVER MUSIC: *If you don't love your water, try Hinckley and Schmitt. Discover how delicious water tastes when it's free of salt, chlorine, chemicals, and additives—a water so good, you'll want to sing its praises, too.*

VOCAL:
Get some pure water
From Hinckley and Schmitt!

I opened my office door. "Renee," I called.

She came in from her office. "This script is charming—when did you write it?" I asked.

"The Water Lilies thing? I put that on your desk a week ago. When you didn't comment on it, I assumed you didn't like it."

"It got buried in the mess. I just found it. It's delightful! The Andrews Sisters thing is brilliant."

"It's sort of based on the song 'I Love My Baby.'"

"I can rewrite the tune. And I can work in some sound effect fills between the phrases. Maybe over the middle part we can add tap dancing. Maybe even gargling. Like they're up on a stage tap dancing and gargling."

"Oh, my God!" said Renee.

I rented a Nagra professional tape machine and worked with my son Chris at home to record some wet sound effects to fill the spaces between the song's phrases. We recorded ice cubes falling into a glass, the glass being filled with water, bubbling sounds, swishing and sloshing sounds in a bathtub full of water.

For the band track I hired a keyboard musician who could play ragtime piano, plus a drummer, a banjo player, and a tuba player to do an oom-pah bass line to enhance the ragtime effect. I booked a local female vocal trio. The studio musicians fell into a happy, fast-paced, flippant ragtime beat. The trio's voices blended perfectly in a saucy version of the Andrews Sisters. The girls had fun gargling in three-part harmony for the bridge. I'd booked a tap dancing instructor from a dance studio in Evanston to do a fast tap dance on a slab of marble.

"Seeking the Bubble, Reputation"

With so much going on in the studio I couldn't bear to stay in the sound booth with the recording engineer, listening on the monitors—I walked into the studio to direct the talent up close.

And something occurred to me there in the studio with the musicians, the trio, and the dancer as they brought my music track to life—*I'm still in theater! I'm putting on a show!*

I'd thought my theatrical career had ended in 1957.

No, this was theater. And I was the *producer,* just as I'd dreamed!

My Atwater Beach resolution of 1944 had finally materialized. I had made it into the performing arts. In fact, I'd been there for some time.

*

One of the sound effect fills I'd come up with for the *Water Lilies* commercial involved tapping out a four-note musical bridge on water glasses. Often I'd done this at dinner parties. I could tune a glass's pitch downward slightly by adding water. Given enough glasses, I sometimes was able to play a bar or two of "Twinkle Twinkle Little Star" to delight my guests.

I headed across Michigan Avenue with a pitch pipe in hand, to check out the immense glassware selection at the Crate & Barrel store. I tapped various glasses with a ballpoint pen, listening for the E, E-flat, D, D-flat tones I needed for my four-note bridge. In no time I found four glasses matching the notes. I bought them, recorded them in the sound studio, and mixed them into the *Water Lilies* sound track as a phrase fill, together with the other wet sound effects Chris and I had recorded.

Then I thought, couldn't I make a separate musical commercial by recording *an entire song* on water glasses? It seemed a natural—pure music tuned by pure Hinckley & Schmitt water. On my piano at home I experimented with the tune of "White Coral Bells," a round that my sister Jane had learned in Girl Scouts in the 1950s. It seemed to work nicely, but it required nearly two full octaves of water glasses.

Heading back to the Crate & Barrel I began tapping on various glasses and comparing their tones to the pitch pipe, setting aside those that were close in tone to the musical scale and marking them with stickers. I could tune them to pitch later by adding water. *Ting Ting* on the glasses. *Toot Toot* on the pitch pipe. After an hour I had twenty or so glasses set aside—nearly two octaves. I'd also attracted an audience of customers and clerks who gathered around me to watch, listen, and wonder what the hell I was doing. One gentleman said to me, "Pardon me, I'm trying to learn something about buying glassware."

Next I needed an arrangement. Something that started out simply, then built into two-part harmony. I met with Judy Godfrey, a former neighbor who was also a classical pianist and composer. Judy created a delightful arrangement that combined the simple tune into an intertwined countermelody that ended with a climactic finale. Her arrangement required *four* octaves of glasses.

Back at the Crate & Barrel store I began blowing my pitch pipe, tinking on glasses with my pen and marking the selects. I chose big wine goblets and oversize snifters for the booming notes below middle C and tiny *Schnapps* glasses for the high tinkling notes that Judy had worked into her countermelody. I must have been there for three hours, once again attracting an audience of curious shoppers. A lady came up to me and said, "Excuse me, my husband and I have been watching you, and we've decided you must have fabulous dinner parties."

Monday I booked a professional percussionist, Bob Wessburg, who was performing in the Chicago production of *Cats*. Over the phone I explained to Bob that I wanted him to play a jingle on four octaves of tuned water glasses. He said, "I've tried this at dinner parties, and it doesn't really work. You'd be better off just having me play your composition on a Celeste."

"I can't. The water that tunes the glasses to pitch is Hinckley & Schmitt Water, the product being advertised. It has to be authentic."

"Seeking the Bubble, Reputation"

"Well, I'll bring an assortment of my mallets and we'll see what we can do."

At Universal Recording Studios I set up the water glasses with the help of my copywriter, Renee. We put the glasses equivalent to a piano's white keys on one level. The black keys, the sharps and flats, we placed behind the row of "white notes" on an elevated panel. I carefully tuned them all to pitch, squirting in or removing water with an ear syringe from Walgreens.

Bob Wessburg came in and began tinking on the glasses with his little wooden mallets. "Hey, this works just fine," he said. And he began playing my water glass piano with the same expertise that he played xylophone, marimba and vibes. In an hour we'd recorded and mixed a thrilling, uplifting rendition of Judy Godfrey's "White Coral Bells" composition, including the harmony tracks and countermelodies.

I turned to Renee, "Now it's your turn. Write the announcer script." In half an hour, Renee, with her limitless creative brilliance, came up with the following:

> ANNOUNCER: *"Hinckley and Schmitt brings you this Water Glass Symphony, played by tapping the rims of crystal glasses filled with Hinckley and Schmitt Water—very clean, pure music for your enjoyment, as pure as the Hinckley and Schmitt water which tunes the pitch of each note—delicious water that's free of the chlorine, salts and impurities of tap water or the chemicals of soft drinks—water that makes beautiful music with your body when you drink it or cook with it at home— water that creates a harmonious work atmosphere at offices when it's close and convenient to work areas.*
>
> *"If you like pure music in a clean world full of healthy people—we're playing your song."*

Renee was a natural. Reading this copy, I realized that I was working with one of the cleverest wordsmiths in the business. All I needed now was to cast the right voice to read Renee's elegant script.

Russ Reed was a Chicago talent I'd been using for years. His magnificent vocal cords could portray a voice that sounded somewhere between God and your favorite uncle—trusting, fatherly, authoritative. Deep and folksy.

In another hour of studio time I recorded, edited and mixed the commercial. I called it "Water Symphony," and I knew right away that our *Water Symphony* and *Water Lilies* commercials would be award winners.

*

To finalize our uncontested divorce, Kathy and I hired Audrey Holzer, a young attorney who was riding upward on the coattails of her father, Reginald Holzer, a noteworthy judge of the Cook County Circuit Court. Those coattails would shred eleven years later when the Greylord scandal would send Reginald Holzer to prison for extortion and mail fraud.

Each December the Chicago legal community staged a major theatrical review in which attorneys played various members of the cast. In 1981 Audrey Holzer was cast to impersonate Chicago's Mayor Jane Byrne. The pressures of her rehearsals, plus her legal responsibilities, coupled with the miserable Chicago winter weather, had Audrey functioning during most of December with a case of the flu. Quite likely her Jane Byrne impersonation was more important to her than Inglehart vs. Inglehart. She put off drafting our divorce agreement until the last minute.

On December 23 Audrey's secretary called me to come into their LaSalle Street offices to sign the divorce agreement. My appointment time was set for 5 P.M. I was ushered into a conference room. Audrey Holzer, sniffling and coughing, brought in the eleven-page document, flipped to the final page and showed me where to sign.

I took the document in hand, turned to page one and began reading.

"It's simply a recap of everything you've already agreed to. Are you going to read it?" snapped Ms. Holzer.

"Yes, I am."

She looked at her watch. "It's already after hours, and I have to appear in court with this thing tomorrow."

Looking her straight in the eyes I said firmly, "Ms. Holzer, are you questioning my wisdom in reviewing this document?"

She marched out of the room, her heels clicking briskly down the deserted hallway. She returned in half an hour to see how I was coming along.

I said, "You left out our agreement to provide health insurance for our two sons."

Again she looked at her watch and snapped, "There are no typists. They've all gone home."

"I make my living with a typewriter, Ms. Holzer. Just lead me to one and I'll retype it myself."

She reappeared in five minutes. "I've found someone to retype it. Give me the thing."

I took a copy of *Newsweek* out of my attaché case and began reading as Ms. Holzer's heels again clicked briskly down the hallway.

On Christmas Eve, 1981, Kathy and I were divorced, just five months short of our silver wedding anniversary.

I closed the books on New Year's Eve with billings down 13% from the previous year. After overhead and expenses I was barely able to pay myself a salary equal to the one I'd been paying myself for the past eight years.

*

January 1982 in Chicago was the coldest in memory. For the first time in my life I experienced an outdoor temperature of minus 27 degrees Fahrenheit.

Renee, dealing with marital problems of her own, plunged herself into her work. She was producing a sales training slide film for Farm Progress Insurance, a new client specializing in primary insurance for farm owners. In the frozen, windswept farmlands of Northern Illinois, Renee and her photographer were capturing some outstanding, sensitive visuals that brought to my mind the Robert Frost poem, *Stopping By Woods on a Snowy Evening*.

In February our Water Lilies commercial was nominated for trophies in three categories of the coveted International Broadcast Awards in Hollywood. I told Renee, "There's no way we can find out in advance if we've won. And it's a black-tie event. Two years ago I was up for three of these awards, and came home with nothing but nomination certificates. I question whether either of us should fly to Hollywood for this event."

"Are any of the other finalists from Chicago?" Renee asked.

I looked down the list. "Joe Sedelmaier is up for several of them for his Federal Express TV commercials."

"Let's see if he's going to the dinner. If we win, maybe he could accept for us."

I phoned Sedelmaier Studios. Joe was sending his svelte blond sales rep, Mason Boyd. She agreed to accept for us if we won.

At the March gala event, Mason Boyd made five trips to the podium—three for her boss Joe, and two for Renee and me. Water Lilies, proclaimed the Best Musical Commercial of the Year, also won for Best Local Market Commercial, and was the only commercial to win trophies in two categories.

There are only eleven I.B.A. radio awards given each year. The rest of the world, from London to Sydney, shared the other nine.

Water Lilies and Water Symphony swept the other award nominations that year. By June we had nominations for three CLIOS, in which Water Symphony won a trophy. In New York, the same two commercials racked up three ONE SHOW and four ANDY nominations. Water Symphony won a Chicago ADDY, then went on to win the three-state regional award, and finally became the national trophy winner.

We wound up with eighteen more gold-framed certificates. I was running out of wall space—and also out of patience. I'd entered the award circuit in order to generate more business, but instead my business had declined steadily each year. All I was generating was an ego trip for myself as visitors gawked at our reception room award wall and trophy case. I'd proven to the world that I was a creative giant—and proven to myself that I couldn't turn national publicity into billings. The words of John Adams rang in my memory: "If I'd had creative this good, I could have gotten a lot more business."

He probably could have. I couldn't.

It was the last year I'd enter my commercials in award competitions. But I was now being invited frequently to *judge* the awards. The New England Ad Club flew me to Boston for a weekend of judging.

In 1983 I was a panelist for both the CLIOS and the International Broadcast Awards.

There had to be a better way to gain recognition. And business.

Chapter 20

Survival

In 1984 I continued prospecting for new business in what seemed a never-ending cycle of gaining clients, then losing them—like an exhausted swimmer who finds a log, grabs it, then feels it sinking beneath him.

In the spring Renee and I did some TV storyboards for Ovaltine, but failed to land the account. We were hired to do a series of radio commercials for Plunkett Furniture, one of which I bartered for a magnificent king-size four poster bed copied after an elegant hand-carved 18th century original.

Merrill Chase Galleries in Chicago hired us to do a qualitative market study involving focus groups, to help them determine what motivated the art-buying public. I farmed the project out to acquaintances I'd worked with previously on John Morrell market studies.

On completion and presentation of the study I billed Merrill Chase $18,000. When payment was not forthcoming after sixty days, I made some inquiries. Merrill Chase was in serious financial difficulty. Dun & Bradstreet had them on their short list of current slow-pay, no-pay businesses.

Survival

I phoned Merrill Chase's headquarters to talk to Robert Chase, the president. *The phones were not working!* Were they already down the tubes?

If I couldn't get cash, maybe I could get Merrill Chase to pay me with artwork. I went to the Merrill Chase gallery on Michigan Avenue. I was somewhat familiar with the value of Rembrandt etchings, but Merrill Chase had none. But there was a 400-year-old Duerer woodcut called *"The Four Horsemen of the Apocalypse"* priced at $40,000. I wondered if I could sell it for about half of that to cover my invoice.

I walked down Michigan Avenue to Stanley Johnson Galleries. Mr. Johnson was an authority on classic prints. After a long discussion I became convinced that Duerer's *Four Horsemen* would fetch me $18,000 to $20,000 wholesale in a gallery in Chicago, New York or London.

I phoned Bob Chase. He wouldn't take my call. I told his secretary that I'd cancel my invoice in exchange for Duerer's *Four Horsemen*.

Bob Chase called me next day. "We normally barter at full retail," he said.

I replied, "I know your company is having cash flow problems right now. My invoice is five weeks overdue. I'm offering you a chance to settle your commitment to me for merchandise rather than cash."

Chase wouldn't part with the valuable and rare *Four Horsemen*. I thought of offering the same deal on a Toulouse-Lautrec poster he had, but it wasn't one of the better Toulouse-Lautrec works, and I didn't like it anyway. Finally Chase offered me a pair of Duerer woodcuts that had been acquired from the Norton-Simon collection in California. They dated from the 16th Century, and each was priced at $9,000 retail. In addition Chase would throw in a large Jules Cheret poster from 1890. I said, "Add in that Buhot *Cab Stand* etching, and you've got a deal." Stanley Johnson was an authority on Buhot, and during our meeting he'd educated me on this fine 19th century print maker.

There was a pause. "Okay," Chase said. "You can drop off a copy of the invoice marked 'Paid' and pick up the art at our Michigan Avenue gallery. I'll call them now."

The Buhot *Cab Stand* etching had been moved that morning to their Oakbrook gallery. The Michigan Avenue gallery manager offered to have it shipped back for me, but I wanted to get this matter wrapped up in one day. The manager then offered me a Francois Millet etching of equal value instead. I was lukewarm on the Millet, and I'd been drooling in anticipation of owning that Buhot etching. But I settled for the Cheret, the Millet, and the two Duerer woodcuts.

I hung the four prints temporarily on the walls of my condo as I examined means of liquidating them. In a matter of days I'd fallen in love with all of them. I couldn't bear to sell them. I still have them. And several years later I purchased a print of the Buhot *Cab Stand* from Stanley Johnson.

Two months after bartering art for research, Bob Chase called me. By selling his elegant offices in Northbrook, he'd managed to make his company solvent again. He was now operating out of unpretentious but functional offices at Sky Harbor office park.

Bob wanted Inglehart and Partners to handle the advertising for Merrill Chase Galleries. "Anyone who can learn as much about art as you did, as quickly as you did, should be handling our advertising."

So we added Merrill Chase Galleries to our client roster.

Early the following year, Hinckley & Schmitt decided to have us handle the advertising for their New Orleans brand, called Ozone Waters. I negotiated a deal to hire Pete Fountain, the famous Dixieland clarinet player, to be Ozone's spokesman, and shot a TV commercial of Pete for Ozone in his New Orleans office.

Three more new clients rolled in. We signed a Denver-based company called Newstrack that produced a weekly audio cassette news roundup for executives too busy to scan the newspapers.

We got a Chicago answering service that was coming out with a beeper pager—the Becker Beeper—which seems so primitive nowadays, when everyone has a cell phone.

Our third new client was a chain of men's clothing stores called Bachrach's. Mr. Bachrach, while commuting by automobile from his headquarters in Decatur, Illinois, to his stores as far away as Milwaukee, had heard our Hinckley & Schmitt commercials on Chicago's Newsradio station, and he'd called the station to find out who produced them. Bachrach's needed an ad agency for radio advertising.

Early in 1984 a substantial new client simply walked in the door—the John Butler Company, a Chicago manufacturer of toothbrushes. We gained this account strictly on the strength of Inglehart and Partners' reputation, the same way we'd gained the Bockman and Bachrach accounts.

Bockman was on a roll that spring—they now had eight Chicagoland stores, all built on funds from Dave Bachmann's inheritance, together with substantial financing from Northern Trust Bank. But Bockman wasn't showing any profits yet.

Neither was Inglehart and Partners. Despite all our hard work, good creative, and new account acquisitions, I generated just over a half-million in billings that year.

I was dating a young lady named Mary Ann Keller who worked for Ogilvy & Mather's Chicago public relations office. It was a small office in one of the Wacker Drive buildings—so small they shared a fax and copy machine with other tenants in the building.

One day while Mary Ann was dispatching a fax at the communal fax machine, a man she'd spoken with from time to time came in for a photocopy. He ran a one-man graphics design studio on the next floor. "Do you know anybody, Mary Ann, who does marketing plans?"

"My boyfriend does marketing plans."

"I have a client, Northwest Community Hospital. I do their brochures. They want a marketing plan."

A marketing plan is a document that sets forth a strategy for marketing a product or service. The plan includes an analysis of the product or service and its competitors, and a study of the strengths and weaknesses of each in the marketplace, then explains how the product or service can be, or should be, positioned to fulfill a marketplace need. The plan explains how the product or service is to be promoted and distributed according to a strategy. Marketing plans can be simple and straightforward, or elaborately supported by extensive qualitative and quantitative research. I'd been exposed to enough marketing plans at Lillienfeld and Young & Rubicam to know how to prepare them. I'd written several for my John Morrell products.

For $5,000 I did a quick market study for Northwest Community Hospital and presented a marketing plan to their executive staff. The plan focused on community newcomers, presumably the only source of increased market share for the hospital, short of putting in a state-of-the-art cancer or cardiac facility and promoting it.

I proposed that they buy periodic name lists of newcomers, and phone those households to tell them about the hospital. I suggested that the newcomers be invited in for a tour and a slide show. I recommended offering the newcomers premiums—perhaps coupons for discounts on school physicals for their kids, or maybe a drug safe for dangerous medicines. The executive staff liked the plan. The marketing director said, "When can you get started on this?"

"On what?"

"Everything. The slide show."

Renee got to work writing a slide show—a fifteen minute study of the life of a newcomer mom who was pregnant. One of her kids gets a high fever in the night and she rushes the child to the emergency room. Her elderly disabled father needs day care. Her husband is a local high school basketball coach, and one of the kids on his team breaks a leg during practice. Eventually mom goes into labor and has her baby at the hospital. Renee covered all the key hospital services in a series of beautifully written vignettes, around song lyrics she wrote, calling it *We're Here for You*.

The hospital quickly approved our script. I set about composing a melody and hired a local studio guitarist, Ray Tate, to play the music in seven or eight different treatments, one for each of the vignettes. He did a remarkable job. I hired a full studio combo and recorded a full band track, and brought in vocalist Judy Maslanka who I'd used on my WBBM-FM commercial years before. Her warm alto voice was sympathetic and maternal—perfect for *We're Here for You*.

I booked my son Christopher to photograph the slide film. For our leading lady we interviewed a number of pregnant women who would be delivering their babies at Northwest Community Hospital sometime that summer. We selected a woman named Pam List because she was photogenic, and also had a couple of cute blond daughters and a good-looking husband, all of whom we could cast in the film. Chris and I began filming the List family in their home, in parks, in the hospital, and at their Lamaze classes. Chris's sensitive photography yielded a huge range of touching scenes.

Chris forewarned me—when Pam List went into labor, he didn't think he'd be up to filming the birth. So he showed me how to use his cameras and his strobe lights and gave me a crash course in professional photography. I would film the birth myself.

I told Pam List to page my Becker Beeper as soon as she went into labor, even before she called her doctor. "I don't even care if it's a false alarm, Pam, I can't risk being late—I've got to be there to set up my equipment."

My grandmother died in Oshkosh, but I couldn't attend her funeral because of the risk that Pam might go into labor when I was three hours away from Chicago.

Pam's labor pains started one evening in early September. I rushed to her labor-delivery-recovery room at the hospital with Mary Ann Keller, who would act as my assistant cameraperson. We dressed in scrubs and began setting up Chris's equipment. We caught some magnificent shots of the couple going through their Lamaze exercises, David looking deeply concerned for his wife as he massaged her back, guided her through the Lamaze breathing and encouraged her, and Pam's pretty face looking alternately pained or calm between contractions. There were touching expressions of trust, sincerity, and love between them. They were in their own world, oblivious to either me or Mary Ann and our intrusive strobe lights. When both of my sons had been born, fathers were not allowed in delivery rooms, which at that time were cold, clinical operating rooms with their sterile white tile walls and racks of intimidating floodlights. By contrast, Pam's labor-delivery-recovery room was comfortable and welcoming, decorated like a room at home.

An obstetrics nurse came in and examined Pam. I caught her expression of urgency as she saw that Pam was fully dilated.

The obstetrician, masked and in surgical garb, entered the room as the crew of attendants quickly, expertly converted the bed and the lighting for delivery. Things began happening rapidly. I was running through a roll of film every couple of minutes, passing the empty camera to Mary Ann, who handed me the reloaded one as she quickly removed the exposed roll and put in a fresh one. *Click! Click! Click! Click! Click!*

I filmed the arrival into this world of Mark Daniel List, their first son, all red and gooky and covered with blood splotches, squirming and screaming his little head off, his red veined umbilical cord still attached to his mother. I filmed David tenderly kissing his wife, and cutting his son's cord, which splashed drops of blood onto his mother's face. Through it all, Mary Ann and I were totally invisible to the couple, the doctor, and the crew of nurses who went through their routine of bathing the boy and putting him into a tiny gown and a cute little cap. I snapped shots of his eyes, moist from the postnatal eye drops.

The nurse snuggled the tiny baby into Pam's arms and I caught a shot in which she looked like Mother Earth, smiling calmly at her husband. I caught the look of pride on David's face.

This was the birth I'd missed—two births, actually—in 1958 and 1961. Finally I got to witness the magic of birth. Today that little kid is probably a freshman in college. With the initials M.D., I wonder if he's destined to be a physician. I'd like to see him. Somehow I feel like family. I am indebted to this couple for allowing me to vicariously fill in two experiences missing from my own life.

By December I had all the actors and actresses recorded for narrations, the sound track mixed, and the visuals edited down into a sensitive two-projector slide film powered by a dissolve unit. Ray Tate's music was moving and thrilling throughout, including a dramatic, climactic build leading up to the birth scene, when I segued to a live track of voices in the delivery room, the doctor encouraging his patient over Pam's agonized cries as her baby emerged into the world. She delivered quickly and naturally, without anesthesia.

*

1985 was a tough year.

Renee left. She was smart enough to see there was no longer enough income to support two writers.

A fellow named Jerry Svec, who ran a one-man marketing firm in Mount Prospect, hired me to produce some radio commercials. I thought for a short time that Jerry might be the "front man" I needed, so I took him with me to Houston to make a new business presentation at the Montgomery County Medical Center. We didn't get the account. And when I received Jerry's payment for the radio production, he'd paid only half of my invoice.

The house in Evanston that Kathy and I had owned was sold after our divorce. I used my share of the proceeds to purchase a lovely condo in a historic landmark building in Evanston. My condo was occupied by rental tenants at the time. I told them I would not be renewing their lease when it expired in May 1985, when I planned to move into the condo myself. But soon after moving in I realized the place was too empty for me to enjoy alone. I rented it out and moved into my downtown office, now in a residential building at 405 N. Wabash, where there were large closets and two bathrooms. I installed a Murphy bed that folded up during the day into what looked like a cabinet for office supplies. For a single man working long hours, living in my office was quite adequate, and the views from the 44th floor were spectacular. By then I was down to a single employee—my administrative assistant, Nancy Linck, who had her own office at the other end of the apartment. I often worked late into the night and slept past 9 A.M. When I awoke Nancy would be at work in her office with the coffee made.

Hinckley & Schmitt had used me for creative development and production for over a decade. This earned regular fees—but the big money in advertising was in placing media. Hinckley & Schmitt placed their own media, using an internal "house" agency.

They had a couple of hundred trucks plying the streets of Chicagoland every day, each truck carrying advertising posters on the back and side panels. Hinckley & Schmitt made estimates of the monthly exposures of their truck posters, compared them with similar rates charged for advertising posters on city busses, and came up with a "value" for this advertising space. They bartered their truck posters for spots on Radio Station WBBM, the only broadcast medium they ever used. To supplement this barter, they budgeted $500,000 additional for cash media buys. At the time, $500,000 was more than my total annual billing at Inglehart and Partners.

I'd been buying WBBM for my other clients for more than ten years. I used the services of independent and freelance media buyers who knew what the bottom prices were because they also bought for much larger advertisers. In 1985 my WBBM buys included Merrill Chase Galleries and the Bockman Company. I had a feel for what we could buy for Hinckley & Schmitt.

I approached the Hinckley & Schmitt marketing manager Gordon Frey, a fellow even more abrasive than myself. He'd just finished negotiating his 1985 media buy with WBBM. I said, "Gordon, maybe I can save you some money. If I can negotiate a better media buy for you, would be willing to place your media buy through Inglehart and Partners this year?"

He scowled at me. "Nobody can buy WBBM cheaper than I can. I've been working with them for years." But he showed me the schedule of time slots he'd negotiated for that season, combined with the barter for his truck posters.

I went back to my office and analyzed Gordon's buy. I was buying the same time slots for considerably less. Next day I came back to Gordon Frey and said, "If you'll let me place this buy at the price you've budgeted, I'll give Hinckley & Schmitt an advertising agency commission of 15%."

"And you'll still make money on it?" I nodded. "What about the truck posters?"

"Well," I said, "you can keep the truck posters to sell as you please."

Frey picked up his phone and called the sales manager of WBBM. He yelled and cursed him out for cheating him, and demanded to renegotiate his buy within the price structure of my buys.

I'd won. But I'd lost. I should have understood that I was dealing with a major ego problem in Gordon Frey when he commented that nobody could beat his WBBM buy. Perhaps I should have found a more subtle way of presenting my buy, rather than hitting him over the head with the fact that I could buy better than he could, and still make a profit, meaning that he'd been wasting at least $100,000 of his company's money each year for quite some time. No doubt the crowning blow was my tactless comment on the truck posters. The poster barter had been Frey's idea years ago, and he believed it gave him a decisive edge in negotiating with WBBM. My comment implied that his poster program was worthless. That was more than Frey could stomach.

So I saved Hinckley & Schmitt a lot of money that year. And I wound up with nothing for myself.

Worse still, my relationship with Hinckley & Schmitt through Gordon Frey became very tense, and deteriorated rapidly.

I had to hand it to the WBBM sales representative that had been dealing with Frey all those years. He'd caused Frey to think that his buys were unbeatable, and that Frey was the best media buyer in town. That's real talent. Maybe *he* should have been my "front man."

The following month Hinckley & Schmitt decided to make my *Water Symphony* radio commercial into a TV commercial. They bartered an arrangement with a Hollywood TV production studio owned by a friend of one of their sources. Gordon Frey may have considered having the studio's director produce the TV commercial without involving me—but when the director confronted the prospect of trying to set up and tune all those water glasses, then finding a percussionist who could play them, he said he wanted me to be involved.

In making the *Water Symphony* radio commercial, I'd recorded a melody track plus a harmony and countermelody track that I'd mixed down to a single track for the finished commercial. To duplicate that on-camera, there would have to be two percussionists. My own percussionist in Chicago, Bob Wessburg, was still involved with the musical *Cats*, but he said he could get away for a day's shoot in Hollywood. I wanted Bob to be paired with a female percussionist on camera.

The studio director sent me test footage of a pretty blonde girl he wanted to cast as the female percussionist—a typical Hollywood model standing in front of several filled water glasses, smiling a plastic smile, tapping the glass rims, pretending to play them. I phoned the director. "She's not even *playing* those glasses! She's no percussionist!"

"True," he replied, "but we can make it *look* like she's playing them."

"It won't fool anyone," I said. That's Hollywood for you. I told him I'd find a female percussionist myself.

In 1984 I'd seen the Chicago stage production of the new *Pirates of Penzance*, the marvelous New York Shakespeare Festival production that virtually re-invented Gilbert and Sullivan. In the orchestra pit I'd watched a female percussionist do a brilliant job. Normally you never notice the percussionist, but this production called for a series of tuned drums, called "Boo-Bams," for the number "A Policeman's Lot Is Not a Happy One." Watching the drums being played is a performance in itself. If she could play boo-bams, she could play my water glasses.

A phone call to the Musicians' Union revealed the name of the *Pirates* percussionist. I called her. She didn't want an on-camera job—she'd put on too much weight during the past year. But she referred me to another young female percussionist she'd worked with, a lady named Theresa Knight who happened to live in a suburb of Los Angeles.

I had the Hollywood studio call in Theresa Knight to record a videotape demo of her and send me the tape. Theresa was an interesting young Chinese-American lady. She looked pretty good. I told the studio to book her for a Friday pre-production meeting prior to a Monday shoot. I packed my four octaves of water glasses into a pair of padded plastic camera equipment cases and flew off to Los Angeles.

Theresa Knight stood up and played my water glasses with the same ease and authority as Bob Wessburg had. I hired her.

Sunday night Bob flew in from Chicago. On Monday, the day of the shoot, the costume crew dressed him in a tuxedo. The studio had hired a very good Hollywood makeup artist plus a hair stylist for Theresa. Together they transformed my interesting Chinese-American percussionist into an absolutely *fascinating*-looking Chinese-American woman. The costume people dressed her diminutive young figure in a transfixing black cocktail dress. Any man seeing this girl in a bar would scramble for an opener to get to talk to her.

It was thrilling to watch my water glass piano being played by a pair of experts who moved through the musical rifts and flourishes with synchronized authority.

On the Wednesday following this commercial shoot, Mary Ann Keller flew to Los Angeles to meet me. We spent the July 4th holiday weekend scuba diving in the Pacific Ocean off La Jolla, California.

Arriving home on Monday, July 8th, I dropped Mary Ann off at her apartment. She began listening to the messages on her answering machine.

Message No. 3 was from my son Jamie, looking for me. He'd been unable to find me at my office, and I hadn't left a number where I could be contacted in California.

Jamie's voice on the answering machine was very strained and distressed as he informed Mary Ann that his brother Chris

Survival

had been in a very serious accident on his motorcycle on Friday evening, July 5th. His life had been saved through open head surgery that night. He was in a coma, in intensive care at Northwestern Memorial Hospital downtown.

Messages 4, 5, and 6 were from Jamie, reporting little change over the weekend in his brother's comatose condition in the intensive care unit.

Message 7 was from my mother, clearly struggling to restrain her tears as she tried to leave a consoling message for Mary Ann to relay to me.

Chris's eyes were closed. He was in a tortured coma. His head was swathed in bandages. The right side of face was battered and disfigured, and his eye orbits looked misaligned. His entire face, as well as his right knee, appeared to be held together with stitches.

He was not resting easily.

But he was alive.

The accident had occurred as he was heading north on State Street on his motorcycle—a heavy, powerful Japanese import. Approaching the busy intersection of Ohio Street, a young man driving a car in the opposite direction had made an illegal left turn in front of Chris, and Chris had plowed into the young man's car.

An ambulance arrived quickly to take my unconscious son to Northwestern Memorial Hospital, the nearest trauma center. The neurological surgeon on call, Dr. Leonard Cirillo, was one of the most brilliant and innovative brain surgeons in the country. He immediately opened Chris's skull to relieve the pressure of internal bleeding that would have otherwise terminated brain functions—and his life—in a matter of minutes.

Had the accident occurred a few blocks further north, Chris would have been taken to a different emergency room—one better qualified for gunshot wounds than brain surgery, and without the services of Dr. Leonard Cirillo. If this had happened, I would probably have only one son today.

My office, where I also lived, was just eight blocks from the hospital, so I was able to visit Chris on a daily basis—sometimes in the morning before work, sometimes midday, sometimes in the evening, often two or three times daily.

On the day of my second such visit, the nurse in the I.C.U. gave me information on the hospital's support group for families of head injury victims. I attended the first meeting the following afternoon, on a Thursday. I sat with parents and siblings whose lives had been damaged or destroyed because one of their family had suffered a head injury. "Well, yesterday was the sixth anniversary of the accident, and also the first time I think he recognized who I am, but I can't be sure..." Until that meeting I had assumed that Chris would eventually recover from his injuries, just as, sixteen years earlier, his broken arm had finally healed after a fall from a porch. The support group forced me to the hard reality that my son might never be the same—might never again communicate or recognize me. He might spend the rest of his life in a care facility attended by nurses.

But by the end of the weekend, three days later, I was noticing changes. His comatose expressions seemed to vary. On Monday he opened his eyes and looked around. He could hear people speaking to him, although he didn't seem to understand what they were saying. That afternoon Chris's bed, together with his feeding tube and I.V., was wheeled out of the I.C.U. to a private hospital room.

By Thursday morning Chris could sit up in a wheelchair for a few hours each day and look at the world around him with groggy curiosity. He could stand up for a few moments with support from two male nurses, but he couldn't take a step.

While he was sitting in his wheelchair, I handed him a package of 35-millimeter film. Chris had worked as a photographer for several years. He held the box in his hand a moment, although his eyes were fixed on the window rather

Survival

than the box of film. His fingers seemed to study and recognize the box without his ever looking down at it. Then suddenly, with one hand, he removed the plastic film canister from the box, popped the plastic lid off with his thumb and dumped the film cartridge into his palm, all in a single, coordinated motion—a motion he'd performed thousands of times in the past years. It seemed promising to me. He could neither speak, nor walk, nor swallow—but his brain remembered how to direct his hand to remove a 35-millimeter film cartridge from its package in a series of smooth motions.

That afternoon, as I sat in the support group discussion, I resolved never to return to that group's meetings again. These meetings were for people with far greater problems than Chris's. My son seemed to be recovering, while their loved ones were not. I didn't belong in this group. My comments, if I made any, wouldn't be supportive, and could perhaps intensify their grief.

In the weeks that followed, under the guidance of a staff of superb therapists, Chris relearned how to walk a few steps each day. And he seemed to be recognizing some habits and patterns he'd known before the accident. He came to expect that when family members visited him, he'd get a hug on arrival and another hug on departure. Soon, when a nurse or therapist attended to him or questioned him, he'd occasionally greet or dismiss them with a hug.

Then he learned that he could pretend to participate in conversations by nodding at the speaker and mumbling brief responses like "Yep!" or "Um-hum." For a day or so he had his brother convinced that he was following conversations, until Jamie realized that he would occasionally nod and say "Yup!" when no one had spoken. And he had little or no understanding of the words being spoken. He seemed to recognize some of them from before, but couldn't attach them to a meaning.

A speech therapist tested his progress with a series of questions:

"Chris, are you in a hospital, or in an airport?" Chris got that one wrong.

"Am I a man, or am I a woman?" Chris got it right. One out of two isn't bad.

"Look out the window, Chris, and tell me, is it day or night?" Wrong again. Oh, well.

Step by step, word by word, Chris progressed in his return to reality. Day by day, a few million of his brain cells would either relearn something, or transfer their functions to cells in another lobe of his brain. Soon he was speaking simple sentences. One day, when his girlfriend, Barb Zaretsky, was visiting, he pointed to the feeding tube stuck into an incision in his abdomen and asked, "How did this get here?" Within a few days he passed the "cookie test," meaning he could now swallow food without suffocating, and the feeding tube was removed.

The trial for the young man who'd turned his car in front of Chris was slated for a date in August. I decided not to attend. I did not want to see the kid that had caused the accident. It wouldn't benefit me to have the image of that boy's face with me for life. He'd made a mistake—a mistake that Chris, or Jamie, or I might have made. And I had no intention of filing a lawsuit against the kid or his family. Chris's medical bills were being covered partially by the other driver's insurance settlement, but mostly by the State of Illinois, and no amount of money awarded by a jury would speed the restoration of my son's damaged brain. He was already receiving the best care that money could buy.

Chris was transferred from the hospital to the Rehabilitation Institute of Chicago, an affiliated organization in a neighboring building. R.I.C. is regarded as the top rehab facility in the country. Chris was lucky to receive such state-of-the-art care. And I would like to be able to say that these fine institutions made no mistakes. But there were two mistakes.

Survival

Dr. Cirillo, the brain surgeon who'd opened Chris's head on the night of the accident, returned after three weeks for a post-op checkup. He was surprised to see that Chris hadn't had facial surgery to repair his eye orbits and the small impact craters denting his skull. Cirillo had instructed that this be done weeks ago, and his instructions hadn't been followed. Such surgery involved wiring the misaligned bones to a metal "halo" mounted around his head, so the bones could knit in correct alignment. Now all the bones had begun to knit incorrectly. They would all have to be *re-broken* in order to be aligned. I asked Dr. Cirillo, "Is this operation mandatory, or is it cosmetic?"

"It's cosmetic."

I turned to Chris's girlfriend. "Barb, take a good look at Chris. How does his face look to you?"

"It's different—but I think it's fine."

"This surgery would be very traumatic, but only cosmetic. Do you think it's worth it?" I asked her.

Barb looked again closely at Chris's face. After a few moments she said, "I think he looks just fine."

Chris's mother agreed with Barb.

The family made a major medical decision on behalf of my son. "Dr. Cirillo," I said, "we're going to pass on that surgery."

The next mistake was the most distressing of all.

Immediately after the accident, Chris's physicians had put him on a daily dose of 100 milligrams of Dilantin, a drug manufactured by the Squibb Pharmaceutical Company to prevent seizures. Dilantin was prescribed routinely in cases of traumatic head injury. Most victims of severe head injury would be advised to stay on Dilantin for life.

Before Chris entered the Rehab Institute, the hospital staff had monitored the level of Dilantin in Chris's blood regularly. The tests had revealed that Chris's blood levels of Dilantin were too low, so they temporarily raised the dose from a maximum dose of 100 milligrams to a double dose of 200 milligrams. The double dose was on his record when he was transferred from the hospital to the Rehab Institute. Unfortunately, the dosage was never questioned at the Rehab Institute, nor did they follow through with blood level monitoring.

Kathy, Jamie, and I had never heard of Dilantin. It was simply one of a veritable cocktail of medicines being given to Chris daily.

After the third week in the Rehab Institute, Chris began to regress. He was losing his coordination. His speech was deteriorating.

I'd been able to withstand the emotional impact of Chris's condition because he'd been making steady progress each day since the accident.

Now he was going in reverse, retreating slowly back toward the vegetative state he'd been in when I first saw him in the I.C.U.

It was more than I could bear. The hopeful, steady progress he'd made was now in reverse. Just like the mental patients under Robin Williams' care in the movie *Awakenings*, Chris's mind was slowly retreating back toward a comatose state.

Accompanying the deterioration was a mounting degree of paranoia in Chris. One night at bedtime I arrived at Chris's hospital room with Mary Ann Keller. Chris was in a state of severe mental anxiety. He spoke in anxious whispers of a nurse hiding in the closet who would come out and harm him if he went to sleep. I tried to calm him, but despite my expertise with words on paper for ads and jingles, I was quite incompetent when it came to finding soothing, calming words for my son. So I said to Chris, "Maybe Mary Ann will sing you a song."

In her lovely, warm soprano voice, Mary Ann began singing softly to Chris—a song about a child growing up in Michigan. *"There's peace in the colors of morning in Michigan where I was born..."*

Slowly Chris relaxed. He fell asleep as Mary Ann sang.

Afterward, driving north on the Outer Drive to take Mary Ann home, I burst into uncontrollable sobs and had to pull over and stop the car. I was losing my son.

A few days later the physician in charge of Chris, an Indian or Pakistani doctor named Singh, finally made the connection between Chris's mental deterioration and the 200 milligram daily dose of Dilantin—an overdose he had never questioned. That day, August 12, he ordered a blood test. The level of Dilantin in Chris's blood was so high, it was off the scale—it couldn't be measured. Dr. Singh immediately took Chris off the drug.

Jamie went to Barnes & Noble and purchased a copy of the *Physician's Desk Reference,* a guide to pharmaceuticals. The description of the symptoms of a Dilantin overdose matched the symptoms of regression Chris was suffering. Jamie showed the description to Kathy and me. I was furious. I was tempted to give a copy of the book to Dr. Singh, but decided that an insult of such magnitude could be counterproductive.

Instead Jamie and I began monitoring Chris's drug intake daily, watching for other errors.

Within a week, Chris's blood levels of Dilantin were normal. His physical and mental deterioration stopped, and he began to improve again.

A week later Dr. Singh's secretary asked me to come into his office. Dr. Singh asked me why my son Jamie and I were monitoring Chris's drugs. I explained that I was concerned about the Dilantin overdose, and thought it might be best if Jamie and I kept an eye on Chris's drugs.

Dr. Singh pulled out a pencil chart he'd made for me, showing that Chris's Dilantin levels had been corrected when the dose was terminated, then resumed at 100 milligrams. Then he said, "I don't want you and your son hovering over the nursing staff like this. You're making everyone nervous."

"Dr. Singh," I replied, "I've dealt with professionals in many fields all my life, and found that the only ones who get nervous when someone is watching them are those who are either inexperienced or incompetent, and fearful of being caught making a mistake. If any members of your staff are disturbed about Jamie's and my questions about Chris's drugs or test results, in the interest of Chris's health, I respectfully ask you to withdraw them from duty on Chris's behalf."

I was *soooo* tempted to add, "Are Jamie and I making *you* nervous, Dr. Singh?" But I held my tongue.

Within three weeks Chris was out of the Rehab Institute.

That December I hired Chris to manage a photo shoot of the rock star, Ace Frehly, for a magazine ad for my client, Fretted Industries, a manufacturer of guitars and mandolins. Chris was still a bit fuzzy at the time, but sufficiently recovered to handle the photographic assignment quite capably.

The remaining clients of Inglehart and Partners were The Bockman Co., The Butler Co., Hinckley & Schmitt, GC Services, Merrill Chase Galleries, and Fretted Industries.

In October, the elderly owner of The Butler Company decided to sell out and retire. In order to get top dollar from any prospective buyer, he followed professional advice in three ways:

He graduated himself to Board Chairman, and installed his son as President and C.E.O. The son was a flaky hippie with no business experience, who walked around the office wearing a belt with a large buckle that had a brass relief of a marijuana leaf. But the son was forty, whereas the father was over seventy. The adviser had said, "Companies managed by septuagenarians don't bring top dollar."

The next piece of advice he followed was to fire the small but dependable accounting firm that had served him for decades. He hired Arthur Andersen.

The final bit of advice was to fire Inglehart and Partners and hire a major ad agency, which he did. The owner sold out to a Japanese firm and, I guess, lived happily ever after.

Survival

By October the Bockman Company was in financial trouble. Dave Bachmann had attempted to do what the dot-coms tried fifteen years later—build the company with no regard for the bottom line. Bockman Company's checks started bouncing. In November, Bockman declared bankruptcy, owing me about $25,000. I took the small cash reserves I had and paid off the small suppliers who'd provided me with services for Bockman. If this bankruptcy took Inglehart and Partners down with it, I wanted to be certain that the only suppliers that got stiffed were those big enough to afford it. There were four I never paid: CBS, ABC, NBC, and the Chicago Tribune Company.

My relationship with Gordon Frey at Hinckley & Schmitt, my oldest client, had steadily deteriorated ever since the fiasco about his WBBM buy. Gordon Frey was a complex character. He was bright, intellectual, and charming. He could win almost anyone with his warm smile and a few compliments. But Frey either respected you or hated you. I'd seen him speak rudely to many of his employees. I'd often seen him humiliate his wife publicly.

In November, I billed him for printing of a massive run of brochures, delivered to eight locations across the country. The bill included $832 for shipping. He called me on the phone, cursed me out and said; "Last August I shipped a fucking *Oldsmobile* to California for less than $300. You're charging me $832 to ship some goddamned *brochures?*"

"How much did that Oldsmobile weigh, Gordon?"

"A ton and a half, maybe."

"Gordon, those brochures weighed five and a half tons. And we shipped them to eight separate plants. I'd say you got a deal." There was a pause. Gordon hated to be proven wrong.

"I'd say you just lost our account."

In December I received a letter from Hinckley & Schmitt announcing the termination of my services.

It was a tough year. But I wasn't ready to give up.

Chapter 21

Scene Change

In the closing months of '85 I thought about the phoenix—the mythological bird that dies and burns, then experiences a rebirth, rising from its own ashes to fly again.

My son Chris had risen from the ashes of his own near-death. The medical records of Northwestern Memorial Hospital described his recovery as "absolutely miraculous."

Looking at the ashes of Inglehart and Partners I wondered if my business could somehow be reborn. The Bockman bankruptcy had put my ad agency on life support, unable even to breathe on its own, much less fly. CBS, ABC, NBC, and the Chicago Tribune Company would soon be filing lawsuits to collect their invoices.

Hinckley & Schmitt, having fired Inglehart and Partners, needed someone on staff to handle their advertising. They hired a young lady with advertising experience named Laura Goldblatt, who would head up the Hinckley & Schmitt in-house advertising agency under Gordon Frey. Before taking the job Laura called me and asked if she could buy me a drink and pick my brains about Hinckley & Schmitt, and particularly about Gordon Frey, a person she'd met and found confusing. Over a

Scene Change

gin-and-tonic I said, "Laura, you've got to handle Frey carefully. He has a giant ego. He'll either charm you or humiliate you. If he starts to charm you, don't let him take you to dinner. If he ever starts to pick on you, it's all over. Get out before he rags you to death."

Just one year later, in mid-December, I heard Renee's Hinckley & Schmitt Christmas commercial on WBBM. We'd recorded the commercial as a Christmas companion to *Water Symphony*. I needed to bill Hinckley & Schmitt for re-use fees for the announcer, as well as for Bob Wessburg, the percussionist who'd played the water glasses on the commercial. Also, as a dues-paying member of the Musicians' Union myself, I was entitled to a handsome quintuple-scale use payment as music director.

I called Gordon Frey to tell him that the re-use fees would come to $880. He said he wouldn't pay it.

"Well," I said, "if I don't pay those talents, Gordon, then Hinckley & Schmitt will be blacklisted by AFTRA, Screen Actors' Guild, and the Musicians' Union. You'd be hard-pressed to produce any decent radio or TV commercials without professional union talent." Frey knew that if he didn't pay, I would probably be the one to inform the talent agencies and get his company blacklisted. He reluctantly agreed to pay. In closing I asked, "How's Laura Goldblatt working out?"

"I fired that fucking Jew-bitch six months ago."

That was my last communication with Gordon Frey.

In January Dave Bachmann came to my office with a plan. The Bockman Company was in reorganization. He'd been contacted by the Maurice Rothschild Company, a firm I remembered from my youth, when Rothschild operated a five-story clothing store on Fountain Square in downtown Evanston. The clothing store had been gone for many years. I was unaware that the principals had entered a different business— that of reviving failed businesses.

The World is a Stage

Rothschild had purchased the Bockman Company. Under Rothschild's ownership, Dave Bachmann was to continue retail operations in his eight suburban stores. Dave wanted me to continue handling the advertising—on a prepaid basis. It sounded pretty good. Together, Dave and I called on my four angry creditors, CBS, NBC, ABC, and the Chicago Tribune Company.

"Look," I said to each of them, "over the course of the past seven years, we've placed a lot of Bockman advertising with you. Now Bockman is bankrupt, and I can't pay the last invoices. But those unpaid sums amount to only about 1.5% of all the Bockman media we've bought from you over the years. Now Bockman is reorganized under Maurice Rothschild. If you'll *forgive* those last invoices and wipe them off your books, it'll be like giving me a 1.5% discount for seven years of prompt payment. And we can begin again under the new Bockman Company. In the course of a few months, you'll probably earn enough from the new Bockman Company to make that 1.5% discount well worth your while."

All four creditors bought the idea. My debts were erased.

Perhaps my little phoenix embryo was stirring.

GC Services had stood by me from the very beginning, providing me with small accounts and projects that helped pay bills. In February of 1986 they came through again. They were standardizing their sales effort, and wanted me to create a notebook-size photographic flip chart to support sales presentations. My son Chris and I set out to dream up the visuals and begin the photography. In three months I delivered 300 copies of a handsome flip chart. And I received some resuscitating income.

Next I thought about that slide show I'd done for Northwest Community Hospital with Renee's lovely story surrounding childbirth, and my son Chris's sensitive, touching photos, coupled with the music track I'd composed and produced. The film could be recast, rewritten and reproduced to work for other hospitals. Perhaps I should try to syndicate the film and the program. Lots of hospitals across the country were desperate to build their market share.

I fleshed out the supporting program I'd built around the film—the brochures, the premiums, and the invitations to newcomers to visit the hospital, to tour the facilities, and to view the film.

I wrote a series of promotional letters and sent them out, starting with hospitals in Texas, a state where business had been good to me. Shortly I had a lot of responses, a lot of interest, and a lot of appointments. I packed up my slide show and flew to Houston where I rented a car and circled the state from Beaumont to Dallas to Midland to San Antonio in an exhausting three-week flurry of presentations, sometimes three per day, in which I set up my cumbersome two-projector show powered by a computer and a tape playback machine.

Then I took the show to the Midwest where, in the freezing cold of late February, I scoured hospitals in Michigan, Wisconsin, Illinois, Indiana, and Missouri.

Early on, Brother Bill had asked a key question: "How many callbacks are you getting?"

I should have paid more attention to Bill's question. New business is built on a good idea, followed by presentations to generate interest and sales. Wherever there is interest, there should be callbacks inviting me to make the presentation to a larger group of higher-ups.

I had assumed the slide show was a good idea. I was getting responses and invitations to make presentations—dozens and dozens of presentations. But I was getting only a handful of callbacks. One in San Antonio. One in Grand Rapids. One in a western suburb of St. Louis.

Not nearly enough. Something was wrong.

Finally, in the redeeming warmth of April, I made a sale to St. Joseph's Hospital in Kirkwood, Missouri, a western suburb of St. Louis. I interviewed and cast a lovely young pregnant lady with a cute animated face, dimples in her cheeks, and lots of curly red hair like Annie in the musical comedy.

Chris and I loaded up his cameras, tripods, and strobes and headed off to St. Louis for two weeks of filming in her home and yard with her husband and children, in the hospital, and in the parks and playgrounds of this pretty suburb. Late in June she went into labor in the middle of the night and phoned me. I called Chris, waking him up. The last flight from Chicago to St. Louis had already departed, so we began the five-hour drive down Interstate 55, arriving just in time to film the birth.

I edited the show together, delivered it to St. Joseph's, billed them, and received some more desperately needed income.

Now I could concentrate on why this program generated interest and lots of invitations to make presentations, but very few callbacks. And only one sale.

Maybe what the hospitals needed more than a pretty slide film was the monthly telemarketing campaign to community newcomers, inviting them in to the hospital to see the show.

But wait!

What these newcomers *really* needed wasn't to visit the hospital and see my lovely slide show. If they'd just moved to a new community, they needed to connect with internists, gynecologists and pediatricians! And maybe dermatologists for a kid's acne. To say nothing of cardiologists for their heart murmurs, gastroenterologists for ulcers, urologists to treat their infertility—they didn't need my slide show, they needed physician referrals! *Health care, not theater!*

Telemarketing to make physician referrals! Now *that* might generate callbacks. This was bottom line stuff. St. Joseph Hospital in St. Louis had just invested $25,000 in a software program to support their physician referral service—as much as they'd spent buying my slide show. How about a telemarketing program to reach the newcomers, offer them physician referrals,

Scene Change

and feed their referral requests into the newly computerized physician referral service?

But who knew telemarketing?

My client, GC Services did. Their business was collecting overdue bills. They had hundreds and hundreds of telemarketers phoning people from offices all over the country.

Including an office in St. Louis.

A call to Brother Bill put me in touch with Harlan Bond, the manager of GC Services in St. Louis. "How do you do telemarketing," I asked Harlan. "What kind of people do you hire? What do you pay them? Where do you get lists of newcomers? What should the telemarketers say to them? If someone wants a physician referral, how do you patch the call into the referral service at the hospital?

"Could I do a test, right here in St. Louis, using a GC Services telemarketer and your sophisticated phone system?" I needed to see if newcomers would respond to the idea and allow us to patch their calls into the referral service at the hospital.

"Indeed we could," said Harlan Bond.

I contacted Beverly Byerly, the marketing director at St. Joseph's. She was skeptical. They'd invested heavily to computerize their referral service, and they'd certainly like to support it with more referrals. But Inglehart and Partners was an ad agency, not a telemarketing firm.

"Tell you what, Barb," I said, "I need a test. With your permission, we'll do the telemarketing for you for free while we get this program started. After that, you can decide whether you want to buy it from us on a continuing basis."

"What would the telemarketers say on the phone?"

I showed Barb my script. *"Welcome to St. Louis, I'm calling on behalf of St. Joseph's, your local hospital. We thought you might want to get the names of some of our staff physicians. Have you found a general practice doctor yet?"*

Barb said, "That sounds pretty good."

"Can I have your permission to do the test from one newcomer list?"

Permission granted.

In September I sat down with Harlan Bond at GC Services in St. Louis to structure the test. He selected Peggy O'Brien, one of his telemarketers, to handle the test. It was fairly cut-and-dried. She would call from the list of newcomers that Bond had secured. When someone wanted a physician referral, Peggy would patch the call into the physician referral service at St. Joseph.

She started calling immediately, with me and Bond listening in on her conversations from a supervisor's office.

On her third call Peggy got a referral request that she patched to St. Joseph.

I ran out onto the telemarketing floor and gave Peggy a hug.

In the course of the next two days, I learned two things that GC Services had known for decades. One thing was telephone personality. Whereas Peggy O'Brien was a bright conversationalist, the referral service girl at St. Joseph had the personality of an earthworm. She answered the phone in a cold, disinterested voice and was unable to maintain a friendly conversation during the long lapses when her slow computer was searching the physician database.

Also, very few people are home during the day. The productive hours for telemarketing are between 5:30 and 9 P.M.

Since the referral service at the hospital closed up at 5 P.M., I told Bond to continue having Peggy make calls during evening hours the following week, starting on Monday, and to give me the names of people who told Peggy they wanted referrals, so I could quickly forward them to the referral service.

The following Tuesday morning I called Bond from my office in Chicago. "How many referral requests did Peg get last night?"

"Let me check..." I was on hold for a minute. "She didn't get any last night."

"Nothing?"
"Nothing."
"But she was getting requests from about a quarter of all the people she reached during the day—what do you think is wrong?"
"I don't understand it."
"I'll call you tomorrow morning."
Next morning—no referral requests.
And none from Wednesday night, either.
At this point I was thoroughly discouraged, and ready to drop the whole business plan as a bad idea. "Look," I said to Bond, "maybe something's wrong with my telephone script, or maybe calling during evening hours isn't right for this. Hold off on the calling for tonight. I'll fly out there. Can I meet with you and Peggy tomorrow morning?"
"Sure. See you tomorrow."

In the meeting I said, "Peggy, something's wrong with that script, if you haven't gotten any referral requests in three nights of calling. Do you have any idea what's wrong?"
"I don't know if anything's wrong with the script. The problem is that the list has no phone numbers, so I have to get them from directory assistance. And there's nobody to patch calls to at the hospital during the evening. I got a patch on my first call Monday night, but the line at the hospital wasn't answered, so I spent the rest of the evening calling Directory Assistance for phone numbers for other names on the list."
"You did *what?*"
"I spent the three nights getting phone numbers from Directory Assistance."
I looked at Harlan Bond. "Didn't you tell her to collect referral requests for me to relay to the hospital for callbacks?"
Bond looked pretty sheepish with so much egg on his face.
I gathered up my lists and scripts and left. I had nearly canceled an entire business plan, only to discover that the

failure was due to a simple but devastating miscommunication. I'd seen enough. I decided to complete the test myself.

I called Brother Bill and explained what had happened. I asked if he would object if I declined to pay GC Services for Peggy O'Brien's three nights. Bill said I was free to deal with them as I would with any other source.

After so many years of loyal, life-giving income from GC Services, I felt bad about stiffing them. But I also felt quite justified.

The bill from GC Services arrived. I sent a letter of explanation as to why I wouldn't pay.

Then came the phone calls. After all, I *was* dealing with a collection agency.

"Would you pay half?"

"Those three nights are not worth half to me, Harlan, they're worth *nothing* to me. Perhaps less than nothing. I nearly abandoned what may be a very promising business plan—all because of a ridiculous miscommunication."

That was the end of the matter.

*

In that autumn of 1986, my other business continued to deteriorate. Merrill Chase Galleries terminated me. Becker Beeper switched to another agency. And I wasn't getting any new assignments from Flavorkist.

But it was Bockman that finally tolled the death knell for Inglehart and Partners. Their September remittance check bounced. I called Dave Bachmann and asked him what had happened.

"Oh, that N.S.F. check we sent you? I learned from the boys at Rothschild that if your checks clear the first time they're presented at your bank, your money isn't working hard enough for you."

"You mean you sent me a bad check *intentionally?*"

"We've got money, it's just in a different account."

Scene Change

"Dave, I'm going to have to cancel your October advertising schedule if I don't get paid immediately."

"I'll send a wire transfer to your bank."

"Today?"

"Yes, today."

Once again I'd been stupid. In March I'd made Bockman prepay. Over the course of the heavy summer advertising schedule, things had begun to look normal again, and I'd started extending them credit.

The following month, the Bockman check for about $30,000 bounced.

I called Dave. He said, "Jerry, I'm sorry, we're out of money. We're going back into bankruptcy."

I called Mr. Rothschild. "I've known of Maurice Rothschild ever since I was a kid when you had that big store in Evanston. I assumed your good name was behind Bockman."

"I'm sorry you thought that, Mr. Inglehart."

So I learned—the hard way—that the Maurice Rothschild Company wasn't in business to *revive* bankrupted companies—they were simply buying the assets (but not the liabilities) of bankrupted companies for a few cents on the dollar, in order to squeeze the final few drops of cash out of them.

I had to act fast. The debtors to whom I owed a little over $25,000 were the same as before—CBS, NBC, ABC, and the Chicago Tribune Company. They wouldn't wait sixty days this time. They'd start legal action immediately.

I got the name of a top bankruptcy firm in Chicago—Siegel, Sloan and Woodward. I wrote a brief letter of explanation of my situation to Mr. Siegel and had it hand delivered by a messenger.

Mr. Siegel didn't return my first call.

Next day he didn't return my second call.

On my third call, Mr. Siegel answered himself. "I'm Jerry Inglehart, I delivered a letter to you about bankruptcy."

"Oh, Mr. Inglehart—I'm standing here at my secretary's desk, on my way out the door. I was expecting a call from a friend I'm meeting for lunch; I thought this call was from him.

"Yes, I remember your letter. Sorry I didn't call back, but I'll give you some free advice. Got a pen? Good. Look, your company doesn't have enough assets to interest any law firm, even a small one; unless you personally guaranteed or prepaid their fees and expenses. I suggest you total up your company's assets, and cut a check to each of your creditors representing their proportional share of those assets—maybe ten cents on the dollar, maybe less. Send out the checks with the following cover letter: 'Inglehart and Partners is terminating business operations due to insolvency. The enclosed check represents your share of the final assets of the company.' "

I was scribbling down his words as fast as I could write. "That's *all?*" I asked.

"Try it, you've got nothing to lose. But I'd be surprised if you ever hear from any of your creditors again. I gotta go. Bye."

I did exactly as Mr. Siegel said. And I never heard from CBS, NBC, ABC, or the Tribune Company. Not a peep.

Mr. Siegel's two minutes of expertise and free advice was so simple—and exceeded what another attorney or law firm might have known. He'd saved me from a phalanx of summonses, responses, defenses and court appearances that might have lasted for months, maybe more. What had that bit of free advice saved me in legal fees—$5,000? $10,000? More?

I sent Mr. Siegel a $125 bottle of brandy, with a note of heartfelt thanks.

With that problem behind me I could concentrate on hospital telemarketing.

ACT II

SCENE 2

PLACE: The United States from coast to coast, but mostly east of the Mississippi River

TIME: The winter of 1986-87 to early July 1998

Chapter 22

The Phoenix

I began poking around in my new pile of corporate ashes, searching again for that phoenix. If he was there, and if I nursed him carefully, perhaps he might come back to life.

Only one thing remained—the germ of an idea, still undeveloped and untested. Telemarketing to promote physician referrals for hospitals. Could it fly?

If it could, it would need a new name. I couldn't very well call on hospitals representing a defunct ad agency.

I decided to call it "The Medical Connection." I applied for a new corporate charter, issued myself 500 shares of stock, wrote a personal check for $500, and opened a new bank account.

Next I'd need to promote my new business. I hired Renee Rockoff on a freelance basis to develop a direct-mail campaign to sell Newcomer Telemarketing to hospitals. She dreamed up a series of three letters. The first letter, on our new Medical Connection letterhead, would have half of a torn dollar bill paper-clipped to it. The copy promised that the recipient would receive the second half of the same bill, with the matching serial number, in another letter in a few days. That first letter suggested that there was a four-word formula by which a hospital could gain greater market share. The first word of the formula was "NEWCOMERS."

Letter Number Two, mailed a few days later with the other half of the dollar bill clipped to it, contained the second word of the formula: "TELEPHONING." The second word of a "fit," just like the two halves of the dollar bill fitting together to form something of value. The letter hinted at the program The Medical Connection offered: phoning newcomers in the hospital's service area.

The letter also promised a third follow-up letter a few days later, containing the final two words that would make the formula worth *more* than the sum of its parts—two more words describing something the hospital already had.

The third letter featured the words "PHYSICIAN REFERRALS" and explained the whole formula—the Medical Connection's program of telephoning community newcomers to promote the hospital's physician referral service.

It also promised a phone call from me in a day or so.

I began sending the mailing out to all hospitals with over 200 beds in the Chicago metropolitan area. The letters were quite effective in piquing interest and anticipation. Soon I had a calendar full of appointments.

My first presentation was to Ravenswood Hospital on Chicago's North Side. The marketing director, Rod Neavill, met with me. He liked the program and set up a meeting for me three days later with six other decision makers including the hospital's president. I had a callback, the vital sign of real interest—from my first presentation.

At the callback meeting I ran through my program description again. They asked about cost. I told them it would cost them about $5,000 a month, depending on the size of each month's newcomer list. The spring and summer lists would be bigger, the holiday season months smaller.

They said they'd let me know.

The Phoenix

I drove back to my office. When I arrived, there was already a phone message for me from Rod Neavill at Ravenswood. They had decided to go with the program.

Rod later told me that after I'd left the meeting and they were discussing the program, the hospital president said, "$5,000 a month? Hell, we *waste* $5,000 around here every day before noon. This program makes a lot of sense. Let's go with it."

I had never closed a sale faster.

By the end of the month I'd signed five more hospitals in the Chicago area, promising each of the hospitals our exclusive Newcomer Telemarketing service in the zip codes of their choice. Condell Hospital in a northern suburb signed for every zip code between Evanston and the Wisconsin line. Humana in Barrington took the entire northwest. Ravenswood took all zip codes in the northern half of the city proper, and Little Company of Mary in Evergreen Park took the rest of the city plus several southern suburbs. Good Samaritan in Downers Grove signed up for the southwestern zips and Silver Cross in Joliet took the rest.

In just three months I'd succeeded in selling our program in every area of the city, from Joliet to Waukegan.

I ordered the lists.

Then I ran a want ad in the *Chicago Tribune* for part-time telemarketers to work evenings.

The response to my classified ad was very large, in fact a little overwhelming. I was looking for very special voices—friendly, talkative, bright, educated-sounding voices. I'd been casting voices for radio and TV commercials for most of my career.

From the first ten words of the phone conversations with these hopefuls, I knew whether or not I had a good candidate. I had only four phone lines in the office at the time, so I hired just three women and trained them myself.

The night following my training session the women began calling. Any call in which the candidate agreed to receive a physician referral was considered a success. We immediately began running a success ratio of about 22%—nothing short of phenomenal in telemarketing. I kept my telephone script short, friendly, and to the point, getting to the offer of physician referrals before the person being called would think we might be trying to sell something.

At the close of each night's calls, I FedExed the referral requests to the physician referral services at each hospital, in order that the callbacks could be made in a timely fashion.

By the end of the first month's list, we'd completed over 7,000 calls, having reached nearly 80% of the households on the list. From this we generated over 1,500 requests for physician referrals. I opted to hand-deliver the final night's batch of Ravenswood referrals to the hospital myself the following morning.

And there, on the desk of the physician referral nurse, was the entire stack of referral requests for the month—over 300 of them—*untouched!*

I asked the referral nurse, "Did these people get called? Did you give them referrals?"

"I've been too busy to get to them. I called a few, but people aren't home during the day."

I went up to talk to Rod Neavill. "Those callbacks for the October list haven't been made."

"Sadly, I know."

"If those requests don't get filled, the program's not worth a nickel, Rod. You've got to let us make the referrals at night, from our office, while we have the patients on the phone. We've got to get information on all your physicians, so we can do the referrals ourselves."

It took Rod a while to convince his physician referral nurse to allow The Medical Connection to make referrals. Most physician referral staffers think nobody can do referrals other than themselves. But the fact that she didn't have time to do the callbacks convinced her to let us proceed.

For this I'd need a computer. And some software.

At the local CompUSA store on Michigan Avenue I secured a copy of the instruction manual for a spreadsheet software product called "Q&A." The book contained about 125 pages.

I understood the first half page. The second half of page one made some assumptions about my computer knowledge that exceeded my understanding. By the middle of page two I was totally befuddled. I'd need more than a computer and some software. I'd need a programmer or adviser of some sort.

My first adviser was a friend of Mary Ann Keller named Bob Binder. He guided me through the purchase of an 8086 computer made by AT&T, plus a Hewlett-Packard ink jet printer, and a word processing software package called WordPerfect.

I turned the whole thing, software and hardware alike, over to my new Administrative Assistant, a bright young lady named Lynda Jo Childs. She attacked the WordPerfect manual and got the thing to compose and print out my new business letters.

She also composed some WordPerfect charts of the Ravenswood hospital physicians, grouped by specialty and containing their office addresses and phone numbers, as well as the insurance plans they accepted.

Until we learned how to use spreadsheet software, we were going to have to do referrals from word processing software.

I needed to convert my big private front office into a call center. I bought several 36-inch-wide desks, assembled them and lined them up against my long window walls. I separated them from one another with fabric-covered office divider panels that functioned as sound barriers. But I needed more phone lines. And this was a residential building, with only five phone lines wired to each apartment. An attorney living in the unit on one side of mine let me take four of his five, and an architect on the other side gave me three. I removed the baseboards and fished out the extra phone lines from these adjacent apartments. This allowed me to construct a total of twelve calling stations. One weekend in December my son Chris and I wired all the phone lines to the workstations, as well as to Lynda Jo Child's office, so that referral requests could be transferred to her, and she could then match the patients up with physicians selected from her database.

Throughout November and December 1987 I continued to run my recruitment ad in the Sunday newspaper, normally getting about four hundred inquiries per week. I had all the ad response calls directed to an unlisted phone line that was always picked up by an answering machine. In this way I could screen dozens of phone calls quickly, selecting out the bright, intelligent, talky voices. From four hundred inquiries I'd select and interview perhaps four, and hire two.

And my three-letter mailing program and follow-up presentations continued to generate new clients. I signed Edwards Hospital in Aurora, Illinois. And St. Mary's Hospital in Racine, Wisconsin. And Deaconess Hospital in a south suburb of Cleveland.

The newcomer lists got larger in the spring when more families moved. By that time I had built and trained an impressive staff of interesting, friendly, talkative women who showed up for work each evening at 5:30 P.M., picked up their lists and phones, and began calling tirelessly through to 9 P.M.

I remember some of those ladies well—Denise McHugh, a lovely, friendly Irish-Italian girl. Natalie DeSurry with her soft, sympathetic alto voice. Caroline Apy, who turned out to be the young daughter of my former client at House of Vision. And Cathy Carroll, a tall, lean girl who seemed destined one day to marry a physician or attorney and live in Winnetka. There was a perky, diminutive young lady, Linda Esau, who worked days as a stockbroker in the financial district. And Lynn Anderson, blond and overweight, with a bubbly laugh so contagious, you couldn't help smiling when she talked. I had an out-of-work actress named Sue McLaughlin, who looked and talked like Lily Tomlin. And Rita Schwartz, an elderly Jewish Mama type who would *kvetch* comically with the people she talked to.

Each request for physician referrals was transferred to Lynda Jo in her office. Lynda Jo had studied premed in college and was sufficiently comfortable with medical terms to handle the referrals capably.

By mid-summer of 1988 I'd convinced all of my clients to share with us their physician databases and allow us to make the referrals from our office at night. Soon Lynda Jo was overloaded and unable to handle each night's flood of referral requests, so I hired a former nurse—as well as the nurse's daughter—to handle the referrals on extra phone extensions in Lynda Jo's office.

I walked around the office each evening like a *maitre d'*, refilling coffee cups for my employees, bringing them new list pages, listening and monitoring their calls closely. By 9:30 P.M. when all the staff completed their reports and went home, I'd pull down my Murphy bed into the middle of the telemarketing bay, undress and fall asleep, quite exhausted from my workday. I was putting in about thirteen hours of work each weekday.

The physician referral nurse at Ravenswood Hospital was planning a three-week vacation in July. Rod Neavill had been pleased with our handling of referrals during telemarketing hours. The telemarketing program had nearly tripled their monthly volume of physician referrals—we were making more referrals at night than they were handling during office hours.

Rod asked if we could handle the referral service full-time during the vacation absence of their referral nurse. The Ravenswood phone system could forward calls from their physician referral line to a dedicated line at The Medical Connection. We could answer each call in their name, just as if we were working on location at the hospital.

I moved Lynda Jo Child's schedule from 1 to 9 P.M. back to 9 to 5 and hired another referral specialist for evening hours.

Even though Lynda Jo had to stumble through her makeshift WordPerfect database, she nevertheless did an outstanding job making referrals to Ravenswood callers. She did it with authority and accuracy, in both English and fluent Spanish. She had a pleasant professionalism that Ravenswood had not been accustomed to. I'm certain she received a few "test" calls from hospital management people, first from Rod Neavill, then from other marketing and management personnel.

Near the end of the three-week period, Rod Neavill asked me if The Medical Connection could continue to handle the Ravenswood Hospital physician referral service permanently. He planned to move his referral nurse to another job.

And so a new chapter in the history of The Medical Connection opened. We now had two telemarketing departments—Outbound (calls to newcomers) and Inbound (incoming calls forwarded to us from Ravenswood's physician referral service).

We were charging our clients $3.30 per completed Outbound call—but the fee for each Inbound call was double that, since the Inbound conversations were lengthier, involving questioning the patient about needs and insurance, plus doing computer lookups of physicians, and providing each caller with the name, office address, and phone number of at least one, sometimes two or three physicians.

The Medical Connection was saving Ravenswood a bundle of money. Their in-house referral nurse had cost them $45,000 a year in salary for the nurse, plus an additional $8,000 in payroll taxes, worker's compensation insurance, and unemployment insurance—as well as contributions to her health insurance and retirement fund. And Ravenswood had had to provide her with an office, a phone line, stationery, and other overhead. And she needed to have someone available to relieve her during lunch, sick days, and vacations.

The Medical Connection could handle all this for less than $25,000 a year, based on their historic call volume of 3,800 calls per year.

And Ravenswood felt that Lynda Jo was friendlier than their own nurse had been. She was projecting a more favorable impression of the hospital. Her proficiency in medical knowledge served her well.

I could see a tremendous potential for the Inbound Department at The Medical Connection. Here was a story I needed to tell to hospitals all over the country.

I could sell Inbound service two ways:

First, as a totally outsourced physician referral service, like Ravenswood. Caroline Apy came up with a name for the service: "Contract Physician Referral Service."

And for those hospitals reluctant to give up an in-house service, we could offer Back-up Physician Referral Service. When a hospital's referral coordinator was handling one call, the phone system could forward additional incoming calls to The Medical Connection. When their coordinator went to lunch or took a coffee break, she could forward all her calls to us. And when she went home at 5 P.M., we'd cover all the calls until 9 P.M.

I hoped that each Back-up client would do what Rod Neavill had done—make test calls to us. Hopefully many of the Back-up clients would discover that The Medical Connection might be out-performing their own internal service with voices that were more pleasant and more professional. *And our service cost them less than an in-house service!*

I'd need an overhead projector to show charts and photos in my client presentations. I'd need mailers. And a brochure. And a new set of solicitation letters.

I told all my staff to come to work the following night in business dress—suits or pantsuits, blouses, and stockings like the women who worked in the brokerage and law offices on LaSalle Street. There would be a moratorium on calls that night—they'd receive full pay for no work, plus a $10 bonus for dressing up. That night I brought in my son Chris with his camera equipment and strobes to take photographs of my staff in business dress, headsets in place, pretending to work at their calling stations.

My Lily Tomlin look-alike actress did a professional hair and makeup job on my Irish-Italian girl. I put one of Chris's photos of her on the cover of an Outbound flyer, which I headlined, *"Phoning Newcomers to Promote your Physician Referral Service."*

I had a staff of *one* referral specialist during the day—and only *three* at night. But I wanted a photo to make it look like my inbound referral staff included a dozen smart-looking women. I selected twelve of my staff to come in for a daytime photo session on Saturday, to represent my Inbound staff. I made this photo into a flyer headlined, *"Introducing the Finest Physician Referral Staff in the U.S.—Yours!"*

I had loads of photos to flesh out my presentations to prospective clients. I could present The Medical Connection as a viable and vibrant telemarketing organization with professional equipment and a staff of pros operating out of a fancy downtown Chicago office.

I elevated Lynn Anderson to Outbound Supervisor, replacing myself. And I sent out brochures with cover letters to hospitals throughout the Midwest, all over Texas, and up and down the East Coast.

Since most hospital marketing departments are staffed by women, most of my presentations were to women. I wanted to train a woman to act as my "front man." I hoped that my lean, aristocratic-sounding Irish lady, Cathy Carroll, would fill the bill. I took her with me on my next round of new business calls, in New York City. I worked with her for a whole evening in a Travelodge hotel room in Manhattan, trying to get her to master my presentation. But while she was easy and authoritative in ordinary conversation, she couldn't relax in a business presentation setting. I sent her alone on a few trips to southern Illinois and Ohio, but she generated no business on her own.

Phoning Newcomers to Promote your Physician Referral Service

THE MEDICAL CONNECTION is a hospital Physician Referral Support organization, founded in 1987 to help hospitals build market share through early contact with community newcomers, to promote the hospital Physician Referral Service.

We maintain a staff of professional hospital service representatives and referral specialists at our hospital service headquarters in Chicago. Each month we generate

Introducing the Finest Physician Referral Staff in the U.S.

...Yours!

It's called Contract Physician Referral Service™. And these are the people who provide it for you.

They're knowledgeable. Authoritative. They've handled millions of physician referrals, as well as community health and education program enrollments. And plenty of crisis calls, too.

They're experienced. They average 2.2 years on the job, doing physician referrals. Each has been certified through The Medical Connection training program – the most comprehensive referral training program in the medical field. They're conversant with medical terminology and know how to recognize emergency situations. They take advantage of cross-selling opportunities. They know what patients need and want, and how to translate those needs into physician appointments and class enrollments.

Continued on back.

Since I'd elevated her to full-time status as an executive, she couldn't go back to part-time calling. I had to let her go.

Late in 1988 I speculated that The Medical Connection would benefit from some exposure at hospital trade conventions. The American Hospital Association sponsored two marketing conventions each year, with accompanying speeches and seminars. I rented a booth for the convention scheduled in Phoenix in February 1989.

Trade show exhibits are costly. In 1988 you'd pay $1,000 to rent a 25-foot-wide booth, and if you didn't have your own display, you'd have to hire a trade show provider to put up a structure with shelves and a lighted back wall to mount your photos, charts or displays. The 3-day-rental, including set-up, removal, and a piece of carpet, was another $1,000.

I made poster-size blowups of the photo of our Irish-Italian cover girl, and the photo of our twelve Inbound Referral Specialists. I hired my perky stockbroker, Linda Esau, to accompany me to the Phoenix trade show. Dressed in one of her stockbroker suits, she talked to the convention visitors about The Medical Connection, and passed out our literature.

The Phoenix show generated about sixty leads for me to follow up. The trade show exposure also stimulated awareness for The Medical Connection among hospital marketing professionals at the convention.

Since I had Linda Esau tending my booth, I was able to attend a couple of the special interest seminars that were offered at this convention. One lecture was billed as "Organizing Business and Projects." Since it was listed under the heading of Management, I hoped I could pick up a few tips.

This particular seminar was very well attended. There must have been over three hundred marketing executives sitting in the ballroom. The speaker, a lady named Sharon Melker, began with an overhead projection showing a typical business pyramid, with seven or eight levels of management, and a

C.E.O. at the top. Sharon called the chart "one of her Melker Management Models." Having seen such organizational pyramid charts many times before, I wondered how Ms. Melker felt she could put her name on it, as if she'd invented it.

I assumed she'd next show a chart with lines running from the C.E.O. to various department heads, then to a larger array of divisional managers, and so on, down to the mass of clerks and go-fers at the bottom who did the actual work. And that's precisely what her next chart looked like. Ms. Melker labeled this chart another of her "Melker Management Models."

Again I guessed what was coming next—pie charts of some sort, showing how each department, job description and task could be broken down into its component parts. And up they came, each one identified by Sharon Melker as another "Melker Management Model," a label I'm sure she changed to "Melker Management *Paradigm*" a year or so later when that noun became the hottest new buzzword of business-speak.

Sharon Melker's *raison d'etre* was *"defining work."* And I realized I had come to a seminar designed to sustain bureaucracies and pacify bureaucrats. I envisioned that some of the women in this seminar would go home to their hospital employers and get their bosses to fund their attendance at a one-week Melker Management Seminar, so they could come back home and spend another four or five weeks "defining their departments," "defining their jobs," and "defining tasks." Maybe they could even get their bosses to allow them to spend a few more weeks creating definitions for other departments and tasks.

A bureaucrat loves to define things, then write up and circulate papers on project definition—anything that postpones actually having to *do* work.

From my dealings with some of my hospital clients, I was aware that bureaucracies crop up in hospitals like weeds in a cow pasture. This practice of hospital management usually creates huge logjams that stand in the way of getting anything done. It spawns unnecessary meetings and subcommittees. I frequently had difficulty reaching my clients and prospects on the telephone—hospital management holds so many meetings that a typical marketing employee will often attend two meetings a day. If there are three or four meetings in a single day, there is no time left to accomplish anything.

It reminded me of a time in the Sears Roebuck Floor Coverings Department when someone decided to bring in a group of Sears laboratory research people to help us in some way. At the end of the week I attended a meeting where we were to review the results of the first week's productivity of this team of research people.

The head lab bureaucrat stood up and said, "Since the basis of floor coverings is *fiber*—cotton, wool, acrylic, polypropylene and such, whether the fiber is used for the pile or the backing of the floor covering—we decided we needed a definition of a fiber. Here's the definition we agreed upon." And he read from a note in his hand:

" 'A fiber is a substance with a length greater than its width, by several hundred dimensions.' "

"My God," I interjected rudely, "you mean Interstate 90 is a fiber?"

The expressions on the faces of the research group suggested that they did not appreciate my flippant evaluation of their week's productivity. And I wondered if they'd go back to their department and spend the following week determining whether or not they could make a carpet out of linguini.

Tact had never been one of my strong suits.

I got up and walked out of Sharon Melker's seminar after ten minutes, grateful that most of my clients had a little more savvy than this roomful of work-evading bureaucrats.

*

My new business presentations around the country continued to generate new clients. By spring I had a total of fourteen hospitals signed for either Outbound Telemarketing, or

Backup Referral Service—and five clients signed us for Full Time Contract Physician Referral Service, the most important and profitable of our services.

From time to time a prospective client would want to visit our offices during evening hours and watch our outbound telemarketing. In anticipation of each such visit I would advise my staff that we would have what I called a "LaSalle Street Night." The employees would receive a bonus of $10 to set aside their jeans, sweatshirts, and sneakers and come to work in smart business dress with suits, blouses and pantyhose, to impress the potential clients. Most of the ladies had such clothes. A few would have to borrow or improvise. The middle-age nurse I'd hired for evenings was an outstanding referral coordinator, but I doubt if she'd ever owned a pantsuit in her life. On each "LaSalle Street Night" she pulled out a black dress she'd probably purchased for a funeral, and came to work looking like a cellist for a symphony orchestra.

*

Now we desperately needed more phone lines for incoming referral calls. Our office was at the far western side of the building, and the building's phone line riser was at the opposite end. Building management would not allow me to run a phone line trunk down the length of the hallway because this was a residential building.

A rental unit at the other end of the building, on the 35th floor, became available in April. There I could tap into as many phone lines as I wished. I leased the unit and ordered service for 24 phone lines, doubling our service.

From a used phone equipment broker I purchased several of those cumbersome old analog phones—huge instruments, 18 inches wide, with 24 lighted buttons and a massive cable containing 24 pairs of wires running from the phone to the wall. I could now dedicate up to 24 phone lines to Inbound and Backup clients.

The Phoenix

One weekend in late April I borrowed a hand truck and a four-wheel dolly and personally moved my entire operation, telemarketing stations and all, including my desk and Murphy bed, down to the office on the 35th floor. Instead of having my "private" office and Murphy bed in the large main office, I put my desk, phone, and Murphy bed in the small end bedroom, leaving the large living-dining-room space exclusively for outbound telemarketing stations. The second bedroom would be for Inbound operations—Lynda Jo's office during the day, and three referral counselors each evening.

My bedroom-office had its own private bathroom, so I could enjoy more privacy with my office door closed. When Lynda Jo arrived at 9 A.M. she could begin her Inbound operations, and I could sleep late in the next room, then shower, shave, and dress before coming out to the kitchen for my breakfast.

We also needed a legitimate database software program to replace our Mickey Mouse WordPerfect physician database.

I began using an independent programmer—a friend-of-a-friend named Bill Rosman. Bill's brain functioned in a cloud of software language somewhere high above the earth in a digital heaven. He found it difficult to communicate with ordinary people like myself who spoke in plain language. He talked in coded statements understandable only to other programmers, and became impatient when I couldn't follow his explanations.

Bill built and maintained a database for us in the Paradox software environment, and we launched our first true spreadsheet software capability that could search the physician tables by criteria.

Our software was finally on the right track.

Meanwhile my lifestyle had become one-dimensional. I lived downtown in a room I converted from a bedroom to an office every morning, and back at night. I put in twelve hours a day, often more. I had no life outside of my work. How long could I keep this up?

Chapter 23

"They Have Their Exits and Their Entrances"

Beware the Ides of March, the soothsayer warned Julius Caesar.

On that day in March 1988, my father was part of a golf foursome in Florida. He swung at his ball and departed this earth—as suddenly as his own father had died a few decades earlier.

The likelihood of stroke and heart attack appears to be a male inheritance in the Inglehart family. Perhaps it's a blessing. Lingering death by cancer or dementia is something I liken to the agony of a hapless actor finishing his scene while watching the disappointed audience file out through the exit doors.

Dad never judged me, whether I was bringing him a substandard high school report card to sign, or calling him for money from a jail in Indiana. Dad always thought I was just fine. His nonjudgmental attitude toward me provided welcome and valuable support in my youth, helping me to withstand the onslaught of berating teachers and school principals, and groaning classmates watching me drop those fly balls in right field. In his youth in Oshkosh Dad had been a star football backfielder and basketball champion, but he never expressed disappointment over my own athletic shortcomings.

The October before Dad's death I broke up with Mary Ann Keller. Ours had been a meaningful relationship, lasting over five years. I learned so much from Mary Ann—including an appreciation for the differences between a man of 50 and a woman in her late 20s. That's when it's often time for a young woman to become a parent—a responsibility I'd happily assumed twice, but was unwilling to repeat. Toward the end of our relationship I reconsidered my position, but Mary Ann turned me down. Thank God! I'd have had a houseful of preteen kids now.

After our break-up, I resolved to date women closer to my own age.

At a party in October 1988, I met Christiane Barber—a delightfully complex woman with a remarkable international background. She was born in Germany in 1940 and raised in Austria and Switzerland. Both her parents had PhDs in chemistry. At age five, even though she'd never been outside of Europe, Christie fell in love with America—because the American occupation forces in Salzburg were so sweet to her. Her father had a photo lab that processed snapshots for the soldiers, and he sent his little 5-year-old daughter to the nearby Salzburg hotel, requisitioned as an officers' quarters, to deliver their photos. Christie looked just like Shirley Temple, with a dimpled laugh and a big crown of tightly curled hair. The homesick officers loved her and played with her. A lieutenant took her for rides on his horse.

When I look at the captivating old black-and-white photos of Christie as a child, it wouldn't surprise me to know that some of those American army officers exposed rolls of film simply for a chance to give them to Christie and have her return with the prints. It was an opportunity to see a sweet, happy, smiling little child who laughed easily and trusted them. Sometimes they'd toss her back and forth between them, making her giggle and scream with delight, helping to remind them that a long and gruesome war was over, peace had come, and they would soon be home.

Christie's irresponsible father had difficulty holding a job. He drank a lot, womanized, and ran up incredible debts that eventually drove him to suicide. At age ten Christie was doing most of the cooking for her working mother, and earning money by sewing clothes for her friends. At fifteen she helped support her family by delivering newspapers and washing dishes in a hotel. At eighteen she studied to be an electrical engineer through a work-study program at Siemens in Erlangen, Germany. Then she immigrated to America as a young bride.

In Chicago in the early 1960's she worked designing electrical circuits for television sets. She earned two degrees at DePaul University and became a professor of electronics at DeVry University.

Christie is irrepressible. I love her positive attitude toward everything—people, animals, children, music, travel, cityscapes, seasons, sunsets—about life itself. And about me.

In 1988 Christie lived in a studio condo in Lincoln Park, where I'd often spend the night. Occasionally she'd stay with me overnight in my home-office downtown. Eventually we moved into my vintage condo in Evanston—I could enjoy it now because I was no longer alone.

In June of 1989 we traveled together to Europe. Christie introduced me to the cities of her childhood—Konstanz, Dessau, Salzburg, and Zurich. And I introduced her to a new way of travel—without an itinerary. For three weeks we explored the Alps in a rental car, stopping whenever and wherever we pleased, staying in charming mountain chalets, bed-and-breakfasts, small hotels and inns, and hikers' huts in the mountains with their soft, welcoming featherbeds. We hiked the trails that lace secretly, endlessly through all of the five nations sharing the Alps. We dined wherever we liked, often on bread, sausage, cheese, and wine on impromptu Alpine picnics where we could look out on the majestic snow-capped peaks, the flowering meadows, the grazing sheep and cattle, and the tiny villages tucked into the mountains.

Together we discovered a heaven on earth, an earth so full of beauty, we'd never run out of places to explore.

Dad, if you'd lived just one more year, you'd have gotten to meet Christie!

Chapter 24

A Different Drummer

In June of 1990 I discovered that I had a competitor—an outfit in Los Angeles called E.R.S. offering out-sourced physician referral service. I found out about E.R.S. as the result of getting an invitation to make a new business presentation at Shore Memorial Hospital in Sommer's Point, New Jersey.

Shore Memorial had no physician referral service. They wanted a proposal for a full-time out-sourced service.

My presentation in New Jersey went quite well. I was invited back to present to a board of twelve decision-makers, including the hospital's president.

They were ready to go with my program, but wanted to visit my Chicago facility first. The marketing director and president decided to fly out to Chicago with their families for a Friday meeting at our office, then spend the weekend seeing the sights in Chicago. I arranged for both families to stay in large rental apartments in my building, so they'd have nice multi-bedroom suites complete with full kitchens, rather than being cramped with a lot of kids in downtown hotel rooms.

At the time, my staff of referral counselors consisted of only three evening referral people handling referrals for the Outbound team, plus Lynda Jo Childs, who handled all daytime

inbound referrals for Ravenswood and a few other hospitals that used us for back-up service.
And I had only one computer.
It was time to revert to my smoke-and-mirrors theatrical background. I had to make it look like I had more staff than I did. I rented two more computers from a shop in Oak Park and had Bill Rosman install our software on them. I paid two of our part-time evening referral counselors to call in sick to their day jobs, dress in business outfits and be stationed at my two rented computers on the Friday when the president and marketing director of Shore Memorial Hospital would show up. It looked like we had a staff of three full-time counselors.

When the Shore Memorial people arrived, I had all three women busily entering data on their computers, two of which were dummy terminals. Lynda Jo handled the few incoming referral requests, which I had the prospective clients monitor on phones in the Outbound room. As always, Lynda Jo did a perfect, professional job.

Then the president of Shore discovered that one of my two "pretend" counselors, a soft-spoken, willowy blond named Lisa Tatoris, was of Lithuanian blood. He himself was a very proud second generation Lithuanian who probably flew a Lithuanian flag in his yard and shot off fireworks when Lithuania withdrew from the Soviet Union. Soon these two loyal Americans of common heritage were chatting about Chicago's only Lithuanian restaurant, and comparing notes on the Lithuanian foods that both their mothers still prepared for family gatherings.

On Sunday I took my prospective clients and their families for a luncheon cruise out on a sunny, placid Lake Michigan aboard the *Star of Chicago* cruise ship out of Navy Pier.

After the lunch cruise, the two executives and their wives thanked me like an old friend for an enjoyable weekend experience. The marketing director invited me to New Jersey the following Thursday, telling me to bring a contract. Then they all bid us good-bye and took cabs to the airport.

I needed this client badly, to expand our Inbound client base. And if ever I was sure I had a new client in the bag, it was that Sunday.

On Monday afternoon I got a call from the marketing executive. "Jerry, have you ever heard of an organization called E.R.S in Los Angeles?"

"Can't say I have."

"Well, they appear to be doing the same thing as The Medical Connection."

"What? Out-sourced physician referral?"

"Yes. We got a mailing from them. And my boss wants to check them out before we hire you, if for no other reason than to prove to the board of directors that we were diligent. The boss and I are flying to L.A. to meet with them on Friday, so we have to hold off on your visit here until the following week."

E.R.S. Where had I heard that name before?

On Tuesday I remembered. E.R.S. had been Emergency Response Systems. Somewhere in my files I had one of their brochures. After an hour I found it. The brochure, which I'd received a couple of years earlier, described Emergency Response Systems as an operation servicing those little beepers you hang around the neck of your aged mother who lives alone with a cardiac condition or some other potentially life-threatening health condition. If she feels a stroke coming on, she squeezes the button on the beeper, and Emergency Response Systems dispatches an ambulance anytime, 24 hours a day, seven days a week.

But that wasn't physician referral! It took a lot more training and savvy to make a competent physician referral than to dispatch an ambulance.

There was a new publication in the physician referral field—an 8-page newsletter called Physician Referral Update, mailed monthly to subscribers. Perhaps they'd heard of Emergency Response Systems. I called their number in San Francisco and talked to the writer-editor, Richard Cohen, who operated the publication from his home.

A Different Drummer

"Do you know anything about Emergency Response Systems?" I asked.

"Yes, that's Paul Spiegelman's operation in Los Angeles. They've recently changed their corporate name to E.R.S. They do out-sourced physician referral."

So I had a competitor.

The following Monday I got a call from the Shore Memorial marketing director. His voice was troubled. "Jerry, this is a difficult call for me to make. We're going to give our referral service to E.R.S. They're a lot bigger than The Medical Connection. They occupy an entire floor of an office building next to Los Angeles Airport. They've got at least fifty employees."

Oh, boy. "Sorry to hear that."

"I'm sorry to have to tell you. We were very pleased with what we saw at The Medical Connection. But E.R.S. is a lot bigger. And they operate 24-7."

I didn't tell him that someone who could dispatch an ambulance might not be competent in making a physician referral. I also didn't tell him that two of the three computers they'd seen in Lynda Jo Child's office were dummies, long since returned to the computer rental store.

But in less than a month I made a presentation for outsourced referral service to St. Francis Hospital in my hometown of Evanston, Illinois. They told me they were also talking to E.R.S.

But they signed with The Medical Connection. One out of two isn't bad. And competition is generally a good thing.

Time would tell.

Meanwhile, I was planning a preemptive strike.

Chapter 25

Rewriting the Scripts

Our regular appearances among the trade show booths at hospital marketing conventions were helping to establish The Medical Connection as a recognized supplier of marketing services to hospitals. Maybe now was the time for something that might establish us as a leader in the industry.

A few years earlier I'd received in my mail a survey questionnaire from the Healthcare Financial Management Association in Westchester, Illinois, a private consulting organization. They were conducting a survey to study salary levels among clerical staffs in hospitals, as well as in businesses that served hospitals. The cover letter promised that, as a survey participant, I would receive a free copy of the published findings.

That was pretty enticing. I knew that hospital management would love to find out what other hospitals were paying their clerical staffs. By sponsoring such a survey, the Healthcare Financial Management Association was building its reputation as a contributor of knowledge to the healthcare industry. And by offering to mail the published findings free to all survey participants, they were assuring a high rate of participation. And new business leads.

Rewriting the Scripts

My brother Ron, a professor of Political Science at the University of Michigan, had built himself a worldwide reputation by conducting attitude surveys in eighty to ninety countries. He'd been analyzing and publishing his survey findings for over 30 years. He'd become the most quoted scholar in the study of world values.

In my advertising career I'd been involved in lots of quantitative research studies. I knew the organizations that could computerize the findings and spew out hundreds of relational charts.

So I structured a study that was heavily skewed toward findings that would support the value of physician referrals, and therefore the value of being sure no physician referral calls were ever missed, i.e. Medical Connection Back-up Service, or Medical Connection Contract Physician Referral Service.

In April I mailed my survey to all 1,800 of the hospitals in the United States with 130 or more beds, as listed in the American Hospital Association Guide for 1989. Prominently clipped to my cover letter was a gold request card with this message: "Enclosed is our completed physician referral survey. Please send one free copy of the published survey results to me:"

There was a line for the recipient to enter his name and title. Below that, our WordPerfect program had preprinted the hospital name and address on the card.

Those names and titles on returned surveys would expand my file of leads.

Within six weeks I'd received 565 completed surveys—a response of 31%, which is remarkable in direct-mail campaigns, where a 3% return is considered good. I packed the surveys off to a service that would computerize the responses and prepare comparison charts. I analyzed the charts for several weeks and wrote up my key findings:

- 86% of all private-sector hospitals had physician referral services.

- There were over 30 referral requests per year per 1,000 homes in any hospital service area. (From this figure, a hospital marketing director could see if his referral service was getting its share.)

- Each referral generated an average of $260 in hospital billings, at a cost to the hospital of $10.88 per referral to run the service—a 24-to-1 return on investment.

- If a referral service received an average of two referrals per hour per staffer, it was approaching peak efficiency, since referral calls come bunched at peak hours, especially on Monday and Tuesday mornings, and during the critical months of January through March.

- For services getting fewer than 200 referrals per month, a full-time staffer was a rarity. Such services were generally staffed part-time.

- Services getting over 250 calls monthly generally had one dedicated staffer; over 600 calls per month typically required the service of two full-time staffers, three staffers over 850 per month, and four over 1,150 per month. (I included a chart.)

Rewriting the Scripts

- Services staffed 40 hours per week by two staffers operated the most efficiently, at a cost-per-referral of $8.26. Services with fewer or more than two staffers cost more per referral. (Another chart)

- The more inbound phone lines there were, the more referrals were handled *per staffer*.

- Use of an answering machine to handle overflow calls actually had the effect to *reduce*, rather than *increase* the number of referrals handled per staffer per hour. (I speculated that people might be reluctant to leave a recorded message regarding anything as personal as their health conditions, especially if they were seeking a urologist or proctologist, or were concerned about an ache in the belly or chest that they feared might be cancer. And those callers who did leave a message for a callback would also probably call a physician referral service at another hospital. Counselors frequently reported that when they got around to making callbacks, the patients often would have already made an appointment with another physician.)

- Computerized services generated more activity with greater efficiency, probably because the decision to invest in costly computers and software accompanied a decision to advertise the service more aggressively, and to add phone lines. (I listed the market share for each of the three major referral service software brands then on the market: Baxter, Healthline, and Referral One.)

I ended with a recap of significant conclusions. I needed to present the findings in a scholarly, objective fashion, avoiding having it look like a sales pitch for The Medical Connection. But any hospital marketing director with a pocket calculator could see from my findings that her physician referral service represented potential pay dirt—it was one of the most productive marketing tools she had. *And that the answering machine at her physician referral service was not helping—in fact, it was counterproductive.* A back-up service could expand her referrals.

And if she didn't have $30,000 to $90,000 to invest in referral service software, she could outsource her service to The Medical Connection, thus becoming instantly computerized.

I had my ten pages of findings printed and handsomely bound with a cover. I titled it, *The Impact of Physician Referral Services: Findings from a National Survey.*

I sent copies to each of the 565 survey contributors. Then I sent copies to all the major health care trade media. That generated four important articles in trade journals that I had reprinted to enclose with subsequent mailings to new business prospects. At the close of each of my new business presentations I'd leave my prospective clients with a copy of the study results and the article reprints.

Now I was equipped to do more than just *exhibit* at the trade shows and conventions.

I could be a featured speaker.

Such publicity could be pivotal in my evolving goals for The Medical Connection. Our future was not with the Outbound Telemarketing program, which tended to be the first item to be cut by the hospitals during a budget crunch because the program's benefits were so hard to measure. Already I'd suffered the loss of a third of my original Outbound clients, reminding me too much of my past experience running an advertising agency, where my income would suddenly and arbitrarily be cut by clients looking to reduce costs, or whenever a change of management resulted in a change of agencies.

By comparison, my Inbound clients tended to stick with me. They knew they had to have a physician referral service, and many of them were recognizing that the referrals could subsequently be traced to profitable inpatient and outpatient services. Our Back-Up Service clients saw that we were significantly increasing the referral activity of their own in-house services. And our Fully Outsourced clients recognized that we could run a service for them more professionally than they could run one themselves, and at far less expense.

The future of The Medical Connection was clearly in Inbound Services. I stopped promoting our Outbound Services entirely, and switched my efforts to the more stable, more permanent, more profitable Inbound Services.

I revised our letter campaign, and sent out hundreds of mailings to hospitals primarily east of the Mississippi. I hit the road in a grueling schedule of presentations in Texas, the Mid-Atlantic States, and the rest of the East Coast from Florida to Maine. Some of my business trips involved jam-packed schedules with two to three presentations a day, requiring that I race from town to town and state to state in rental cars. Typically I'd finish up my last presentation of the day at about 5 P.M., then drive into the night to my next hospital appointment, often in another state, arriving late at night and flopping down exhausted in a Motel 6 room.

Two such trips kept me out-of-town for two entire weeks. After a week on the road, I'd park my rental car at an airport late on Friday, fly home for the weekend, then fly back to my rental car on Sunday evening to begin my next full week of presentations. One two-week trip involved driving through eleven southern states, traveling from Georgia to Texas to Florida to North Carolina. When I returned the rental car in Atlanta at the end of the second week, I'd put 4,000 miles on the odometer.

During 1991, I logged 71 out-of-town travel days, thus spending over 25% of that year's business days on the road in a wide assortment of rental compacts and hatchbacks, and sleeping each night in budget motels.

And it was paying off. I was reeling in new clients. I signed hospitals in San Diego; Austin; Corpus Christi; Omaha; Jacksonville; Miami; Trenton; Boston; Brooklyn; Queens; Lancaster, Pennsylvania and Nashua, New Hampshire, plus a few closer to home in the Chicago suburbs of Berwyn, Highland Park, and Blue Island.

Whenever I completed an out-of-town presentation that felt very promising and seemed likely to yield another new client, I'd check the neighborhood of the hospital for a nice nearby motel or hotel in a safe neighborhood, and make a note of its name and location. If we signed that client, I'd want a decent place for Lynda Jo Childs to stay when she visited the hospital to gather information for the physician database. Her installation of the service involved loading our "monitoring" software, together with a modem, on a computer at the hospital so we could transfer the records of our daily referral activity to allow the hospital to generate reports and print follow-up letters to the patients who'd received our referrals. Each installation was a three-day job for Lynda Jo. The motels I chose for myself were usually low-budget lodgings, occasionally in questionable neighborhoods. But I wanted decent, safe, nearby lodgings for any female employee of mine.

*

By then I'd expanded the daytime Inbound staff from a solo operation handled by Lynda Jo Childs, to four full-time counselors. I purchased a pair of the new, faster "286" computers and had my programmer, Bill Rosman, convert to a "Local Area Network" (LAN) computer system. We also needed more phone service at The Medical Connection in order to have additional lines to dedicate to incoming calls from the new clients.

Lynda Jo Childs left me in June to become a housewife and get pregnant. I advertised for another supervisor and hired Debbie Maturo, an unassuming girl who, I would soon discover, had a remarkable talent for training, managing, and inspiring a large staff of referral specialists. She set out at once to structure a formal training program to allow the counselors she hired to develop the medical proficiency they needed to handle physician referral questions comfortably and authoritatively.

Very early in her career with The Medical Connection, Debbie would come to me with questions: "Should I hire this applicant?" "Should the training be broken down into easy-to-handle modules?"

In my advertising years I had developed a lot of award-winning commercials based on a simple formula: hire the best, then let them do their thing, their own way. I applied the same strategy to Debbie's questions.

"I could decide this for you, Debbie, but I'm at least a step away, maybe several steps away from it, and you're right on top of it. So whatever you decide, it's going to be a better decision than one I'd try to make for you. Whether you make a good decision or a bad one, I'll stand by your decision because, right or wrong, yours is a better decision than the one I'd make myself."

This statement became a mantra for my management style at The Medical Connection. And its effect on Debbie was amazing. Debbie came to realize that the Inbound department was *her* department, to run and develop in her own style. She took personal pride of authorship, achieving results that at first were remarkable—and eventually, astonishing. I came to realize that the professionalism of the counselors she hired and trained, and her careful supervision and inspiration was one of the key foundation stones on which The Medical Connection stood and grew. It allowed me to be out of town making sales, rather than in the office trying to micro-manage her department.

It also allowed me to say to prospective clients, "We have a staff of committed career specialists who have been carefully selected and exceptionally trained. Pick up your phone anytime you like—call the referral service line of any of our Fully Outsourced clients. Ask for a referral. See for yourself." And no matter *which* of Debbie's counselors picked up the prospective client's call, I was never disappointed. At random, at any time of day, whoever picked up the test call would be bright, courteous, professional, knowledgeable, and confidence-inspiring.

Soon we had more Inbound counselors than would fit in Debbie's office, so I moved her department, phones, computers and all, into the large living-dining-room area of the apartment, which had previously been our Outbound telemarketing bay. Debbie continued to hire and train Inbound counselors as they were needed to support our expanding client base, and I bought more computers to add to the network.

I removed the old 36-inch call station desks and put them in storage. I installed a handsome, wide butcher-block counter along the entire 50-foot window wall looking out on Michigan Avenue. I stored the room dividers and replaced them with sound barriers mounted on the counters between the stations. I had the barriers upholstered in a pleasant green fabric matching our logo color. Debbie sat at a desk in the center where she could watch each counselor and monitor each conversation on her phone.

By the time Debbie's staff had grown to eight counselors, we had outgrown the outdated analog phone system with its huge 24-button phones. I purchased a modern digital phone

Rewriting the Scripts

switch that could identify each incoming call by hospital name, and sequence the calls to each counselor. Now, instead of all calls ringing at all stations, calls would be routed to the counselor who had been idle the longest.

Not too many years earlier, long-distance telephone rates had been absurdly high. But federal legislation had broken up "Ma Bell" resulting in deregulated long-distance telephone service. This deregulation is what permitted the very existence of The Medical Connection. By 1991, three independent long-distance companies—AT&T, Sprint, and MCI, competed with one another, forcing rates as low as 12 cents per minute, later to 9 cents a minute. By the end of the decade long-distance rates hovered at 6 cents a minute. At these rates our out-of-town client hospitals could afford to forward their local referral calls to Chicago. A typical referral call averaged six minutes in length, so the long distance costs-per-call were only 72 cents in 1990, soon afterward dropping to as low as 36 cents. The Medical Connection could never have existed at the sky-high long distance rates of the mid 1970s, prior to deregulation.

*

I received a letter from Paul Spiegelman, my competitor at E.R.S. in Los Angeles. He'd been working to sign Mount Sinai hospital in New York City—a hospital where I'd also made a presentation.

I had told the Mount Sinai marketing director, "Well, E.R.S. is a fine operation. "E.R.S." stands for "Emergency Response Systems," one of those outfits that dispatches ambulances. Of course, there's a world of difference between dispatching an ambulance and making a physician referral.

"The Medical Connection is the leader in this business. We invented out-sourced physician referral, and we've made the most contributions to it."

The marketing director relayed these statements to Paul Spiegelman who wrote me a scathing letter, stating that *all* his referral counselors were professionals, they weren't dispatchers. And he added, "By what right do you call The Medical Connection 'the leader in the field?' "

I wrote back, apologizing if I had incorrectly described the capabilities of his counselors. And I added, "I refer to The Medical Connection as the leader in the field simply because we are. We invented this field, and have made the greatest contributions to its development." And I enclosed a copy of our research study booklet, together with reprints of articles written about my study in *Journal of American Medical Association, Crain's Business Review* and *Physician Referral Update.*

*

I decided it was time to consolidate the Medical Connection's new recognition by speaking at upcoming trade conventions on the survey and its findings. I wrote up a resume of my experience and of the study and sent them off to The American Hospital Association, together with a copy of the study booklet and the press clippings.

I was accepted as a featured speaker at both of their marketing conventions—one in Orlando in May, the other in Phoenix in October.

Years before I'd sought attention for Inglehart and Partners by winning advertising awards. I'd won plenty, but they were presented to me in front of audiences consisting of my *competitors.* Now I had two big opportunities to be recognized in front of my *prospective clients.* This would be far more valuable than all those trophies I'd won.

But, I also realized, I would be presenting research findings. Dry stuff. The findings are valuable, extremely important in fact—but my experience in both theater and advertising told me that whenever there's an audience, I should give them a show. Research findings aren't exactly Tennessee

Williams. And I couldn't get them all singing a jingle. As I scripted my one-hour presentation I agonized over how to make it come to life.

Then I hit on an idea—an idea I developed, then scripted, then rehearsed and perfected like an out-of-town pre-Broadway show tryout.

As I stood in front of my first convention seminar audience in Orlando, before a group of perhaps 75 health-care marketing professionals, I described the situations that called for my study. Hospitals needed to find out what their physician referral services were doing right, and what they were doing wrong.

Computerized studies that matched referrals to subsequent hospital billings suggested that each referral would yield an average of $260 in subsequent hospital billings. For every ten referrals made, one of those referred patients would eventually yield an average of $2,600 worth of inpatient or outpatient billings—or $5,200 of hospital billings for every twenty referrals made. The physician referral service was one of the biggest profit centers in the hospital. What, according to my survey findings, were hospitals across the country doing to get more of these referral-generated billings—and what were they doing *wrong?*

- Each 1,000 homes generate 30 referral requests annually. How many should *your* service area yield? How many are you getting now?

- This chart shows how services of various sizes are staffed. How much staff do *you* have? How many calls are *you* missing?

- This next chart shows how much each referral costs the hospital. How much are you paying *your* referral coordinator?

- Here's how many phone lines you need to handle various call volumes. How many phone lines do *you* have?

Then I came to the issue that played right into my hands—the lodestone upon which the future of The Medical Connection Back-up Service rested: those answering machines. According to the survey there were more than 1,200 hospitals using answering machines to handle overflow calls to their physician referral services. My overhead chart showed that, everywhere in the country, services with answering machines handled *fewer* referrals than services without them. The machines were absolutely *counterproductive*. "Why?" I asked. "It's really quite obvious. The patient got your phone number from the Yellow Pages. She called and got an answering machine. Maybe she left a message, maybe she hung up. But she's calling on her lunch hour, and there are eight other hospital referral services listed in the Yellow Pages. *So she calls another hospital.*

"Or maybe she saw blood in her stool that morning, and she's scared to death. She's not going to ask an answering machine whether she should see an oncologist or a gastroenterologist. And she's not going to wait for your referral coordinator to phone her back, possibly at a time when she can't talk privately. She needs to get to a doctor—*now!*

"So," I said from the podium, "all of you have been here at this convention since Wednesday afternoon. Tomorrow you fly home. And I just want you to know that, of all the things you'll remember from these three days here in Orlando, *what you're going to see in the next three minutes you will remember more than anything else you saw or heard in the past three days.*"

I had their full attention.

"Ready?" I said.

I hit the play button on my tape recorder, which was connected to the meeting room's sound system.

Rewriting the Scripts

My audience heard the sounds of touch-tone dialing. Then a pause. Then a ring and a pause. A second ring and a pause.

As the audience listened to this, they saw me step from the podium holding one of those zipper bags that a retailer uses to take cash deposits to the bank. The front of the zipper bag read, "First National Bank of Chicago."

They heard a third ring on the speakers, as I lifted from the zipper bag a pair of thick, banded packets of fresh one-dollar bills, all uncirculated, crisp and consecutively numbered. I broke the bands on both packs.

A telephone voice came over the speakers.

"You have reached the physician referral service at St. Mary's Hospital. We can't take your call right now, but it's very important to us. Please leave your name and number and we'll call you back as soon as possible."

As the message began, I started throwing the dollar bills—over two hundred of them—above the heads of the audience on both sides of the aisle. As the bills floated down onto the audience, everyone began laughing.

"A MISSED CALL," I shouted over the laughter, "REPRESENTS NEARLY THRE HUNDRED DOLLARS IN HOSPITAL BILLINGS *WASTED! LOST FOREVER!* THE COST OF YOUR EXPENSIVE YELLOW PAGES AD IS *BLOWN!* AN ANSWERING MACHINE AT A REFERRAL SERVICE IS LIKE *THROWING MONEY AWAY!*"

Walking back to the podium amid the pandemonium of audience laughter I had just created, I turned and addressed the audience again. "As you all know, marketing is about getting *attention*. DO I HAVE YOUR ATTENTION?"

This final comment drew loud applause in both of my A.H.A. presentations.

Back at the podium, I needed to assure my audience that I wasn't expecting them to return my two hundred bills, so I quipped, "I think I've just subsidized several cab rides back to the airport."

I was there to present important research findings, not to sell The Medical Connection. In fact, I never even mentioned The Medical Connection services.

But any marketing executive could read between the lines: Get rid of your answering machine. Hire more counselors. Or hire The Medical Connection for back-up service. *Don't miss calls!*

At this point in my presentation I'd have the audience in my hands. They were relaxed. More important, I was relaxed with them. I'd gotten them responding. I'd gotten them to "sing my jingle."

And that was just Act One of my show. I had even more theatrics up my sleeve.

Prior to the presentation I'd arranged for the local telephone company to install a private phone line in the hotel meeting room to which I'd been assigned—a phone line on which I could make long-distance calls.

And I'd brought with me a young lady named Dana Klein, one of my most experienced referral specialists.

The meeting room was cordoned off from the hotel ballroom by a series of moveable walls that folded into wall pockets. When the walls were extended out of these wall pockets, the pockets themselves provided a small separate room right off of the conference room. The area had no windows or ventilation, but it was soundproof—inside the "pocket room" you could carry on a telephone conversation without hearing anything in the adjacent meeting room.

Into this little wall pocket room I installed the telephone plus a desk, a chair, a light, and an electric fan.

At the close of my presentation of facts, figures, tables, charts, and floating dollar bills, I introduced Dana as one of The Medical Connection referral specialists. I'd explain about her private phone booth in the hidden wall pocket, where her

Rewriting the Scripts

telephone conversations could be heard on the speakers in the meeting room. I explained that she would now enter the wall pocket room to make some *live calls* to physician referral services around the country. She would ask for a physician referral, and the audience could listen in.

Of course I'd pre-selected the hospitals to call. Some, I knew from previous test calls, were very good. Others were pretty bad.

As Dana's dial-ups connected to these hospital physician referral services, I'd comment on the calls from the podium. One referral coordinator might sound like she'd been up all night, or perhaps as if Dana's call was interrupting her from an article in *People Magazine.* "Does she sound interested in serving Dana?" I'd ask. "She knows her business, but what about her personality? Listen to her—is this someone you'd want to ask about anything as personal as a physician referral?"

I could count on at least one of Dana's calls being picked up by answering machine. "There's another $260 shot to hell," I'd quip.

Then Dana would connect with a good one—a counselor who was friendly, confidence inspiring, and proficient, and concerned with Dana's needs. I'd point out the counselor's strengths as the call progressed.

At the first presentation in Orlando, Dana connected with a hospital in Nashville that I knew from my test calls was very good. The call proceeded nicely. The counselor remembered Dana's name and used it in her conversation. She checked Dana's insurance. She chatted with Dana as her computer did a lookup. "This is good," I commented to my meeting room audience. "She's friendly. She asks the right questions. She calls Dana by her name. She inspires confidence. This is a referral Dana can trust."

From the middle row of my audience, a lady jumped to her feet. "THAT'S *MY* HOSPITAL!" she exclaimed happily.

I hadn't planted her there. It was just luck.

At the end of that meeting, a marketing director walked up to me with a fistful of my dollar bills that she'd gathered off the floor. "I'll trade you these for one of your calling cards," she said.

After each seminar, The American Hospital Association passed out surveys to the attendees, to gauge their evaluations of the speakers and the presentations, and the value of the information. For both of my presentations my scores were very high.

I'd just received the Healthcare industry's equivalent of a pair of CLIO awards.

*

Physician Referral Update was the new industry newsletter published out of Richard Cohen's apartment in San Francisco. By 1991 Richard decided to have his publication sponsor its own convention. He booked a large conference room at St. Francis Hospital in San Francisco and sent out invitations for a two-day conference in June. I made a reservation for myself and booked an airline ticket to San Francisco. About 150 marketing managers attended. At this conference I met several new business prospects.

Also I met two women who would both have a major impact on The Medical Connection, although I didn't know it at the time. One such impact was very positive. The other—well, that one I regret, even to this day.

One of the women was Jan Swan, a marketing director at a sizeable hospital in one of Chicago's northwest suburbs. I'd sent a new business mailing to Jan in May, and had been trying to reach her by phone at her office for several weeks. Just before I left for San Francisco, I called her office again. Her secretary said, "Jerry Inglehart? Oh, Jan's not here, she's left for the convention in San Francisco. But she does want to meet with you. She saw your name on the roster of conference attendees, and told me to tell you she'll be looking for you."

I met Jan and took her to dinner at the Tadisch Grill, made famous in the San Francisco detective novels of Dashiell Hammett. Jan and I enjoyed a world-class fish dinner in this delightful classic restaurant with its paneled booths, charming old light fixtures, and historic windows looking out on San Francisco's historic district.

We talked about The Medical Connection.

Four weeks later Jan hired The Medical Connection, and Debbie Maturo installed the service.

The other woman was Madeline Levy, a marketing director at an Atlanta hospital. She was a tall, skinny girl with an intense face and a head of tightly curled shoulder-length black hair that made her look a little like Andie MacDowell. She was one of the speakers in San Francisco, and made an interesting presentation on ideas for motivating physician referral counselors. I'd be seeing more of Madeline.

Richard Cohen was pleased with the attendance at his San Francisco convention, and decided to have an East Coast convention in Atlanta in mid-October.

I offered to present the Medical Connection Survey findings, but Cohen did not want to use speakers who represented suppliers to the industry.

One of his speakers was Larry Kessenic, a San Francisco attorney specializing in hospitals and health care. He spoke on a subject which had been puzzling the industry since January— the new "Safe Harbor" guidelines for hospital physician referral services, issued by the U.S. Department of Health and Human Services.

A "Safe Harbor" is a guideline that, if followed, protects against prosecution under a specific law, thus providing a "safe harbor." The Miranda Rights that policemen read suspects upon arrest could be construed as a "Safe Harbor" for the lawmen because it protects them from possible charges of misleading the suspect, or having the case thrown out of court. If, upon being arrested, you are told you have the right to remain silent, and that you have the right to an attorney, but you then fail to get an attorney and incriminate yourself in interrogation, the charges against you can't be dropped on the basis that you weren't informed.

Soon after the enactment of Medicare legislation in 1965, a number of fraudulent activities surfaced in the health care industry. Among them were several cases in which physicians prescribed such things as physical therapy, or the use of equipment such as oxygen, whether or not it was needed, simply because the doctors were receiving handsome kickback payments from the suppliers of equipment or therapy.

Federal legislators became concerned that physician referral services might receive kickbacks from the physicians, even though no such cases had surfaced. In an effort to regulate the referral services, the government provided a "Safe Harbor." The service was protected from prosecution if it disclosed to the patient all of the following information when making a referral:

- How the physicians were selected for referral by the hospital.

- Whether or not the physicians had an ownership position in the referral service.

- Whether or not the physicians paid for referrals.

- The criteria used by the service in selecting a physician for referral.

- Any restrictions that would exclude a physician from receiving referrals.

These guidelines told the hospitals *what* their referral services must disclose to the patients, but it failed to tell them *how* to disclose the information. This resulted in total confusion, and a hodgepodge of complicated and non-uniform efforts at compliance.

Larry Kessenick's speech at the Atlanta convention described the dilemma.

My Medical Connection clients were thoroughly confused by the guidelines. Every week I'd get calls from clients and prospects asking what the Safe Harbor meant, and how to comply.

I met with Larry and asked him several questions. His knowledge and guidance helped cut through the cloud of confusion surrounding the issue. I told Larry that I planned to study the matter further, and then write and distribute a booklet explaining the standards, with recommendations for compliance. I asked him if I could hire him to review my work when I finished it, and put his professional stamp of approval on it. Larry said yes, he'd be happy to work for me—but if I made him a coauthor of the book, he'd review it without charge.

I sent him a written proposal. Then in January and February of 1992 I donned my paralegal hat and began a two-month-long project of sorting out the facts and organizing them into a scholarly, yet easy-to-understand-and-follow document of analysis and recommendations based on Larry's comments. I faxed sections of the document to Larry as I proceeded. He got back to me with concise corrections and recommendations.

The greatest single accomplishment of the document was that Larry and I rendered *all five* of the requirements down to a single 25-word disclosure statement to replace the jumble of complicated and lengthy disclosures that had been prepared by various hospital attorneys. Our disclosure could be read to each patient over the phone in about eight seconds. In Larry's educated opinion, the following statement did it all:

"We operate a referral panel for physicians who are on our medical staff, without charge to them. Selection is based on your needs and preferences."

If William Shakespeare has his *"That time of year thou mayst in me behold..."* sonnet engraved on his tombstone, perhaps I should have this 25-word phrase engraved on mine. It proved to be the most permanent and influential thing I'd ever write in my life—because it became the *standard for the industry!*

I titled my book *Coping with the New Safe Harbor Standards for Hospital Physician Referral Services.* It was the first treatise explaining the Safe Harbor regulations, and how to comply with them. It was well crafted, authoritative, and *legal.* It fulfilled a crying need. The book was widely distributed by me to The Medical Connection clients and prospective clients, and was written up in several trade journals. As such, it *became* the industry standard—meaning that if any legal action arose against a hospital regarding compliance, if the hospital could prove that it had complied with *my* recommendations coauthored by Larry Kessenick, the hospital could demonstrate that it had followed the accepted standards for the industry.

This made me and Larry Kessenick the country's leading authorities on Safe Harbor Compliance—a rather satisfying *coup* for me, because at the time of publication, the clients of Paul Spiegelman's E.R.S, my major competitor and arch rival, were using a complex eighty-word disclosure that took nearly a minute to read to each patient. *And Paul Spiegelman was an attorney!*

There was one other notable recommendation in our book. The Department of Health and Human Services, in its wisdom, had specified that, in order to comply with the Safe Harbor, each disclosure to each patient had to be written out with the patient's name, the date the referral was made, and *signed* by the person making the referral. Needless to say, there was no time for the referral specialist to accomplish this on a busy

Rewriting the Scripts

morning handling one call with two others on hold. Consequently she was likely to print all the statements for the week on Friday afternoon, then sign and file them as a batch.

But we were now in the age of computers. So in our book we built a case for the fact that, by hitting a function key on her computer after reading the statement to the patient, the counselor was in fact "signing" a document which, although it existed only electronically, could in fact be printed out at any future time, with the patient name and referral date included.

The question was—is electronic notation in an electronic age the same as the written, dated, and signed document required by the government? In our publication, Larry and I stated that it was indeed, with the disclaimer that some future court decision would be needed to test and verify our conclusions. Meanwhile, we recommended to our readers that they ignore the "written, dated, and hand-signed" requirements of the guidelines and instead allow electronic notation to constitute compliance with the guidelines. This, too, became the "standard for the industry," eliminating the printing, signing, and filing of nearly ten million pieces of paper per year by hospitals across America.

In June of 1992, *Physician Referral Update* held its second San Francisco conference. Attendance was triple that of the previous year's conference. Larry Kessenick was a featured speaker. After he presented our findings and recommendations, a marketing director in the audience asked, "Where can we get our hands on a copy of this book?"

Larry at the podium addressed me, sitting at our Medical Connection booth in the back of the ballroom. "Jerry, how can people get a copy of our book?"

"BY RAISING THEIR HANDS," I called out.

About 130 hands shot up. Dana and I rushed into the audience, our arms loaded with copies of the book, which we distributed to both sides of the aisle in a matter of minutes.

I couldn't speak at this convention. But I was getting everything I could have hoped for if I had been a speaker. In the eyes of over 400 hospital marketing directors, The Medical Connection was the leader in the field.

Walking back to my booth, I shot a glance at Paul Spiegelman sitting in the E.R.S. booth. He was pretending not to notice.

A two-hour lunch break followed Larry's presentation. I'd arranged for a Medical Connection bus tour of San Francisco, having booked one of those wide, comfortable European tour busses with huge windows. We'd sent invitations to the list of conference attendees. The bus tour was fully booked. As the driver drove our guests through the streets and sights of San Francisco, Dana and I walked up and down the bus aisle serving our guests a nice deli lunch and lots of bubbly champagne.

One guest, seated near the front of the bus, was Madeline Levy from Atlanta, the young lady with the Andie MacDowell hairdo who had delivered the presentation on motivation the previous year.

*

After the San Francisco convention, I'd get at least one call per week from a hospital seeking a copy of my Safe Harbor book, and questions as to how their referral service could quickly begin adhering to the standards. My response became:

"The book is fairly easy to understand. We wrote it in layman's language. It's important that you read it. For immediate compliance I suggest you turn to page 21, where you'll find the 25-word disclosure statement. This has to be read over the phone *verbatim* to each patient before you give a referral. Modify your software so that the counselor can make an electronic notation that the disclosure was read to the patient. *Don't* include the disclosure in your follow-up letters to patients; it will simply cloud the question of how and when the disclosure was made.

"Then turn to Appendix A in the back of the book. This is a four-page 'Letter to File' which you can copy and have signed and filed by anyone in authority at the hospital—perhaps yourself. This document establishes how your hospital is complying with the standards. If you want legal counsel to review your compliance letter, be certain you give them the copy of the book along with the letter. When they see the book, they'll probably sign off on the letter.

"And that's it. You can be in compliance as soon as your compliance letter is signed and filed."

"Can't you just give me the disclosure statement over the phone now?" many callers would ask.

"I can't. Using the disclosure statement without understanding how it complies with the guidelines could get you in trouble. And this is an area where you want to follow the guidelines exactly. The guidelines actually include criminal penalties, including fines and jail terms for non-compliance. I know of no instance where anybody has been imprisoned for noncompliance, but there's always a first time, and I wouldn't want to be phoning you in a jail cell."

As we mailed out each booklet that was requested, we enclosed some of our Medical Connection brochures. And I'd follow up on these leads.

A self-ordained paralegal, I was now dispensing legal advice to hospitals all over the country.

It was time to consolidate my company's leadership position. I'd need to make some additions to my cast of characters, including that "front man."

Chapter 26

Madeline and Other Challenges

I resumed my intensive and exhausting schedule of new business travel throughout the eastern half of the United States, lodging each night in humble Motel 6 and Red Roof Inns with their tiny bathrooms and modular shower stalls. Coach seats on commercial aircraft would serve me as temporary offices where I could set up my laptop to organize notes and write follow-up letters.

By late 1992, hospitals were rushing to computerize their in-house physician referral services. Each hospital would spend anywhere from $30,000 and $90,000 to purchase a referral software package. The leading brand with a 40% market share was called Healthmatch, developed by Baxter Laboratories, and subsequently sold by Baxter to an independent marketing organization. An outfit called Healthline had purchased a software product that had been developed for Scripps Medical Center in La Jolla, California. The product gained a 20% market share. Referral One, sold by an organization in Phoenix, was an also-ran contender with a 7% market share. Meanwhile, 13% of the hospitals hired independent programmers to develop custom packages based on off-the-shelf spreadsheet software like

Madeline and Other Challenges

Paradox and Q&A. All of these software products were very rudimentary when measured against the software capabilities of today. They were cumbersome, slow, and full of glitches.

I used a laptop computer to demonstrate our own software capabilities to prospective clients. I wanted them to understand how our software aided our counselors—and also to see how our own software was *superior* in many ways to the software they might have purchased or developed themselves. For clients seeking our Back-Up service, we were able to transfer our back-up referrals by modem to their own systems each night, in order that the hospitals could send out patient follow-up letters the next day. They could also monitor our back-up activity closely.

I began bringing Dana Klein along on my trips to handle the software demos. As an experienced counselor, she was far more proficient with the software than I was. And the presence of a woman in my presentation was valuable, since the majority of our prospective clients were female marketing directors.

But I was still hoping for my female "front man."

In September I made a call to Madeline Levy, the marketing director of a large Atlanta hospital whom I'd seen at two of the *Physician Referral Update* conferences. I spoke to her very briefly: "Madeline, The Medical Connection is growing rapidly, and we're looking for a marketing vice president to handle our new business efforts. I don't know whether you are seeking a career change, but if you are, perhaps we should talk."

"Interesting," she said. "I'll think about it."

A week later Madeline accepted my invitation to fly to Chicago, see our operation, and talk with me about the position. I was impressed with her. She was knowledgeable in all aspects of hospital referral service. She was heading a large referral service with a staff of four counselors. I offered her a choice of a salary or a commission on future sales, and told her I'd pay to move her to Chicago. I took her on a tour of neighborhoods where I thought a young single woman might fit in—the high-rise apartment buildings in nearby Streeterville, the vintage townhouses of Old Town and Lincoln Park, and the apartments around Northwestern University in Evanston. I wined and dined her at the 95th floor restaurant of the John Hancock building.

She joined The Medical Connection in late November.

On the morning of her arrival, I introduced her to a piece of business software in which she could record all her new business activity—solicitation letters, follow-up calls, appointments, evaluations, and client acquisitions. I told her I'd expect a printout of each week's activity on my desk every Friday afternoon.

At the end of her first week, Madeline came into my office. "I don't have any new business activity to report because what with moving and getting settled in here, I didn't have a chance to organize a new business mailing. But I spent some time this week looking over the mailing you've been using. And I think the mail-back postcards we enclose should be postage-paid, with a business reply indicia."

"Did you organize a mailing list for your first batch of letters?"

"I'm working on that."

"I want you to report your progress on that list. That will constitute your first week's activity report."

"What about the business reply card?"

"Well, Madeline," I began, "I gave that some thought when I put that mailing together. I don't think it's a major issue."

"It makes us look so cheap, that they have to use their own postage to request more information."

"Madeline," I said, "you're a marketing professional with a great deal of knowledge and experience in this field. We need that knowledge. You're a vice president here. I think you should evaluate our new business efforts from a more far-reaching and insightful viewpoint than whether or not we should be using a business reply card."

I've often wondered whether this comment marked the beginning of the end of my relationship with Madeline. I

Madeline and Other Challenges

intended to challenge her. But no doubt she took my comment as a put-down. I'm no Dale Carnegie. Or Henry Kissinger. Maybe this was the problem. How could I have rephrased my criticism?

"Madeline, if you think a business reply card would help, do it—but I'd hoped for a little more from you after one week."

Maybe.

"Madeline, you're a very bright woman, that's why I hired you. You know this business better than most of the people you'll call on." Then smile at her, with a little twinkle in my eyes. "I'll bet you can think of a lot more significant ways to improve our mailings than by enclosing a business reply card."

Better.

At the end of Week Two, Madeline came in with her first new business report. She'd succeeded in getting a mailing out. She said to me, "We need to have a marketing plan."

"Have you ever prepared a marketing plan before?"

"*We* don't prepare it. We hire an advertising agency to write one for us."

"I think you should know, Madeline, that I spent over twenty years generating marketing plans for advertising clients. I can write the marketing plan for The Medical Connection on the back of a matchbook. And here it is: 'The Medical Connection seeks income from hospitals by performing physician referral services that are more professional and less costly than services the hospitals can or might provide internally.' "

"But every serious business has an ad agency," she replied.

I looked at her. Did I detect a Melker Management Paradigm?

Apparently Madeline was another of those bureaucrats who hoped to spend ten days at a seminar to learn how to *define* work, then waste several more weeks *defining* her job—anything to postpone actually *doing* her job. Now she wanted to hire an outside firm to do her work for her. She was just too steeped in the routines of hospitals that were large, bureaucratic, and submerged in traditions of endless meetings and exhaustive memos, to ever be able to succeed with the real work of making calls, lining up presentations, and signing new clients. Would she ever understand what business was all about in the real world?

I'd already noticed how Madeline often reflected on her past career success not in terms of what she'd accomplished, but in terms of how many people reported to her. If she had four people working for her, then her job seemed four times more meaningful than if she had just a secretary.

Now she wanted an advertising agency to report to her.

Dale Carnegie, what do I do now?

The following Wednesday, around 5 P.M., I passed her office. For some reason, I got the impression that she was waiting for me to leave the office. I closed the door to my private office next to hers, then said goodnight to her, and left. I stood by the elevator, thinking, pondering, and wondering.

I turned around and returned to the office suite very quietly, closing my office door behind me. I left my light off. I picked up my phone and dialed the code to monitor Madeline's phone line.

She was on the phone talking to a girlfriend. What I heard was shocking and disappointing. Madeline was complaining about me to her friend, disparaging me, even doing a parody my voice to make me sound stupid and incompetent to her girlfriend.

I wondered, if she feels this way about me personally, how might she present us to prospective clients? If she was bad-mouthing The Medical Connection, I'd better find out about it fast.

That night after she left to go home, I wired a separate phone extension in my office to a voice-activated tape recorder. I drilled a hole in a file cabinet, ran the phone line through the hole, placed the phone extension and tape recorder in one of the

Madeline and Other Challenges

drawers and locked the cabinet. I left this hidden phone coded to monitor Madeline's line.

During the next ten days I took the cassette from the voice-activated tape machine each evening and listened to it on my car's tape deck while driving home to Evanston. Her work pattern was proving to be deplorable. Although she came into the office each morning on time, she'd make only two or three new business calls, then spend the rest of the morning calling girlfriends and boyfriends, to chat or to line up a lunch date. Each afternoon after lunch, she'd make two or three more business calls, and then lapse back into the marathon calls to girlfriends and boyfriends until quitting time.

On one occasion—perhaps the sixth or seventh day of my monitoring—she made a new business call that was truly outstanding. Talking to a prospect at a hospital in Philadelphia she spoke easily, comfortably, like two executives networking. She was very convincing as she explained what The Medical Connection could do for this marketing director. She had remarkable confidence and authority. I was convinced she'd be able to sign this hospital shortly after her first visit.

Here was the talent I'd hoped for when I hired her—a real pro, the "front man" I'd been seeking for decades. What could I do to motivate this woman to do what she did so easily, but so infrequently?

For the following week I'd organized a schedule of East Coast new business presentations, beginning in Maine and working down the coast to Philadelphia. Madeline would accompany me, to learn how to make presentations on her own.

Each night that we were in the East, I'd pull up to a motel where I'd made a reservation for Madeline. I'd drop her, explaining that I was staying with friends in town that night. Then I'd drive to another motel and check in. I did this for four consecutive nights, in Falmouth, Massachusetts; Bridgeport, Connecticut; Yonkers, New York; and Trenton, New Jersey. I figured that if I had to fire Madeline, I didn't want to have to deal with some sexual harassment charge she might trump up, claiming I'd fired her because she refused to sleep with me. By pretending to spend each night with friends, I presumably had witnesses to testify that I never spent a night in a motel with her.

I didn't trust this woman.

Two weeks later, Madeline had finally organized her own new business trip from the prospects she'd generated herself. She'd be making calls in Pennsylvania and Washington, D.C.

She booked herself into a fancy hotel in Georgetown.

My cassettes of her monitored phone conversations revealed that she'd also lined up a weekend at this hotel with a boyfriend.

A major January snowstorm hit the D.C. area the Wednesday evening she arrived there. On Thursday morning she phoned me from the Georgetown hotel to advise me that she was snowed in, and had cancelled all her appointments for Thursday and Friday.

Madeline returned to the office on Monday and submitted her expense account for the trip. I examined the bill from her Georgetown hotel. Whereas cheap hotels like Motel 6 and Red Roof let you make local and credit card calls free of charge, the fancy hotels tack 75 cents to a dollar onto the bill for each "connect," whether it's a local or credit card call.

Each of these calls was itemized on Madeline's Georgetown hotel bill, revealing that while she was snowbound in her hotel that Thursday and Friday, she'd made twenty-six calls from her room. Only two of them were to hospitals. *She'd made 24 calls to boyfriends, girlfriends, and family!*

That Monday my hidden voice-activated tape recorder captured the piece of straw that broke this camel's back. Madeline's major interest in life was networking with girlfriends and dating boyfriends. In airplanes she apparently enjoyed getting hit on by young male passengers. Madeline would give her business cards to these men who would then call her when she returned to the office. One of her cards went to a

Madeline and Other Challenges

fellow passenger on her flight back from Washington D.C. He called her that Monday.

In his conversation with Madeline, the gentleman said something about "...you can't go on working for a misguided company with a stupid boss who won't even get a marketing plan."

So Madeline was bad-mouthing not just me, but The Medical Connection as well—and not just to her girlfriends—to total strangers! This called for damage control. I had to fire her—fast.

I lined up a new business presentation for Madeline at a hospital in Rockford, Illinois. I told her that since I'd called on this prospect for several months, I would come to the presentation to introduce her.

At the presentation I made note of any and all errors, omissions and deletions Madeline made in her presentation. Actually, she made a fine pitch, but I needed solid evidence to justify firing her.

In two days Madeline was scheduled to fly back East for more hospital presentations. I called her into my office, explained to her the errors, omissions, and deletions I'd witnessed at the Rockford presentation, and told her that she'd need retraining. I said I would accompany her on her East Coast trip, to supervise her until she was performing up to the standards of The Medical Connection.

I was almost certain that Madeline would refuse to travel with me under such demeaning circumstances. Maybe she had social plans made for that trip that she didn't want me to know about. And I was right. She said that if I went on the East Coast trip, she wouldn't go.

Next I called Debbie Maturo into the office to witness what I was about to say. "Debbie," I said, "yesterday Madeline demonstrated in a Rockford presentation that she is missing a great many important sales points in her Medical Connection presentations. I told her she needed retraining, and that I would accompany her on her East Coast trip tomorrow. She has refused to go. Therefore I am firing her, effective immediately. She is to leave the office as soon as she can pack her personal things."

Madeline was furious. She started screaming at me and calling me names—loud enough to disturb the counselors handling referral calls in the front room. Next she went into her office and began stuffing company files from her desk into a box. I forcibly stopped her. "Those files belong to The Medical Connection."

"They're mine. These letters bear my signature."

"I paid you to write those letters. They belong to The Medical Connection."

"I WON'T LEAVE WITHOUT THESE FILES!"

I said to Debbie, "Call the Chicago Police Department on 911. Tell them we have a former employee creating a disturbance, disrupting our office, and trying to steal files."

Two cops arrived in less than ten minutes, during which time Madeline and I had stood in a silent face-off. "This bastard just fired me," Madeline said to the cops, "and he won't he let me take my files."

To my amazement, the Chicago cop proved to be quite knowledgeable in such matters. He said to Madeline, "The law allows you to take your coat, your photos, your personal effects, and nothing else. Everything else belongs to the company."

"These letters are personal effects," Madeline screamed at the cop. "They have my signature." She thrust one of the letters in the cop's face.

"They're business letters," the cop said. "They belong to the company. You can't remove them."

Madeline grabbed her coat and purse and left in a huff, the cops right behind her. She'd been in my employ for only a few weeks.

Three days later I got a call from Richard Cohen, the editor of the newsletter, *Physician Referral Update.* Richard wanted some information for a follow-up article on Safe Harbors. At the end of the conversation I mentioned that I'd fired Madeline Levy.

"Madeline told me she'd *quit* The Medical Connection," Richard Cohen replied.

"Did she, now? Did she happen to mention that we had to call the police to have her removed from the office?"

So Madeline was still bad-mouthing my company and misrepresenting facts—this time to the editor of a trade journal.

I phoned my law office, Lord, Bissell and Brook, and talked to Katherine Montgomery, an attorney specializing in employee relations. She drafted a letter to Madeline and had it delivered to her apartment that day by special messenger. The letter read, "It has come to our client's attention that you are misrepresenting the facts surrounding your departure from The Medical Connection. This letter is to inform you that you will be held personally responsible for any damages that occur to The Medical Connection as a result of your misrepresentations."

I still feel disappointment when I think about Madeline Levy. She could have been so perfect for The Medical Connection—exactly the person I was looking for, had she been willing to take her work seriously. The Medical Connection could have eventually made her a very successful and fabulously wealthy woman. She had everything I needed—everything except the Yankee Work Ethic.

Two years later I was tending a Medical Connection trade show booth at a convention in Atlanta. Madeline was then employed in that city by Scottish Rite Children's Hospital. She wandered into my booth. "Hello, Jerry, how have you been?"

"Fine, Madeline—how about you?"

"Great—I have a staff of twenty-two people reporting to me now."

So Madeline's life was now twenty-two times more meaningful than when she worked for me. And she'd come clear across the convention hall to let me know. Madeline had found her niche!

*

Throughout the rest of 1993 and well into 1994 I continued my intense pace of business travel, viewing the world through the windshields of economy rental cars as cities and towns flew past me on the interstate highway system.

By then I was proficient in ferreting out cheap airfares. I knew which cities were serviced by discount airlines, creating a competitive situation that forced down all the fares to that city. Newark Airport was always a bargain, while LaGuardia and Kennedy were not. To get to noncompetitive Pittsburgh I'd save several hundred dollars by flying to Cleveland and driving a rental car to Pittsburgh. If I had an appointment in Pensacola or Mobile I could save plenty by flying to Birmingham and driving the rest of the way. To get to Boston it was considerably cheaper to fly Southwest Airlines from Chicago to Columbus, then catch America West from Columbus to Boston. Baltimore was so much cheaper than Washington National or Dulles that I'd use Baltimore as a "hub" to get to Washington—or even to Richmond. I probably knew more about discount travel than most travel agents. Of course, a travel agent's success rested on selling the *costliest* fares, paying top commissions. They worked at odds with travelers like me.

By 1993 The Medical Connection enjoyed enough income to have enabled me to travel more comfortably. But by that time, economical travel had become a part of my business philosophy. True, I could have afforded to book myself into more elegant hotels and to rent cars that were larger and more comfortable. But whenever I compared the prices of the fancier accommodations, I'd think about my hard-working counselors coming in to work promptly each day, sitting for eight hours with their eyes glued to their computer screens, listening to patients on their headsets, earning money for The Medical

Connection. The difference in price of a typical first-class upgrade ticket for one of my frequent trips to New York or Atlanta would absorb all the profit generated by one of those counselors in two or three days. And the upgrade would give me no more than a couple of hours of extra leg room, a couple of free drinks, and an ego boost that I neither needed nor wanted. I preferred to use my travel savings to fund employee bonuses and raises that would make my staff feel appreciated. Their loyalty yielded far more to The Medical Connection than a luxury hotel room, a bigger rental car, or a first-class airline seat.

I signed new clients in Knoxville, Indianapolis, St. Louis, and towns in West Virginia, Massachusetts, Virginia, and Florida. Whenever my new business calls brought me nearby an existing client, I'd call on that client to deliver reports, share important events in the industry, or outline any new services or features we were developing—but mostly just to say hello and keep my face before them. Their calls were being handled by our counselors hundreds of miles away, and I wanted to make sure they saw me often enough to recognize that The Medical Connection valued them as clients, and to give them an opportunity to tell me about any problems or complaints that might have cropped up.

I discovered I had a valuable booster in New York City. His name was Thomas Cooperman, the Yellow Pages rep for Reuben H. Donnelley. Cooperman handled all hospital clients in the New York Metro Area. He'd found out about The Medical Connection, as well as E.R.S, on learning that when a hospital hired either of us, they generally increased their Yellow Pages advertising.

Cooperman was a masterful networker who managed to get the inside line on everything that was going on in the marketing departments of New York hospitals, including the names of key people to be writing and talking to. He was also quite a conversationalist. When my staff told me he was on the line, I could count on being on the phone with him for at least half an hour.

For the first half-year of our relationship, Thomas advised me that he'd be referring his Yellow Pages clients not only to me but also to Paul Spiegelman at E.R.S. But eventually, after learning that his clients were generally more satisfied with service from The Medical Connection, he stopped referring E.R.S. and gave his leads to me exclusively. Cooperman proved to be a key ingredient of our success in getting leads and signing clients in the New York Metro Area. On my frequent commutes to The Big Apple, I'd often take him to dinner, to pick his brains. One weekend Christie and I met and dined with him and his family at a mid-town brunch. Could Cooperman be the "front man" I'd been seeking for so long?

*

New York Cornell Medical Center went on a merger binge. They purchased several New York area hospitals, including two of my oldest New York clients. One was Methodist Hospital in the posh Park Slope neighborhood of Brooklyn, just below Prospect Park. The other was Booth Memorial Hospital in a charming Archie Bunker neighborhood in Queens where the streets were lined with tiny two-bedroom bungalows. Booth had been owned and operated by The Salvation Army. We'd provided full-time service to both Booth and Methodist hospitals for many years. After the merger, the hospital names were changed to New York Methodist and New York Hospital of Queens.

From my advertising agency days I'd learned that when a client was sold, merged, or hired a new marketing director, you could kiss that client good-bye—you'd have a letter of termination in a matter of weeks. It had happened to me with both WBBM-FM and The Butler Company.

But while ad agencies are as disposable as paper towels, my value to my New York hospital clients was great. They both retained me after their big mergers with New York Cornell. Furthermore, after evaluating the physician referral activity at both hospitals, New York Cornell invited The Medical Connection to make a presentation to them.

In the years when I had run Inglehart and Partners, I always felt that when I retired, the agency would be worthless in the sale or merger market. I suspected one day I'd simply be taking my Inglehart and Partners sign down from my office door and tossing it in a trash barrel. Without me, there was no Inglehart and Partners.

But The Medical Connection seemed to represent permanence—clients that stayed because of all those superb, well-trained and experienced Medical Connection referral counselors—plus our superior software.

For the first time in my life, I had the satisfaction of knowing that I was building something that might exist after I retired. It felt good.

*

By September Debbie had expanded her staff to eleven counselors. And I was deeply proud of every one of them. Debbie had screened each candidate extensively. She had an instinct for determining which applicants would study her training manuals carefully and become proficient in medical terminology. And she could spot the serious applicants who would become career employees and stick with The Medical Connection for years. This was important because each candidate needed six to eight weeks of full-time training and monitoring before she could begin to handle calls on her own. Debbie couldn't afford to waste her time with fly-by-nighters.

Whenever I walked into our call center, I felt pride as I listened to each of my expert counselors chatting like old friends with the patients, entering their demographic and insurance information on the computer terminals, making the referrals and answering patient questions proficiently. Debbie's crew of experts was the foundation of our success, and no competitor could match them for personality and professionalism.

I regularly boosted our charges to our clients by 4% or 5% annually in order to fund handsome raises to reward loyalty, and to pay Debbie huge annual bonuses that soon amounted to 40% of her income.

I purchased a refrigerator for the ladies' soda pop and bag lunches. I instituted a program of birthday gifts for each employee. One year each of them received on her birthday a handsome, comprehensive Webster's dictionary with an enclosure card in which I had written in longhand the following melodious speech of Professor Henry Higgins in his effort to inspire his student, Eliza Doolittle :

> *"Eliza, yours is the language of Shakespeare and Milton. The majesty and grandeur of the English language is the greatest possession we have. The noblest thoughts that have flown through the hearts of men are contained in its extraordinary, imaginative and magical mixture of sounds."*
> -Alan Jay Lerner, *My Fair Lady*

One autumn, as we changed our clocks from daylight saving time and ushered in the months when most of my staff would leave the office in darkness, I brought in a lecturer from the Chicago Police Department to talk to the women about street safety, and how to avoid or foil an attacker. I gave each of them a pocket aerosol of pepper spray.

Before Thanksgiving I told the staff that I'd be bringing in a load of 15-lb. Butterball Turkeys, one for each of them. I handed them out on the Wednesday before Thanksgiving in canvas shopping bags so they could carry their big birds home on the busses.

Each year I'd reserve tables for them at a nice restaurant for a Christmas party. I'd give my credit card to Debbie for the tab.

Madeline and Other Challenges

I'd come in at the start of the party, buy a bottle of champagne for each table, then lead a toast to tell them that they were the best referral counselors in the country, and that I was very proud of them all.

I'd hold up the restaurant menu and say, "Tonight, you order anything you want. Lobster? Filet mignon? *Nothing's* too good for you people." And indeed, they'd all order the most expensive things on the menu. This was their night to live high on seafood and champagne.

Right after my toast I'd leave the restaurant and go home so they could get drunk and giggle among themselves without worrying about making a good impression on the boss.

They were an incredible bunch. Debbie had built an unbeatable staff that was delivering a quality of service no competitor could match. And I dearly respected them all.

My sincere appreciation of them was reaping a valuable side benefit for The Medical Connection—*loyalty*. They liked their bosses, both of us! They liked working at The Medical Connection where they felt properly appreciated. They'd convince their friends, sisters, and cousins to apply for work at The Medical Connection. The word was out—The Medical Connection is a great place to work!

I heard a radio interview appealing to employers to hire handicapped people. Our building, office, and lavatories were all wheelchair-accessible. What an opportunity I had for paraplegics! I called the phone number cited in the radio interview. No one called back. Six months later I heard another radio appeal encouraging employers to hire handicapped people. Again I called the organization cited. I described the requirements for the job. The organization sent out only two applicants. Both were hopelessly inadequate—not just physically challenged, but mentally challenged as well.

In the laundry room I occasionally saw a man in a wheelchair—a resident of an apartment in the building. I asked him if he knew of any organizations I could contact to interview paraplegic job candidates. He said he'd look into it. He never did. When I next saw him in the laundry room, he said he wasn't really interested in returning to work.

I thought of how often miscommunication caused failure. I remembered Harlan Bond at the St. Louis office of GC Services, and how his miscommunication to his telephone counselor had nearly caused me to abandon the business plan for The Medical Connection.

*

Our computer LAN system grew to fourteen stations plus a file server. The newer, faster computers with "486" chips had come on the market, making the old "286" and "386" machines seem woefully slow and inadequate.

We now had the capability to crank out quarterly reports for each client. The reports contained analyses of our referral activity with respect to several criteria. We included color charts. The addenda to these reports had listings of every patient, including address and insurance—plus a separate compilation of the patient comments recorded by the counselors from every referral. These reports were ½ inch to ¾ inch thick. The reports let our clients know that we were handling a lot of activity for them.

Whenever a hospital provided us with a magnetic tape or series of discs listing all of their inpatient and outpatient billings by patient name and address, our software could do a "Billings Match" report, matching the names and addresses on the billings to referrals previously made. These reports were very time consuming for our programmer, Bill Rosman, and I had to charge $1,000 for each Billings Match report. But these reports constituted the first quantitative proof of the dollar value of our service. The published national average at that time was $260 in hospital billings for every referral made—that is to say, if the service made ten referrals, the patient names ultimately matched up to an average of $2,600 in hospital billings. But our own matches were yielding an average of $407 dollars, and on reports for some of the hospitals, the matches occasionally exceeded $800 per referral made.

These reports were very effective in proving the value of our contribution to hospital profits. I decided to subsidize their high cost by reducing our charges from $1,000 per report to $500, and ultimately to $200, simply to get the clients to let us do them so they'd appreciate the dollar value of our services.

We were quickly running out of space in the apartment at 405 North Wabash. I began looking for legitimate business space in an office building. Operating out of an apartment in a residential building may have been acceptable for a one-man advertising agency. But as The Medical Connection grew into a business with fifteen employees, having our clients and prospective clients visit us in an apartment building was something of an embarrassment.

I found a nice office space at 625 North Michigan Avenue. It was double the size of our North Wabash space. It had a huge bay for the computer stations. Off of this room was a doorway leading to three private offices—a quiet corner office for me, an office for any future assistants, and an end office that I could make into a lunch room where the staff could dine on bag lunches, have coffee breaks and make personal phone calls.

A few weeks earlier I'd monitored a personal call in which one of my bilingual Hispanic counselors had an agonized discussion with her Latin boyfriend. The boyfriend had become very abusive on the phone, swearing at her in Spanish and threatening her. This concerned me. Most of my counselors were young women with boyfriends. My brother had described a time at his own company when an angered boyfriend had broken into their office with a gun. What if something like this happened at The Medical Connection?

I installed a deadbolt lock on the main entrance door from the elevator lobby and put in a peephole with a lens so the staff could see who was at the door. If threatened, the staff could retreat through a second door to the private office area where I installed another inside deadbolt and peephole on the door. In the end office I placed a sledgehammer, and marked the drywall separating this office from the next tenant. If necessary, the drywall could be smashed with the hammer so the staff could escape into the offices next door and retreat to the stairway or elevator bank.

Then it occurred to me that if I ever had a disaffected or unbalanced employee on my own staff, she could use that sledgehammer to damage our computers and phone switch. So I hid the hammer where only Debbie Maturo and Barbara Barth, Debbie's evening supervisor, could find it.

Five or six weeks before our move to 625 North Michigan, I had my new landlord rewire the office. We needed a separate electrical circuit for every five computers, to avoid overload and blowing of fuses. I had the phone company run a fifty-line trunk up to the office.

Then I began worrying in earnest.

How do you move a telemarketing service from one building to another, when it's operating seven days a week?

The move would have to take place overnight—between close of business on Sunday evening and opening early Monday morning. That meant a great deal of rushing, and paying a lot of overtime to union contractors and suppliers. Our entire digital phone system, as well as our fourteen-terminal LAN computer system would have to be disassembled and reassembled—overnight—because there was no way in the world that we could declare a moving day. Those incoming calls were our lifeblood—and they came in nearly 100 hours per week. If we missed an hour, patients would be complaining to our client hospitals. If we missed two days, our clients would have to find other sources to handle their calls. We'd be out of business.

Burrows Movers in Rogers Park agreed to handle an overnight move at double wages.

Bill Rosman said he could disconnect, move, and reconnect the computer system overnight.

Madeline and Other Challenges

The outfit that sold me the phone system arranged for two technicians to relocate the system in the new office overnight. I made certain I had the home phone numbers of their boss as well as that of the owner of the company from whom I'd purchased the phone system.

My paranoia built. Could so much complicated electronics be moved successfully between dusk and dawn? What if something went wrong?

By 3 A.M. the movers had transferred our furniture, cabinets, supplies, and potted plants to 625 North Michigan. And Bill Rosman had the computers up and working in the new office.

But the phone switch wouldn't work. The technicians reported that a motherboard had burnt out. They woke up their parts department. There was no replacement board in Chicago. One could be flown in from a supply depot in Denver overnight, arriving by 10 A.M. on Tuesday. I explained that The Medical Connection would be out of business by 10 A.M. on Tuesday. Someone in Denver would have to be awakened to retrieve the part, drive it to Denver International Airport immediately, and put it on the next plane for Chicago. I would personally receive it at the airport.

The technicians looked at me in disbelief. I pulled out the phone number of the owner of their company. "If I have to call this number, I'll be getting your boss out of bed at home. But I have no other choice. We need that part now. Our incoming calls start four hours from now, and we're going to be ready. I'll go downstairs to a pay phone now and make this call."

"Hold on," the head technician said. He thought maybe they could borrow the motherboard from the phone system of another Chicago client. He didn't want to face what would happen to him if I woke up his boss's boss.

Meanwhile, I was so upset I was afraid I was going to vomit. My fears were realized. I was living a nightmare. Our client's patients would complain to our hospitals, the marketing directors would call our line and receive a recording, "The number you have dialed is not in service." NO! NO! NO! I'd worked too hard for too long.

My threat worked. Somebody hopped in a cab and went to the overnight office of another client, cannibalized the motherboard, and brought it to our office by 5 A.M. When the ladies showed up for work at 7 A.M., the phones were working.

I was physically and mentally drained. I stayed and watched my business swing into action in the new office. Just a few hours earlier it had hung by a thread. When I was assured nothing else would go wrong, I went home to a day of tortured sleep.

*

My next project would be to revise our Inbound brochure. I'd produced it just a few years before when I had only one counselor, and I needed a photo to make it look like I had a dozen counselors. Now I actually *had* a dozen, and I needed a brochure to make it look like I had about thirty. My archrival, E.R.S. reportedly had a *whole floor* of counselors in a building near Los Angeles International Airport.

I held a "LaSalle Street Day" early one Sunday morning before call time. For this I told my staff to dress in suits and blouses for the photo, and to bring their sisters, cousins, and girlfriends as well—each woman would sign a release and receive a payment of $30 for her trouble.

I also brought in my daughter-in-law, my girlfriend Christie Barber, and Melissa Lain, head of the graphics design studio that prepared our brochures.

On the wall above the heads of my staff I'd mounted six big wall clocks that I'd labeled with the four U.S. time zones plus two labeled "Indianapolis" and "Phoenix,"—the two cities that didn't go on daylight saving time, but bounced back and forth each year between one time zone and another. We didn't have a client in Phoenix, but this was showbiz.

Madeline and Other Challenges

The new group photo didn't have quite the spontaneity and personality of the old one. With so many people it looked more like a class reunion. But my new brochure had the impact I wanted. The Medical Connection is BIG. And it's NATIONAL.

*

Our software development had always lacked continuity. It had evolved through a veritable chorus of independent software engineers. It performed a lot of innovative tasks, but like anything else designed by a committee, it had glitches and failings that had us constantly on the phone to any independent programmer who was available.

For most of 1994 we'd gotten satisfactory results from a competent independent programmer named Mary Sue Honigschmidt, whom I'd paid over $80,000 during that year to bandage our glitches and keep things running. But she told me she needed to spend more time with her larger clients. (I was taken aback, wondering how much she was billing her more important clients.)

Mary Sue had a close friend—a programmer named Ken Whittenhall who worked for Household Finance Company. Whittenhall was looking for a change. I talked to him and hired him—our first full-time, on-staff programmer.

When Ken sat down at a computer keyboard to write code, it was like watching Bach at a harpsichord composing fugues. With amazing speed and talent, he surgically extracted our glitches and rewrote new code that was more streamlined and easier for the counselors to use. Then he began to dream up additional software features that would improve our service and increase our reporting capabilities.

Ken was vastly different from other computer programmers in another way, too—he was communicative. He could talk to ordinary, non-electronic people like myself, providing explanations and instructions that *people* could easily understand. We'd learned to live with computer programmers who seemed to exist only in their own lofty, ethereal worlds of code. Many of them echoed the rude, impatient programmers one often had to deal with on the various tech support lines—service technicians who grow testy when you don't understand things at their level and soon make you feel like a hopeless idiot, unworthy of their advice.

Ken was friendly, talkative, and could explain things in terms I could understand.

And, as with Debbie, I gave him full rein. I recited my mantra of business management philosophy: "Any decision you make is better than a decision I could make for you, so even if you make the *wrong* decision, I'll stand behind it, because, right or wrong, it's a better decision than one I'd make myself."

Ken quickly recognized that he was building a software product that was clearly superior to the software being sold directly to hospitals by three referral software companies. And he enjoyed pride of authorship.

Through Ken's software I could see another marketing breakthrough for The Medical Connection.

The industry for physician referral service software was dominated by three companies: Healthmatch, Healthline, and Referral One. They sold their products directly to hospitals for anywhere from $30,000 to $90,000, depending on features and capabilities. And our software product under Ken's design was superior to all of them.

Should we start marketing our software to hospitals? Should we enter our product in competition with the other three brands on the market?

A strategy occurred to me—a totally unbeatable strategy that our competitors could never match in any way, shape, or form.

Let's give our software away!

If a hospital was struggling to decide which of the three software products to buy, and discovered that they could have Medical Connection software—*for free,* in conjunction with our

Back-up Service—which they needed anyway—our software could gain us new Back-up Service clients. They'd get the benefit of our wide range of experience—helping them to select hardware, printers, phone systems, and phone lines, teaching them the latest methodology for running their service, printing confirmation letters, and following the Safe Harbor guidelines.

Then we'd install our software on their machines *for free!* We'd train their counselor *for free!* Technical support? *Free!* It's easy for us to service software in a hospital that's hard-wired to The Medical Connection for Back-up Service. Our software competitors had to service freestanding software installed in a hospital—a far more difficult task for them. We could easily monitor our clients' activity, correct their glitches, and help them over their growing pains.

Most important, all of the complex functions of the software, which cause 90% of the problems—the daily reports, the quarterly reports, and the Billings Match reports—would be done at The Medical Connection. The software we'd install at the hospital could be a very simple, trouble-free edition of our software. It wouldn't need to turn out any complicated reports. All that the clients would need to do locally would be to update their physician databases, enter the referrals they made, print out and mail the follow-up letters daily, and go home at five o'clock. All the fancy, complicated reports would come out of our offices in Chicago.

The hospitals would have a professional, computerized referral service with the least problems, with no investment for software, and with our Back-up Service. And The Medical Connection would have a steady stream of income from new clients.

These new clients would be more permanent. If a hospital decided to give up our Back-up Service, they'd be giving up our lovely, trouble-free software as well. They'd have to head back into the market to shop and learn.

This was a proposition no one could match. Even my arch-competitor, E.R.S. couldn't copy it because they used the Healthline software package, which they didn't own.

Ken would be a key person in this business plan. He was the ideal tech support person for The Medical Connection. He could talk to *people*.

Once again I donned my paralegal hat. The Medical Connection now needed a software licensing agreement.

Before I went on the road to sell our new Service-Plus-Software package, I began thinking about the Internet. It was revolutionizing the world of communications. *Expedia.com* and *Travelocity.com* were putting travel agents out of business. One day it would put many other businesses into the unemployment lines.

Would it put The Medical Connection out of business too? Would a day come when people would go to the Internet for their physician referrals?

Probably.

The Internet could do everything my counselors were doing—presenting every detail about the physicians, their backgrounds, their experience, and the insurance coverages they accepted. And it could do a few things that our counselors couldn't—like showing *photos* of the doctors.

It could even provide brief *videotaped messages* from each physician, personally detailing his or her background and practice philosophy—in his or her own on-camera voice. This could be very helpful to patients trying to reach decisions about a very personal matter. It could short-circuit the disappointment many patients suffered when they finally met the doctor face-to-face in his or her office.

The Internet was *show biz!*

Some of the older physicians would hate me for this—especially the ones with sour, scowling faces and self-infatuated voices, or thick, hard-to-understand foreign accents.

But it would benefit the patients. And the future of The Medical Connection lay in satisfying patients. Every year those patients became more sophisticated in the questions they asked. They read *Time* and *Newsweek*. They listened to NPR and watched *60 Minutes*. They already knew to ask about each physician's Board Certification status. One day they'd be asking about experience, lawsuits, and disciplinary actions. Was the physician a graduate of Johns Hopkins or Yale—or one of those schools in a Caribbean nation that accepts applicants who can't get admitted to a medical school in the United States?

I remembered an anecdote, told to me by one of my brothers. "What do you call the guy who finished at the bottom of his class in medical school?"

"Doctor."

A patient has but one husband, perhaps just one son or daughter. And only one pair of lungs. One heart. One colon. An unqualified physician could destroy any of these things with a clumsy stroke of a scalpel.

Which surgeons were truly qualified? How many open-heart procedures has this or that cardiologist performed in the past year? According to the Board of Cardiologists, an open-heart surgeon should be performing a *minimum* of five open-heart procedures *per week*, just to stay qualified. If this particular cardiologist had performed only fifteen procedures in the past *year*, why was he allowed to perform any at all? Does the caller want that doctor messing around with her husband's cardiac arteries?

The hospitals paid my bills. But my future and the future of my company would ultimately be determined by *patients*.

And one day, many of those patients would want to make their physician selections slowly, carefully, working with the hospital referral service that had the best Internet site, and taking advantage of another thing my counselors couldn't easily offer—the luxury of *time* to ponder their decisions at length, and privately—something they can't do when they're talking on the phone to a live counselor.

But they can do it on the Internet.

If the Internet was the wave of the future, it was a wave I wanted to be riding. I was damned if I'd end up like the buggy whip and harness salesmen of the 1920s—or for that matter, the pocket pager salesmen of the 1980s. I wanted The Medical Connection to be able to put its hospital clients on the Internet.

Could we make any money from the Internet? I didn't really know. But I set Ken to work developing an Internet package. Ken hired an experienced web site designer named Harold Driscol. And I set to work on a new brochure.

I'd never been a software person. I was a product of theater training.

I'd simply discovered the drama in software.

Chapter 27

The Big Apple

I awoke on Friday, January 11, 1996 to a typical Midwestern winter day—cold and gloomy with an overcast that had been with us since New Year's Day. If this was going to be a typical Chicago winter, the sun would be shrouded until at least six weeks after Groundhog Day.

But I was too buoyant and busy to dwell on the clouds overhead. Like so many of the days of my life, I had a plane to catch. Heading toward O'Hare Field, I exited the Kennedy Expressway in Park Ridge and drove into the huge parking lot of the Marriott Hotel, where I'd been parking my car for a couple of years, and riding the hotel's courtesy van to the airport. My car was safer in Park Ridge than at the airport parking ramp, where I'd suffered two break-ins in previous years. If a Marriott executive happens to read this, please accept both my apology and my thanks—your free Park Ridge lot saved me about $1,500 a year in parking fees, and who knows how many break-ins—and your courtesy vans are frequent, fast and comfortable.

Later, aboard my American Airlines flight bound for Newark, I tilted my seat back for a power nap. I had two appointments that day. The first would be at Englewood

Hospital in Englewood, New Jersey, just a bit north of the George Washington Bridge. There I would meet with Barbara Ettington, a marketing director I'd met the previous year when she worked at Lenox Hill Hospital in midtown Manhattan. She had liked the idea of using The Medical Connection for Back-Up Service, but the referral counselor at Lenox Hill had been too protective of her job to risk having anyone other than herself handle referral calls.

Barb had invited me to present my program to her new management team at Englewood Hospital.

After this presentation I would drive my rental car across the George Washington Bridge where the Hudson River separates two pieces of earth that are a world apart—suburban New Jersey and Manhattan Island. There I'd turn south for half a mile to Columbia-Presbyterian Hospital where I was to follow up on a lead given me by Thomas Cooperman of the New York Yellow Pages.

Columbia-Presbyterian would be a stretch for The Medical Connection. All of our clients were medium-size hospitals with less than 800 beds. Columbia-Presbyterian was one of the nation's major tertiary care hospitals with thousands of beds and a worldwide reputation, in a league with such institutions as Johns Hopkins and The Mayo Clinic. Cooperman said Columbia-Presbyterian had never had a physician referral service and was considering installing one. If they did, it would yield Cooperman a juicy advertiser for the Yellow Pages.

At Columbia-Presbyterian I was to meet with Deborah MacGregor, a marketing vice president. This was a good sign. Vice Presidents usually have the authority to make their own decisions. I could quickly tell if I was sitting across from a decision maker, based on the questions he or she asked. Decision makers wanted information they would personally evaluate. Gatekeepers simply gathered facts to pass along to someone higher up. Gatekeepers were authorized only to say "no"—all "yes" decisions had to be made by someone a level or two above them.

The Big Apple

The meeting with Barb Ettington at Englewood went very well. She was quite impressed with our new Internet capability. Her hospital was in the process of developing a web site, and if we could hot-link her referral service to their home page immediately, she'd be pleased.

I left Barb shortly after lunch. She asked me to send a proposal, a contract, and a licensing agreement. A great start for a day that was just as cloudy and gloomy in New York as it had been back in Chicago. I was properly psyched to try for Columbia-Presbyterian, potentially my biggest bite of the Big Apple. I headed toward the ramps of the George Washington Bridge.

I found a parking lot a block from the hospital entrance. The receptionist directed me to the fifth floor.

I arrived at Deborah MacGregor's department. She was in a meeting somewhere. I got her secretary's permission to set up my laptop in Ms. MacGregor's office, and plug her computer monitor into my laptop for the demo.

I was ready at 3:15 but Ms. MacGregor's meeting was still in progress. I told the secretary I had no other appointments scheduled for that day, and I'd be happy to wait.

At 4:30 Deborah MacGregor finally came in. She had a medium complexion and brown hair. She didn't appear to be Irish; MacGregor was probably her married name. She seemed to be in her early forties and had a relaxed face and pleasant smile—another good sign since it suggested that she'd been in a position of authority long enough to have become comfortable with it. Younger, less experienced executives tended to be insecure and liked to act tough in order to be impressive.

The bad news was that Ms. MacGregor had only thirty minutes to spare—she had to leave at five to catch a commuter train home. I hid my disappointment, saying, "If you like what I tell you in the next thirty minutes I can arrange to come back to finish my presentation on another day." I launched into my prepared, rehearsed, standard pitch and software demo.

After about twenty minutes when I was describing our staff of referral counselors in Chicago, Ms. MacGregor looked a little confused and interrupted me. "Let me see if I understand—you're *not* here to sell me a referral software package?"

And I realized that I'd just blown twenty of my precious thirty minutes, and failed to clarify how The Medical Connection was unique. I'd sent her a letter and brochure, and assumed she'd read them, which she hadn't. Now she was confusing The Medical Connection with Healthline or Healthmatch or Referral One, any of the vendors she may have seen who wanted to sell her software to support an in-house referral service—which Columbia-Presbyterian hospital did not have.

In the ten minutes that remained I'd have to perform a miracle.

I set my entire rehearsed presentation aside in my mind, sat back and said, "Let me tell you what The Medical Connection does. We're an *outsourced* physician referral service. We have a staff of referral specialists in Chicago who handle all your incoming referral calls, which you forward to a dedicated phone line at The Medical Connection in Chicago…"

I went through a rapid, condensed checklist of the differences and advantages of our out-sourced service over an in-house service.

Normally I would have felt nervous and insecure in a one-on-one presentation unless I was following a rehearsed script. A lifetime of theater and advertising had caused me to crave an audience of at least three listeners so I could stand up, pace back and forth, and speak and gesticulate with dramatic intensity, moving my gaze from one set of eyes to another as I followed my scripted, practiced monologue. I felt most at ease playing out a drama of my own making before a large group—getting the audience to sing my jingle, or making dollar bills rain down on them—things I couldn't do in a one-on-one conversation where I had to stay seated, maintain eye contact, and speak directly to an individual, adjusting my words to the reactions

The Big Apple

and responses of one person. That usually made me uneasy. I preferred my script.

Now I was speaking to Ms. MacGregor off the top of my head, condensing my presentation down to the bare bones, reciting facts and scenarios strictly from my knowledge of the business, my company, and what I perceived to be Ms. MacGregor's needs.

There was a clock on her wall. I dared not glance at it. I read it in my peripheral vision. The clock soon read five. Then five after five. The sky outside her window was now black. She had been anxious to end this busy week and grab a cab to the railroad station and home to have dinner with her husband and kids somewhere in the suburbs. But she was giving me her full attention. She listened. She nodded. I continued my point-by-point explanation in a clear, collected, cogent narrative. Oddly, I'd never in my life felt so confident in a one-on-one presentation. My voice was so relaxed, I hardly recognized it as my own.

At a quarter past five I began showing Deborah MacGregor the daily reports on referral activity that The Medical Connection would download into a computer in her department each night for her immediate review and evaluation, and for her department to use in generating the follow-up letters to patients.

The clock swept toward five-thirty as I began explaining the new Internet capability. I still had her full attention. She occasionally asked questions, which I answered. We discussed anticipated call volume and price, which, for a hospital of this size and reputation, would be considerable. I told her she could probably expect 3,000 to 4,000 calls per month. For that kind of volume our charges would be somewhere in the neighborhood of $24,000 to $32,000 monthly. And the Billings Match reports were likely to demonstrate that our referrals would support an extra $12 million to $18 million in hospital billings each year—possibly even more. I said, "Our clients at New York Methodist and New York Hospital of Queens regularly show matches far above the national average—sometimes as high as $800 per referral."

There was a pause as she mulled these figures over in her head.

Then she looked at the clock. "I have to run now, Jerry, I can still make the 6:30 train—but I think I'm going to go with this program. Please call me on Monday, I want to get moving on this."

I think I'm going to go with this program! Her comment rang in my head like the cymbal crash in a Wagner finale. This bright, sophisticated, knowledgeable and experienced health care executive, possibly with an M.B.A. from Wharton or Yale, could see that the physician referral service she needed already existed at The Medical Connection in Chicago—a service she could supervise easily, daily, from a computer terminal in her department. She didn't need to create, staff, and supervise a cumbersome in-house referral service.

In the space of 75 minutes I'd solved a major problem for her.

Ms. MacGregor had never met me before today, but after just an hour and a quarter she had said "yes" to investing over a quarter million dollars annually in the services of my company, my software, and my staff of counselors. Indeed, she would have us checked out thoroughly before she signed anything, but her investigation would reveal that everything I had just told her was true.

I had just made the most effective and convincing presentation of my life.

I stayed that weekend in Manhattan with Jack Waterman and his wife in their rambling, Salingeresque co-op on Riverside Drive. Lying in bed on Saturday morning, I continued to puzzle over my Friday presentation. I'd been on stage most of my life—why had this last performance been such an improvement over all the others? What had I done differently?

The Big Apple

At breakfast I discussed the meeting at length with Jack and his wife.

On Sunday's plane ride home to Chicago, I continued to think, to analyze. *Why?*

I thought about my first exposure to a lifetime of performing from center-stage. At the age of twelve I'd been seduced by the world of theater. I'd played a Victorian schoolboy to a paying audience for Threshold Players. Then I'd performed as a 19th century British sailor, playing my guitar and dancing a hornpipe before my peers and their parents. Next came years of creating stage sets for Lake Shore Players and *Lagniappe*, and moving on from there to professional theater in college.

Had I *advanced* into this magical, mystical world of drama? Or had I simply *retreated* into theater, escaping from teachers who hated me, from grades that doomed me, from the repeated humiliation of dropping one fly ball after another in right field, and from a mother who judged me relentlessly?

In theater I had found a place where I could create and control perfection with pretend canvas sets and backdrops and mystical lighting effects that could change a bright yellow noonday to a haunting blue-green dusk by turning a series of dimmer switches.

At age 16 I learned to purchased beer and liquor with a phony I.D. coupled with my ability to appear to be five years older than I was. At two different masquerade parties I'd worn motorcycle garb and faked a Marlon Brando impersonation to appear sexy and mysterious.

When I was 25 I assumed the role of a writer to get a job creating copy for Sears. Then I pretended to be a salesman to get a better-paying job in the Sears Coldspot national marketing department. Then I was miscast as a rug buyer.

From there I'd advanced to the world of advertising agencies where I could manufacture even more magic and mystery with music, actors, and lovely models with flawless figures and faces, and voices that made unrealistic promises about everything from cosmetics to toaster pastries to sliced bacon.

I'd spent a lifetime performing slight-of-hand tricks, controlling a collection of images to entertain and mystify—images that never really happened, and ended when the final curtain came down. And always before an audience, rarely in one-on-one situations.

The answer finally dawned on me in my American Airlines coach seat somewhere above Ft. Wayne, Indiana. It was such a simple answer, I wasn't certain I could trust it:

In less than a decade, I'd become the nation's prime authority in my field.

This was a new role for me—a role I didn't have to rehearse or act because it was a role I'd earned and for which I was recognized. *It was real.* And it inspired a feeling of confidence that I'd rarely felt, and which I nearly distrusted because it was so unfamiliar to me.

A voice echoed to me from the past...

"Now you've got a Tom I can believe in."

It was the voice of Alvin Sargent Clinton, my drama coach during high school. Clinton's comment referred to my acting interpretation of Tom Wingfield in *The Glass Menagerie*, after Clinton had coached me to a clearer understanding of the agony and guilt Tom suffered after he abandoned his sister Laura. I now realized that Mr. Clinton's lesson transcended my Tennessee Williams interpretation.

The lesson was so simple: credibility and believability. The stuff that actors like Alec Guinness and Dustin Hoffman had learned at the *beginning* of their careers. The talent to touch emotions and move people, either to tears or to signing a commitment for $30,000 a month, whether they were watching Tom Wingfield's failure or Jerry Inglehart's triumph. I'd devoted several years to crafting and polishing a drama in which the stage set consisted of telephones, computers and butcher-block counters. I'd cast and directed a star-studded

The Big Apple

company of counselors and software wizards. My drama had turned out brilliantly, every bit as viable and dramatic as *The Glass Menagerie*, except for one glaring flaw—I hadn't understood how to play the leading role as president and C.E.O. Mr. Clinton had showed me how to do a convincing Tom Wingfield, and his coaching had paved my way into college—where I promptly forgot the lesson and lapsed into a lifetime of over-dramatized presentations just like my first improbable attempt at Tom Wingfield, strutting across the stage like Napoleon. All those years of hyped-up sales presentations had probably caused many of my prospective clients to wonder, "Why the dramatics? What's the catch?"

So, 41 years later, Mr. Clinton's message finally clicked into place—without a script, without a rehearsal, at center stage in Deborah MacGregor's office. And I hadn't even created the show-stopping line, which had come from Deborah MacGregor:

"I think I'm going to go with this program!"

I was no longer a showman. I was now a professional. For the first time since high school, I totally believed in my script—and in myself.

And Deborah MacGregor believed in me too.

Brother Bill was right. The "front man" I'd been seeking throughout my career was right there in my mirror. Of course, that "front man" hadn't been ready in 1971. Or ten years later. Not even in 1990.

But he was ready now.

*

Barbara Ettington at Englewood Hospital signed us up in late February. Debbie Maturo installed the program in March. By the end of the month, our counselors were taking calls for Englewood.

The World is a Stage

In March 1996 I got a call from Integra Health System in Omaha, a holding company controlling a number of hospitals in Nebraska. I was invited to present to a panel of seven people.

In Omaha I sensed that the jury of seven had already decided to sign with The Medical Connection. I'd sent them all brochures, plus cover letters listing our clients, including Columbia-Presbyterian and the two New York clients who had become part of the New York Cornell system. Perhaps they felt that if The Medical Connection was good enough for such large, prestigious tertiary care health systems, it was good enough for Integra. The jury signed off on our proposal within three weeks. Debbie Maturo and Ken Whittenhall had the system installed for them by late April. Their calls began in May, and the volume proved to be huge. Soon we were handling over 2,000 calls a month for Integra.

The speed with which Integra moved astonished me. Big organizations tended to move at a more glacial pace due to more layers of bureaucracy. Columbia-Presbyterian was moving far more cautiously. I'd had my paperwork on Deborah MacGregor's desk in mid-January. Then in May I had the first of several conversations with Linda Ryland, an attorney at Columbia-Presbyterian. We went over several points in detail. I'd boiler-plated all of my contracts and licensing agreements myself, drawing on language existing in legal documents I'd gathered. Lynda negotiated several points in the documents with me, some of which I reviewed by my law firm, Lord, Bissell & Brook.

In June, Linda Ryland dropped a bombshell. Her department had unearthed a New York law that *prohibited* an out-of-state contractor from handling physician referral calls for any New York hospital. It appeared as if 40% of our total Medical Connection billings were illegal!

I called Larry Kessenick, the health care attorney in Los Angeles who coauthored the Safe Harbor book with me. He

The Big Apple

referred me to Alan Reardon, a health care attorney practicing law in New York City.

Reardon was familiar with the New York law, passed in 1988 amid the flurry of anti-kickback legislation coming out of Washington at the time. These laws attacked abuses in the medical profession. Reardon felt the New York law, as written and passed, was somewhat misguided, and was never intended to affect the operation of a legitimate hospital physician referral service, whether the service was internal or outsourced, within or outside of the state. He said the law was unknown to most hospitals, several of which were currently outsourcing their referral services to organizations outside of the state. The law, he said, had never been enforced, probably because it was unreasonable and poorly drafted. He felt any attempt at enforcement would result in a major defense by several hospitals as well as their out-of-state services, and that a high court would most likely shoot the law down.

In short, Reardon felt the law could probably be ignored.

I paid him to draft his opinion in a letter. I forwarded his letter to Linda Ryland at Columbia-Presbyterian. Her department accepted Reardon's opinion, knowing that their efforts at any future defense would be supported by a virtual phalanx of New York hospitals currently using out-of-state services, including Mount Sinai Hospital which employed my competitor E.R.S., as well as the great and mighty New York Cornell system, in which two of their hospitals had been using The Medical Connection for several years.

Columbia-Presbyterian signed off on my documents. Together we would be co-conspirators in crime. And I breathed a mighty sigh of relief.

Within two months Debbie Maturo and Ken Whittenhall had our program installed at Columbia-Presbyterian—just in time for the appearance of the new Yellow Pages directory containing the big new ad Thomas Cooperman had sold them.

The calls for Columbia-Presbyterian began pouring in. Fortunately, Debbie Maturo had anticipated this new call volume, as well as the new volume coming in from Integra in Omaha, Englewood in New Jersey, and another new client—Miami Children's Hospital. She'd expanded her staff of counselors to eighteen very competent pros.

*

That spring I initiated an annual reward for our top-performing counselors, to be chosen by Debbie for the best service based on professionalism, number of calls handled, attendance, whatever criteria Debbie felt was most important.

The reward for the two winning counselors was a three-day expense-paid weekend in the client city of their choice, where they'd stay in a first-class hotel or bed and breakfast, dine at the restaurants of their choice, and take in a show or tour of their choosing, all at Medical Connection expense. The only requirement was that they would meet with our client's marketing director sometime on Friday, and possibly take a hospital tour. This would have the benefit of exposing some of our important clients to a couple of our best counselors. Also I felt that the winners would enjoy a degree of prestige among their peers, having actually visited a client hospital and seen the town where so many of their callers lived.

I assumed the winning counselors would choose The Big Apple. But the first winners selected by Debbie happened both to be Mexican-American. About ten percent of our calls came from Spanish-speaking patients, and our many bilingual women possessed talent we needed, and often sought in job applicants. The counselors chose Corpus Christi, Texas, where they could spend the weekend with relatives across the border.

The following year the winners chose Charlotte, North Carolina, where we served Presbyterian Hospital.

*

The Big Apple

I got a call from Thomas Cooperman in late June. He had an urgent lead—Maimonides Hospital in Brooklyn, another huge hospital that could result in large income for The Medical Connection—and a big Yellow Pages ad for Cooperman.

I said, "I've been trying to get in to see Maimonides for nearly a year."

"Who have you tried to contact?"

"A lady named Rose Caldwell."

"Rose Caldwell is in the public relations department. She's not the one you want to talk to. The person who's calling the shots is Margarite Corda in marketing. But you'd better hurry—she's about to sign up with E.R.S."

"Oh, Lord!" I'd spent a year barking at the base of the wrong tree.

I FedExed some literature and a cover letter to Margarite Corda, and called her the next day. She said, "Thomas Cooperman mentioned your name. But I just got our contract with E.R.S. back from legal. I was going to sign it and send it out today."

"If you see The Medical Connection before you do that, it might confirm that you made the right choice, based on reviewing all your options. Then again, it might not."

"The new Brooklyn Yellow Pages comes out in September with our ad in it. I have to move quickly. How soon can you be here?"

"How's your schedule look for tomorrow?" She paused as she consulted her calendar.

"Can you be here in the morning?"

"9 A.M.?"

"Make it 8 A.M. I have a meeting to go to at 9:30."

Three hours later I was on a flight to Newark. I arrived in Brooklyn about 9 P.M.

Maimonides is the name of a 12th Century rabbi who had been very influential in medieval medicine—sort of the Jewish equivalent of Hippocrates. The area of Brooklyn served by this hospital is almost entirely Jewish. As I pulled up to my hotel two blocks from the hospital, I noticed that at least ten percent of all the male pedestrians on the street were dressed as Orthodox Jews wearing black suits, prayer vests with braided tassels, full beards, and black homburg hats perched on top of their yarmulkes. This was clearly a New York neighborhood where one would be safe on the streets after dark.

And my travel agent had booked me into a *kosher hotel!* I'd always prided myself in knowing more than the average gentile about Judaism. I understood a few words of Yiddish. I'd attended at least six Jewish weddings and one seder. But I never knew there was such a thing as a kosher hotel.

It was pretty much like any other small, clean, budget-priced urban hotel except that all the guests and desk clerks were Orthodox Jews. Each room had a kosher kitchenette and no Gideon's Bible. During the *Shabbos* the elevator would run automatically, stopping at each floor so passengers could board and exit without having to push the floor buttons—an Orthodox definition of "work" which is forbidden between sundown Friday and sundown Saturday.

Next morning at 7 A.M. I checked out of the hotel and schlepped my presentation equipment on foot to Maimonides Hospital a block away, where I located the cafeteria. Behind the grill was a huge black man dressed in a white chef's jacket and chef's hat, with a spatula in his hand. I asked him for two eggs over easy with bacon. "No bacon," he said.

"Of course not. My mistake. Can I have—ummm—maybe a hamburger patty with the eggs?"

"No meat with dairy. We don't serve meat until after breakfast."

How silly of me. I'd grown up in a Jewish community, and I was being out-koshered by a black man! I got my eggs with a glass of milk.

I presented to Margarite Corda and two of her colleagues, including Rose Caldwell, who'd been ignoring me for nearly a year. I think Rose was hoping I'd not mention my letters and unanswered calls to her. Ms. Corda had expected to view all legitimate sources, and Rose Caldwell had failed to forward my information to her.

I guess my presentation was another showstopper. Like my historic performance on January 11 to Deborah MacGregor at Columbia-Presbyterian, I was able to build a strong case for The Medical Connection in just 75 minutes. Once again I quoted performance figures from my important New York clients, except that now I was able to include the giant Columbia-Presbyterian Hospital in that client mix.

Ms. Corda was something of a showstopper herself. She was about thirty with a perfect figure clothed in a smart pinstripe business suit. And very attractive. Her eyes looked Mediterranean, not Hispanic like her last name, which I assumed to be a married name. I guessed her maiden name might be something like Micheletti or Conforti—her eyes were clearly Italian.

When I'd run Inglehart and Partners, all my client contacts had been male. But in the health care field there seems to be no glass ceiling for women, so many executive positions are held by women. Through the years, half of the women I contacted were fairly young, and a quarter of them distractingly attractive. It was very important that nothing I said could be interpreted as even remotely patronizing by these women, since it could blow my presentation out the door. In such situations I would run an old Woody Allen quote through my mind: "God gave Man a brain and a penis, but only enough blood to use one of them at a time." Whenever speaking to a client as stunning as Margarite Corda, I learned to keep my eyes focused on her eyes. This rigid discipline allowed me to stick to my presentation and respect these women as the bright, talented Masters-of-Business Degree holders that many of them were.

It also gave me something of a talent for guessing nationality from the eyes alone.

"Well, Mr. Inglehart," she said, "your eleventh-hour appeal is pretty convincing. My question is, where were you three months ago when I decided to outsource?" I avoided glancing at Rose Caldwell, and changed the subject.

Ms. Corda would need to investigate The Medical Connection, but a few calls across town to Columbia-Presbyterian, New York Queens, New York Methodist and Lutheran would nail this new client down for me. Local clients make much better references than those out of town. "How fast can you move on this if we decide to go with it?"

"Well, Ms. Corda, I presented to Englewood Hospital in New Jersey on January 11th, and we were signed, installed, and taking calls in less than eight weeks. Depending on the speed with which you can handle our contract and licensing agreement, I'd say we could be taking your calls a few weeks before that Yellow Pages book delivers."

"When can I receive these documents?"

"It's all boilerplate. I can have them to you by overnight courier day after tomorrow. Maybe even tomorrow if I can get back to the airport in an hour or so."

"Do it! Go! Get out!"

Eight weeks later Ken and Debbie installed our service at Maimonides Hospital.

I'd pulled this client right off the table in front of E.R.S. And theoretically, they had an advantage. The hospital is Jewish. E.R.S. already served Mount Sinai, the other Jewish hospital in New York. Paul Spiegelman is Jewish. I'm not.

But then, neither is Margarite Corda.

*

By now our growing client list represented a rather interesting mix of people and ethnicities. I thought it might be interesting to mount a set of *Family of Man*-type photos on the walls of our call center where the counselors could see them and appreciate the worldly mix of people they were serving.

The Big Apple

Naturally my photo gallery would include a folksy *Fiddler-on-the-Roof*-type photo of Orthodox Jews of Brooklyn with their full beards, black coats, *tsitsit* vests, and homburg hats.

Next I'd find a warm family shot of a black couple playing with their little baby, to represent Howard University Hospital in Washington, D.C.

Lancaster General is in the heart of Bucks County, Pennsylvania, where many of the patients are Amish—folks you aren't supposed to photograph. But I could buy a stock photo of these Amish farmers in their carriages, the women in bonnets, the bearded men wearing wide-brimmed hats.

It'd be easy to find an endearing shot of happy children in a playground. That would do nicely for Miami Children's.

And Mercy Miami is near Cuban Florida. Certainly there must be some impressive photos of upper-middle-class Cubans, many of whom are physicians themselves.

Along the Texas border are thousands of photogenic Mexicans working hard in America in order to send money each month to their families south of the border. These Latinos often have intense, sun-weathered faces, the men with their black moustaches, the women and girls with long braided black hair and embroidered blouses and dresses. That would represent Corpus Christi.

MacNeal Hospital in Berwyn, Illinois, is in the heart of one of Chicago's big Eastern European neighborhoods. Bohemian, Slovak, Czech, and Polish people with serious, intense, beautifully sculptured features—people who grew up on tasty, lard-laden sausages and potato *latkes*.

What about Omaha, Nebraska and Nashua, New Hampshire? Both are in America's rural heartland, one with Wheat Belt farmers living amid the amber waves of grain, the other heavy with Down-East New England blood. Rural faces can be fascinating! Maybe my photographer friend Archie Lieberman could sell me one of his swarthy Midwestern farmer photos he'd published in his book, *Farm Boy*. For the New England photo I'd need subjects with more Yankee heritage—

people who looked like their ancestors had been cod fishermen or Revolutionary War minutemen.

Chestnut Hill Hospital is in one of Philadelphia's crusty upper class suburbs. I'd need a photo of an impeccably dressed Brooks Brothers and Bonwit's couple stepping out of a big BMW sedan.

Stereotypical, every one of them—yet real in their combined diversity. The Family of The Medical Connection—The Family of Man.

*

Our new income allowed me to make improvements in our equipment. Years earlier I'd "Jerry-rigged" a system for recording inbound calls, using a bank of individual Radio Shack voice-activated cassette recorders. Now we needed a far more sophisticated system. I studied options and decided on a TEAC system. In September I flew to Los Angeles to examine it. The system could record up to forty simultaneous phone conversations. I bought it for $20,000 and had TEAC install it in October.

The major benefit of recording calls was to be able to review problem conversations. If a client hospital received a complaint or a threat from an angry patient, it was useful to be able to review and download the call in question. Most often the tape would speak for itself and exonerate our counselors against occasional accusations made by irate callers.

A month after the TEAC system was up and running, we received just such a call. A patient calling on the Columbia-Presbyterian line had been abusive to our counselor named Martha. Debbie said she'd found Martha crying in the lunchroom. Debbie listened to the recording of the call that had upset Martha and decided to draw it to my attention.

The woman caller had a heavy Long Island accent and a chip on her shoulder from the beginning of the conversation. She whined at Martha for taking too long with her computer

The Big Apple

lookups. She berated Martha for asking too many questions. She refused to give certain information Martha asked for. She chided Martha relentlessly. As the call progressed, her language became so abusive, I could understand why a sensitive counselor like Martha had gotten upset. Nevertheless, Martha continued to ignore each of the caller's nasty comments and stuck calmly and politely to her work, in keeping with her training and our set policies. Toward the end of the conversation I heard the lady snap at Martha, "Young lady, how long has it been since you've had an enema?"

Taken aback, Martha said "What?"

"You're so full of shit it's unbelievable. I happen to be recording this conversation, and I'm going to send copies of this tape to the *New York Times* and all the radio stations in town." The woman slammed her receiver down.

I FedExed a copy of the tape to my client with a cover letter in which I said, "From time to time we receive a threat from a patient like the one contained in this conversation recorded by our system on the Columbia-Presbyterian referral line this morning, October 12th.

"As a standard practice, The Medical Connection wants you to hear any such threats from our recording of the actual conversation, in order to be able to respond quickly and authoritatively to any issue that might arise."

I was particularly proud of Martha's handling of the call, never once losing her calm in the face of unreasonable abuse. And I was especially anxious for our client to hear the tape, to be reassured about the quality of our counselors who, even in the most outrageous situations, remained professional.

*

Toward year's end in 1996 I tallied the net profits for the year and was amazed to see that they were *five times greater* than the profits Inglehart and Partners had generated during its most successful year. Our staff was up to nineteen counselors.

Payroll was our biggest expense, absorbing well over half of our gross receipts. During the year I'd spent a hefty chunk on outside consultants for our software development. Rent was $31,000. Health insurance for my staff was $45,000.

On the bottom line was an amount left over that overwhelmed me. It was equal to *more* than the entire year's billings at Inglehart and Partners the year before it went belly-up.

It was time for me to cut my once-a-year New Year's Eve paycheck. I called my accountant, David Blockowicz, and told him about the figure at the bottom of the page.

"What do I do with it, Dave?"

"You cut yourself a check for that amount. That's your pay for the year."

"Take it in *salary?* The income tax liability on that amount would be phenomenal!"

"Then you cut two checks—one for yourself and one for the Internal Revenue Service. It's a lot cheaper than the alternative, which is a corporate dividend that gets taxed *twice.*"

David had several clients who earned a lot of money. He said, "When you earn big money, you pay big taxes. You have to get used to that. You're shouldering the tax burden for yourself plus over a hundred other people."

Then he added, "Jerry, you pay me to tell you what to do with your money. You haven't given yourself a single raise in at least thirteen years. Now you're approaching retirement age. You've got a lot of catching up to do."

I followed Dave's advice. I made a gigantic tax deposit to the I.R.S. Then I cut myself a paycheck so huge it intimidated me. Was it possible for someone to earn this much money in a single year—*legally?*

I certainly hadn't broken any laws. Perhaps I did deserve it.

So my phoenix had become a goose—a goose that laid golden eggs.

*

The Big Apple

By 1997 the management of The Medical Connection had evolved into a troika.

I was responsible for product development and sales, like a ship's captain who watches the compass, and sets the course.

Debbie Maturo was our boatswain, managing the counselors and carefully, tirelessly monitoring their quality, enlarging the staff as needed by screening applicants and hiring and training new people.

Down in the engine room Ken Whittenhall kept the software functioning flawlessly, removing bugs, developing new reports and capabilities, and keeping the growing number of client Internet sites functioning. I quickly discovered that the Internet sites were bringing us steady income because the physician databases were constantly changing with new doctors, revised insurance, new offices, new partners, and changes-of-address. These updates were done at The Medical Connection for a modest fee of $2.00 per addition or alteration. Ken now had an assistant, Juanita Martin, who spent endless days at her keyboard operating this new profit engine.

By now our voluminous monthly and quarterly reports were generated automatically, making our fast printers belch forth reams of paperwork, all of which Juanita would assemble, bind into booklets and ship U.P.S. to our clients.

Ken asked if he should begin having these massive reports spit out by the computer terminals on-site in our client's offices instead. I said, "I don't think so. There's an element of psychology at work here. These reports are important in evaluating our performance and productivity. The department clerks in each hospital might not bother to print them out on time, or at all, and they certainly won't bother to bind them and present them to the marketing directors, as we are doing. Each month we can enclose monthly reports with our monthly invoices, showing what the clients got for their money.

"If I haven't met with a client for some time, the quarterly report is an excuse for me to show my face.

"And the most important reports we do here are those annual Billings Match Reports. In each case I want to hand-deliver them and call the marketing director's attention to the dollar value of each referral we made. Sometimes the marketing director will call a meeting to have me present the Billings Match report to a lot of important decision makers who might be her bosses. It's a chance for them to see me and ask questions. It's a chance for me to find out if there's anything wrong. When I visit our clients, it means we're not just some hidden group of anonymous people somewhere in Chicago. We're part of their management team.

"You and Juanita keep printing and binding the reports right here. I'll keep delivering them myself."

*

More than a year earlier, when New York Cornell Hospital had purchased our client hospitals in Brooklyn and Queens, the parent hospital had expressed an interest in the services of The Medical Connection, and had invited me in to make a presentation. But they had never hired us. New York Cornell had its own physician referral service, handling over 4,000 calls a month with a staff of six counselors. Hospital management at Cornell could see what an outstanding job we were doing in Brooklyn and Queens. Perhaps some of them even reviewed our reports, which were superior to the ones their own computer system could generate.

But wherever a hospital had an in-house referral service, The Medical Connection would make their referral staff nervous. Would our counselors in Chicago show them up? Would our reports and our professionalism put their own jobs at risk? Sometimes the supervising marketing director would value her fiefdom of people reporting to her. She didn't want any comparisons drawn between her people and ours.

Winifred Lowenstein, the marketing director at New York Cornell, wasn't like that. I'd talked to her a couple of times on

The Big Apple

the phone. She was a vice president and a business person. But she was also in a lofty position, and very difficult to reach. Twice I'd had appointments to meet with her. On both occasions she'd deferred my presentation to the head of her physician referral service—a total waste of my time.

By April of 1997 we had several hospital Internet sites up and running—including another hospital affiliate of New York Cornell, a small specialty hospital in Brooklyn that I'd signed in January. Perhaps an Internet presentation would clinch an opportunity for me to meet with Ms. Lowenstein.

I very much wanted New York Cornell to hire us. At any point in time, the inpatient roster of New York Cornell read like a Who's Who in the worlds of government and the entertainment industry. Mayors, senators, and movie stars regularly checked into New York Cornell to take advantage of the services of some of the world's most outstanding surgeons. It was not uncommon to see private security forces and bodyguards hovering around the corridors of New York Cornell, protecting the safety and privacy of prominent figures.

If we could serve New York Cornell, it would help to consolidate our position with four of their affiliate hospitals, including three that were major clients of ours. And it would give The Medical Connection a lock on the two biggest, most prestigious tertiary care hospitals in America, representing the lion's share of referral activity in the New York Metro Area.

I sent Ms. Lowenstein some Internet literature and performance figures for our Internet clients. She could visit our client Internet sites from a computer at her home or office.

Then I phoned her. She was interested.

In an effort to try to clinch her presence at a meeting I told her I'd bring to the presentation my programmer, Ken Whittenhall, and our Internet developer, Harold Driscol. "When's a good time for you?" I asked.

"I'm pretty tied up for the next few weeks."

"How about a luncheon presentation? We'll bring lunch for everyone."

A pause. She said, "That might work. How's Thursday?"

"That works for us. Do you prefer corned beef or pastrami?"

"I'd really like to get our referral service on the Internet. Maybe I can get a few other people to attend this meeting. Lunch is a good idea; people are usually available. Figure on (a pause) maybe about four of us.

Ken, Harold, and I touched down at Newark airport at 9:30 on Thursday morning April 10th, 1997, and picked up an Avis car. Our next stop was the Carnegie Deli in mid-town, where I'd called ahead for eight of their famous, gigantic corned beef sandwiches to go. Bringing food from Carnegie Deli was part of my strategy to demonstrate to the executives at New York Cornell that we at The Medical Connection in Chicago understood the mystique of their fabled city. We were familiar with New York's remarkable streets and restaurants and personality, even to the extent of our choice of take-out sandwiches from Carnegie Deli.

Winifred Lowenstein showed up with two key vice presidents in tow, including the vice president of data processing. And also her referral department head that I'd met with twice before.

I took a back seat as Ken and Harold, my two brilliant cast members, ran through the Internet presentation with perfect clarity and authority. They had answers to all the questions I could never have handled alone—"How do those hot links work?" "Is this Y2K compatible?" (In April, 1997, the term "Y2K" was just beginning to be used.)

What a brilliant supporting cast I had! Could we land Cornell? Time would tell.

Chapter 28

Right on the Money

In September 1997 I received a two-color brochure in the mail at home. It was from a Toronto-based travel outfit called Marine Expeditions. I'd written to them a half-year before, inquiring about their fascinating cruises from Patagonia down to the Antarctic Peninsula.

Marine Expeditions was organizing an Around-the-World cruise out of Athens in November of 1999, returning to Athens four months later. The cruise would touch on all seven continents, *including a landing in Antarctica*, plus a millennium New Year's Eve celebration in Buenos Aires—all at an unbelievable starting price of $9,000 per passenger! Food, lodging, and seven continents for four months for as little as $9,000—Christie and I spent more than that living at home.

I rushed to get a Dun & Bradstreet credit report on Marine Expeditions in Toronto. I went to Barnes & Noble for a guide on cruise ships that included information on the *Aegean I*, which was the ship booked for this trip by Marine Expeditions. The ship was owned by a tour company in Greece. It had been built in Romania and renovated a few years earlier. It was small by cruise ship standards. And out of eighty cruise ships listed in the guide, it was the only one built in Romania. *And it had never sailed out of the Mediterranean!*

Would Christie and I be safe on a warm water ship with an eggshell-thin hull dodging icebergs in the Drake Passage? The movie *Titanic* had been released that year. Christie and I saw it and loved it, but didn't necessarily want to live it.

I called the offices of the U.S. Department of Transportation in Washington, D.C. and talked to a man there who knew about cruise ship standards. After fielding several of my questions, he said, "When a cruise ship goes down, it's not like when a Boeing 747 goes down. Even in the worst scenario you still have time to get into a lifeboat. My advice—when you board the ship in Athens, pay careful attention to the mandatory lifeboat drill. Then relax and enjoy your cruise."

Well, Marine Expeditions had organized Antarctic trips for nearly ten years. Presumably they knew what they were getting into. But how could they do this cruise for only $9,000 per passenger? Would we be living on Shredded Wheat? Would the company go broke in the middle of the cruise? At that price, these were definite possibilities.

They needed a deposit of $1,000 for two passengers. And our reservation would be so early, we'd probably be able to pick a cabin near mid-ship, where wave motion would be minimal. We upgraded to an outside cabin. I sent in the reservation and check. And I purchased trip cancellation insurance.

Then I made a big mistake.

I was so excited and buoyant about the prospect of sailing with Christie around the world and visiting Antarctica, I couldn't help mentioning the trip to people at the office.

The following week Ken and Debbie came into my office and closed the door. "Can we talk with you?" Of course—what's going on?

"We were wondering if we could purchase The Medical Connection from you."

Right on the Money

My God, what had I done? My two most valuable employees were afraid I was about to sell the company and retire. I'd failed to let them know that the reason I felt safe about booking a four-month cruise was because of my confidence in their ability to run my corporate ship while I was off on a cruise ship.

That night I called my brother Bill, now retired and living in California. "I've made a major blunder, Bill. Debbie and Ken know that I'd booked a four-month cruise, and they're worried that I might sell the company. I can't risk losing either of them—what do you think I should do to reassure them?"

Next day, following another piece of my brother's extraordinary business advice, I called Ken and Debbie into my office.

I said, "It is not on my agenda to sell this company and retire. However, if and when I should decide to sell the company, upon successful completion of such a sale, you each will receive a bonus of one year's salary." And I pulled out two copies of a signed and notarized statement to this effect, handing one to each of them.

One year's salary! That's worth sticking around for.

Bill's advice had satisfied them both and defused the situation. My irreplaceable boatswain and my engineer were happy.

*

At the same time, a thought began to take seed in my head.

My company was now riding the crest of a huge wave. Gaining Columbia-Presbyterian Hospital as a client in 1996 had had the effect of reassuring other big hospitals I'd been calling on. Soon afterward we signed Integra Health System in Omaha, Maimonides Hospital in Brooklyn, and New England Medical Center in Boston, bringing us considerable additional call volume and billings. A number of other new clients were with us as well. The impact of all this new business would increase our 1997 billings about fifty percent above the previous year. And those billings were proving to be very profitable. Any potential buyer could read that upsweep in our billings figures and project the natural acquisition of future clients, based on our growing reputation alone.

With the future looking that good, perhaps I could get a handsome price for The Medical Connection now.

In October of 1997 I'd celebrated my 60th birthday. Christie and I had been together for nine years. Christie's two annual vacations from her job as a professor at DeVry University afforded us two yearly opportunities for world travel. It began in the summer of 1990 when we traveled together to her native Germany. In the years that followed, we'd motored through the charming medieval walled towns of northern Italy. We'd lived in quaint thatched farmhouses in the Yorkshire Dales of England—visited the studios of Mozart and Beethoven in Vienna—drunk beer with students in Poland—swum in the warm blue waters of the Aegean Sea—hiked from village to village in the Pyrenees—viewed 10,000-year-old paintings deep inside a cave in Southern France—slept on futons in traditional Japanese ryokans in Tokyo. We'd traveled on state ferries up to Alaska, flown to the Bering Sea and toasted the midnight sun as it circled the sky above a lonely, lovely Arctic Ocean beach where polar bears sometimes came to give birth to their cubs.

We were eager students of the world—and yet, four of its seven massive, glorious continents still awaited us. There were mountain ranges and volcanic ridges, fjords and glaciers, tidal plains and a Serengeti we'd never explored—creatures like kookaburras and wombats and zebras we'd never seen—cultures from Lapland to Nepal to Peru we'd never visited. So much earth, so much beauty to explore, so many things to learn and experience—and so little time left to do it! Such heady ambitions demanded the luxury of huge open blocks of time—far more time than either of our demanding careers could spare.

At the same time, I worried about a life of retirement with so much free time and no supporting career to justify my

Right on the Money

existence. Should I remain a lifelong career-aholic, clinging to the importance that my position provided? Many people did.

My own field was progressing with the speed of a thoroughbred racehorse. In just a few years I had personally made many of the contributions that had caused sea changes in that field, and the changes would continue after my retirement. It bothered me to realize that just 24 or so months into my retirement, my knowledge of this field would be so hopelessly outdated, I wouldn't be fit to serve in it, even as a consultant.

But more than that I wanted to travel with Christie—and to do it while I was still in good enough health to enjoy it. How many years might it be before some unanticipated ailment or infirmity, physical or mental, might close the doors of the world to us?

There was a company with offices near O'Hare Field known as The Geneva Company. Their business was to represent companies for sale, and market those companies to buyers. I met with them. For an up-front fee of $25,000, they could do an analysis of The Medical Connection, put together a prospectus, and seek out buyers.

I faced one of the major questions of my life—was this the right time?

Then on the last day of the year, my phoenix-goose dropped another gold egg in my lap—half again larger than the one last year.

What a thoughtful, considerate, generous bird!

*

At that moment however, I didn't have time to think of either retirement or The Geneva Company. A more daunting and agonizing task faced me. Once again The Medical Connection had outgrown its office space. Like a growing hermit crab unable to move in the confines of its old borrowed shell, we needed to quickly find larger space and duck into it—a task I feared because of the agony I'd suffered during the move just a few years before, when our disconnected phone system wouldn't work, and it threatened to dissolve my company to a pile of dust by dawn. Could I handle the strain once again? Move we must! There was no available space large enough for us at 625 Michigan, and no adjacent offices that we could expand into.

After a brief search I found an ideal location around the corner on St. Clair Street, in a handsome, relatively new building with a twelfth floor space that was just right—a huge 3,000 square foot open area lined by windows and a pleasant view to the east. That could be our call center. And there were four private offices bordering the space—a corner office for myself, a large office to serve as Ken's "engine room," a lunchroom for the counselors, and a utility room to house the phone system, the file server, and our TEAC voice recording system.

We could move in without changing the space at all. Therefore I could negotiate a short-term lease. I'd learned *never* to sign a long-term lease. 26 years of experience as an entrepreneur had taught me that business is either expanding or contracting. After a year or so, you either have too little space to function in, or more space than you can afford. I'd started a business in 1971 in a tiny 180-square-foot office with a single window. My needs had grown quickly to 1,500 feet—and then collapsed. I'd started The Medical Connection in an 800-square-foot office that doubled as my bedroom. Now I needed over 3,000 square feet. Volatility on that scale made a one-year lease ideal, and a two-year lease acceptable.

So when I looked for new office space, I took a lesson from the lowly hermit crab. Find a space you can move right into, and ask for a rental quote on an "as is" basis. Pay any necessary and minor build-out expenses in *cash*, at the time the work is completed.

Right on the Money

I sketched out a floor plan with thirty calling stations—ten along the window wall, and twenty in two rows facing one another, running down the center of the room. If needed, I could add four more stations along the back wall. Thirty-four counselors at 34 call stations could handle double our present call volume. And that was about the maximum number of callers one supervisor could manage. If we needed more than thirty-four stations we'd need another supervisor. For that we'd either expand into more space on the same floor—or, with another supervisor managing another calling team, they could function from an office on a different floor. Or a different building. Even a different city. Like New York City.

I liked the butcher-block counters we'd always used for our workstations. The heavy, thick oak surfaces were warm and personal. I decided to continue using them for the call room at the St. Clair office, and for the massive work surfaces Ken and his assistant, Juanita, would need in the engine room. I ordered more than two dozen twelve-foot slabs of beautiful solid oak butcher-block countertops from a supplier in Michigan, and hired a cabinetmaker in Northbrook to construct the supports and the call station dividers, to be upholstered in green.

We'd outgrown our phone system in just five years. Debbie and Ken had done some shopping and found a system they liked from Lucent Technologies, the phone hardware company that had emerged from the breakup of Ma Bell. It was a remarkable system. It could use T-1 phone service, recently made available in this area of the North Michigan Avenue neighborhood that now had nearly sixty high-rise office buildings. T-1 service can handle up to 16 simultaneous phone conversations on a single pair of copper wires, each conversation operating on a separate frequency. We could run our entire operation on three pairs of copper wires fed into our suite. The technology of T-1, as well as the complex software needed to run it, was way beyond my understanding—but not beyond Ken's. I was grateful for his remarkable technical understanding that allowed us to make a wise buying decision. The phone system was an $80,000 investment.

As it happened, buying a new phone system at this time eliminated the nightmare I had experienced during our last move. Ken could have the new phone system installed at St. Clair as we continued to use the old one at the Michigan Avenue office.

Ken also made the switchover of his huge LAN computer system easy, too. He'd been purchasing new Pentium-chip computers regularly as we hired more counselors and activated more workstations. He needed a new, larger file server, which he ordered and installed at St. Clair. Then he and Juanita installed six new computers at St. Clair and activated them on the new file server. When the new Lucent phone system was up and running, Ken and Debbie relocated six of our counselors to the new office where they worked alone for a week. They were able to test out the new phone and computer system and work out the bugs. So there was no gut-wrenching, nerve-wracking night when everything was moved, leaving us all to hope it would be working when calls started coming in the following morning. It was already working! Throughout the week before the move, Ken and Juanita transported four to six computers over to the St. Clair office each night. By the end of the week we were fully operational at St. Clair. All that was left for the movers was office furniture for Ken, Debbie, and myself, plus our printers, cabinets, plants and supplies.

The move I had dreaded turned out to be a piece of cake.

On Monday morning following the move, I looked out from my private office onto the vast new Medical Connection call center where 24 of my counselors were busily handling dozens of incoming calls, each counselor's face concentrated on her computer screen, each mind focusing on the patients on their headsets—a scene of intense, prideful productivity in a quiet, acoustically pleasant setting. On a slightly raised platform was Debbie at her desk, tirelessly monitoring calls to maintain her high professional standards. And to my left, through the engine room door was Johann Sebastian Whittenhall and his assistant, Juanita, clicking away at their keyboards, creating their magnificently perfect digital concertos and cantatas that expanded our software and Internet capabilities and made them more user-friendly.

In both my theatrical and advertising careers, my greatest strength had been casting. And now, before my eyes, I was seeing my lifetime's greatest accomplishment in casting—the staff of The Medical Connection. The scene before me was as thrilling to me as any awe-inspiring vista that Christie and I had viewed from Alpine cable cars drifting quietly upward through flower-strewn meadows and green pastures toward the majestic snow-capped peaks.

God created the Alps.

But, by God, I created The Medical Connection.

*

On Valentine's Day of 1998, just four weeks after the final move to St. Clair, I received a phone call from a former client—Jan Swan.

Jan had been progressing in a career that led from job to job. She was now the Midwest Sales Representative for Call Connect, the 1-800-D-O-C-T-O-R-S outfit in Boulder, Colorado, that billed itself as a "Physician Appointment Service" and sold their services directly to physicians. Jan operated out of a study in her home in a Chicago suburb. Recently she'd worked for an outfit in Aurora, Colorado, which was a subsidiary of Laidlaw, a large Canadian company that was traded on the New York Stock Exchange. The Laidlaw subsidiary was a company called American Medical Response. They owned and operated a nationwide network of ambulances staffed by paramedics. They had a telemarketing division called American Medical Pathways, providing nationwide dispatching services for the ambulances and paramedics.

Jan Swan had worked for a Pathways marketing vice president named Bob Watson. The parent company had enjoyed a rather profitable year with income up 47%, putting them into an acquisition mode. And Bob Watson's job was to acquire companies in related businesses.

Jan told me about her previous affiliation with Watson at American Medical Pathways. "Jerry," she said, "Bob Watson wanted me to call you and ask if you might be open to a discussion about a possible merger or acquisition."

Happy Valentine's Day, Jan!

"Possibly," I said, hiding my enthusiasm, pausing just long enough before answering to make it sound like the thought had never occurred to me.

"Then he'd like to call you. Are you going to be in for the rest of the day?"

"Yes."

"Expect a call then, from Bob Watson."

I met with Bob Watson the following day for lunch at Sayat Nova, an Armenian restaurant down the block from our office. I liked Sayat Nova for business meetings because it was quiet.

Watson was in his late thirties, thin, unpretentious, with short hair. He had an M.B.A. from Wharton. He gave me a brochure describing American Medical Response, and a copy of the annual report from the Canadian parent company that had enough disposable assets to buy The Medical Connection many times over. In return I showed him a set of our brochures together with the booklets I'd written on Referral Service Impact and Safe Harbor Compliance. He reviewed the brochures quickly but with interest, and asked me questions about the scope of our services.

Bob described his company's desire to acquire or merge with related companies in the health care field. He talked about his own company's experience owning and dispatching ambulances. The Medical Connection seemed to him to be a logical area for expansion. If I was interested, he wanted to see balance sheets for 1996 and 1997, and some sort of client list.

"I can't give you a client list, Bob."

"We don't need client names. Just some idea of how many clients, how much income from each of them, and a general breakdown as to which regions of the country your clients are located. Is that okay?"

"I think I could do that. Balance sheets aren't too confidential. And billing by region doesn't reveal anything that would be of much use to a competitor."

"And can you give us some idea of how long you've had each of these clients?"

"Probably—in general terms." I began taking notes on a paper napkin.

"I'll be in Colorado the rest of the week, then back in Chicago for the weekend. Could we get together on this on Saturday morning?"

I decided to do something risky—to let him take a quick peek our office. "Would you like a very brief tour of our call center?" I asked. "We're just a block and a half away."

"I'd like that very much."

"I'd just like to ask you not to listen in on the phone conversations. You can understand my not wanting to reveal names of our clients until we've prepared some sort of nondisclosure agreement."

"Of course."

I took him up to our lovely new offices. As I hoped and expected, the phone lines were humming and all of the counselors were busy. I didn't take him around the call stations—he could see them all at a glance. I walked him past Debbie's desk and introduced him. Then we dropped into the utility room where I could show off our new Lucent phone system, our state-of-the-art file server, and our TEAC voice recording setup.

Then I introduced him to Ken and his assistant, Juanita. By keeping him away from the call stations, he was unlikely to hear anyone say something like "Columbia-Presbyterian Physician Referral Service."

Five minutes had plenty of impact. Watson could see that The Medical Connection was for real, that it was clean, that our staff was bright, nicely dressed, and professional.

I couldn't help remembering a time, not that long ago, when I had only one counselor, and needed to rent computers and bring in two of my part-time employees to sit at them, in order to impress a potential client from New Jersey.

I took Bob Watson to the elevators and said good-bye—until Saturday morning.

Ken Whittehall came into my office. "Is Watson a prospective new client?" he asked.

"No, Ken, his company is a prospective *buyer*. They may want to buy The Medical Connection."

I saw a little glint in Ken's eyes as he smiled and thought about his possible one-year bonus.

I began preparing statements for Bob Watson. The Medical Connection's bottom lines for both 1996 and 1997 looked very impressive. I broke our billings down by size category and region of the United States.

22% of our billings came from clients we'd had six years or more.

44% came from clients gained in the past year.

43% of billings came from Midwestern clients.

50% of billings came from clients in the Northeast, from Washington D.C. to Boston, with our biggest clients in New York City. That surprised even me. We needed a New York call center.

My Saturday morning meeting with Bob was brief. We met for coffee at a café in Northbrook. He looked over my figures with an eye that was obviously experienced at reading corporate balance sheets.

Right on the Money

He said, "Good. Just about what I expected."

I momentarily recalled the visit John Adams had made to my office eighteen years earlier, as he contemplated joining me at Inglehart and Partners. He'd reviewed my books, then looked up and said, "I thought there'd be more."

Just about what I'd expected sounded better. Not a showstopper, but nicer. Of course Inglehart and Partners had been in freefall in 1980. By contrast, the 1998 Medical Connection figures soared like a falcon.

"Now we need to come up with an offer," said Bob. "Do you plan to retire, or stay on with the company?"

"Which would you prefer?"

"Either way is fine with us."

"Does it affect the price?"

"Well, our offer would be quite a bit higher if you retired."

I smiled. "Bob," I quipped, "I've been asked to leave some of the finest restaurants and hotels in America and Europe—but never my own company."

"Your company is paying you a rather sizeable salary. If we purchased the company and you retired, we'd probably replace you with an administrator earning a small fraction of what you pay yourself."

"In that case, I'd retire on selling the company."

"Will you be around next Thursday?"

"Thursday I'll be in New York. Here's a phone number where you can call me." I wrote down Jack Waterman's home phone number on Riverside Drive in Manhattan. "What time do you expect to call?"

"I'll be in Colorado. Let's say—about 11 A.M. Eastern."

"I'll be there."

The following Tuesday I got another call from Jan Swan. "You're quite a popular guy—now my boss at Call Connect wants to talk to you."

Jan had obviously mentioned my discussions with Bob Watson to her boss at Call Connect. And I hoped that, in her conversations with Bob Watson, Jan would let Bob know that there might be another offer on my table. Competition for the purchase of The Medical Connection would work in my favor of course, possibly even initiating a bidding war. But I didn't want to have to mention Call Connect's interest to Bob Watson myself.

That afternoon I flew to Newark for a Wednesday meeting at Columbia-Presbyterian. I drove my rental car north on Interstate 95 through New Jersey to the George Washington Bridge. As I passed beneath the two proud towers of this engineering marvel, strung with huge cables set into massive concrete anchors in two states, I thought about my first crossing of that bridge forty-two years earlier as a road-weary, slightly Brando-esque 18-year-old hitchhiker seeking a quick-fix Western Union money order from Jack Waterman at Harvard.

Before me was the city of my hopes, the island of Damon Runyon and Holly Golightly, the impossible dream of success in a hard-nosed metropolis populated by the finest talents in theater. I had nothing going for me then but my own untapped talent and my youth—luxurious decades ahead of me, years and years that had since sifted through the sands of time.

I never did become a David Merrick with three simultaneous hits running on Broadway. Nor did I conquer New York in the make-believe advertising world of David Ogilvie and William Bernbach.

I had conquered it as Jerry Inglehart, nationally recognized authority in the field of hospital physician referral services, a calling I'd never dreamed of, and in 1956 didn't even exist. Had I been able to read the future back then, perhaps my star-struck eyes, peering at Manhattan from the George Washington Bridge, would not have sought out the sights and sounds of Broadway, the great old theaters named after famous actors like Ethyl Barrymore and Helen Hayes, and Lindy's Restaurant and the theatrical bar at Sardi's. I might never have looked up at the awesome steel-and-glass Manhattan towers along Madison Avenue—the temples of those big ad agencies where, through photos, films, glamour, and illusion, the tastes and preferences of a post-war nation of big spenders were shaped and dictated.

No—instead I would have looked fondly and hopefully toward the buildings of Columbia-Presbyterian Hospital, visible from the center of the bridge along the east bank of the Hudson River. Inside these buildings, and in several others scattered across this city, there were theaters of a different sort—surgical theaters where dramatic human tragedies and miracles played out daily. There I would act out my ultimate professional role— my *opus magnum!*

New York, New York! *If you can make it there, you'll make it anywhere.* That was Sinatra. And I'd made it there, all right.

On Thursday morning I was in the living room of the Waterman's Manhattan co-op. I sat nervously waiting for the call from Bob Watson. I'd tried to think through every possible scenario, and how I should respond. The best response, of course, would be easy— "Give me a few days to think about this."

Watson's call came promptly at 11A.M. Based on the preliminary figures I'd given him, he made me a dollar offer.

I promised to get back to him.

I hung up the phone and let out a joyful whoop! I had a legitimate offer! Perhaps a little less than I'd hoped for, but nonetheless *on the mark.* And it was a *cash* offer. Not some complicated offer stretched out over time, contingent on future performance—not some awkward stock trade—but *cash,* from a big blue-chip corporation with cash to burn.

Back in Chicago on Friday I called The Geneva Company. In past months my mind had been occupied by the move to St. Clair. I'd never signed their agreement or paid them their up-front fee of $25,000.

"I have an offer from a potential buyer for The Medical Connection," I told the sales rep.

"It happens," he replied, "and invariably, the seller settles for only a fraction of the real value of his company. You need our analysis to know what your company is really worth." He was hungry for that $25,000 fee.

"I may or may not accept the offer. If not, I'll be back to talk with you."

On Monday I called Bob Watson back. "I think your offer is probably fair and legitimate, even though I'd be hard-pressed to come up with any standards on which to base it. The problem, Bob, is that I've played around with some figures over the weekend, and in order to fund my retirement the way I'd hoped, and do the things my wife and I want to do, I'd need—a third more than you're offering me. If this poses a problem for you, I'll understand." Nervously, I wondered if Jan Swan had told him that I had another offer pending.

"Give me a couple of days," Watson said.

He called back on Wednesday. "We'll meet your price, Jerry."

"Then I guess we have a deal. What's the next step?"

"Next we sign a nondisclosure agreement, which I can fax to you. Then we begin what's called 'discovery.' Are you familiar with the discovery process?"

"At this point I think I'll involve my law firm. They'll probably be able to advise me on all these things."

In discussions with Call Connect on Thursday and Friday, I'd decided their offer wasn't appealing. They could match the dollar offer from American Medical Pathways, but not as a buyout of my stock. They wanted to pay to buy "the assets but not the liabilities" of The Medical Connection, the same arrangement Maurice Rothschild had made with the Bockman Company. Selling the assets by themselves would subject me to ordinary federal tax on the income, whereas by selling the company stock outright to Pathways, I'd pay simple long-term capital gains tax on the 500 shares of stock I'd sold myself at a dollar a share in 1987. This difference in tax liability alone made the Call Connect offer trivial in comparison to the Pathways offer.

Over the next few days I began to agonize over my decision, and again called my brother Bill for advice. Bill's business knowledge was extensive and sophisticated. He had no M.B.A., but with his successful business experience, he could probably have done a better job of *teaching* M.B.A. courses than most of the professors at Stanford or Yale. Many large companies would have happily called him out of retirement and paid him $1,000 per hour as a consultant. And I got his counsel for free.

I told Bill, "I thought they'd respond to my counteroffer with another figure, like meeting me halfway. But they accepted my price almost immediately without further negotiation That makes me wonder if I'm selling out for too little. How do I know they're offering me a fair price?"

"You don't. You never will. But it's the better of two offers. And if you take the offer, *you'll have what you wanted.* So don't agonize over it. Never look back."

Good point.

"I also worry that I might be selling at the wrong time," I told him. "New clients have come to us more easily since Columbia-Presbyterian. If I continue to sign new business at this rate, I could possibly get three or four times this offer in as many years."

"The question," said Bill, "is what you want out of those three or four years. Do you want all that extra money at age 63 or 64, or would you prefer, in 2002, to be able to look back on four years of world discoveries with Christie?"

Excellent point.

"And here's something else for you to think about, Jer. I see the lifestyle you and Christie enjoy. I've admired the way you and she share your travels together. You both seem to be living and traveling exactly the way you want to. You don't seem to be denying yourselves anything you really want. If you got three or four times as much for The Medical Connection, I frankly question whether you'd ever spend it. Most of it would end up as a massive gift to the Internal Revenue Service when you died."

That was the clincher.

But this wasn't an M.B.A. course. This was a course in psychology.

In the next few weeks I'd discover just how closely related psychology is to business. My law firm, Lord, Bissell & Brook, is one of the major Chicago law firms. They assigned my project to a young attorney with a Hollywood-sounding name: Brett Pritchard. Brett had spent a solid decade dealing exclusively with mergers and acquisitions—possibly hundreds of them. From Brett I learned not only the legal steps of an acquisition, but equally important, the psychology. Brett informed me and rehearsed me on questions to expect from my buyer and how to be prepared for them, for their possible parries, and for counteroffers. Brett's experience actually kept me a move or two ahead of Laidlaw in a complex game of high-stakes poker. Just as a good trial attorney never asks a question he doesn't know the answer to, there was never a single question put to me by the Pathways attorneys and executives that Brett hadn't anticipated and rehearsed me in my response.

Brett provided me with an exhaustive list of categories for disclosure—facts that, if I neglected to remember them, look them up and reveal them, could upset or destroy my position, possibly even the price. One of the thorny issues was that little-known New York State law that declared my services in that state to be illegal. I found the written opinion of Alan Reardon, the New York health care attorney, who advised me and my prospective client, Columbia-Presbyterian, that the law could probably be ignored because any efforts to enforce it would likely result in its being shot down in a higher court. I showed that Columbia-Presbyterian Hospital was aware of this opinion at the time their legal department signed off on our service contract.

The Pathways attorneys were satisfied. Negotiations were complete. On Friday, May 15, 1998, at about 4 P.M., in the offices of Lord, Bissell & Brook, notification of a wire transfer of American funds reached my personal checking account from a bank in Canada. I endorsed the back of my 500-share Medical Connection stock certificate. Pathways stamped the certificate "Cancelled" and returned it to me as a souvenir.

Christie gave notice of her own retirement from DeVry University the next day. She completed the semester and turned in her final exam grades on June 17th.

The final twenty days of my service constituted my last whirlwind business tour, as I introduced my clients to Bob Watson. We covered Illinois and Indiana first, then Boston, New York, Atlanta, Miami, Charlotte, and several cities in between, completing our trip in Washington, D.C. On Thursday, July 2, 1998 I boarded a United Airlines flight out of Washington National Airport, touching down two hours later at O'Hare and joining the ranks of the unemployed.

Then on Monday, July 20th, Christie and I showed up at O'Hare. The previous January we'd booked a flight to Europe for a three-week tour of the Normandy invasion beaches of France. We simply extended the return flight from three weeks to *three months*, and spent the balance of the summer and early autumn in a lovely, leisurely tour of northern France, Holland, and Belgium, enjoying the first months of a new life.

Chapter 29

"Last Scene of All, that Ends this Strange, Eventful History"

So there you have it—my life in performing arts, from "Casey Would Waltz" in 1941 to my Grand Farewell Tour 57 years later. It's not so much the story of a life in the performing arts, as it is the saga of my performances in the art of life—or perhaps the art of business. But when does art become a business? And when does business become an art? I never abandoned the performing arts. I simply molded them to my needs and responsibilities.

Responsibilities. That's the thread that holds this story together. And since it includes my premarital performance, it's the story of *Irresponsibility and Responsibility*. But that sounds as dull as a Lutheran sermon. I could divide the book into a trilogy, calling my school years *Crime and Punishment*, my years as an employee *War and Peace*, and my entrepreneurial years *The Agony and the Ecstasy*.

But those responsibilities, and this story, come to a sudden end in July 1998 when the lives of Christie and me suddenly contained no more responsibilities than a pair of trees has to the squirrels.

There are a few interesting postscripts—

By the time I reached age 45, my hair and beard had become so gray, I looked older than either of my brothers. At 50 I decided I looked too old to be the C.E.O. of an emerging company staffed with young people, selling to youthful hospital executives. My hairdresser, Barb Honn, said she could dye both my hair and beard to relieve me of a few years.

She applied her witches' brew, heavy with hydrogen peroxide, to all the hair on my head and face, and then had me sit for an agonizing 30 minutes as the stuff burnt in. When she washed it all off, my hair and beard were a youthful shade of brown, although my cheeks were red from the chemicals. After a day or so my facial skin healed, and I looked a lot healthier.

In three weeks' time the gray roots would grow out evenly, giving my hair and beard an appealing salt-and-pepper appearance. But then it was time to return to Barb's torture chamber for another thirty minute "burn." I stuck to this painful regimen every three weeks for the next ten years. Each time I suffered through the excruciating half-hour, I swore I would stop this nonsense immediately upon retirement.

The Tuesday after I touched down at O'Hare and entered retirement, I came for my appointment with Barb. "I've sold my company, Barb. I'm retired. No more hair dye. *Cut off every bit of brown hair!*"

She gave me the shortest haircut I'd had in decades, and my trimmed beard made me look a little like those unshaven characters in *Miami Vice*. And suddenly I was an elderly man again.

That afternoon I dropped by my office to pick up my possessions—and chuckled as I watched my staff stare at me with their mouths open in shock. All these years they'd been working for an *old man!* Ah, show biz!

A year later I heard from Ken Whittenhall. He told me that Pathways had also purchased a small new referral service in Seattle, which had been folded into The Medical Connection. Bob Watson had even tried to purchase E.R.S. but that had failed.

Ken also mentioned that New York Cornell purchased Columbia-Presbyterian. Within months New York Cornell hired The Medical Connection to replace its in-house physician referral department. So we ultimately got New York Cornell.

Bob Watson had rehired Jan Swan to have her attempt to fill my shoes at The Medical Connection.

Ken also mentioned that he'd seen a lot of financial statements of Pathways and its subsidiaries. And The Medical Connection had proven to be the most profitable venture Pathways owned, by a large margin. It was more profitable even than Pathways itself. This didn't surprise me. During the acquisition talks, Pathways had flown Ken, Debbie, and me to Denver for a meeting. They delivered us airline tickets they'd purchased from a travel agent at *full price!* I could have purchased the same three coach seats for $2,400 less. But it amused me to examine full-price airline tickets, which I'd never seen before. They looked exactly like the cheap tickets I'd always bought.

I framed the cancelled Medical Connection stock certificate and hung it in my den as my personal lifetime achievement award. During the next decade, many dot-com founders made huge paper fortunes on their own stock, but for all their wealth, none of them came even close to the *percentage* of increase I'd achieved with my own 500 shares.

Since this is a work of nonfiction, my publisher has advised me to double check all the facts. I changed several names to protect the guilty. And anyone who's ever received an ANDY Award knows that, unlike the CLIOs, you don't go home with the ANDY statuette they give you at the podium on awards night. After your photo is taken, you hand the ANDY back, and they ship it to you after they've engraved your name on it. So my description in Chapter 16 of toting that ANDY statuette all over Manhattan during that crazy night with Jake is fiction. But I thought my tale would have more continuity if, while I was basking in the morning-after glory of being an ANDY winner, I'd find Renee's *Water Lilies* script as I pushed aside papers on my desk to position my ANDY statuette. *Water Lilies* would prove to be the ultimate award winner.

Other than that, it all checks out—except, of course, that thunderstorm I dreamed up for the beginning of Chapter 1—but that's a rather transparent fabrication. I mean, who ever heard of a thunderstorm in Wisconsin in mid-October?

*

Since every ad man knows that sooner or later he'll get fired, every agency writer, art director and producer keeps samples of his or her work, either at home if his job is secure, or in a bank vault downtown if he's sneaking out to job interviews during lunch. I had reels containing over 2,000 of my radio and TV commercials stored away in boxes in my garage. They were valuable in reconstructing the story of my advertising career. Researching them brought several rushes of nostalgia, reviewing dialogues, lyrics and melodies I had agonized over so long ago, and the brilliant cast of actors, announcers, musicians, arrangers and sound engineers I'd worked with.

Eventually I decided to select out 25 of the commercials that best supported the thrust of my broadcast advertising career and put them onto a CD that could be tipped into the inside front cover of this book. Then my publisher advised me that the logistics of including the CD would be costly, pushing the book price up well over $50.

The CD includes the following 25 tracks:

The World is a Stage

U.S. Navy	*Poundin' Streets*	Page 202
U.S. Navy	*Girl in the 9-to-5 World*	Page 204
Partridge Meats	*Talkin' Sausage Blues*	Page 208
Katz Drug	*Katz as Katz Can*	Page 218
Katz Drug	*John and Myrna*	Page 219
Partridge Meats	*Grillwork*	Page 209
WBBM-FM	*Meet Me Every Morning*	Page 240
Downyflake Waffles	*Sleepyhead*	Page 241
Downyflake Waffles	*Cup of Tea*	Page 241
House of Vision	*The Eyes Have It*	Page 252
House of Vision	*Psychiatrist*	Page 252
Killen Savings	*Money Tree*	Page 253
Leaf Confectionery	*Charles Dickens*	Page 254
Autotronics	*Snooper XK*	Page 255
1st National Killeen	*The First Thing*	Page 256
Chrysler-Plymouth	*Come On Up*	Page 262
Magicolor Paints	*Rhythms to Paint by*	Page 254
Toast'Em	*Andrew*	Page 262
Hinckley & Schmitt	*Witches' Brew*	Page 277
Hinckley & Schmitt	*30 Days*	Page 278
Bockman	*Granddad*	Page 276
Becker Beeper	*Larry Moran*	Page 299
Hinckley & Schmitt	*Water Lilies*	Page 287
Hinckley & Schmitt	*Water Symphony*	Page 289
Hinckley & Schmitt	*Christmas Card*	Page 319

Anyone wishing to order this collection of 25 minutes of commercials uninterrupted by program material, send $5 to:

Inglehart CD Offer – PMB 603
88005 Overseas Highway, Suite 9
Islamorada, FL 33036

Please allow 5 weeks for delivery. The $5 includes shipping.

So now Christie and I are into an adventurous retirement of world discovery—a set of experiences quite foreign to this tale of responsibility and irresponsibility. Maybe it's the start of a new book.
That's another story.
This one is told.

—FINAL CURTAIN—

Index

A

Abrams, Chuck..........................261
Adams, John..........273-5, 280-1, 295, 441
Adams, Mason 277
Alderman, Betsy......................105
Altorfer, John 184
Anderson, Lynn...............336, 340
Apy, Caroline 336, 339
Arey, Dave 56, 74-5
Arnold, Joe 44, 56, 71-2
Auxer, Ed 195, 197

B

Bachmann, Dave......274-6, 280, 299, 317, 319, 326-7
Bachrach, Ed 299
Baima, Tom.............................144
Ball, William....................95, 109
Barber, Christiane......347-9, 398, 429-30, 432-3 437, 447-9
Barth, Barbara 396
Bates, Sharon 42-5
Berman, Marshall.. 58-9, 65, 80-1
Bernbach, William .176, 222, 442
Bernstein, Jordy................ 263-4
Bevilaqua, Ray 109
Binder, Bob 335
Binns, Ed 275-6, 278
Binzer, Rollin 221
Black, Eli............................ 248-9
Blask, Bill............................. 50-1
Blockowicz, Dave 424
Blondell, Joan.................118, 121
Bloom, Frank 231, 234, 236
Boll, Carl 170-1, 187
Bond, Harlan 323-5, 394

Bonhivert, Ernie 36
Bosley, Rev. Harold............... 131
Boyd, Mason.......................... 294
Boyell, Dick...........202-4, 218-19
Bradley, Joe 31
Brando, Marlon......74-5, 93, 102, 121, 411, 442
Breskin, Sally 109
Brodie, Steve 256
Brown, Cal............................... 37
Brown, Mark and Michael..... 246
Brown, Penn 36
Buck, Doug..........24-5, 53, 58-9, 64, 70-4, 80-1, 85-8, 92, 94, 96, 100-1, 105-6, 108, 111, 114, 117-18, 123, 125-6, 138
Bucknell, Peter 109
Burdis, Bert......................216-17
Burkhardt, Paul....57-8, 81-2, 88, 98, 105, 117-18, 122, 126
Byerly, Beverly...................... 323

C

Caesar, John........................... 229
Caldwell, Rose..................417-20
Callahan, Doug...................... 208
Calvi, Jane 35
Carlisle, Guy.......................220-1
Carney, Bob........202, 204-5, 210
Carpenters, The..................236-7
Carr, Alan 81-2, 86
Carroll, Cathy 336, 340
Casker, Tom 102, 108
Cellier, Frank............... 161-2, 169
Chambers, Patricia................... 76
Chase, Bob.........................297-8

Childs, Lynda Jo.......335-8, 345, 350-1, 353, 360-1
Christopher, William................37
Churchill, Mac 216
Cirillo, Dr. Leonard........310, 313
Clignet, Remi 192
Clinton, Alvin Sargent....... 78-9, 93-4, 96, 412-13
Cohen, Richard... 352, 370-1, 386
Collins, Eleanor..................18, 37
Collins, Gretchen............ 37-9, 86
Compton, Ann..........................46
Connagan, Eileen 41
Cooperman, Thomas.....389, 406, 415, 417
Corda, Margarite 417-20
Cotterill, Bill 234
Coyle, Ann 194, 196
Cusak, John 127, 193

D

DeHart, Jon 110
Dennis, Barbara......................111
Dennis, Tom...................110, 133
DeSurry, Natalie.....................336
Diamond, Art 145
Dickens, Charles 72, 198, 451
Diedrich, Horst.........................30
Donaldson, Bill 149
Doolittle, Eliza 66, 392
Driscol, Harold........... 404, 427-8
Dussault, Nancy 122

E

Eden, Barbara.........................267
Edmonds, Howie..............63, 105
Esau, Linda....................336, 341
Ettington, Barbara 406-7, 413

F

Farnham, Walt............56, 75, 106
Fell, Abe 86, 97

Fletcher, Alan 123
Forler, Dorothy 18
Fountain, Pete 298
Fourgis, Kris........................... 96
Frehley, Ace 316
Frey, Gordon..........305-6, 317-19
Frickie, Janie.................253, 257-8
Frommer, Arthur.................155-6
Fuller, Candy 75-6, 79
Fullerton, Dave 199, 216

G

Gahagen, Winnifred................. 85
Gavin, John...........................76-7
George Washington Bridge .. 115, 155, 406-7, 442
Godfrey, Judy 290-1
Goldberg, Sue 56, 118
Goldblatt, Laura................318-19
Goldswig, Ron 109
Golightly, Holly............. 155, 442
Goodman, Steve.......200, 202-4, 219, 241
Gootsan, George 267, 269, 278
Grant, Mel...................... 194, 196
Green, Gayle......................... 137
Guthrie, Arlo.. 200, 203, 208, 241

H

Hague, Joe 139
Hanson, Pearl........................... 9
Harris, Jack and Judy............. 152
Harvey, Paul 161, 235
Hawkins, Charlotte 92
Heiser, Bill............................. 98
Helms, J.D. 56
Henry, Martha................. 95, 109
Heston, Charleton 46, 117, 123
Hollingsworth, Elbert..178, 183-4
Holzer, Audrey 292-3
Honigschmidt, Mary Sue 399
Honn, Barb 449

Index

Horberg, Susie 35
Horn, Gladys 10
Houseman, Ron 122
Huelster, Peter 50-1
Hunter, Holly 95, 109
Huyler, Jerry 234-6, 238, 242, 251, 261, 267
Hyman, Mike 261, 266, 270

I

Inglehart, Bill 7, 12, 21, 28, 30, 32-4, 36, 192, 222, 253, 281, 321, 323, 326, 395, 413, 431, 445-6
Inglehart, Chris 154, 288-9, 301-2, 309-18, 320, 322, 336, 339, 340
Inglehart, Gerald A 3, 9, 20, 23, 28, 32-4, 40, 56, 62, 91, 142, 148, 150-1, 158, 346-7, 349
Inglehart, Helen 3, 14, 16, 20, 23, 28, 41, 56, 85, 87, 309
Inglehart, James 141, 143, 155, 165-6, 308, 314-15
Inglehart, Ronald 7-8, 10, 26, 41, 56-8, 63, 78-9, 81, 88, 98, 105, 116-17, 133, 147, 165, 355

J

Jacobson, Walter 46
Jake 284-5, 451
Johnson, Babs 35
Johnson, R. Stanley 297-8
Jones, Pete 36

K

Kahler, Dean 72
Kase, Jane Inglehart 35-6, 46, 289
Kaufherr, Jerry 278
Kazan, Elia 60-1

Keller, Mary Ann 299-300, 302-3, 308, 314, 335, 347
Kessenic, Larry 372-6, 414
Kincella, Tom 236
Kinsey, Dr. Alfred 68
Kitkat, Cecil 113-14
Klein, Dana 368-70, 379
Klein, Suzy 56, 81
Knight, Theresa 308
Koulous, Lefty 134-5
Kraus, Alvina 123
Kroc, Ray 214

L

Lacey, Bill 199, 212-13, 216
Lahr, Bert 118
Lain, Mel 206, 261, 265, 276
Lain, Melissa 398
Lake Shore Players 56-60, 65, 74, 79, 81, 85-6, 95, 98, 105, 107-8, 117-18, 149, 201, 206, 411
LaKundt, Eva 18-19
Lazarus, George 247
Levy, Madeline .. 371, 376, 379-88
Lieberman, Archie 421
Lief, Todd 216-18, 220-2
Linck, Nancy 304
List, David and Pam 301-3
List, Mark Daniel 302-3
Lowenstein, Winifred 426-8
Lynd, Robert 181

M

MacGregor, Deborah 406-10, 413-14, 419
Mallery, Sam 169
Martin, Juanita . 425-6, 435-7, 439
Martin, Nicholas 109-10
Maslanka, Judy 240, 301
Masterson, Sky 286
Mathis, Donald 145

Maturo, Debbie..361-3, 371, 385-6, 391-3, 396, 400, 413-16, 420, 422, 425, 430-1, 435-6, 439, 450
Mays, Ron 118, 121
McCann-Erickson...82, 105, 121, 274-5, 280-1
McHugh, Denise 336, 340-1
McLaughlin, Sue 336
McMillan, Frank 210, 216
Melker, Sharon 341-3, 381
Montgomery, Katherine 387
Montgomery, Lavinia 29
Morris, Mary 95, 123
Mull, Steve 213

N

Nader, Al 217, 221-2
Neavill, Rod 332-4, 337, 339
Nicholson, Erika.......................... 8
Nicklaus, Jack 283
Nolan, Laurie 197

O

Oakes, Dave 267, 269, 278
Oakland, Simon 238, 256
O'Brien, Dave 93
O'Brien, Peggy 324-5
Oldendorf, Walt 53, 70-1, 80-1, 88, 123, 125

P

Parker, Jim 63-4, 116
Parton, Dolly 263, 281-3
Paul, Albert 247-8
Perreault, Chuck 254
Perry, Gregg 236-7, 239-41, 253, 257-9, 263-5, 281-2
Petersen, Rex 76-7
Peterson, Cindy .. 261, 264-7, 270
Pfeifer, Dr. Heinrich 5, 6
Pickens, Slim 236

Piven, Byrne 193
Piven, Jeremy 193
Poor, Martha 102-3
Post, Jim 202-4
Potts, Mary Beth 132
Price, Grace 133
Prine, John 200, 203
Pritchard, Brett 446

R

Rahn, Dr. Grant 27-9
Ramanouskas, Vito 229
Reardon, Alan 415, 446
Reed, Russ 294
Rengland, Byron 109
Rieger, Judy............................ 86
Rockoff, Renee......280, 283, 286, 288, 291-2, 294, 296, 301, 303, 319-20, 331, 450
Roesch, Larry 273
Roewade, Paul 239
Rogers, Gerald....................... 195
Rosman, Bill.........345, 351, 361, 394, 396-7
Rumsfeld, Donald.................... 46
Runyon, Damon........55, 104, 115, 442
Ryland, Linda 414-15

S

Salinger, J.D. 60-1, 410
Schallert, William............... 278-9
Scheinfeld, Danny 57
Schmidt, R. G. 148
Schmitt, Gladys 106, 112
Schneider, Al......231, 235-6, 243, 245-9
Schneiderman, Bob................ 123
Schneiderman, George... 196, 198
Schultz, Carl 56
Schwartz, Rita....................... 336
Sedelmaier, Joe............. 276, 294

Index

Sheffler, Bill............................122
Singh, Dr. 315-16
Smith, Gordon........108, 110, 137
Sobin, Frank....................... 151-2
Sommer, Al..........82, 97, 105-6, 132, 139-40, 142, 274
Sommer, Connie.............105, 132
Sommer, Dave................105, 185
Sommer, Jane...97, 121, 126, 142
Sommer, Josef..................95, 109
Sommer, Kathy.......74-5, 77, 79, 82-3, 88, 97, 105, 121-2, 126-7, 131-3, 136-41, 143, 147, 152-3, 155, 157, 164-5, 192, 201, 213, 230, 242, 244, 246, 248-9, 251-2, 259-60, 270, 280, 282, 284, 292-3, 314-15
Sommer, Kim........... 139-40, 142
Sommer, Mary 145
Sommer, Rick.........................105
Spiegelman, Paul......353, 363-4, 374, 376, 390, 420
Stramp, Joey.......................... 50-1
Strohmeier, Gloria.. 59, 66-70, 74
Sutton, Linda...........................82
Svec, Jerry.............................304
Swan, Jan......371, 437-8, 441-2, 444, 450
Swan, Winnifred 29
Swensen, Ezra 182

T

Tate, Ray 232, 301, 303
Tatman, Joan 77-8
Tatoris, Lisa......................351
Telfer, Bob 149-50
Terrana, Angela.............231, 245
Terrill, Bill 149-50, 156
Threshold Players....37, 55-6, 78, 107, 117, 410

Tippens, Marty ...59, 73-4, 84, 86
Tuhill, Betty............................ 11

W

Wade, Roland 189
Wahlen, Don........................50-1
Walgreen, Cork...................46
Warner, Florence ... 258, 263, 265
Waterman, Esther 71, 133
Waterman, Jack....53, 58-9, 70-1, 74, 80-1, 85, 88, 105, 114-16, 123, 132, 155, 252, 410-11, 441-3
Watson, Bob 438-44, 447, 450
Weisner, Bernard......230-1, 233, 251, 261
Wessburg, Bob......290-1, 307-8, 319
White, Palmer 35
Whittenhall, Ken...........399-404, 414-15, 420, 425-8, 430-1, 434-7, 439-40, 450
Williams, Tennessee...61, 93, 98, 107, 365, 412-13
Winston, Gail......................... 149
Witt, Denny 196
Worthington, Bill.................... 12

Y

Yale, Merritt 178
Young, Janet............................ 96
Yousi, Harold 157

Z

Zaretsky, Barb 313
Ziebell, Don............................ 10
Zimmerman, Don.......211-13, 216

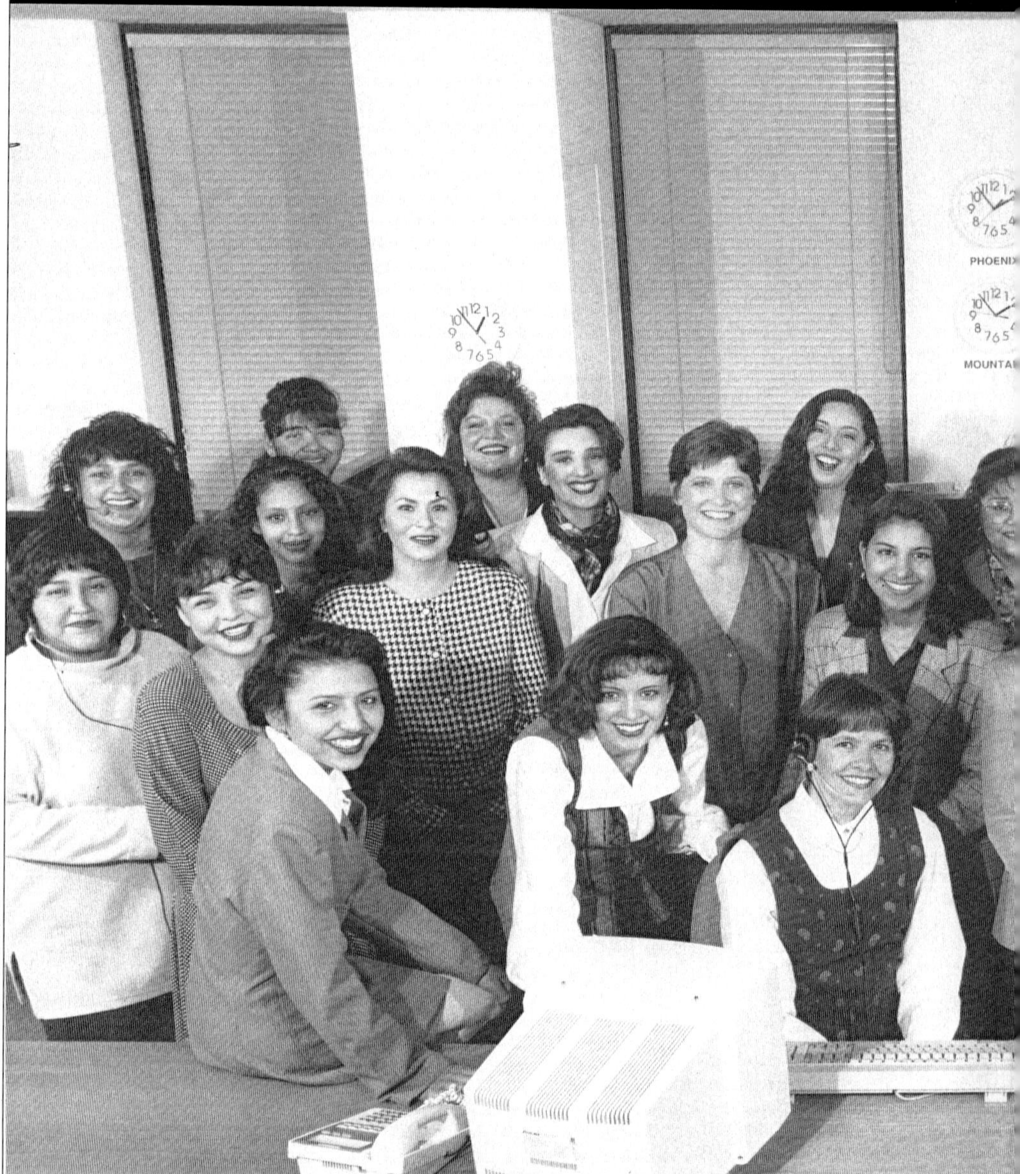